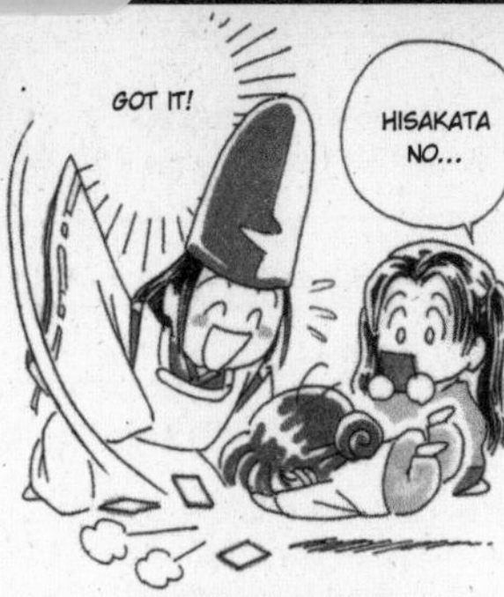
HISAKATA NO...
GOT IT!

Yumi Hotta

If one were to play Hyakunin Isshu with Sai, he'd be merciless and not let you get a single card. Meanie!
—Yumi Hotta

It all began when Yumi Hotta played a pick-up game of Go with her father-in-law. As she was learning how to play, Ms. Hotta thought it might be fun to create a story around the traditional board game. More confident in her storytelling abilities than her drawing skills, she submitted the beginnings of **Hikaru no Go** to **Weekly Shonen Jump**'s Story King Award. The Story King Award is an award that picks the best story, manga, character design and youth (under 15) manga submissions every year in Japan. As fate would have it, Ms. Hotta's story (originally named, "***Kokonotsu no Hoshi***"), was a runner-up in the "Story" category of the Story King Award. Many years earlier, Takeshi Obata was a runner-up for the Tezuka Award, another Japanese manga contest sponsored by **Weekly Shonen Jump** and **Monthly Shonen Jump**. An editor assigned to Mr. Obata's artwork came upon Ms. Hotta's story and paired the two for a full-fledged manga about Go. The rest is modern Go history.

HIKARU NO GO VOL. 5
SHONEN JUMP Manga Edition

This graphic novel contains material that was originally published in English from
SHONEN JUMP #29 to #33.

STORY BY YUMI HOTTA
ART BY TAKESHI OBATA
Supervised by YUKARI UMEZAWA (5 Dan)

Translation & English Adaptation/Andy Nakatani
English Script Consultant/Janice Kim (3 Dan)
Touch-up Art & Lettering/Adam Symons
Additional Touch-up/Josh Simpson and Walden Wong
Cover & Interior Design/Courtney Utt
Editors/Livia Ching and Yuki Takagaki

VP, Production/Alvin Lu
VP, Sales & Product Marketing/Gonzalo Ferreyra
VP, Creative/Linda Espinosa
Publisher/Hyoe Narita

Published by VIZ Media, LLC
P.O. Box 77010
San Francisco, CA 94107

10 9 8 7 6 5 4 3 2
First printing, November 2009
Second printing, February 2010

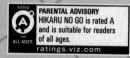

PARENTAL ADVISORY
HIKARU NO GO is rated A
and is suitable for readers
of all ages.
ratings.viz.com

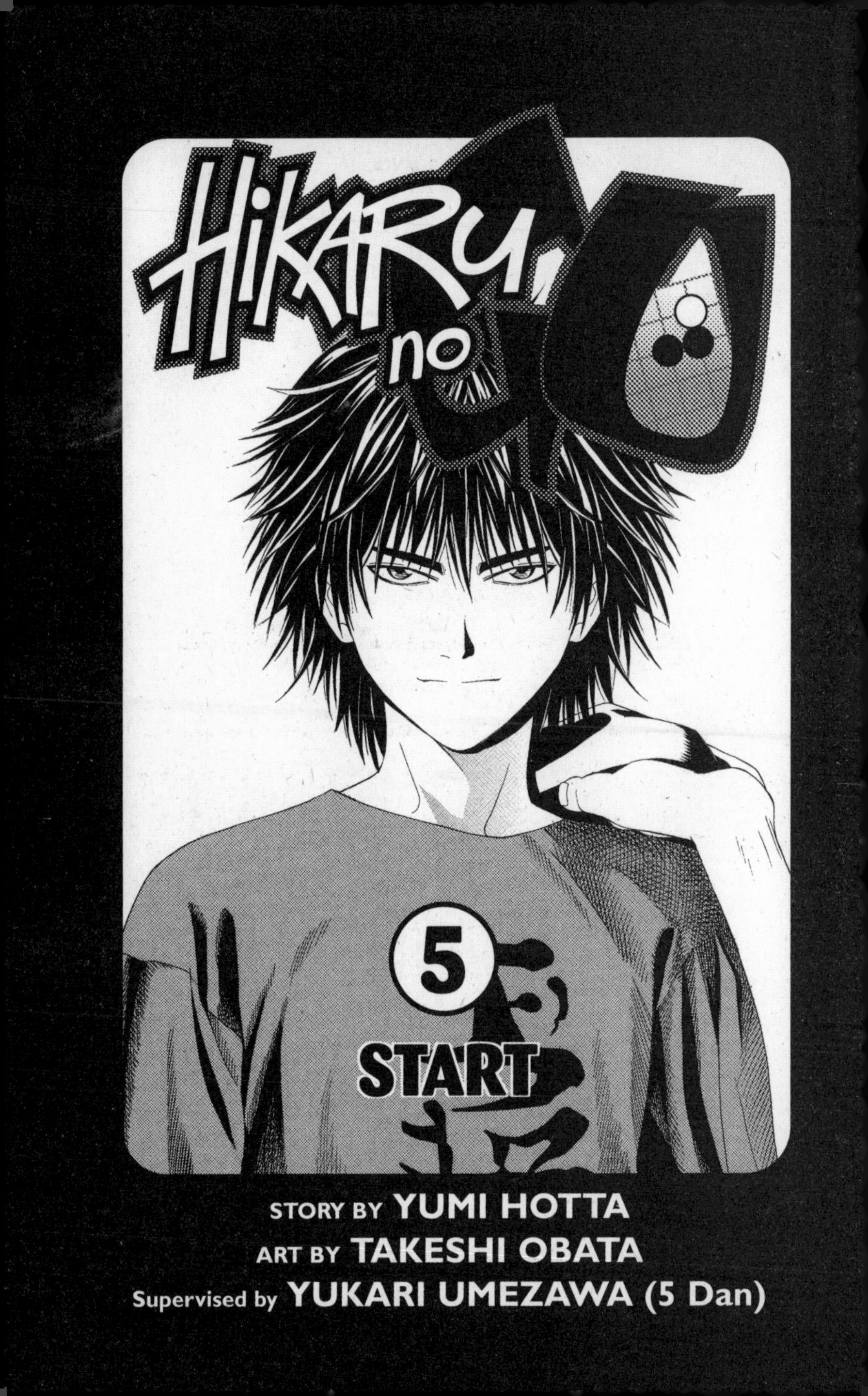
HIKARU
no
5
START

STORY BY YUMI HOTTA

ART BY TAKESHI OBATA

Supervised by YUKARI UMEZAWA (5 Dan)

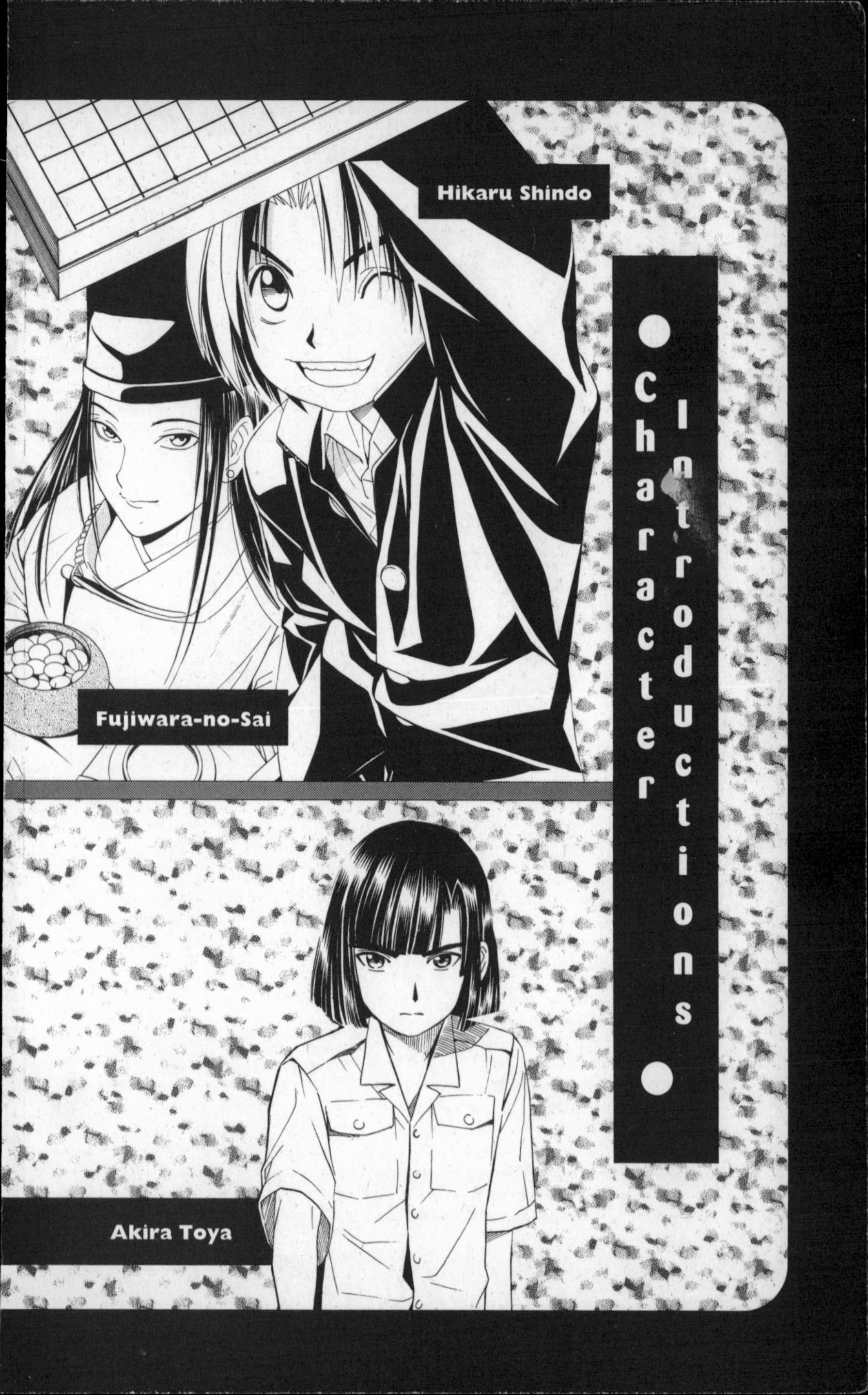
●Character Introductions●
Hikaru Shindo
Fujiwara-no-Sai
Akira Toya

Yuki Mitani
Tetsuo Kaga
Kimihiro Tsutsui
Akari Fujisaki

Story Thus Far

One day, Hikaru, a sixth grader, discovers an old go board in his grandfather's attic. The instant Hikaru touches the board, the spirit of Fujiwara-no-Sai, a genius go player from Japan's Heian Era, enters Hikaru's consciousness. Inspired by Sai's love of go, and by his encounter with the prodigy Akira Toya (son of go master Toya Meijin), Hikaru is slowly drawn to the game.

Hikaru and Akira face off for a third time at a middle school go tournament. Hikaru is determined to play Akira by himself, but he ends up letting Sai play instead. Midway through the game, however, Hikaru thinks up an interesting move and decides to play it. Naturally, he loses the game. Both Kimihiro and Yuki lose their games, too, and in the second round Haze Middle School is eliminated from the tournament. Akira is so disappointed by Hikaru's true abilities that he makes up his mind to take the pro test. With the onset of summer vacation, Hikaru begins playing Internet go as "sai" and defeats strong players around the world one after another. At the World Amateur Go Tournament, Akira learns of Sai's online presence, and his subsequent match with the anonymous player takes an unexpected turn—Akira resigns from the game and requests a rematch. But the day that the two have set for the next game is the first day of the pro test. Akira skips the test and prepares to face "sai" instead.

CONTENTS

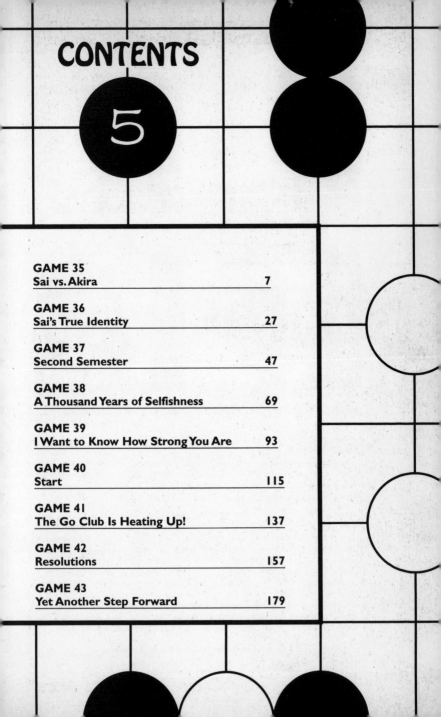

5

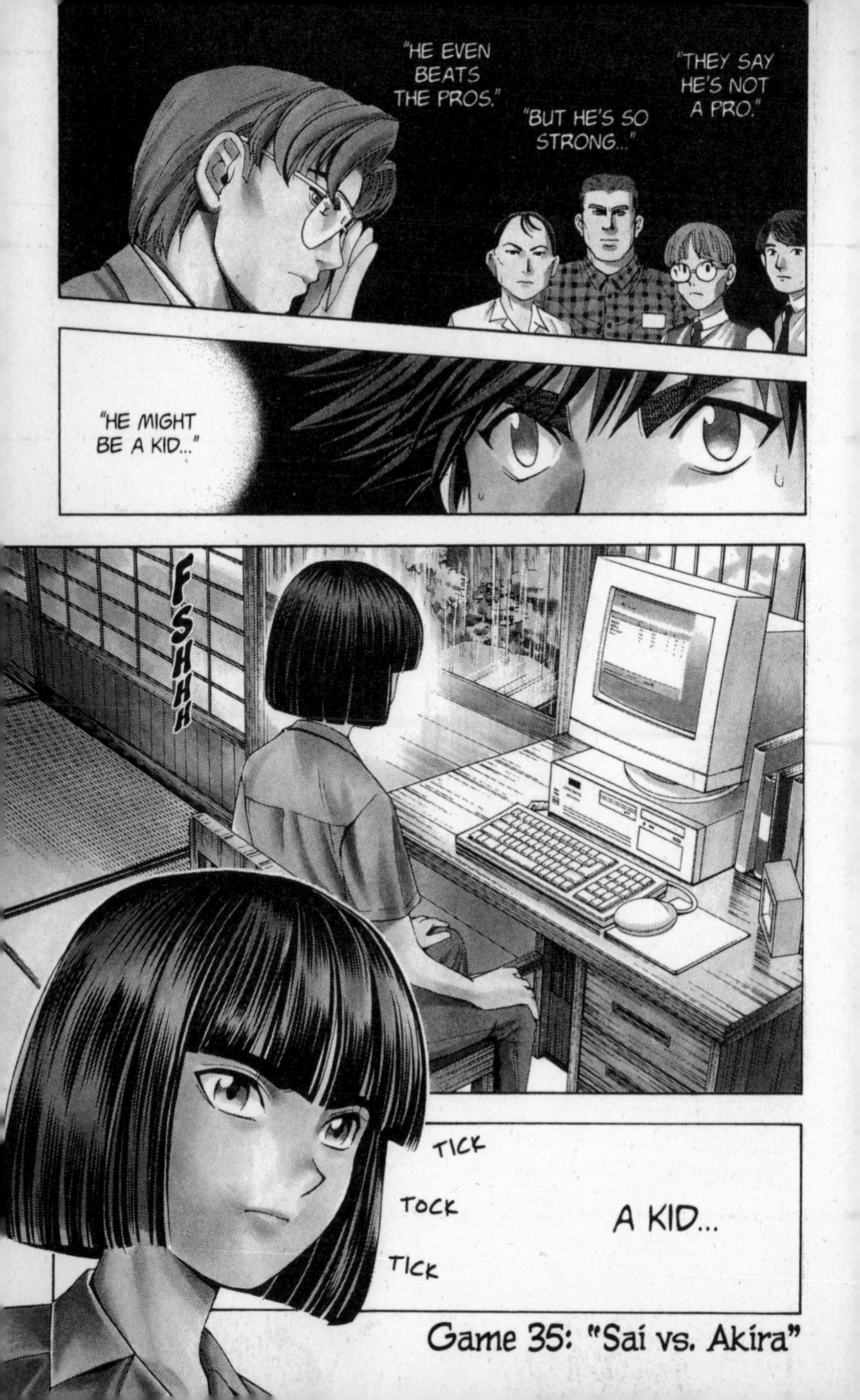
"THEY SAY HE'S NOT A PRO."
"BUT HE'S SO STRONG..."
"HE EVEN BEATS THE PROS."
"HE MIGHT BE A KID..."
FSHHH
A KID...
TICK
TOCK
TICK

Game 35: "Sai vs. Akira"

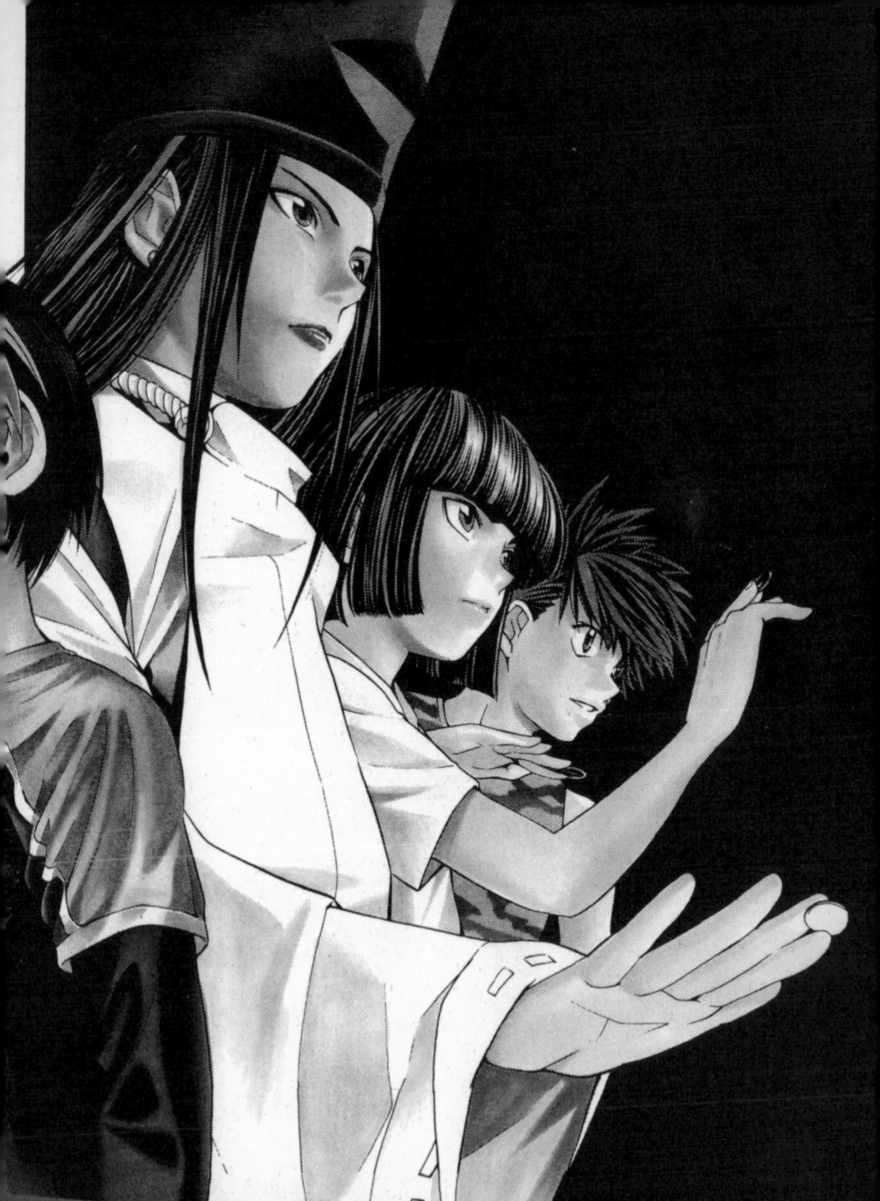

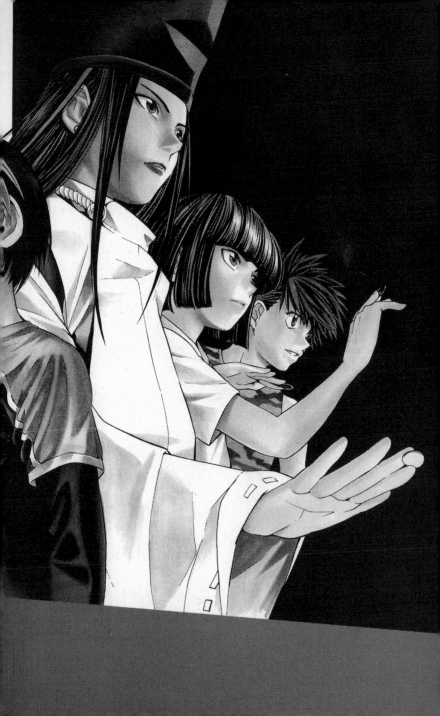

Game 35 "Sai vs. Akira"

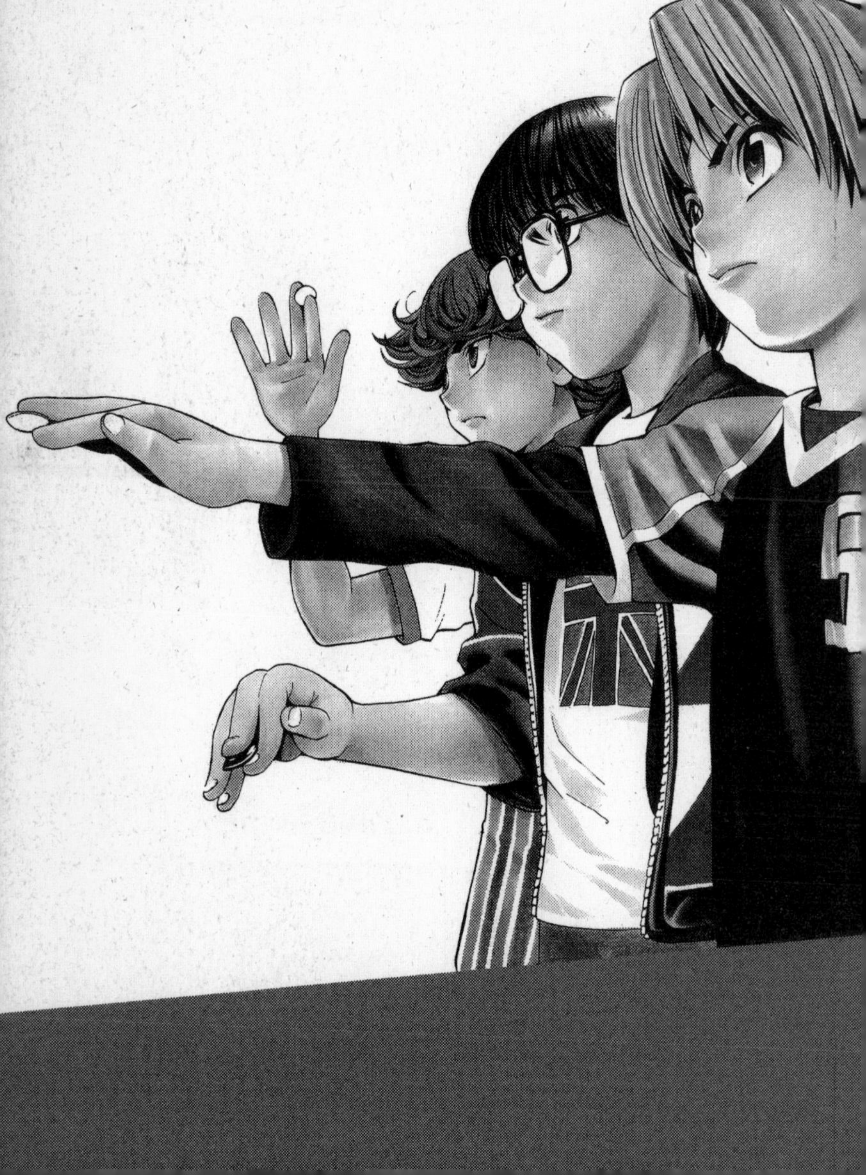

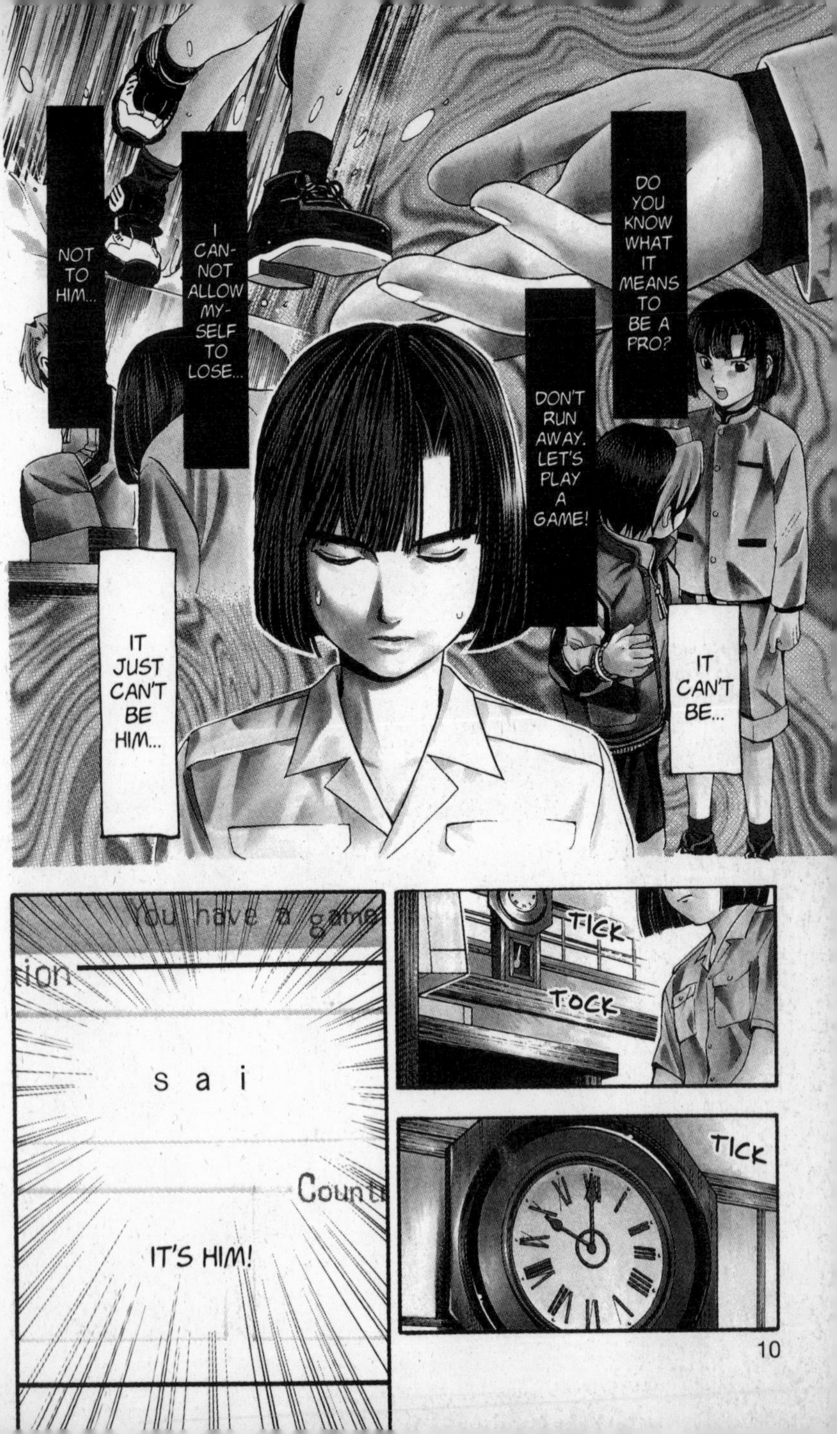
DO YOU KNOW WHAT IT MEANS TO BE A PRO?
DON'T RUN AWAY. LET'S PLAY A GAME!
I CAN-NOT ALLOW MY-SELF TO LOSE...
NOT TO HIM...
IT CAN'T BE...
IT JUST CAN'T BE HIM...
TICK
TOCK
TICK
You have a game
ion
s a i
Count
IT'S HIM!

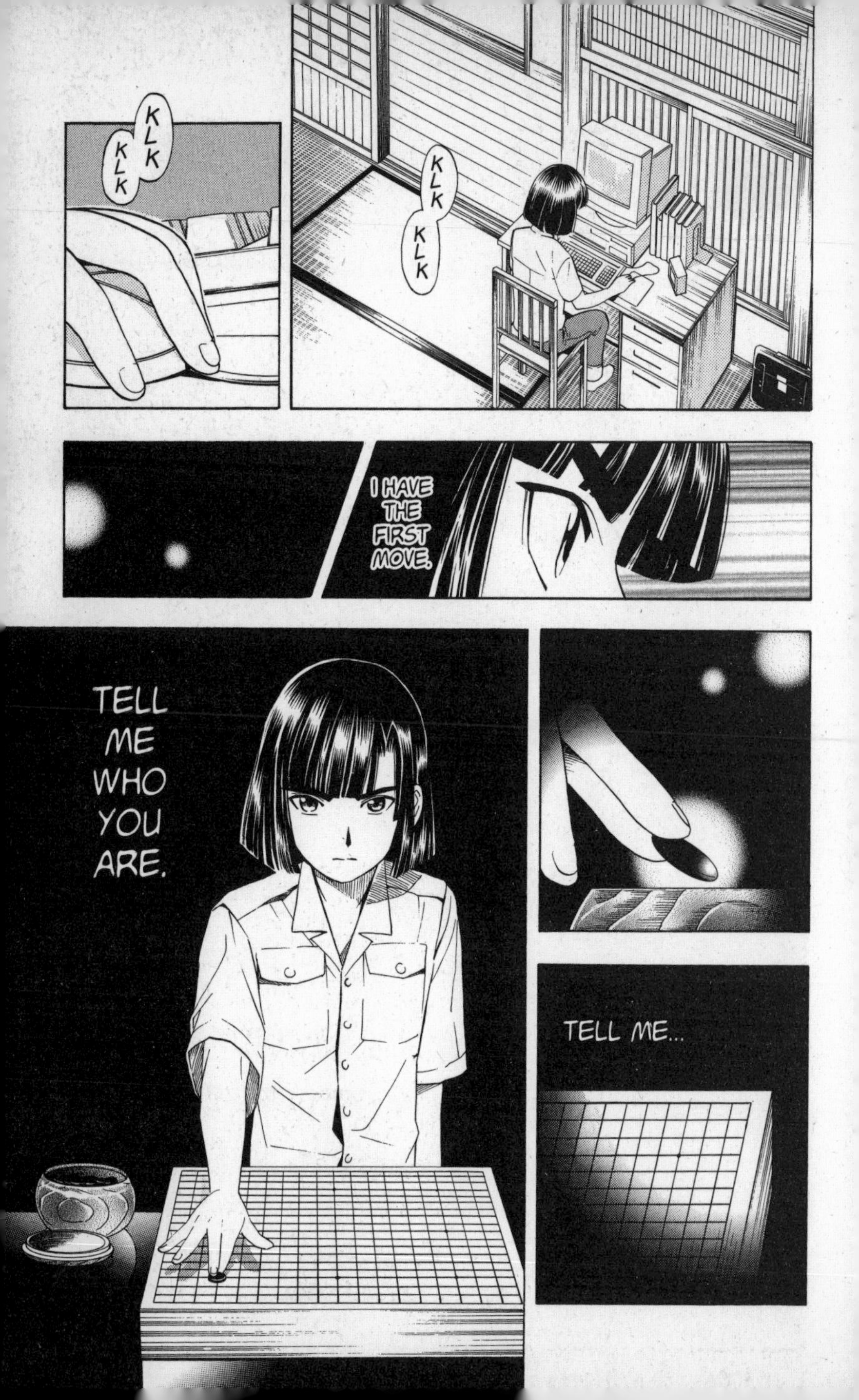
KLK
KLK
KLK
KLK
I HAVE THE FIRST MOVE.
TELL ME WHO YOU ARE.
TELL ME...

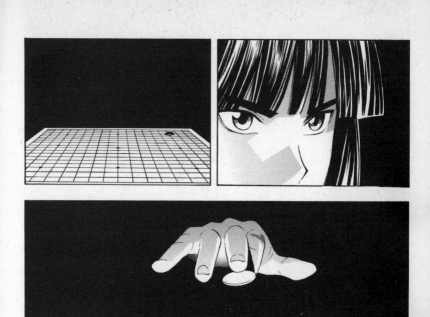

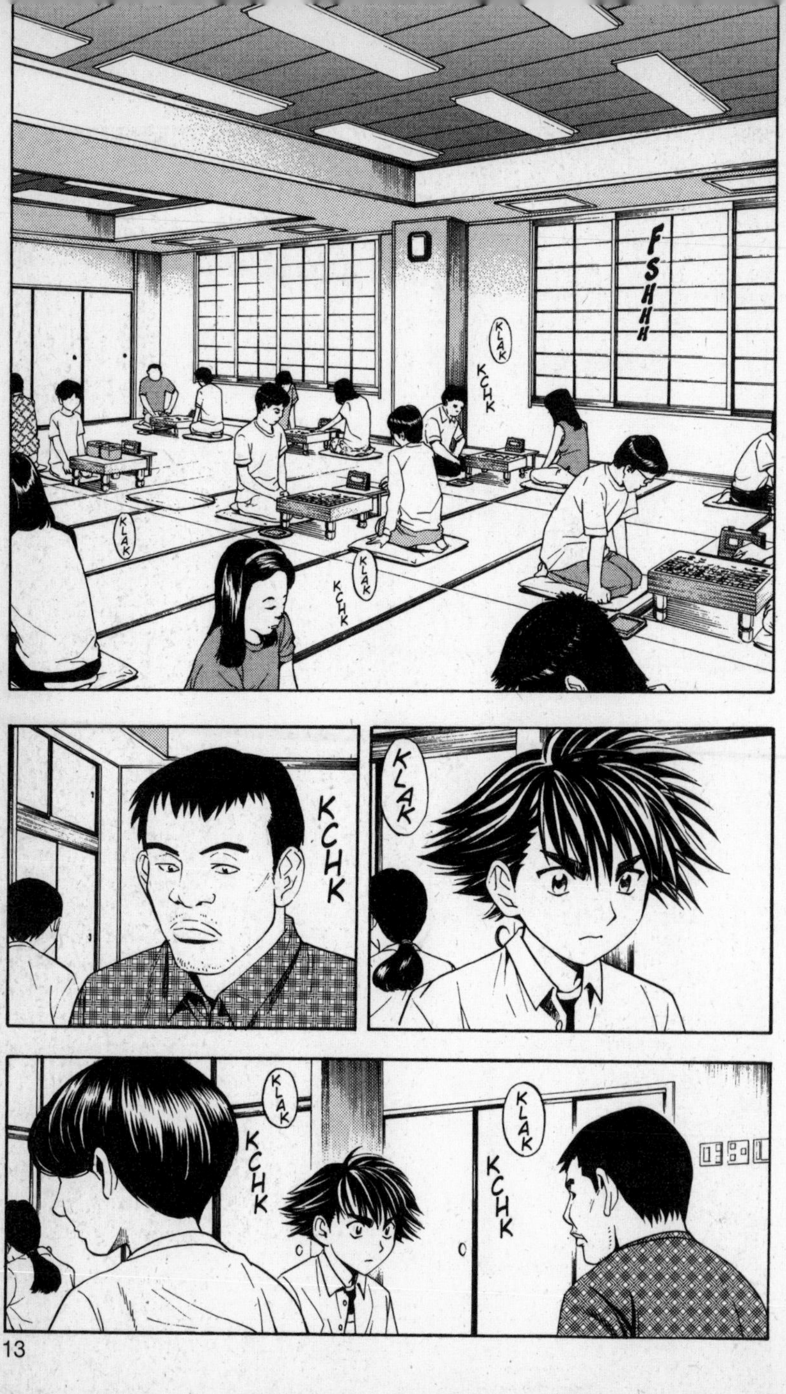
FSHHH
KLAK
KCHK
KLAK
KCHK
KLAK
KLAK
KCHK
KLAK
KCHK
KLAK
KCHK

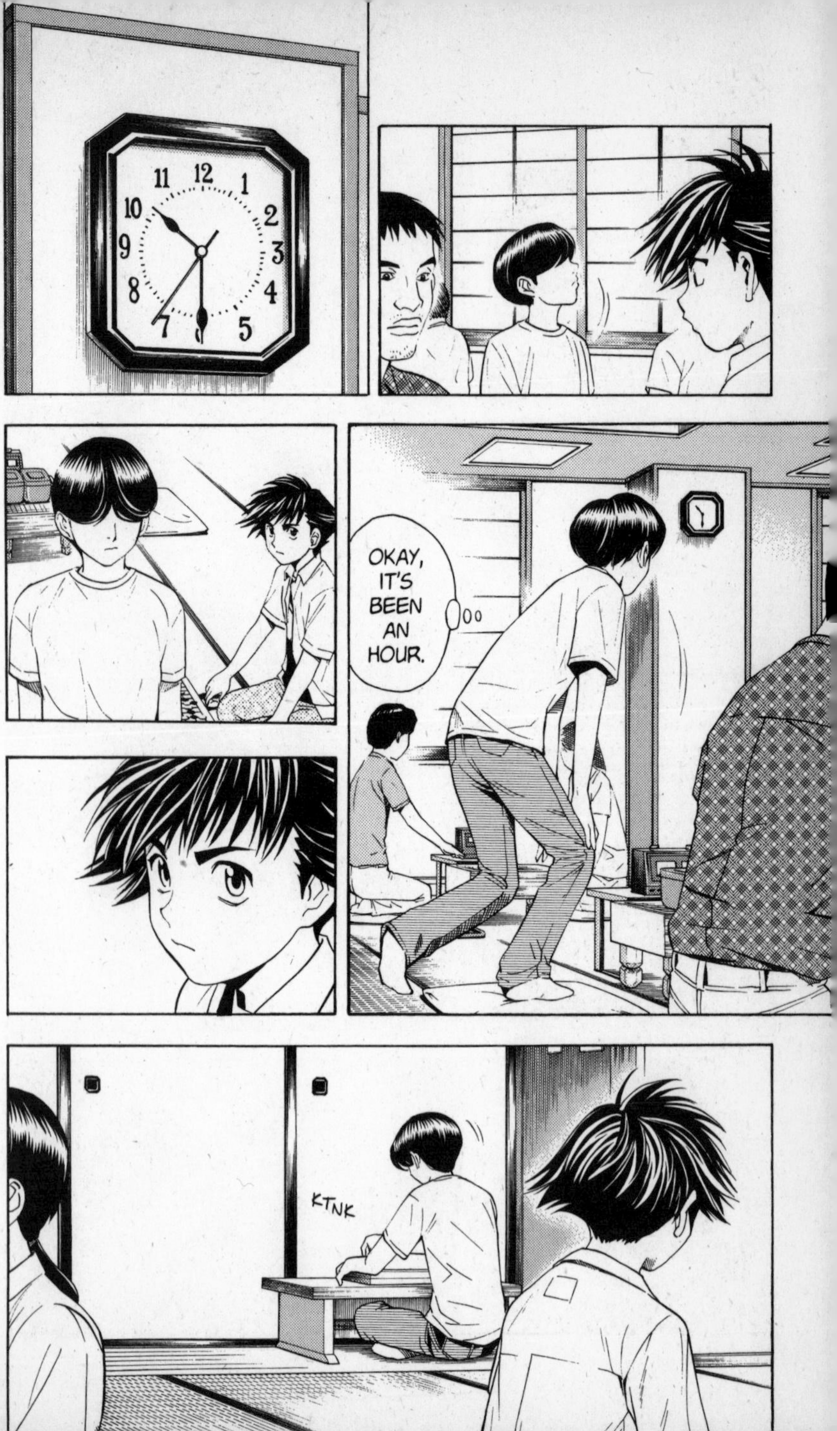

OKAY, IT'S BEEN AN HOUR.
KTNK

READ THIS WAY

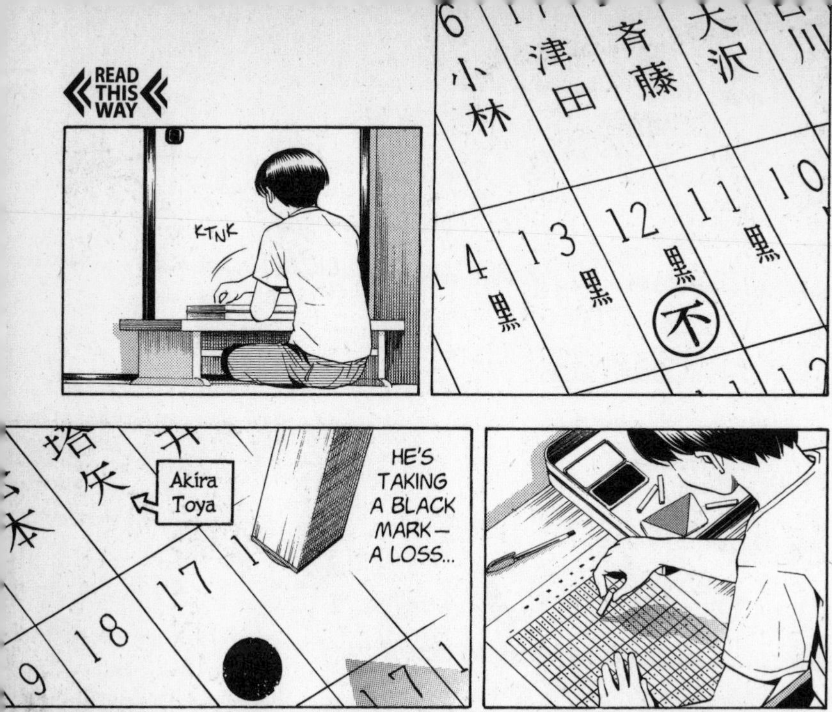
小林
津田
斉藤
大沢
黒
不
KTNK
Akira Toya
HE'S TAKING A BLACK MARK— A LOSS...

Akira has a black mark next to his name now.

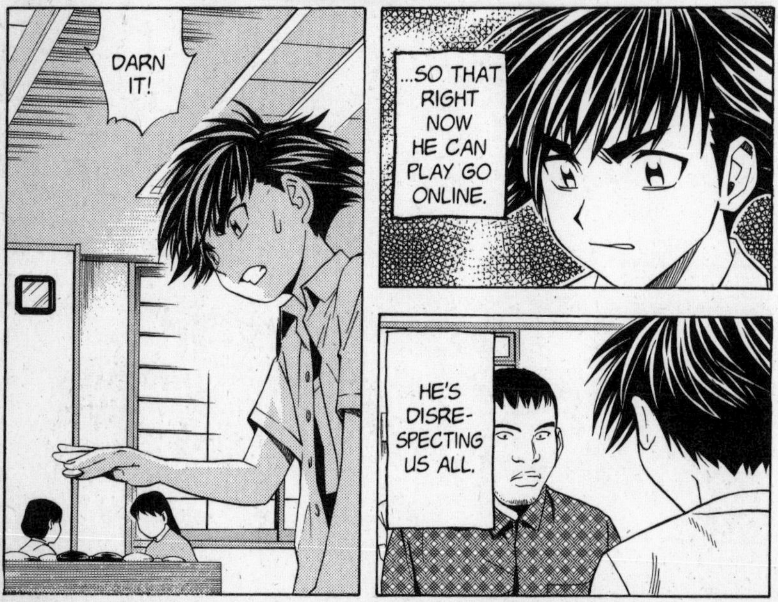
...SO THAT RIGHT NOW HE CAN PLAY GO ONLINE.
HE'S DISRE- SPECTING US ALL.
DARN IT!

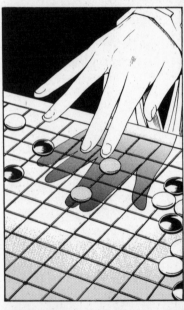

HE'S STRONG.

COULD IT BE...

I SENSE A GREAT WALL EVEN MORE DIFFICULT TO OVERCOME THAN THE LAST TIME I LOST TO HIKARU SHINDO.

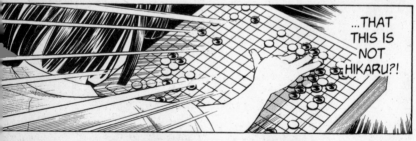

...THAT THIS IS NOT HIKARU?!

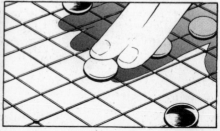

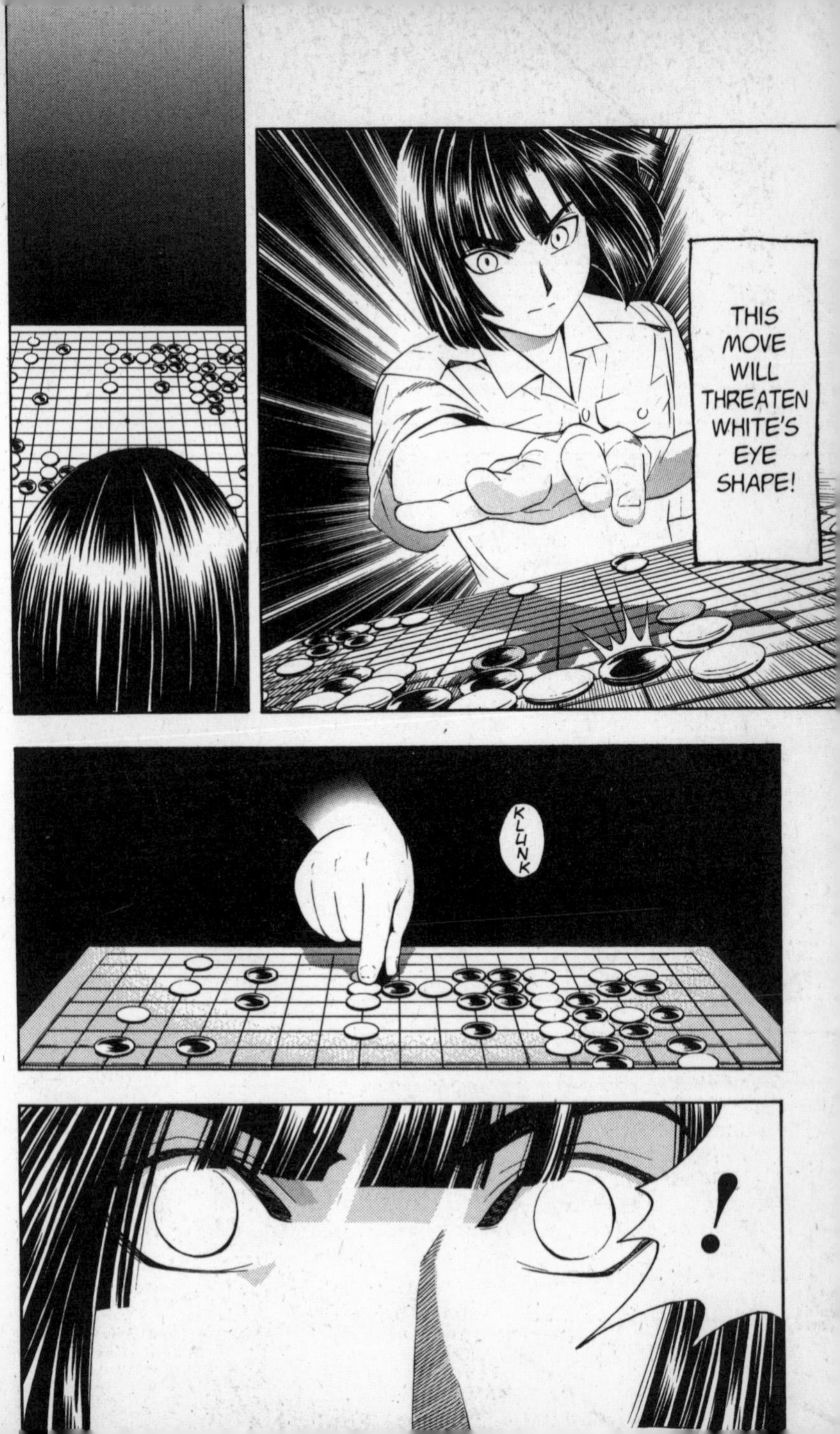
THIS MOVE WILL THREATEN WHITE'S EYE SHAPE!
KLUNK
!

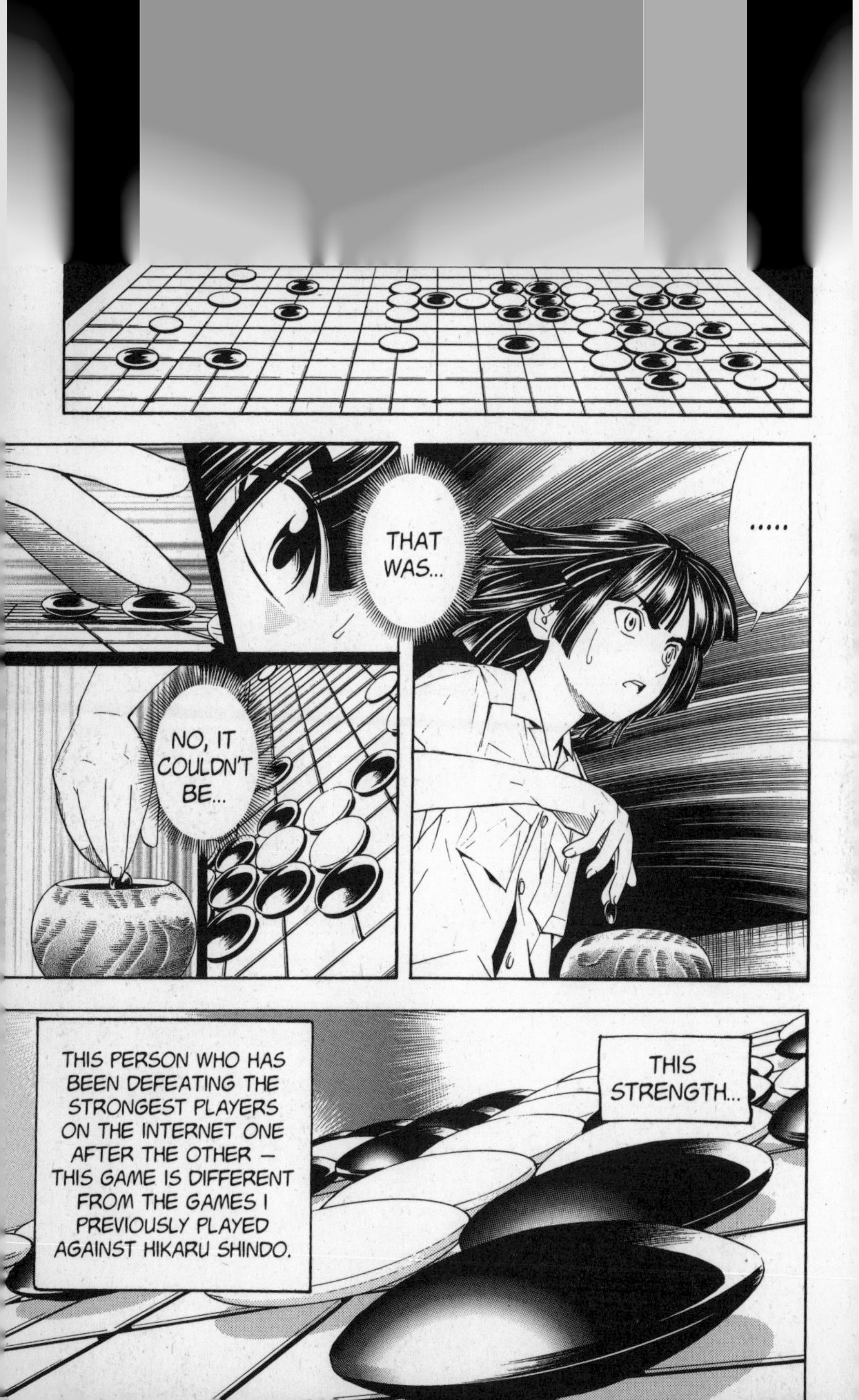
.....
THAT WAS...
NO, IT COULDN'T BE...
THIS STRENGTH...
THIS PERSON WHO HAS BEEN DEFEATING THE STRONGEST PLAYERS ON THE INTERNET ONE AFTER THE OTHER — THIS GAME IS DIFFERENT FROM THE GAMES I PREVIOUSLY PLAYED AGAINST HIKARU SHINDO.

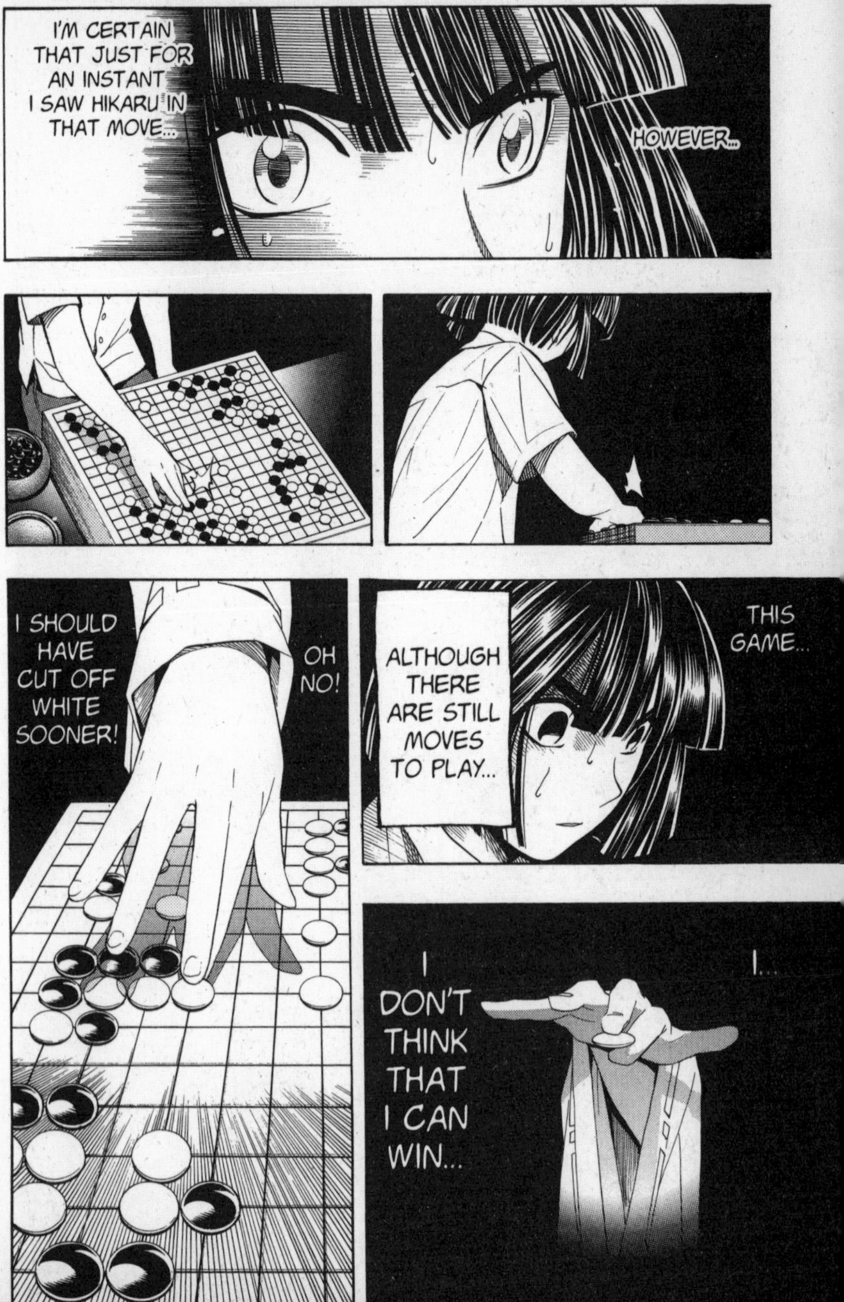

I'M CERTAIN THAT JUST FOR AN INSTANT I SAW HIKARU IN THAT MOVE...
HOWEVER...
THIS GAME...
ALTHOUGH THERE ARE STILL MOVES TO PLAY...
I...
I DON'T THINK THAT I CAN WIN...
OH NO!
I SHOULD HAVE CUT OFF WHITE SOONER!

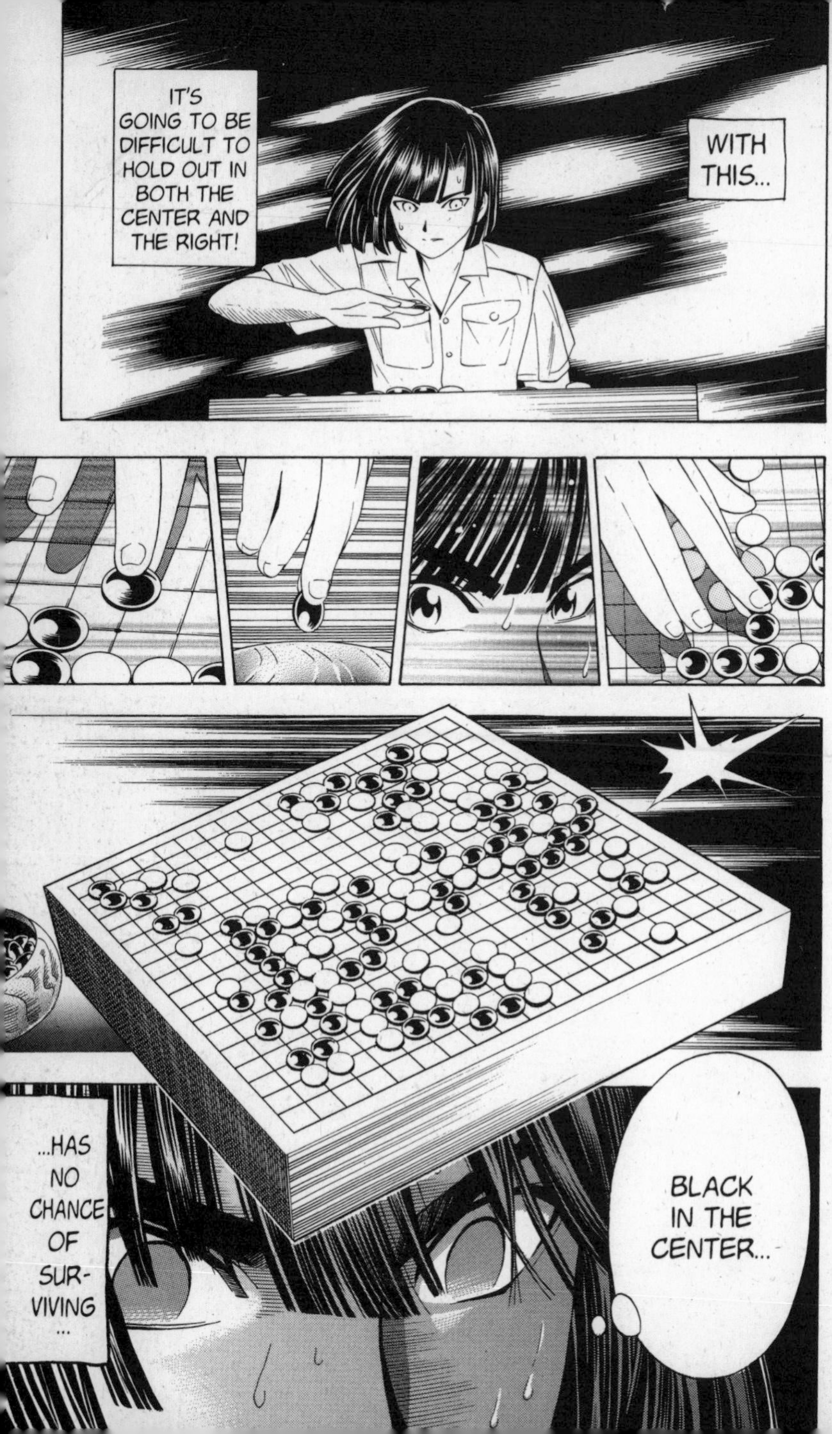
WITH THIS...
IT'S GOING TO BE DIFFICULT TO HOLD OUT IN BOTH THE CENTER AND THE RIGHT!
BLACK IN THE CENTER...
...HAS NO CHANCE OF SUR-VIVING ...

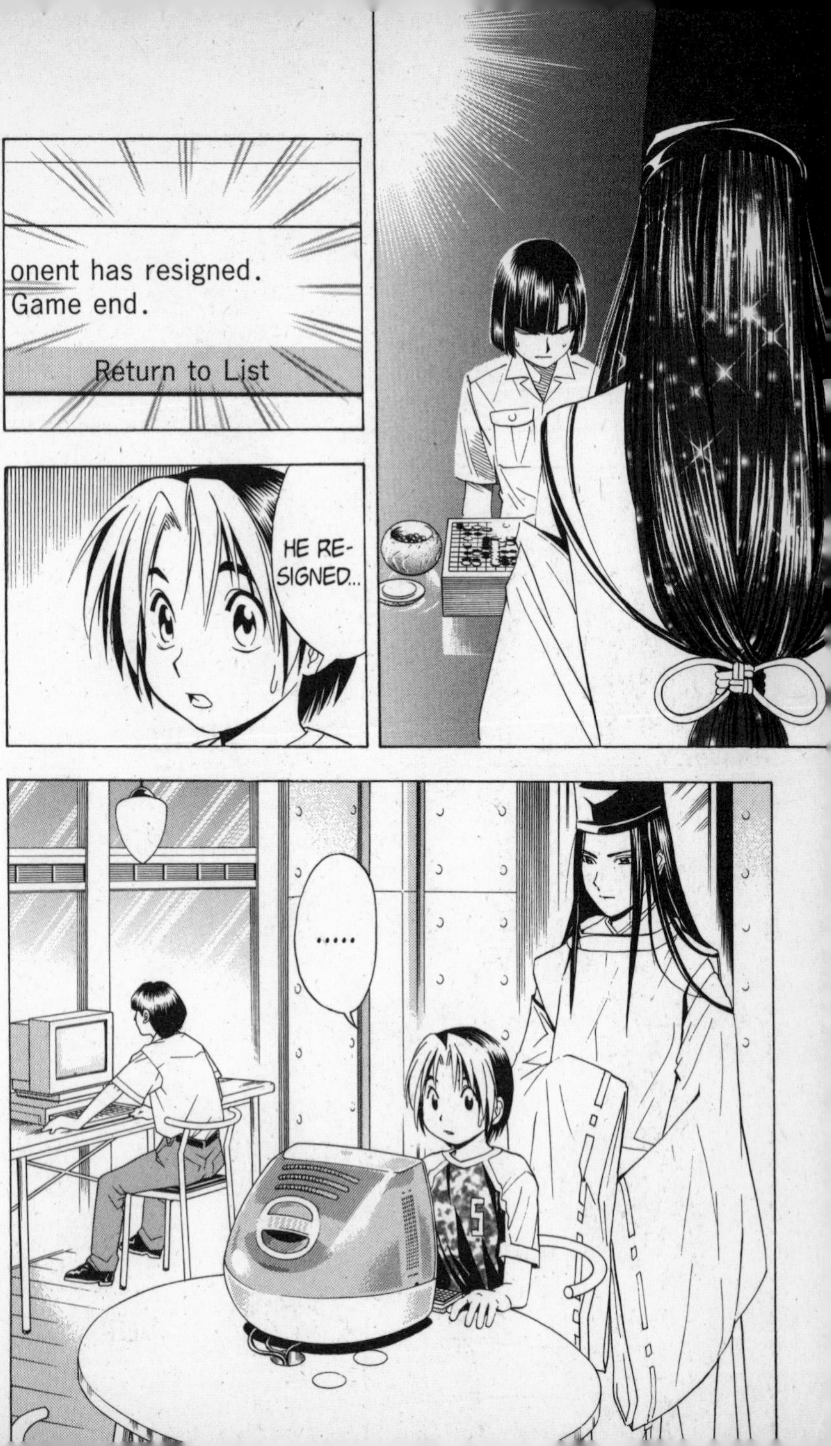

onent has resigned.
Game end.
Return to List
HE RE-SIGNED...
.....

READ THIS WAY

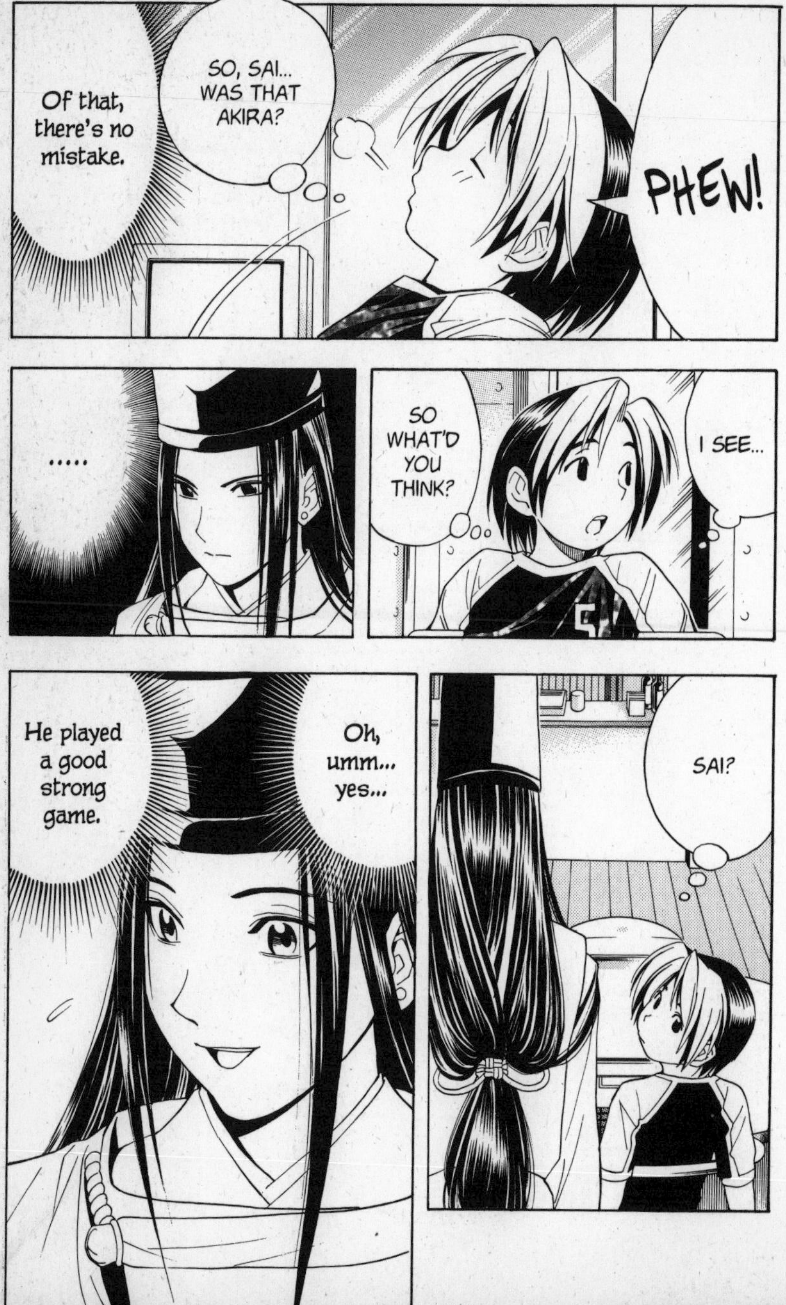
PHEW!
SO, SAI... WAS THAT AKIRA?
Of that, there's no mistake.
I SEE...
SO WHAT'D YOU THINK?
.....
SAI?
Oh, umm... yes...
He played a good strong game.

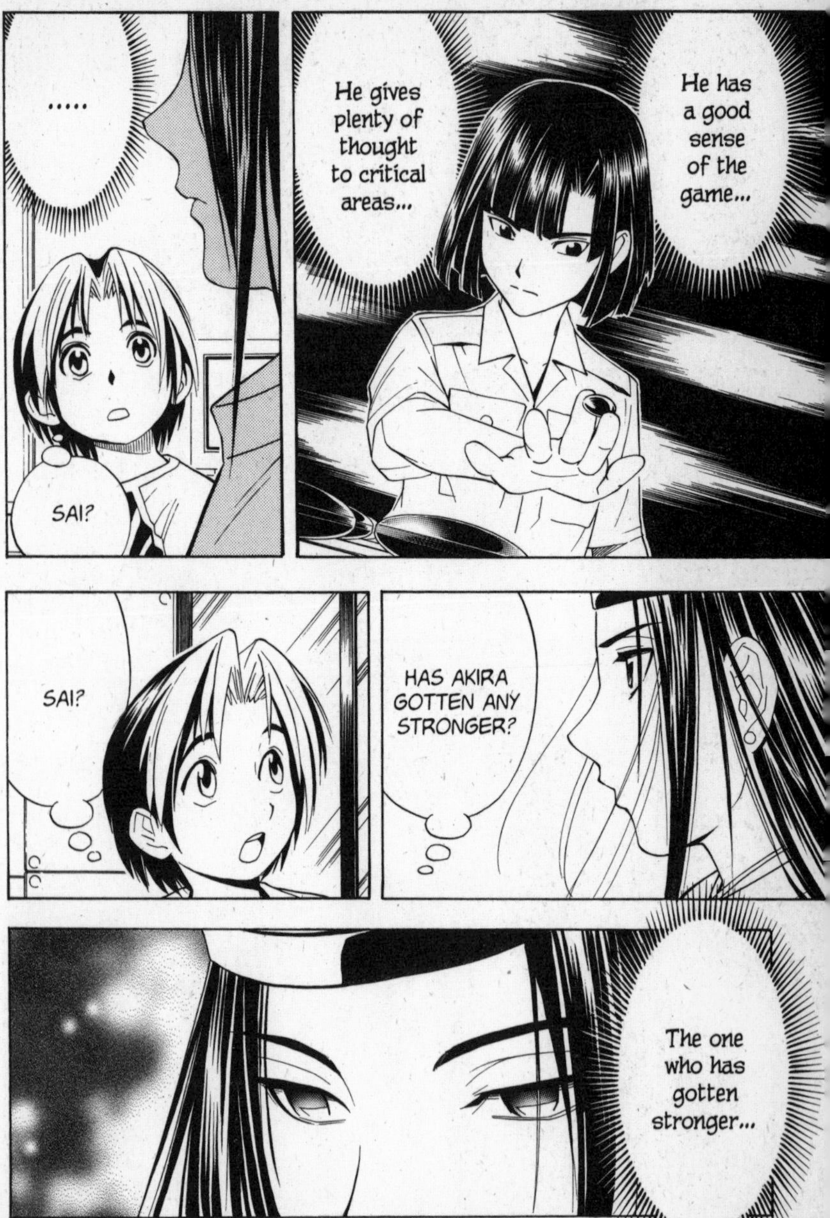
He has a good sense of the game...
He gives plenty of thought to critical areas...
.....
SAI?
HAS AKIRA GOTTEN ANY STRONGER?
SAI?
The one who has gotten stronger...

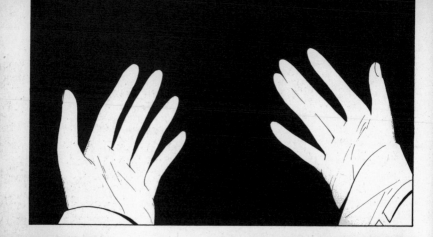

IS ME...

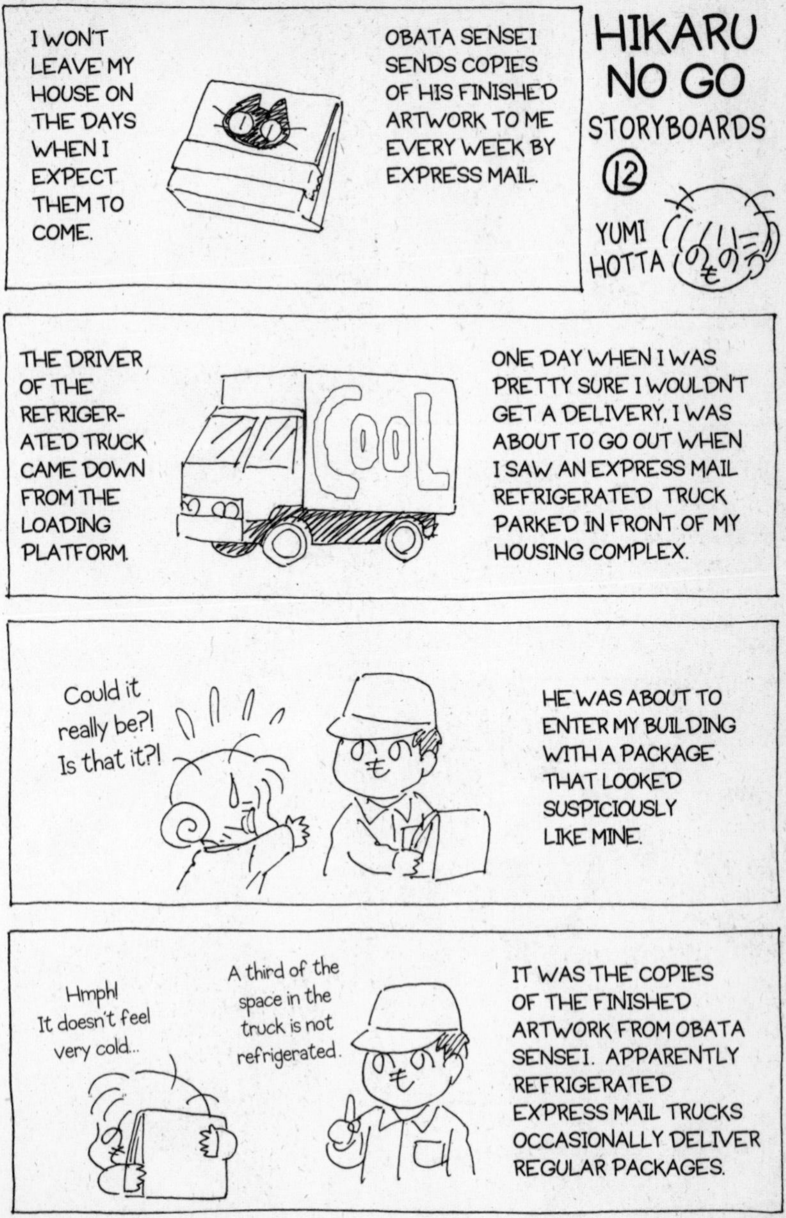

HIKARU NO GO STORYBOARDS ⑫
YUMI HOTTA
OBATA SENSEI SENDS COPIES OF HIS FINISHED ARTWORK TO ME EVERY WEEK BY EXPRESS MAIL.
I WON'T LEAVE MY HOUSE ON THE DAYS WHEN I EXPECT THEM TO COME.
ONE DAY WHEN I WAS PRETTY SURE I WOULDN'T GET A DELIVERY, I WAS ABOUT TO GO OUT WHEN I SAW AN EXPRESS MAIL REFRIGERATED TRUCK PARKED IN FRONT OF MY HOUSING COMPLEX.
COOL
THE DRIVER OF THE REFRIGER-ATED TRUCK CAME DOWN FROM THE LOADING PLATFORM.
HE WAS ABOUT TO ENTER MY BUILDING WITH A PACKAGE THAT LOOKED SUSPICIOUSLY LIKE MINE.
Could it really be?! Is that it?!
IT WAS THE COPIES OF THE FINISHED ARTWORK FROM OBATA SENSEI. APPARENTLY REFRIGERATED EXPRESS MAIL TRUCKS OCCASIONALLY DELIVER REGULAR PACKAGES.
A third of the space in the truck is not refrigerated.
Hmph! It doesn't feel very cold...

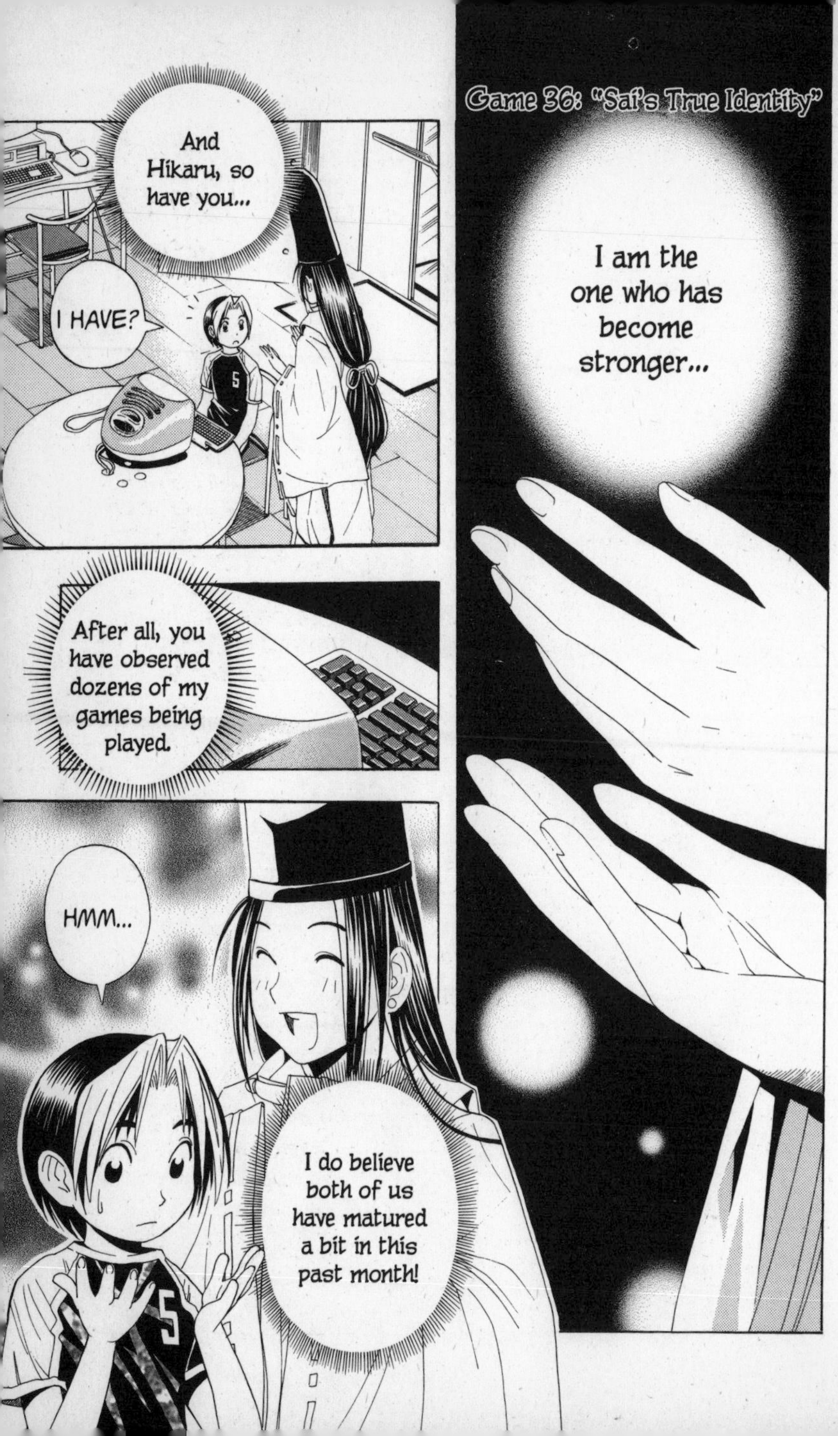
Game 36: "Sai's True Identity"
I am the one who has become stronger...
And Hikaru, so have you...
I HAVE?
After all, you have observed dozens of my games being played.
HMM...
I do believe both of us have matured a bit in this past month!

Game 36 "Sai's True Identity"

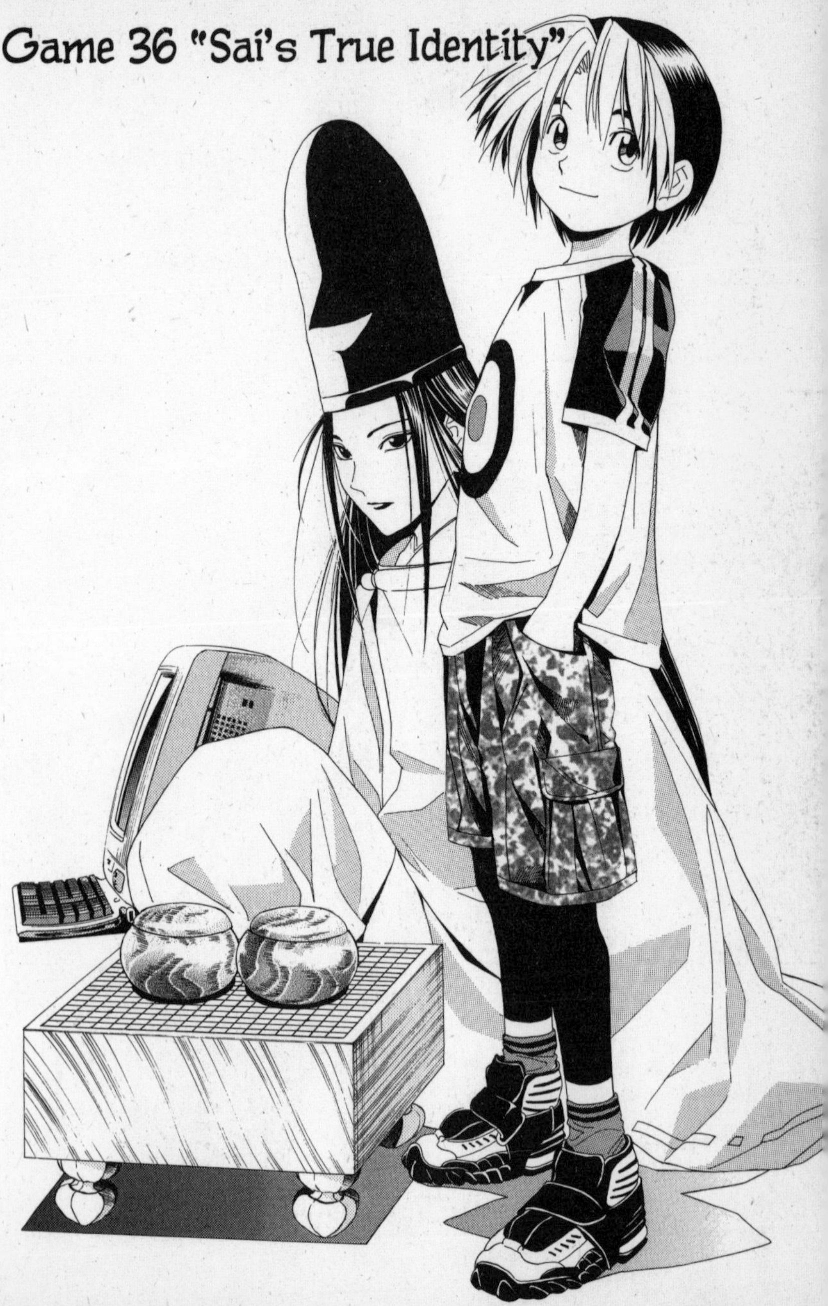

READ THIS WAY

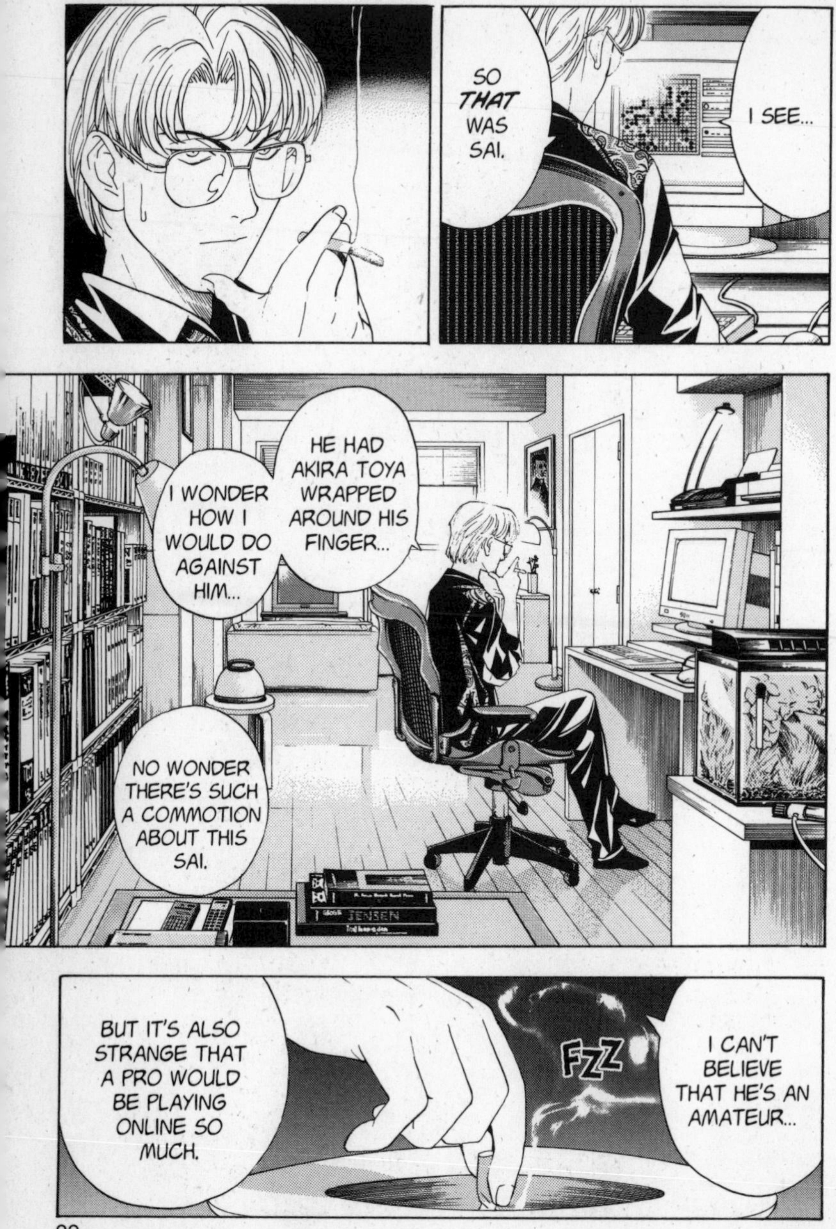

I SEE...
SO THAT WAS SAI.
HE HAD AKIRA TOYA WRAPPED AROUND HIS FINGER...
I WONDER HOW I WOULD DO AGAINST HIM...
NO WONDER THERE'S SUCH A COMMOTION ABOUT THIS SAI.
I CAN'T BELIEVE THAT HE'S AN AMATEUR...
FZZ
BUT IT'S ALSO STRANGE THAT A PRO WOULD BE PLAYING ONLINE SO MUCH.

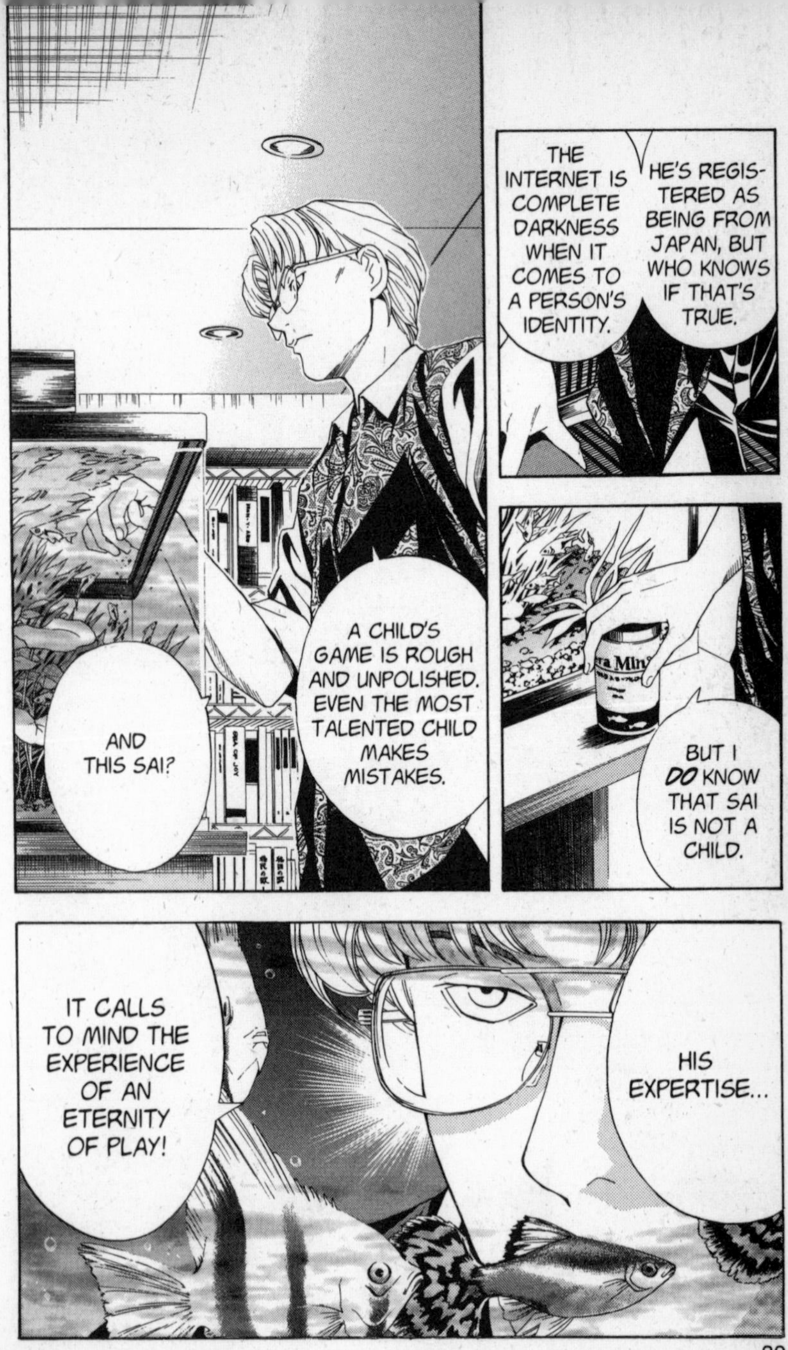
HE'S REGIS-TERED AS BEING FROM JAPAN, BUT WHO KNOWS IF THAT'S TRUE.
THE INTERNET IS COMPLETE DARKNESS WHEN IT COMES TO A PERSON'S IDENTITY.
BUT I *DO* KNOW THAT SAI IS NOT A CHILD.
A CHILD'S GAME IS ROUGH AND UNPOLISHED. EVEN THE MOST TALENTED CHILD MAKES MISTAKES.
AND THIS SAI?
HIS EXPERTISE...
IT CALLS TO MIND THE EXPERIENCE OF AN ETERNITY OF PLAY!

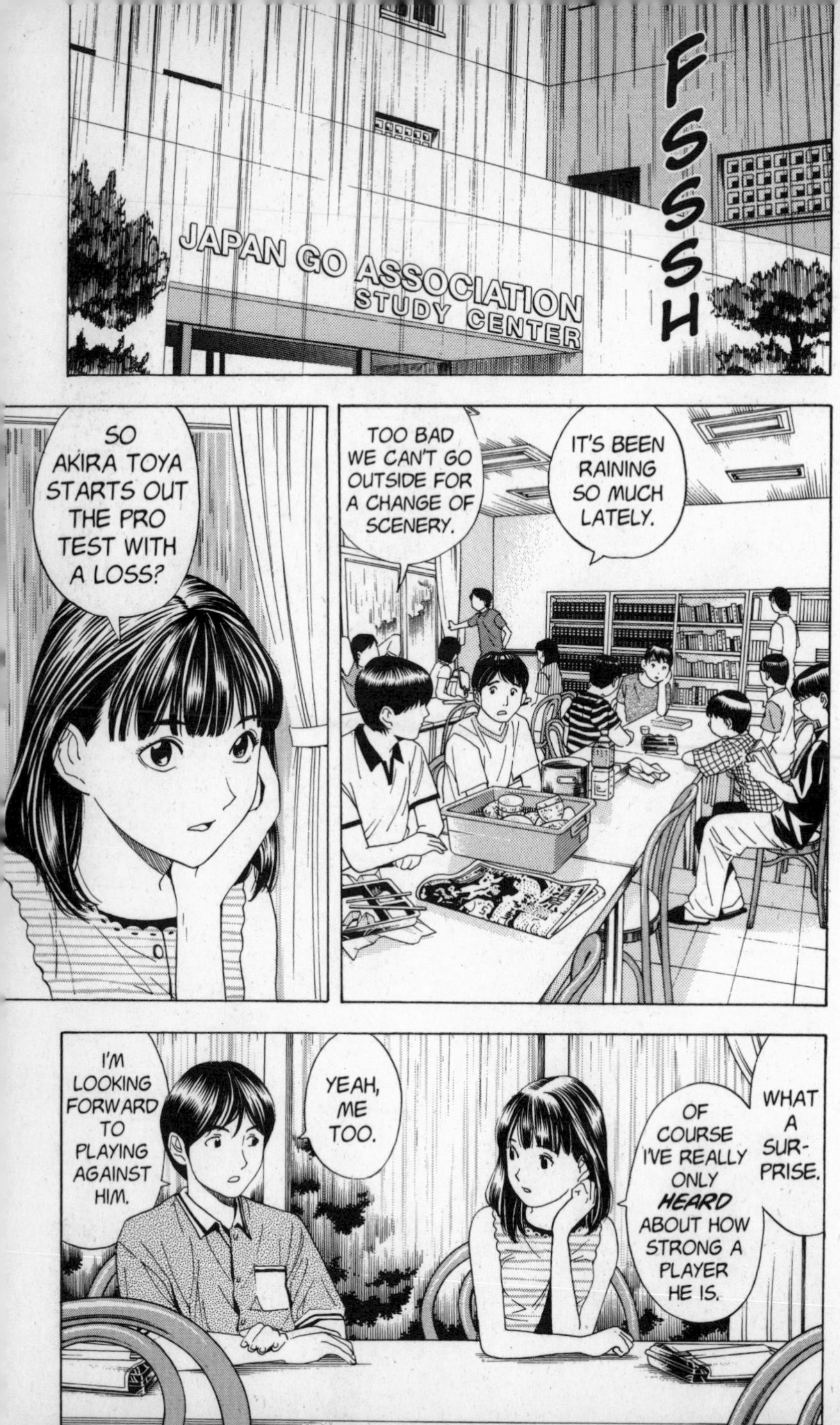
JAPAN GO ASSOCIATION
STUDY CENTER
FSSSH
IT'S BEEN RAINING SO MUCH LATELY.
TOO BAD WE CAN'T GO OUTSIDE FOR A CHANGE OF SCENERY.
SO AKIRA TOYA STARTS OUT THE PRO TEST WITH A LOSS?
WHAT A SUR-PRISE.
OF COURSE I'VE REALLY ONLY *HEARD* ABOUT HOW STRONG A PLAYER HE IS.
YEAH, ME TOO.
I'M LOOKING FORWARD TO PLAYING AGAINST HIM.

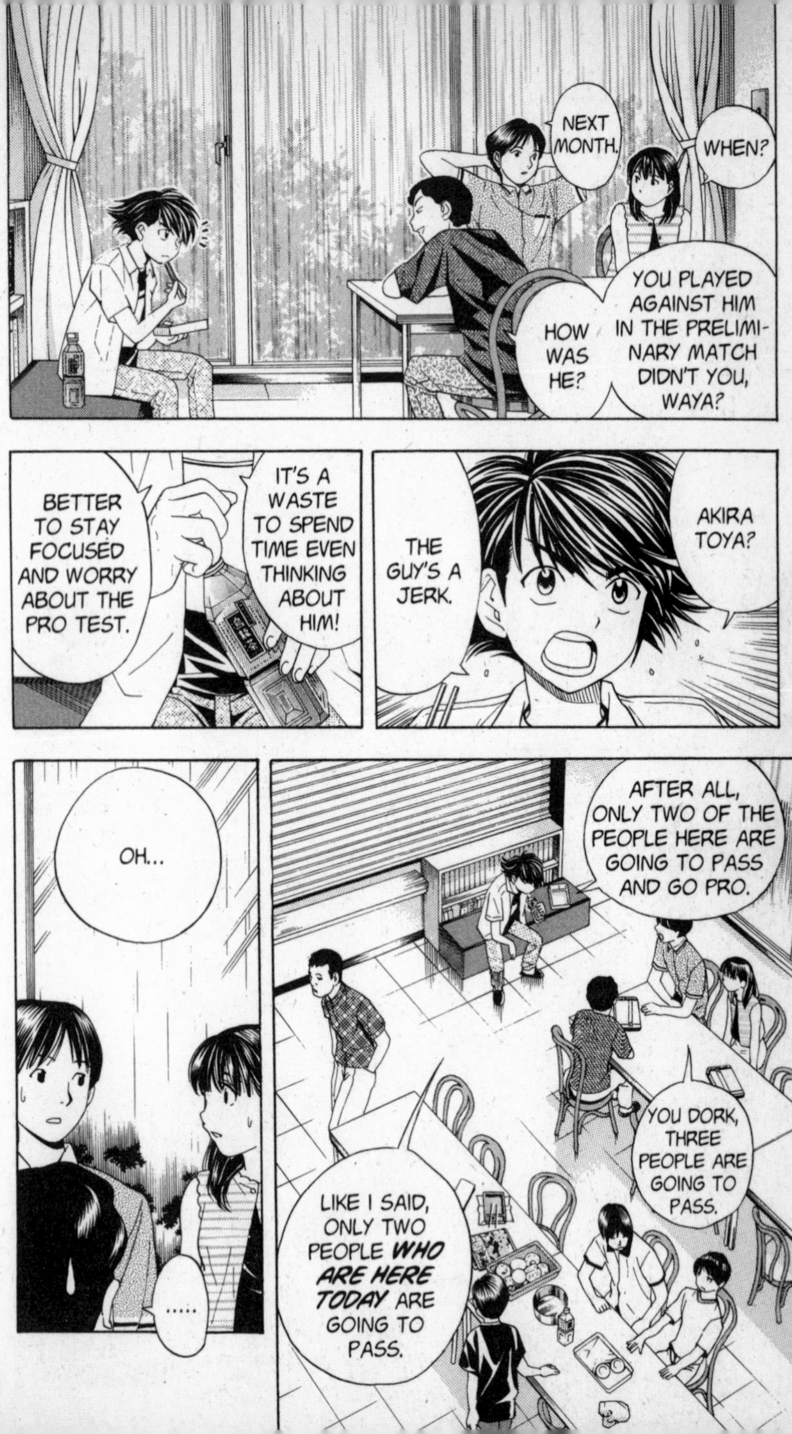
WHEN?
NEXT MONTH.
YOU PLAYED AGAINST HIM IN THE PRELIMINARY MATCH DIDN'T YOU, WAYA?
HOW WAS HE?
AKIRA TOYA?
THE GUY'S A JERK.
IT'S A WASTE TO SPEND TIME EVEN THINKING ABOUT HIM!
BETTER TO STAY FOCUSED AND WORRY ABOUT THE PRO TEST.
AFTER ALL, ONLY TWO OF THE PEOPLE HERE ARE GOING TO PASS AND GO PRO.
YOU DORK, THREE PEOPLE ARE GOING TO PASS.
LIKE I SAID, ONLY TWO PEOPLE ***WHO ARE HERE TODAY*** ARE GOING TO PASS.
OH...
......

READ THIS WAY

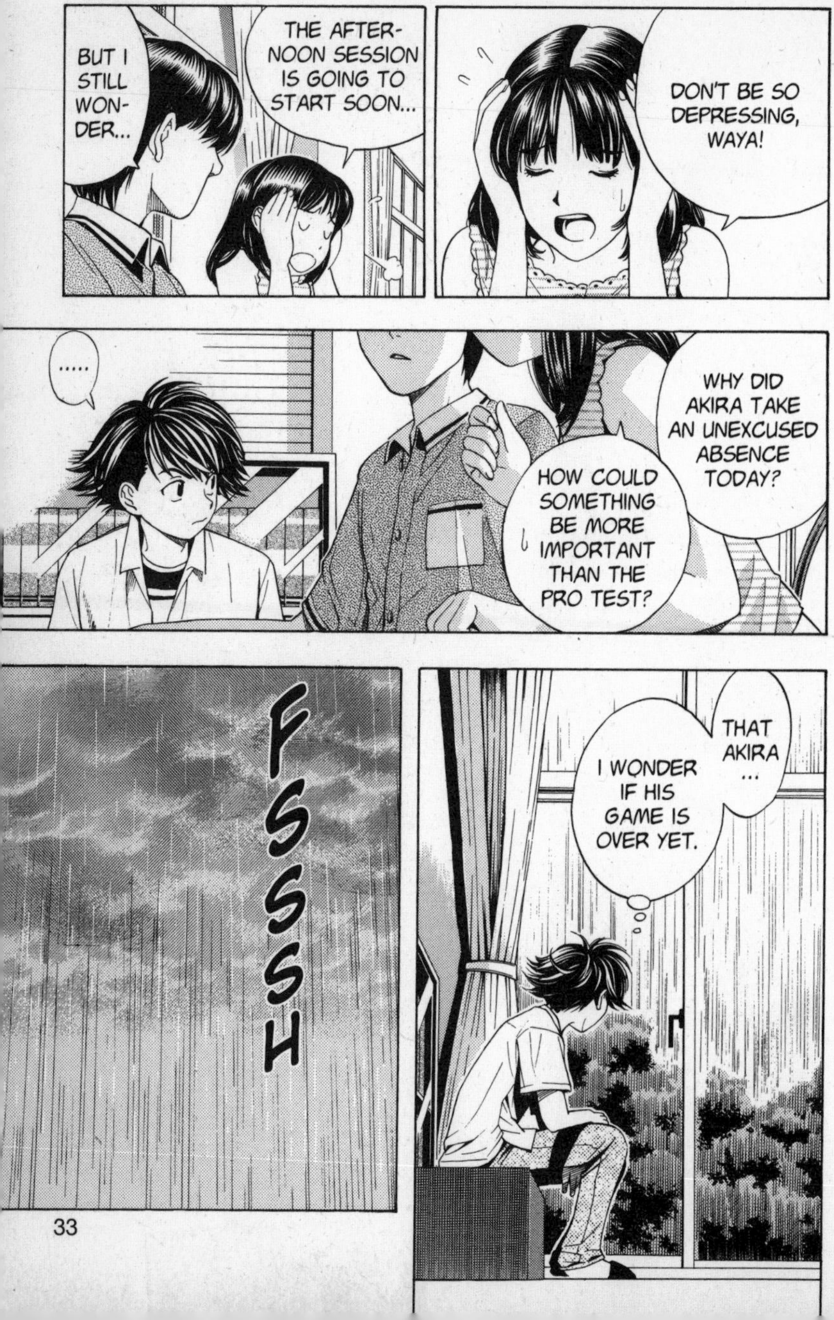

DON'T BE SO DEPRESSING, WAYA!
THE AFTER-NOON SESSION IS GOING TO START SOON...
BUT I STILL WON-DER...
WHY DID AKIRA TAKE AN UNEXCUSED ABSENCE TODAY?
HOW COULD SOMETHING BE MORE IMPORTANT THAN THE PRO TEST?
.....
THAT AKIRA ...
I WONDER IF HIS GAME IS OVER YET.
FSSSH

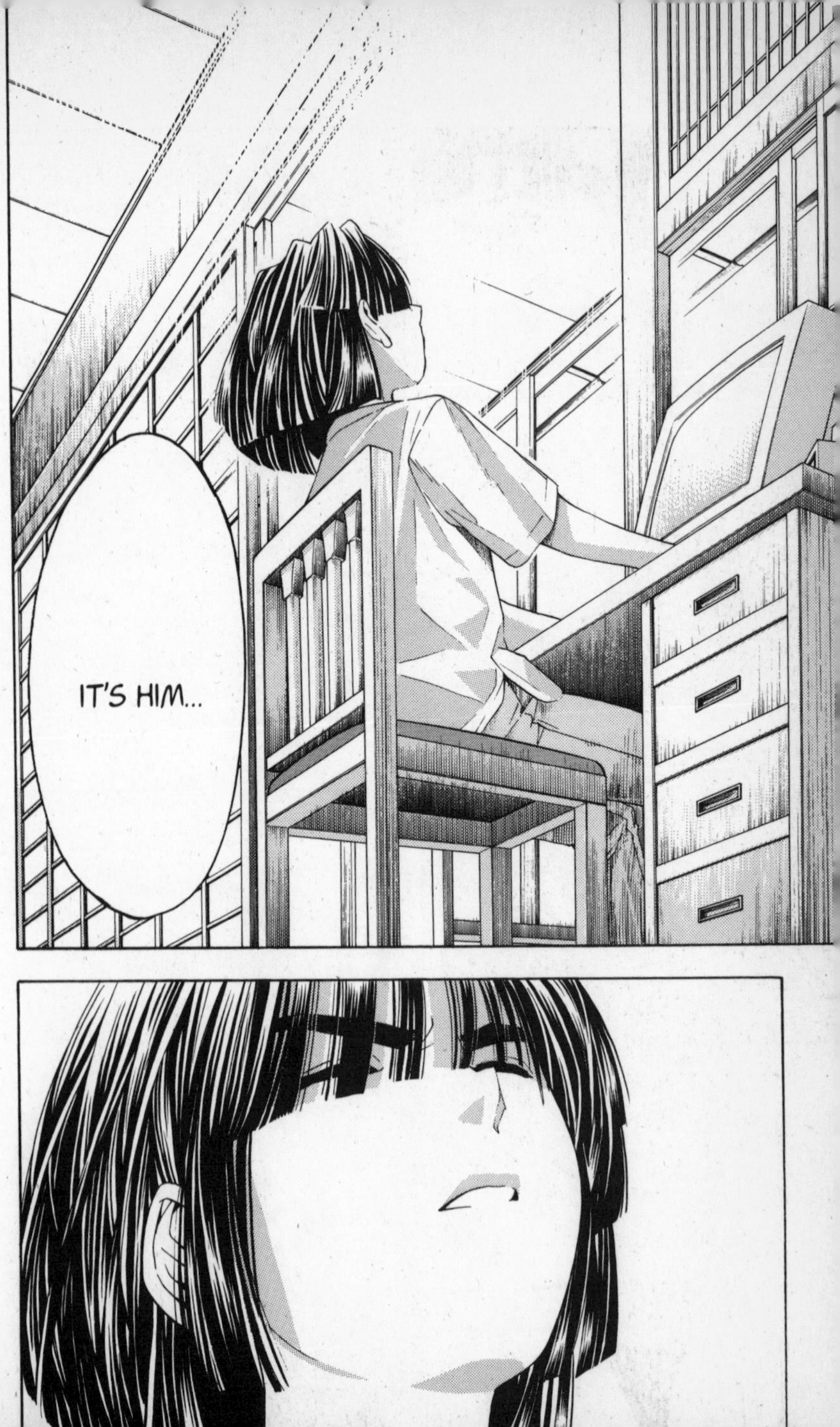
IT'S HIM...

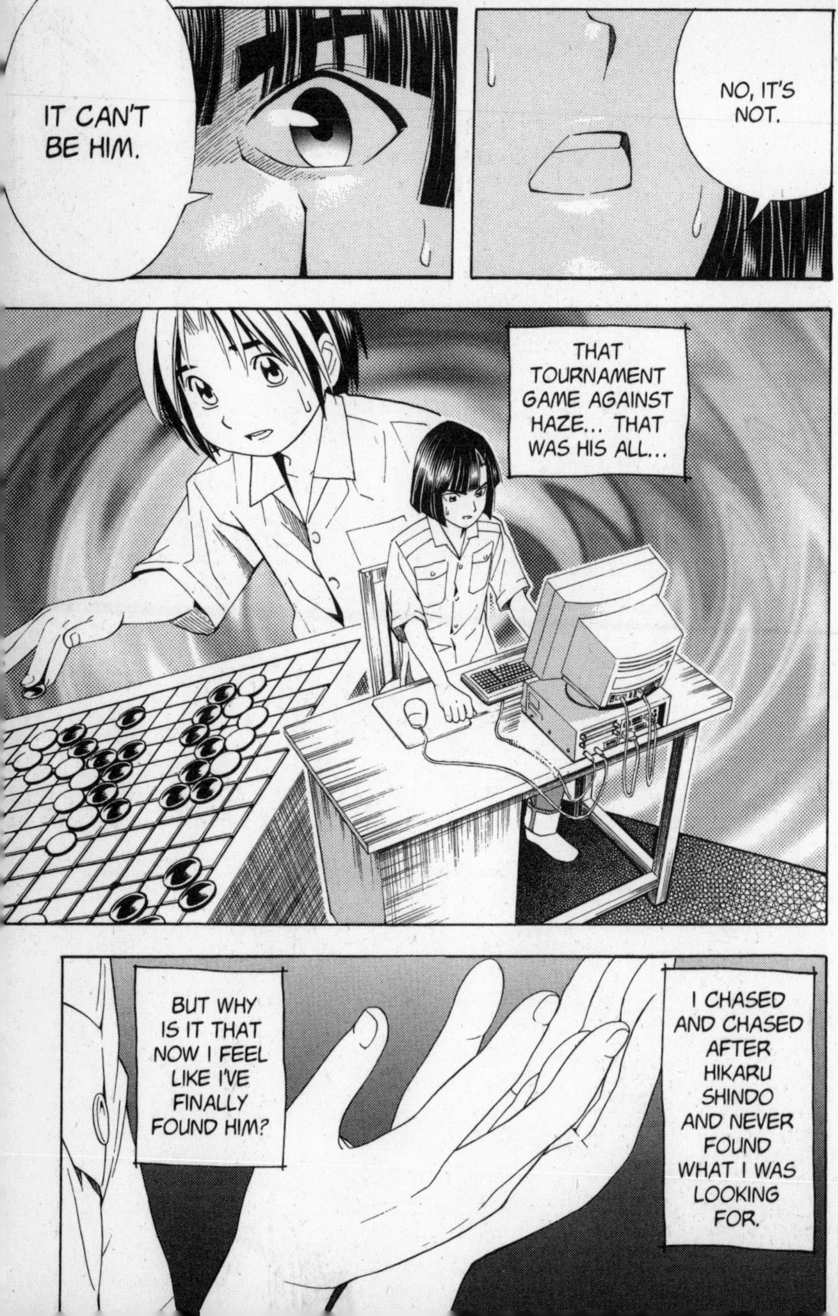
NO, IT'S NOT.
IT CAN'T BE HIM.
THAT TOURNAMENT GAME AGAINST HAZE... THAT WAS HIS ALL...
I CHASED AND CHASED AFTER HIKARU SHINDO AND NEVER FOUND WHAT I WAS LOOKING FOR.
BUT WHY IS IT THAT NOW I FEEL LIKE I'VE FINALLY FOUND HIM?

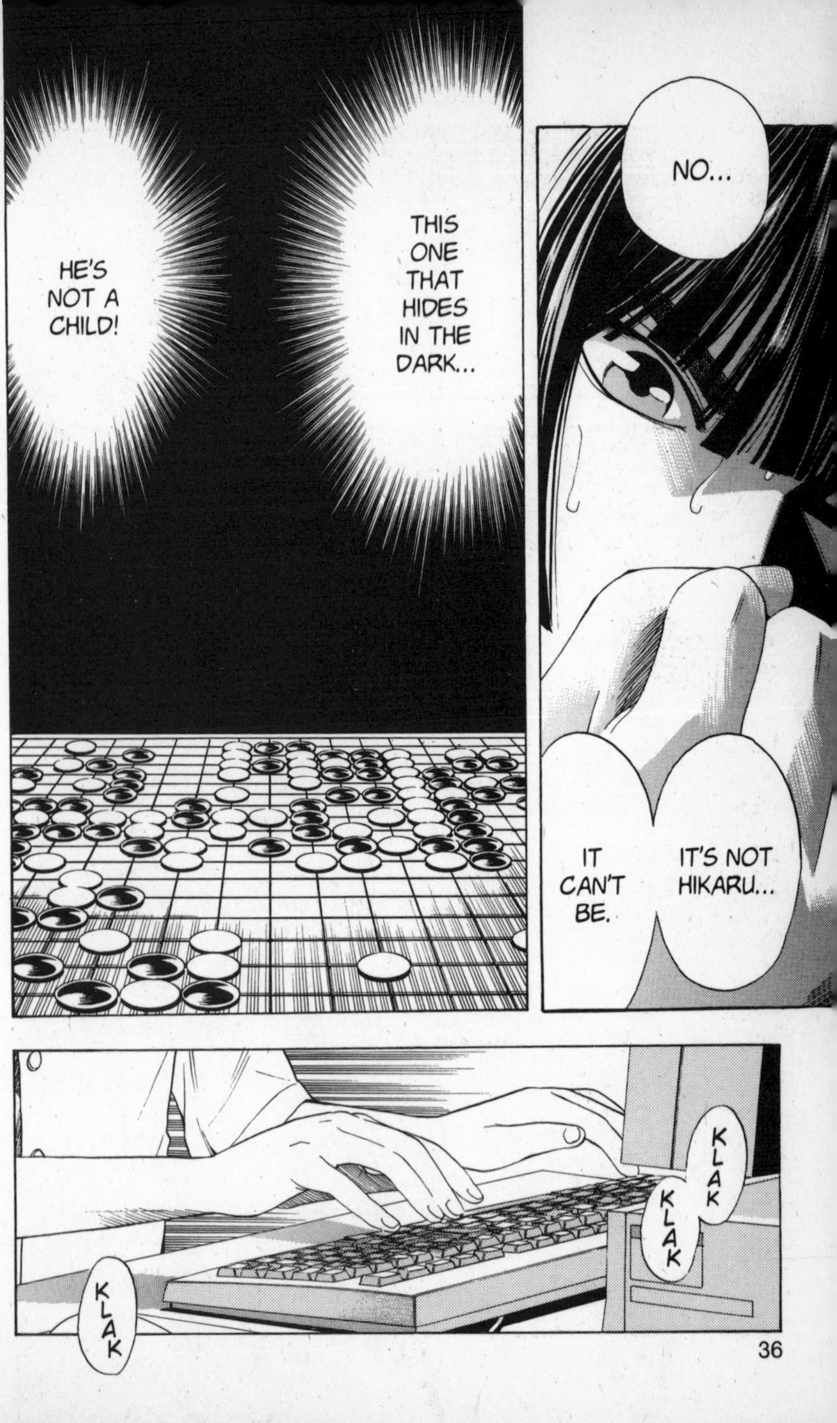
NO...
IT'S NOT HIKARU...
IT CAN'T BE.
THIS ONE THAT HIDES IN THE DARK...
HE'S NOT A CHILD!
KLAK
KLAK
KLAK

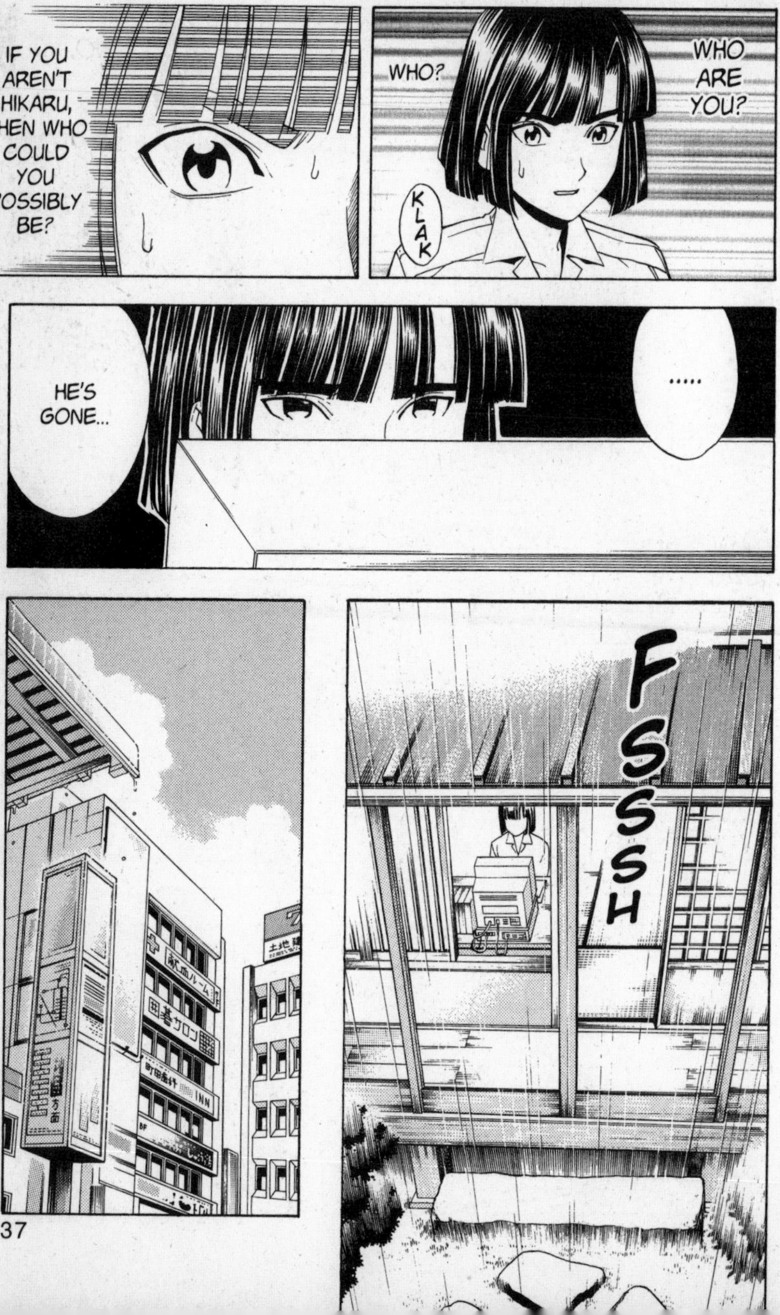
WHO ARE YOU?
WHO?
KLAK
IF YOU AREN'T HIKARU, THEN WHO COULD YOU POSSIBLY BE?
.....
HE'S GONE...
FSSSH

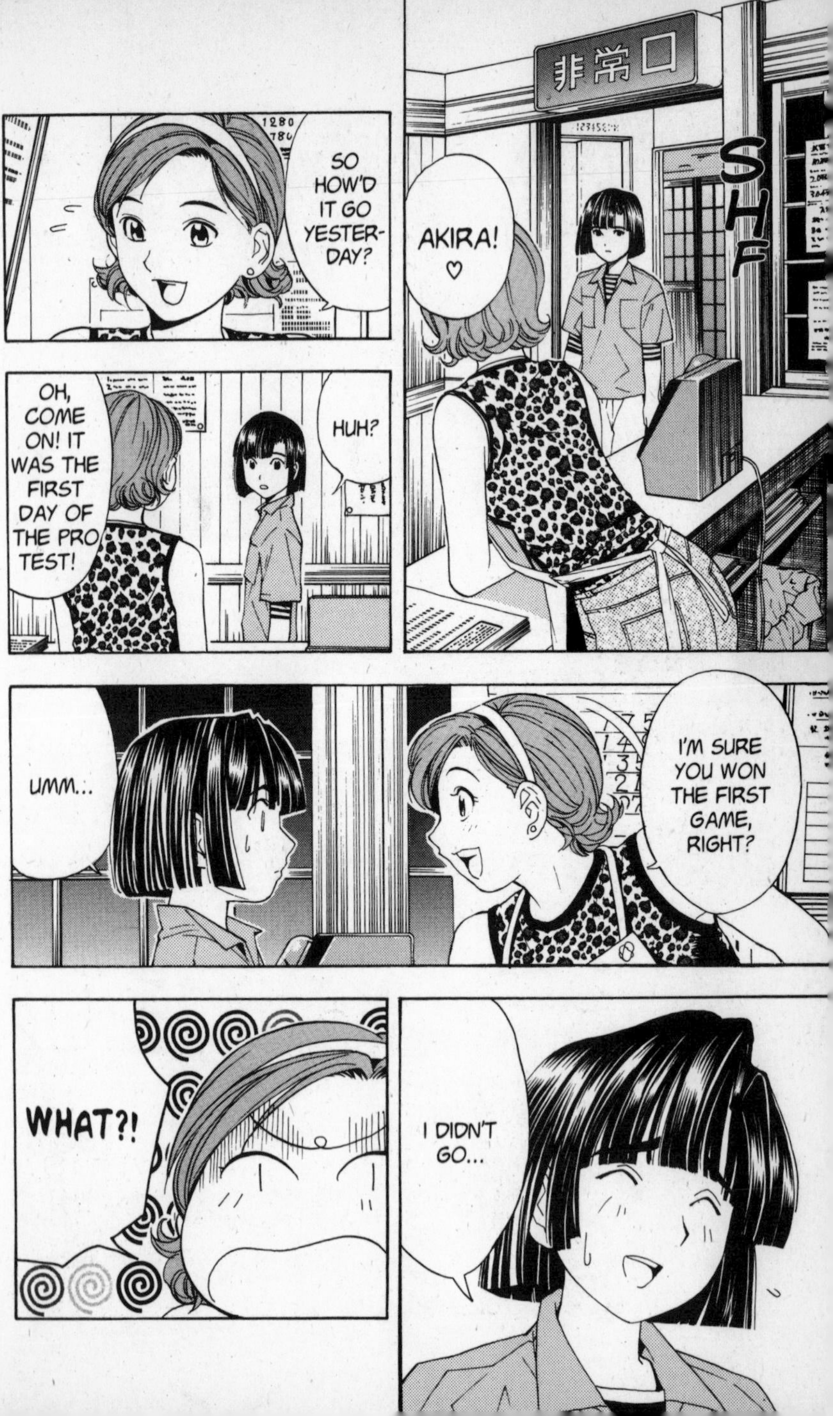
非常口
SHF
AKIRA! ♡
SO HOW'D IT GO YESTER-DAY?
HUH?
OH, COME ON! IT WAS THE FIRST DAY OF THE PRO TEST!
I'M SURE YOU WON THE FIRST GAME, RIGHT?
UMM...
I DIDN'T GO...
WHAT?!

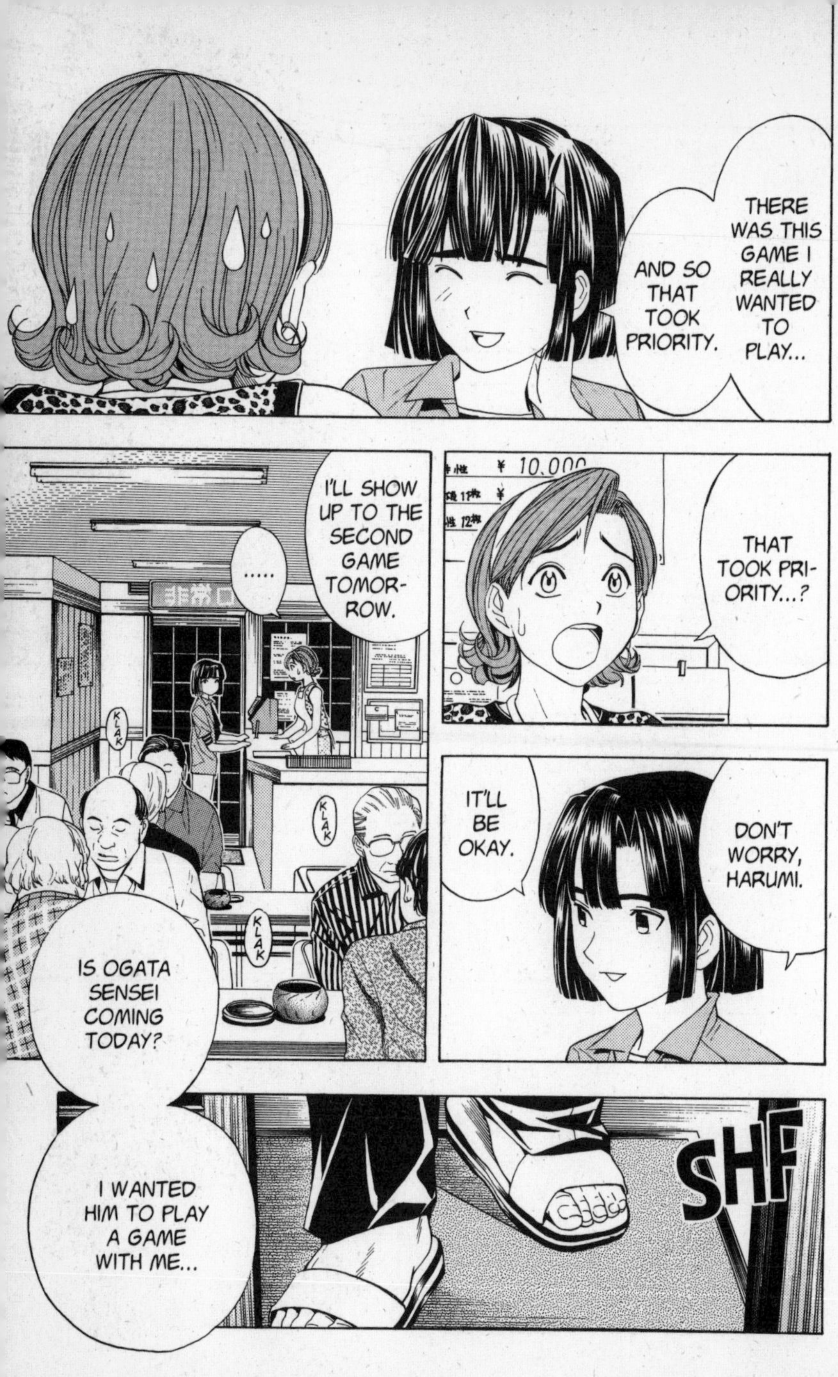
THERE WAS THIS GAME I REALLY WANTED TO PLAY...
AND SO THAT TOOK PRIORITY.
THAT TOOK PRI-ORITY...?
I'LL SHOW UP TO THE SECOND GAME TOMOR-ROW.
......
KLAK
KLAK
KLAK
DON'T WORRY, HARUMI.
IT'LL BE OKAY.
IS OGATA SENSEI COMING TODAY?
I WANTED HIM TO PLAY A GAME WITH ME...
SHF

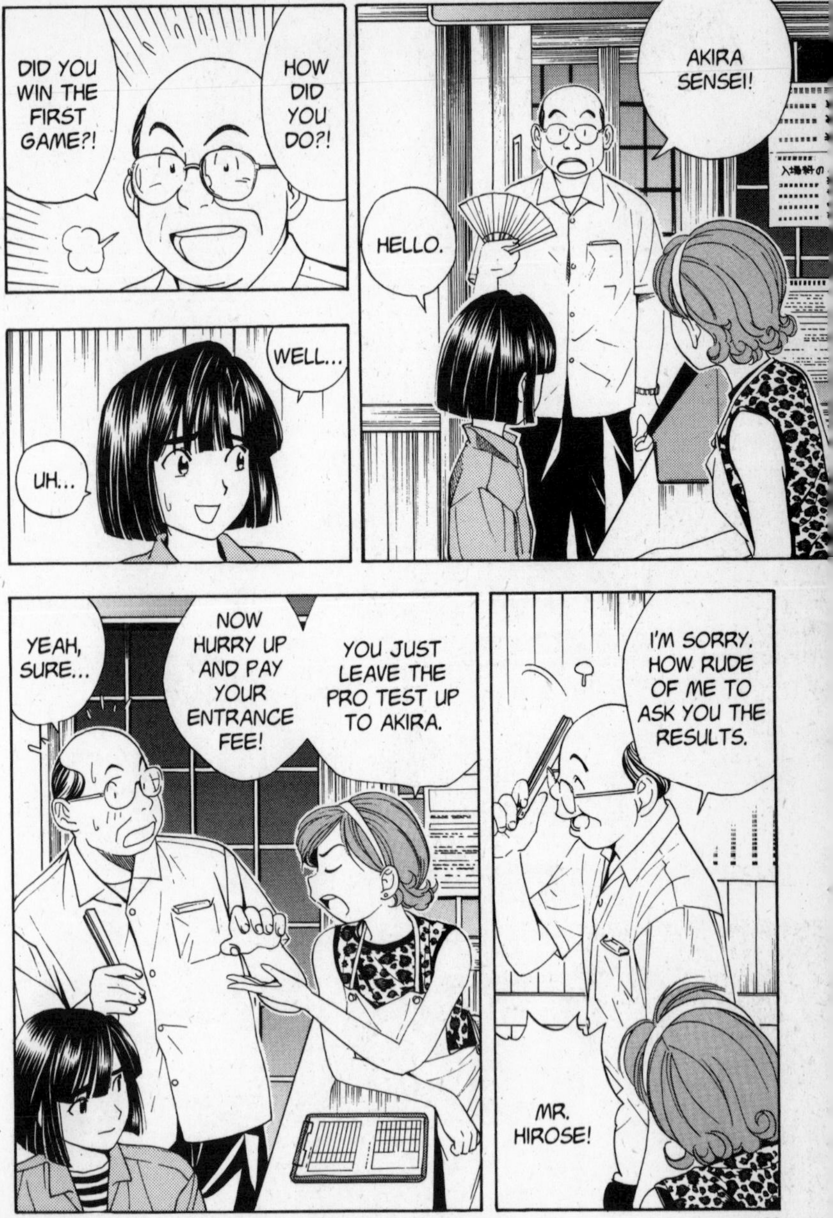
AKIRA SENSEI!
HELLO.
HOW DID YOU DO?!
DID YOU WIN THE FIRST GAME?!
WELL...
UH...
I'M SORRY. HOW RUDE OF ME TO ASK YOU THE RESULTS.
MR. HIROSE!
YOU JUST LEAVE THE PRO TEST UP TO AKIRA.
NOW HURRY UP AND PAY YOUR ENTRANCE FEE!
YEAH, SURE...

READ THIS WAY

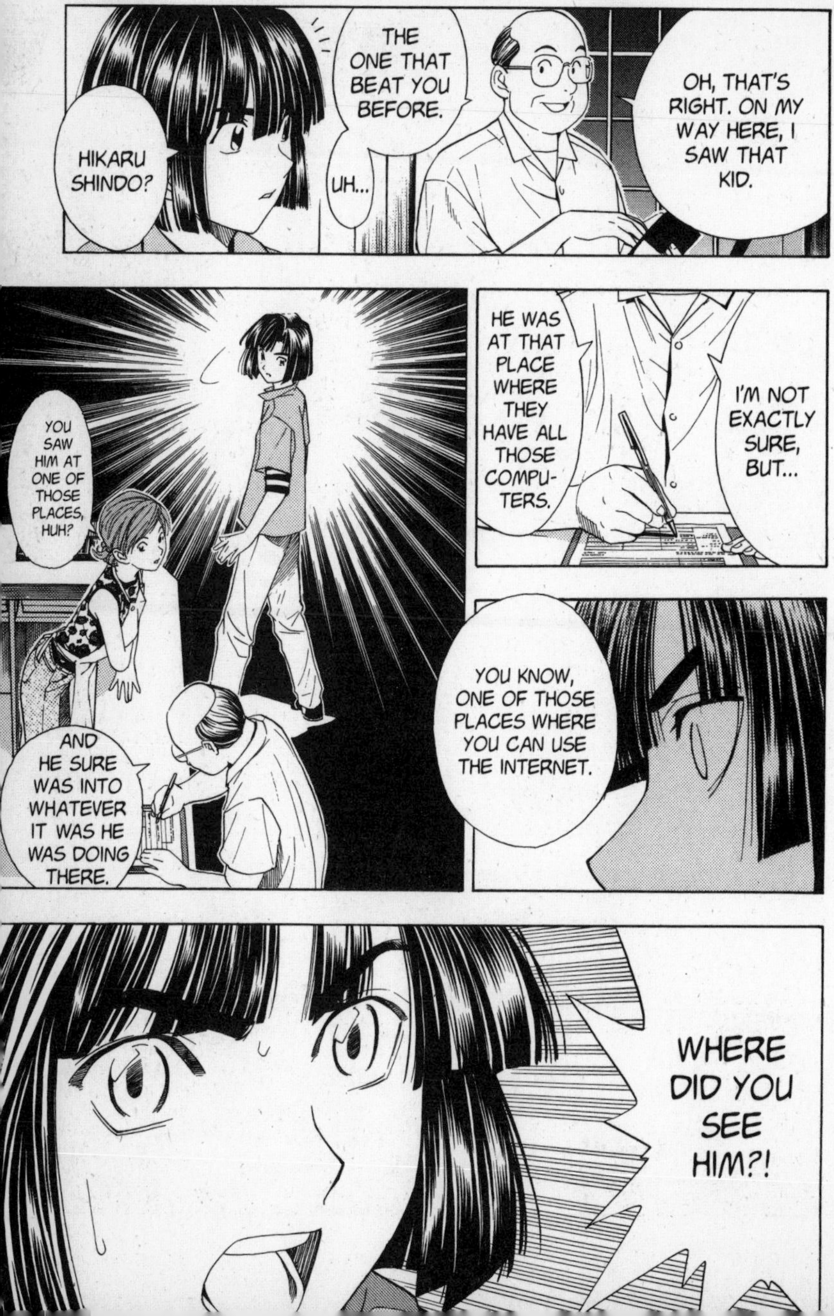

OH, THAT'S RIGHT. ON MY WAY HERE, I SAW THAT KID.
THE ONE THAT BEAT YOU BEFORE.
UH...
HIKARU SHINDO?
I'M NOT EXACTLY SURE, BUT...
HE WAS AT THAT PLACE WHERE THEY HAVE ALL THOSE COMPUTERS.
YOU KNOW, ONE OF THOSE PLACES WHERE YOU CAN USE THE INTERNET.
YOU SAW HIM AT ONE OF THOSE PLACES, HUH?
AND HE SURE WAS INTO WHATEVER IT WAS HE WAS DOING THERE.
WHERE DID YOU SEE HIM?!

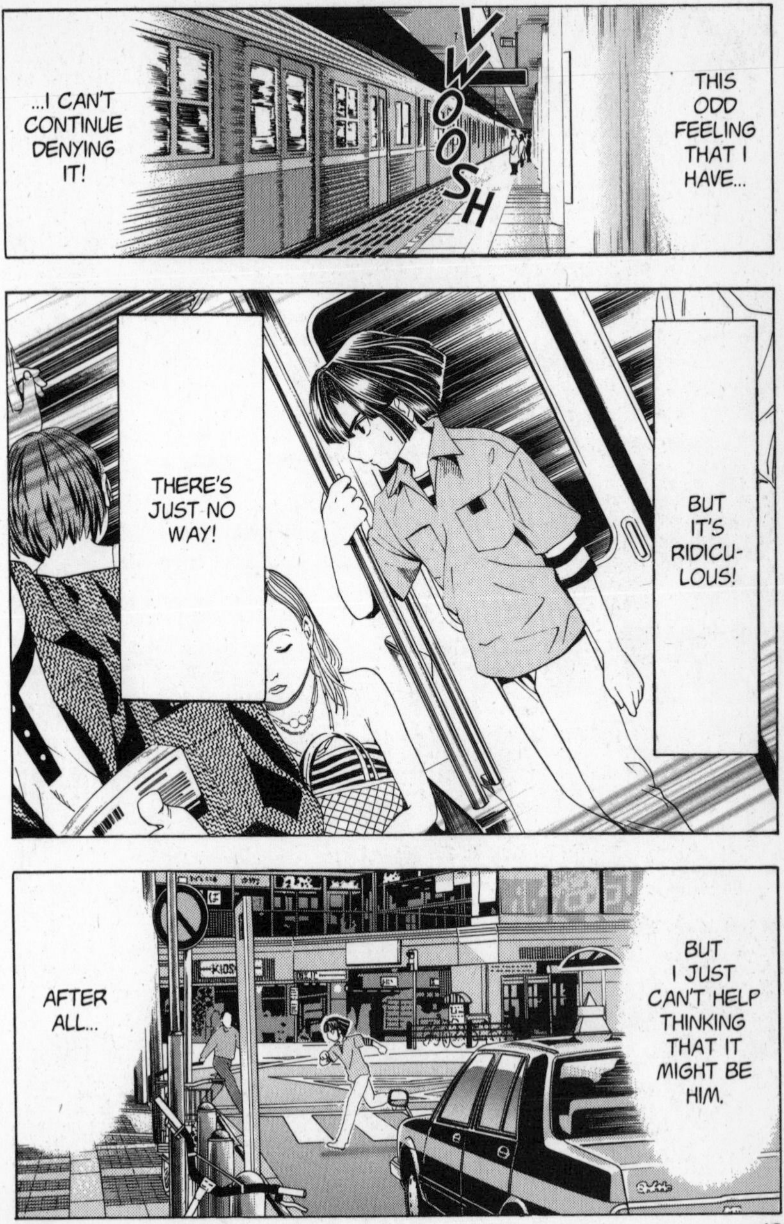
THIS ODD FEELING THAT I HAVE...
VWOOSH
...I CAN'T CONTINUE DENYING IT!
BUT IT'S RIDICU-LOUS!
THERE'S JUST NO WAY!
BUT I JUST CAN'T HELP THINKING THAT IT MIGHT BE HIM.
AFTER ALL...

READ THIS WAY

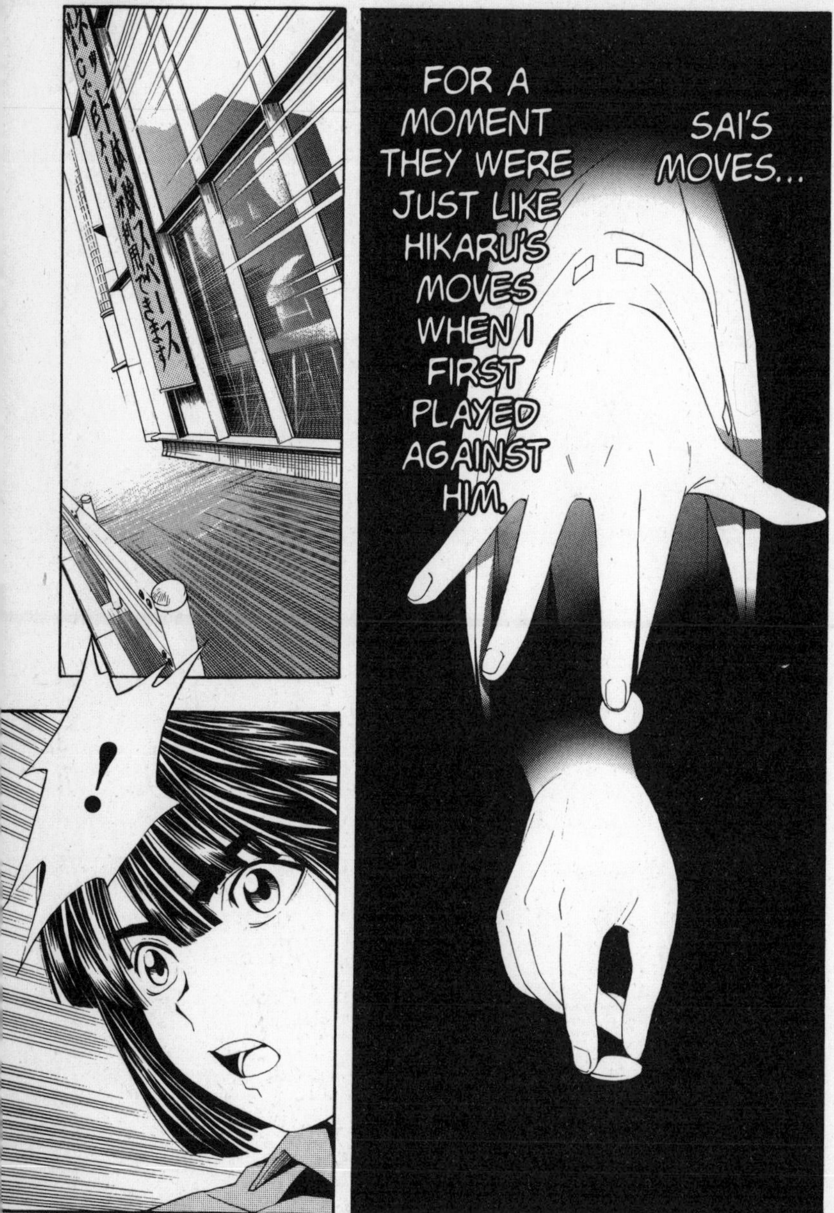
SAI'S MOVES...
FOR A MOMENT THEY WERE JUST LIKE HIKARU'S MOVES WHEN I FIRST PLAYED AGAINST HIM.
!

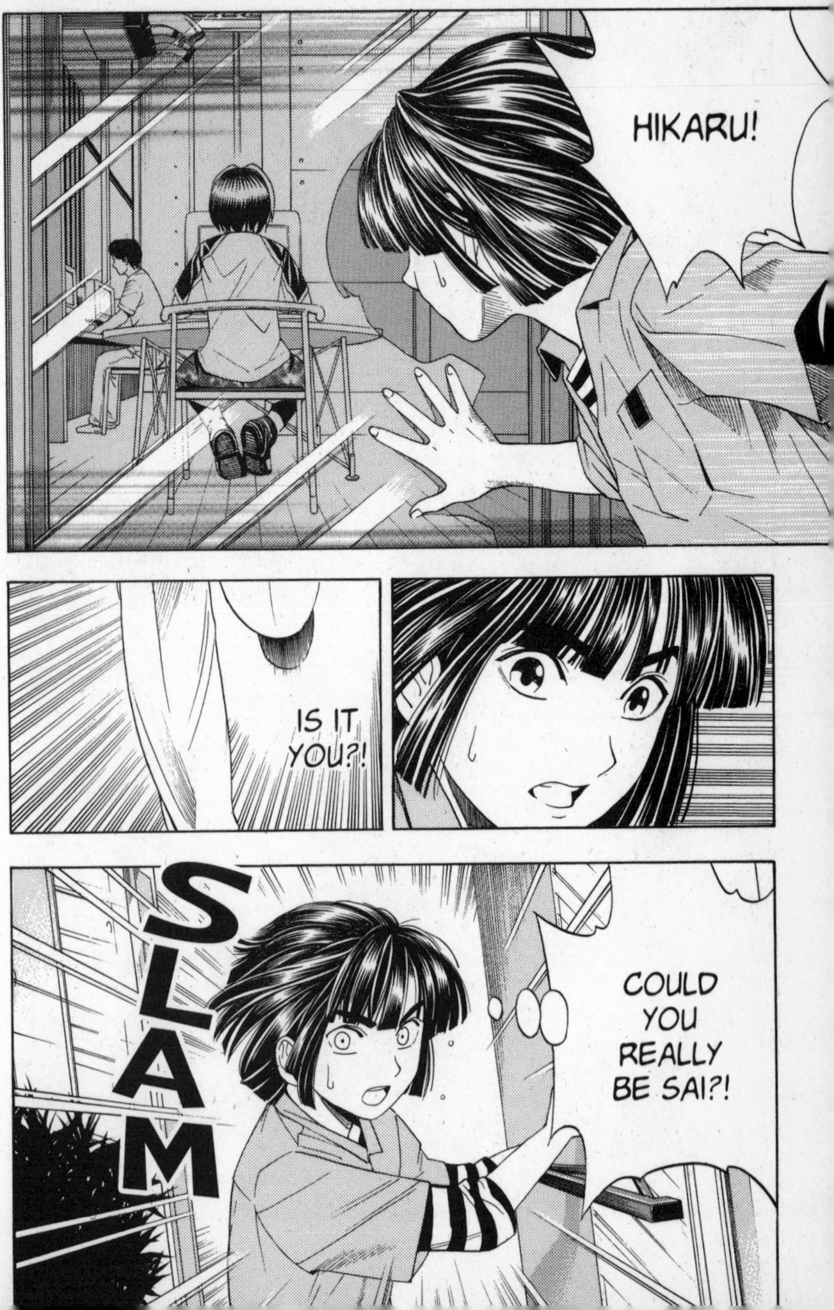
HIKARU!
IS IT YOU?!
COULD YOU REALLY BE SAI?!
SLAM

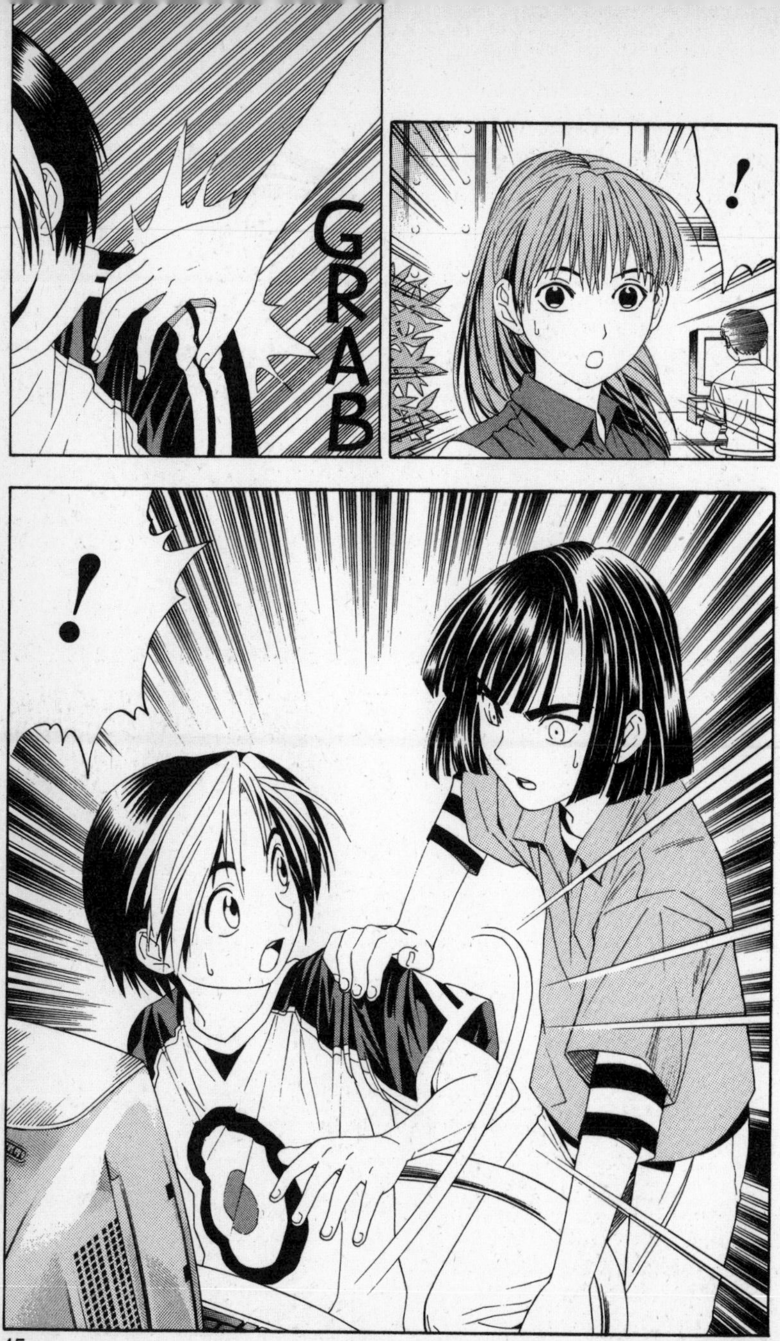
!
GRAB
!

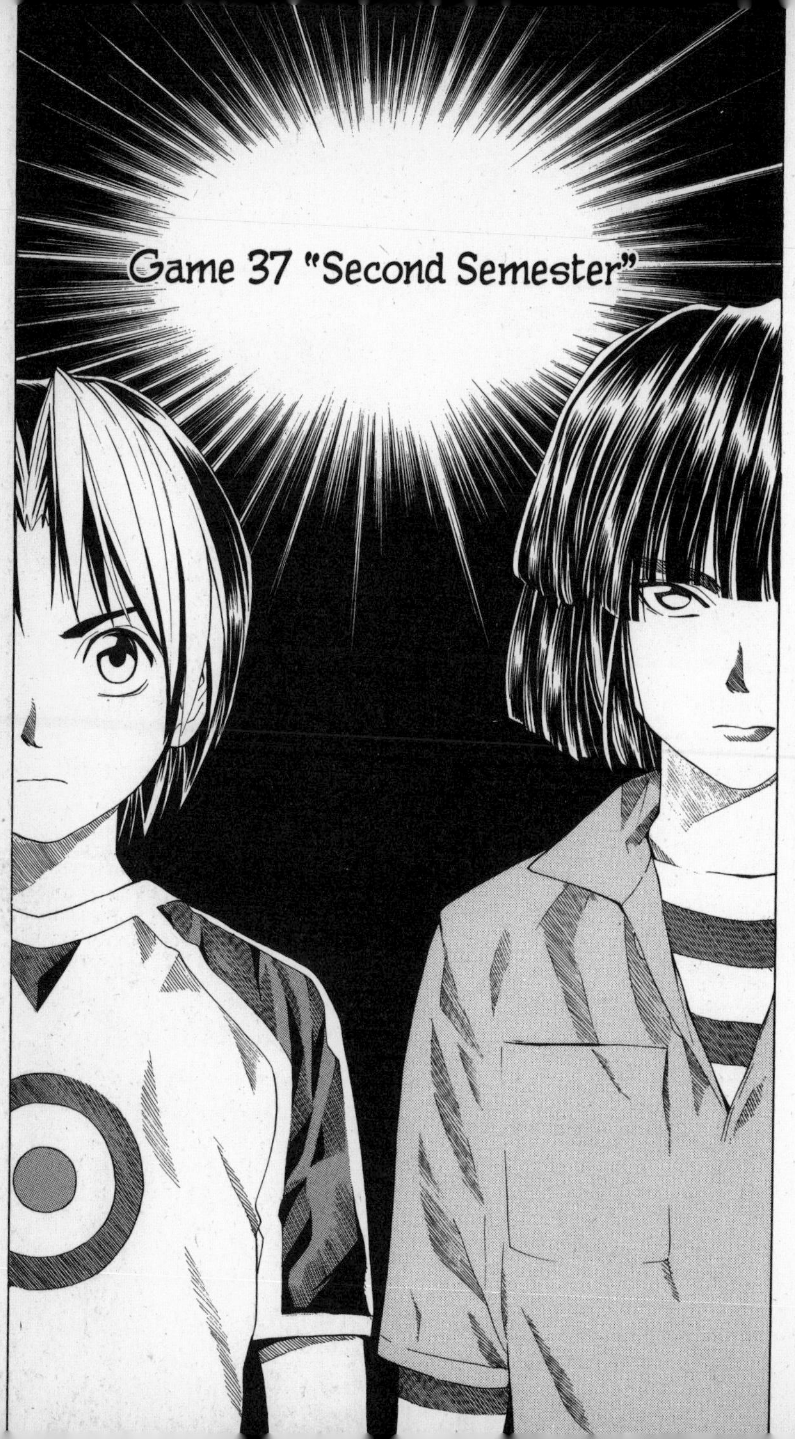
Game 37 "Second Semester"

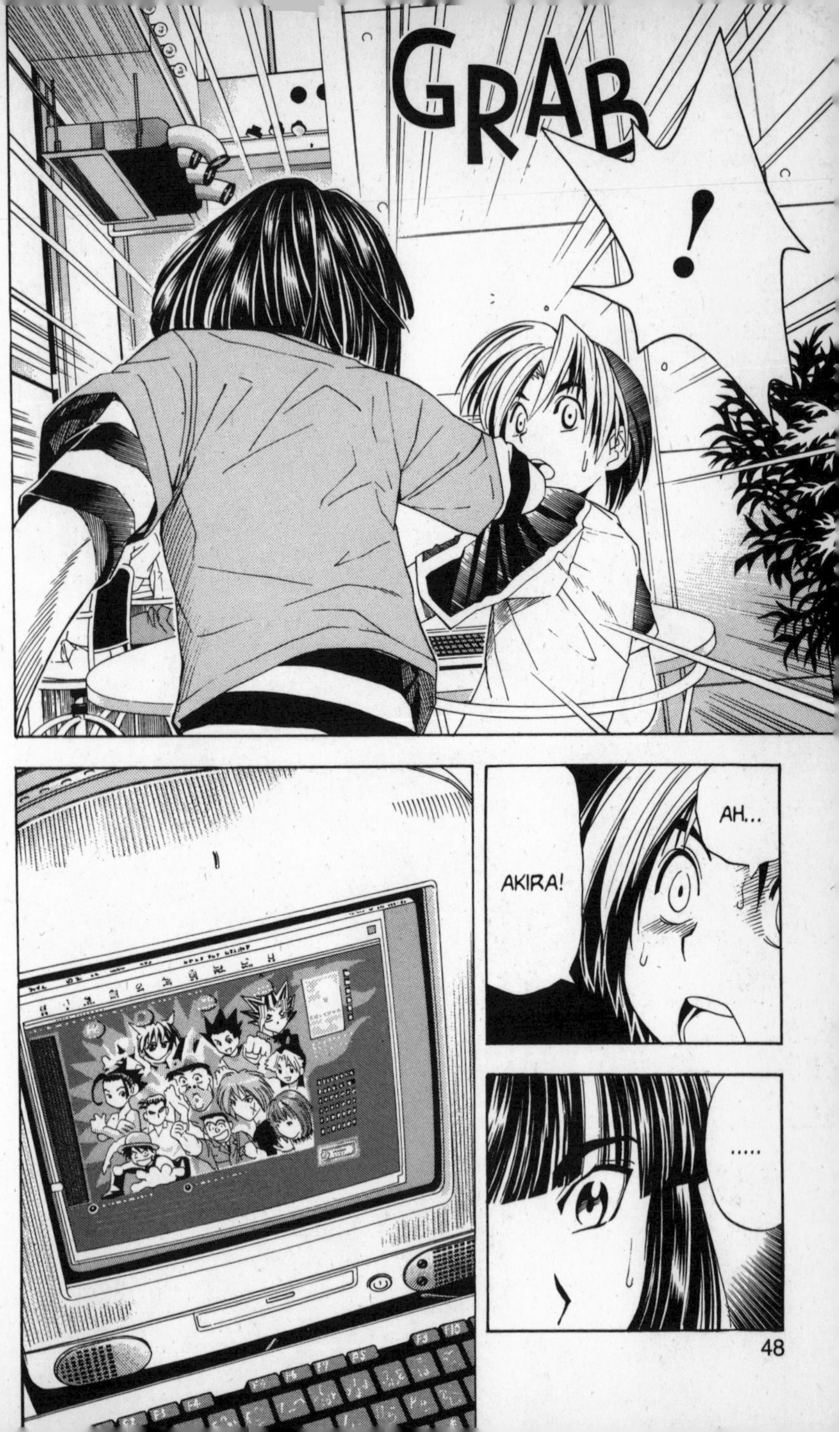
GRAB
!
AH...
AKIRA!
.....

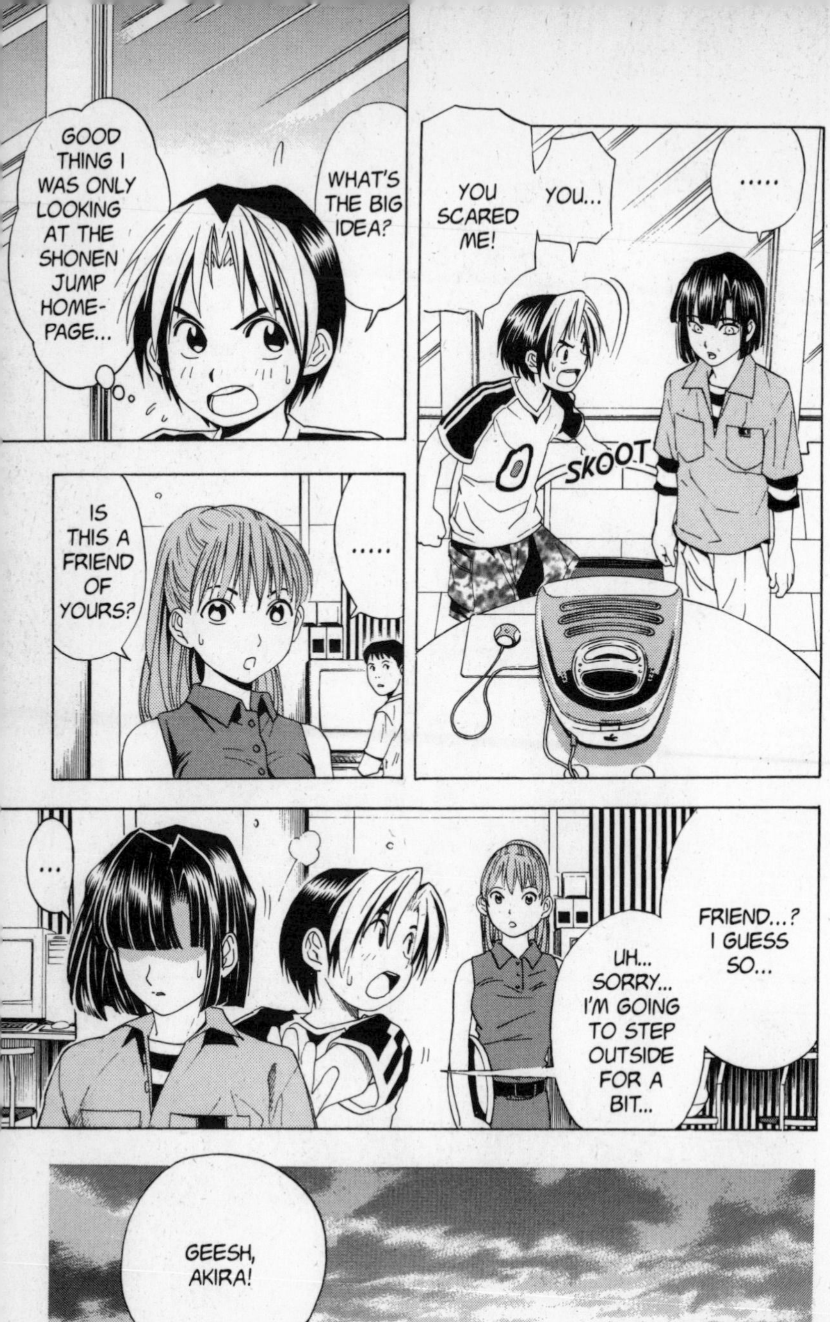
.....
YOU...
YOU SCARED ME!
SKOOT
WHAT'S THE BIG IDEA?
GOOD THING I WAS ONLY LOOKING AT THE SHONEN JUMP HOME-PAGE...
.....
IS THIS A FRIEND OF YOURS?
FRIEND...? I GUESS SO...
UH... SORRY... I'M GOING TO STEP OUTSIDE FOR A BIT...
...
GEESH, AKIRA!

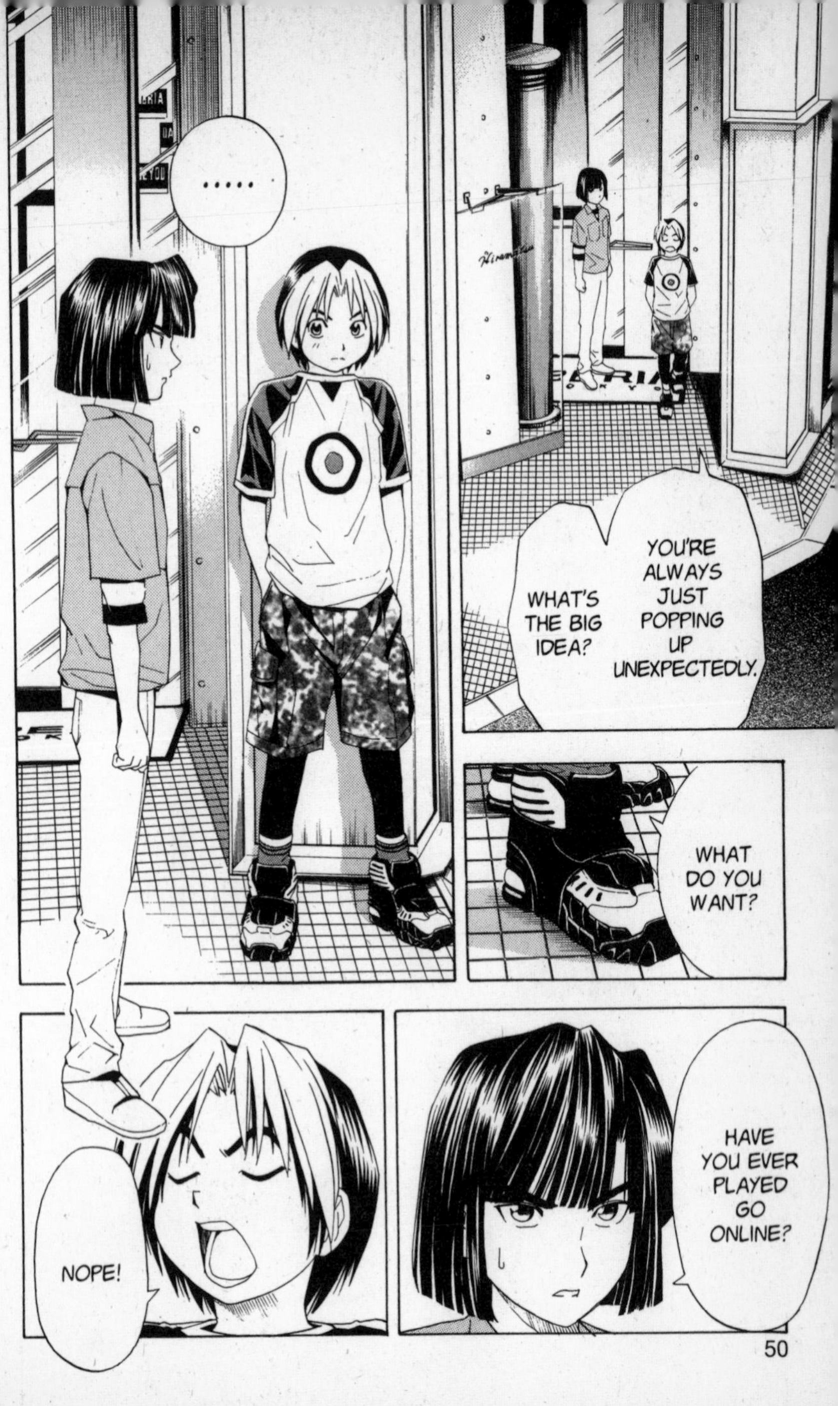
YOU'RE ALWAYS JUST POPPING UP UNEXPECTEDLY.
WHAT'S THE BIG IDEA?
WHAT DO YOU WANT?
......
HAVE YOU EVER PLAYED GO ONLINE?
NOPE!

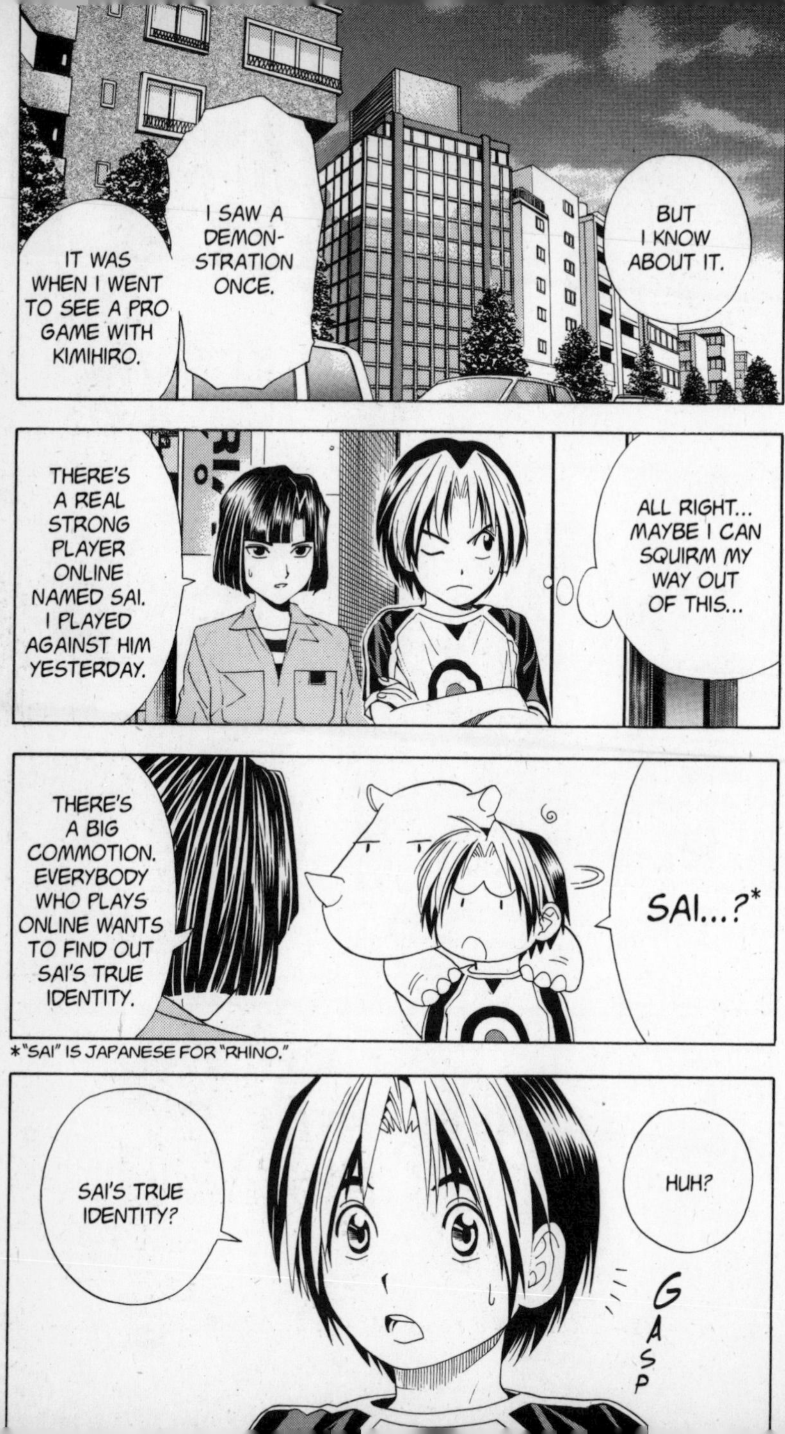
BUT I KNOW ABOUT IT.
I SAW A DEMON-STRATION ONCE.
IT WAS WHEN I WENT TO SEE A PRO GAME WITH KIMIHIRO.
ALL RIGHT... MAYBE I CAN SQUIRM MY WAY OUT OF THIS...
THERE'S A REAL STRONG PLAYER ONLINE NAMED SAI. I PLAYED AGAINST HIM YESTERDAY.
SAI...?*
THERE'S A BIG COMMOTION. EVERYBODY WHO PLAYS ONLINE WANTS TO FIND OUT SAI'S TRUE IDENTITY.
HUH?
GASP
SAI'S TRUE IDENTITY?

*"SAI" IS JAPANESE FOR "RHINO."

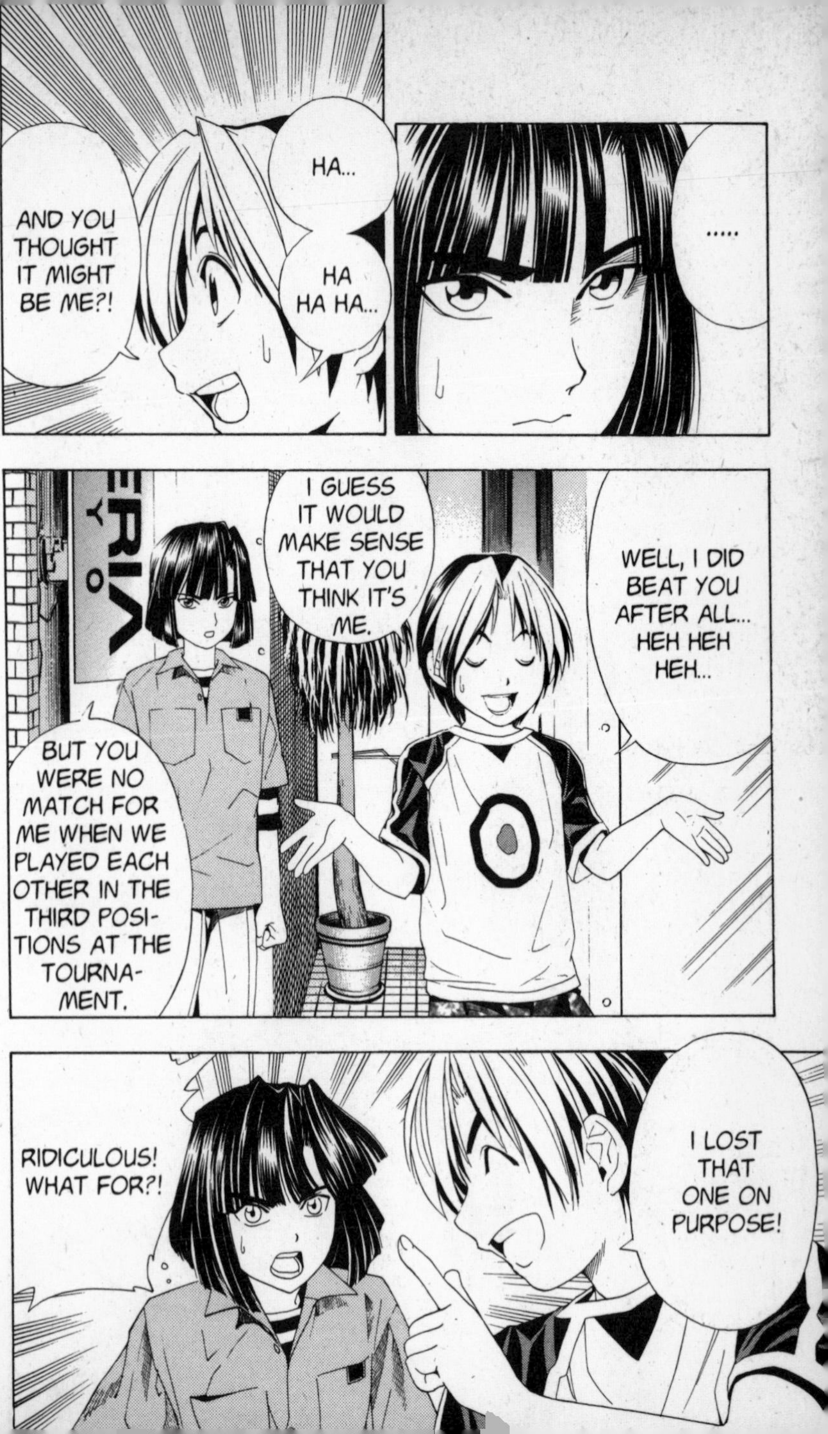
.....
HA...
HA HA HA...
AND YOU THOUGHT IT MIGHT BE ME?!
WELL, I DID BEAT YOU AFTER ALL... HEH HEH HEH...
I GUESS IT WOULD MAKE SENSE THAT YOU THINK IT'S ME.
BUT YOU WERE NO MATCH FOR ME WHEN WE PLAYED EACH OTHER IN THE THIRD POSITIONS AT THE TOURNAMENT.
I LOST THAT ONE ON PURPOSE!
RIDICULOUS! WHAT FOR?!

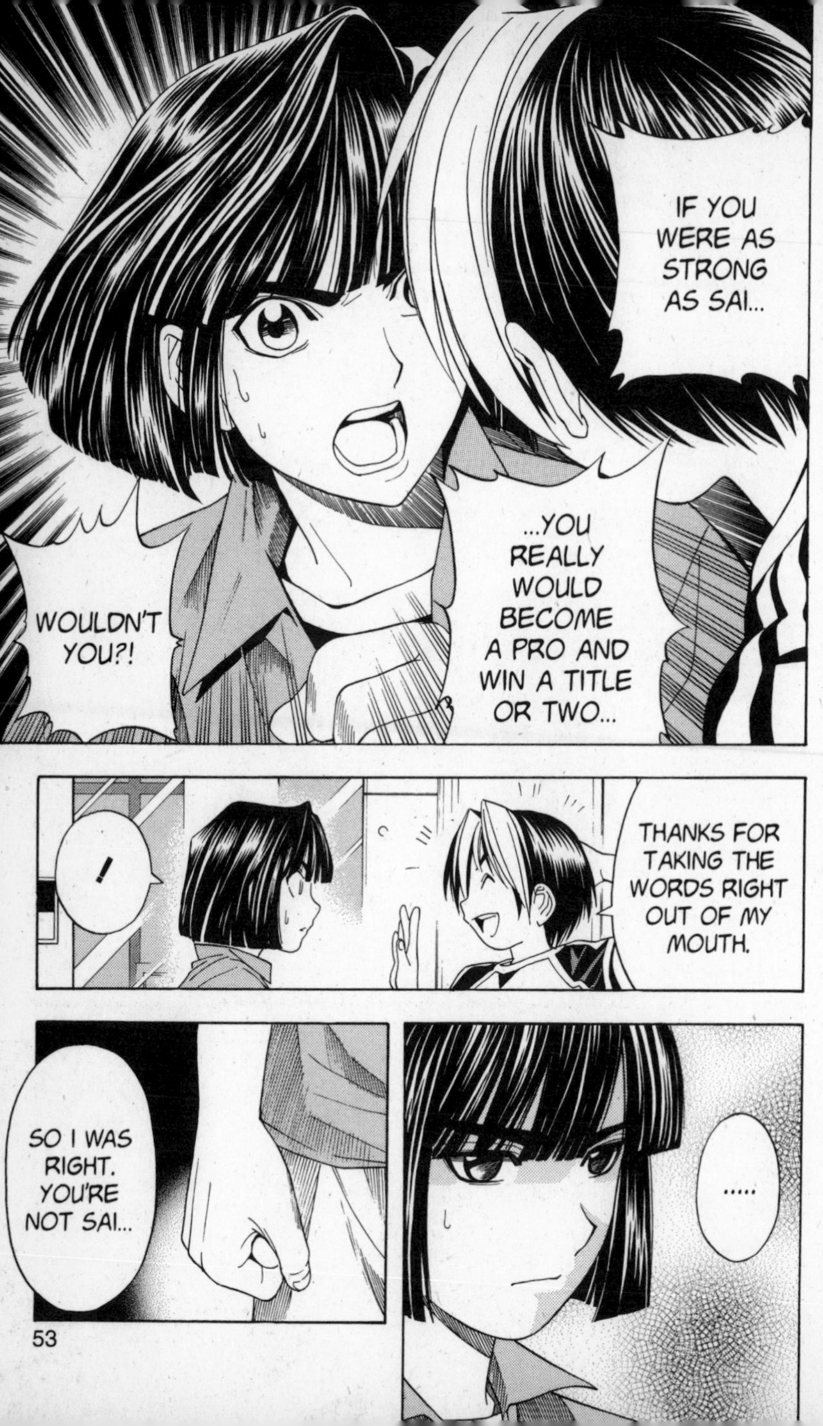
IF YOU WERE AS STRONG AS SAI...
...YOU REALLY WOULD BECOME A PRO AND WIN A TITLE OR TWO...
WOULDN'T YOU?!
THANKS FOR TAKING THE WORDS RIGHT OUT OF MY MOUTH.
!
.....
SO I WAS RIGHT. YOU'RE NOT SAI...

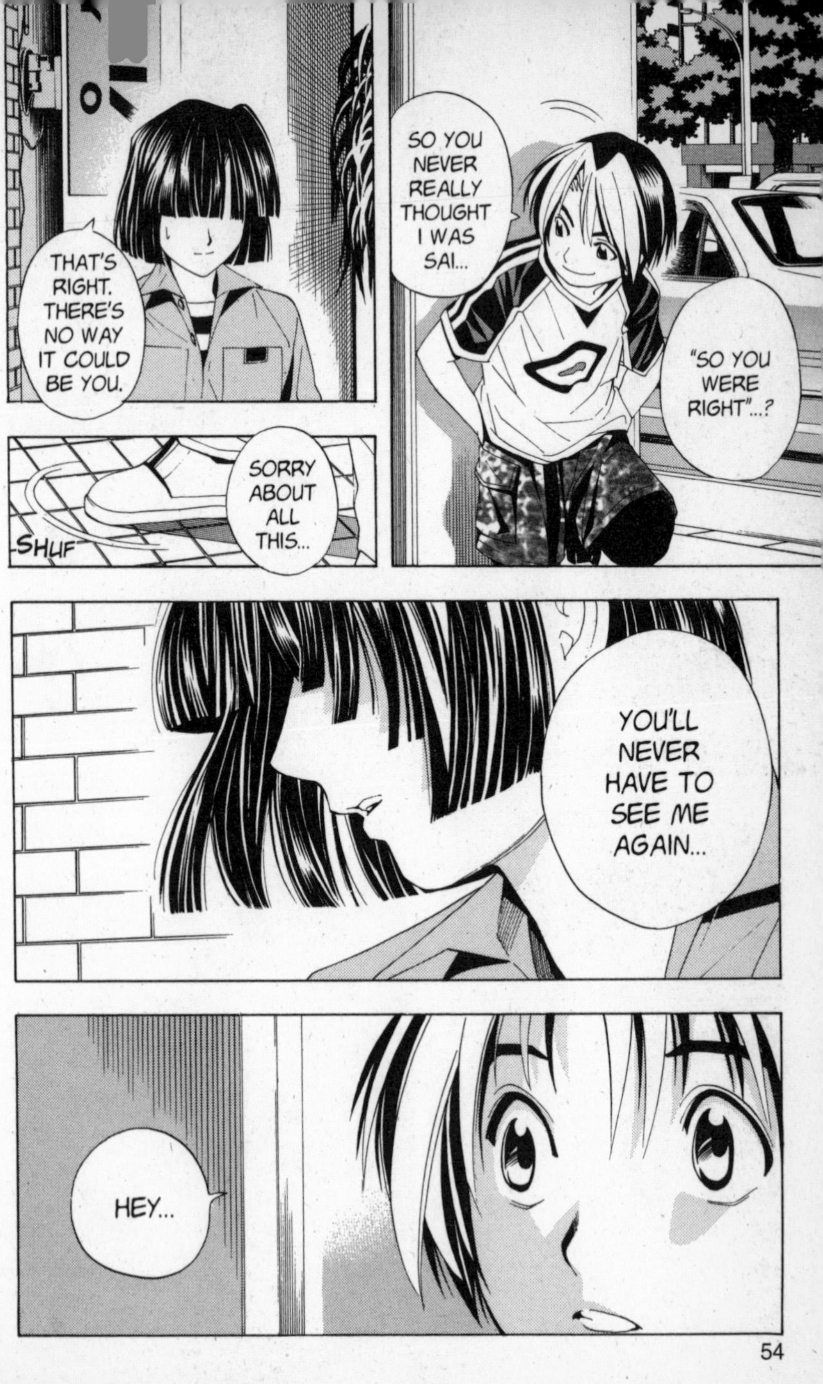
SO YOU NEVER REALLY THOUGHT I WAS SAI...
"SO YOU WERE RIGHT"...?
THAT'S RIGHT. THERE'S NO WAY IT COULD BE YOU.
SORRY ABOUT ALL THIS...
SHUF
YOU'LL NEVER HAVE TO SEE ME AGAIN...
HEY...

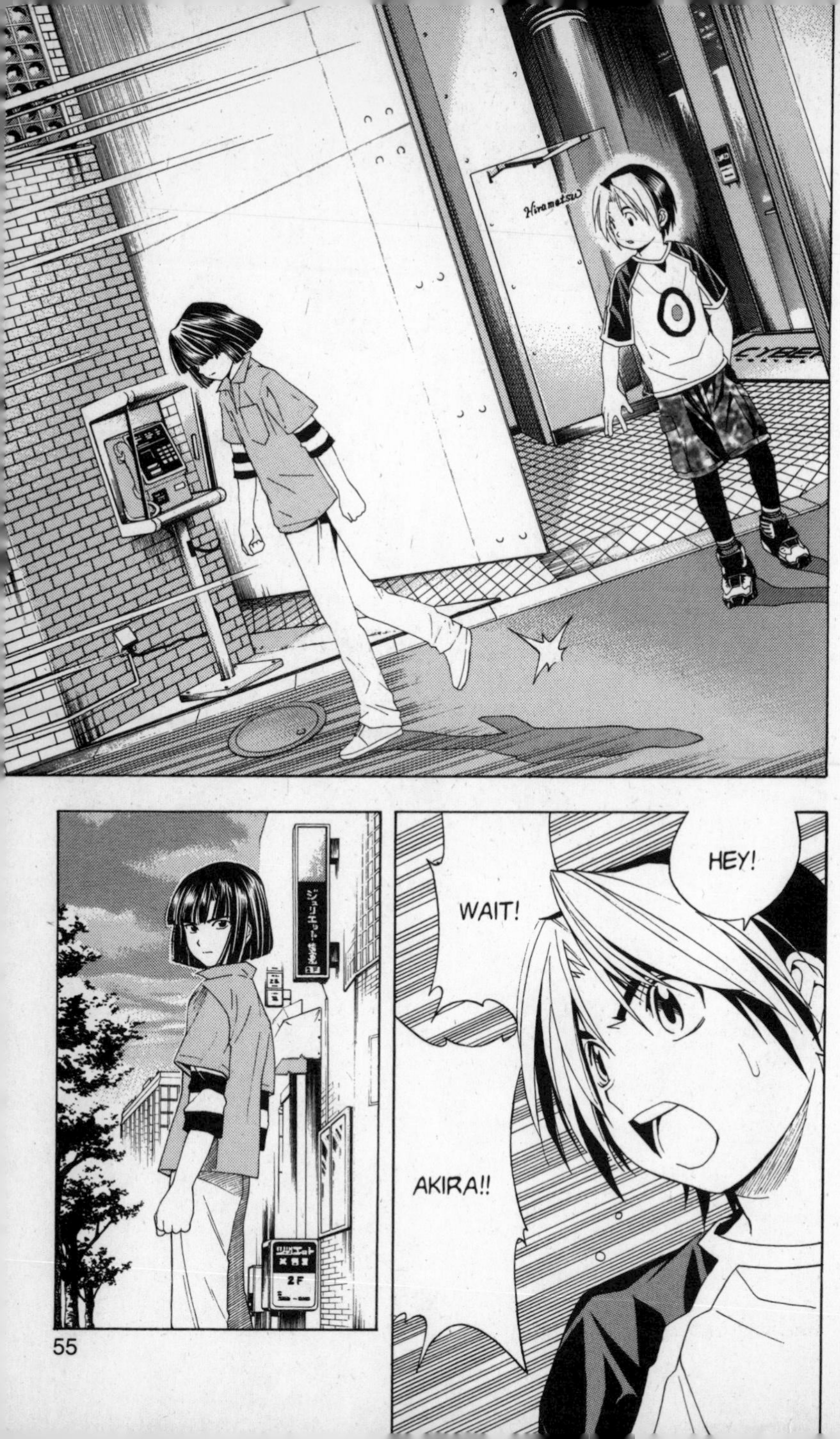
Hiramatsu
HEY!
WAIT!
AKIRA!!

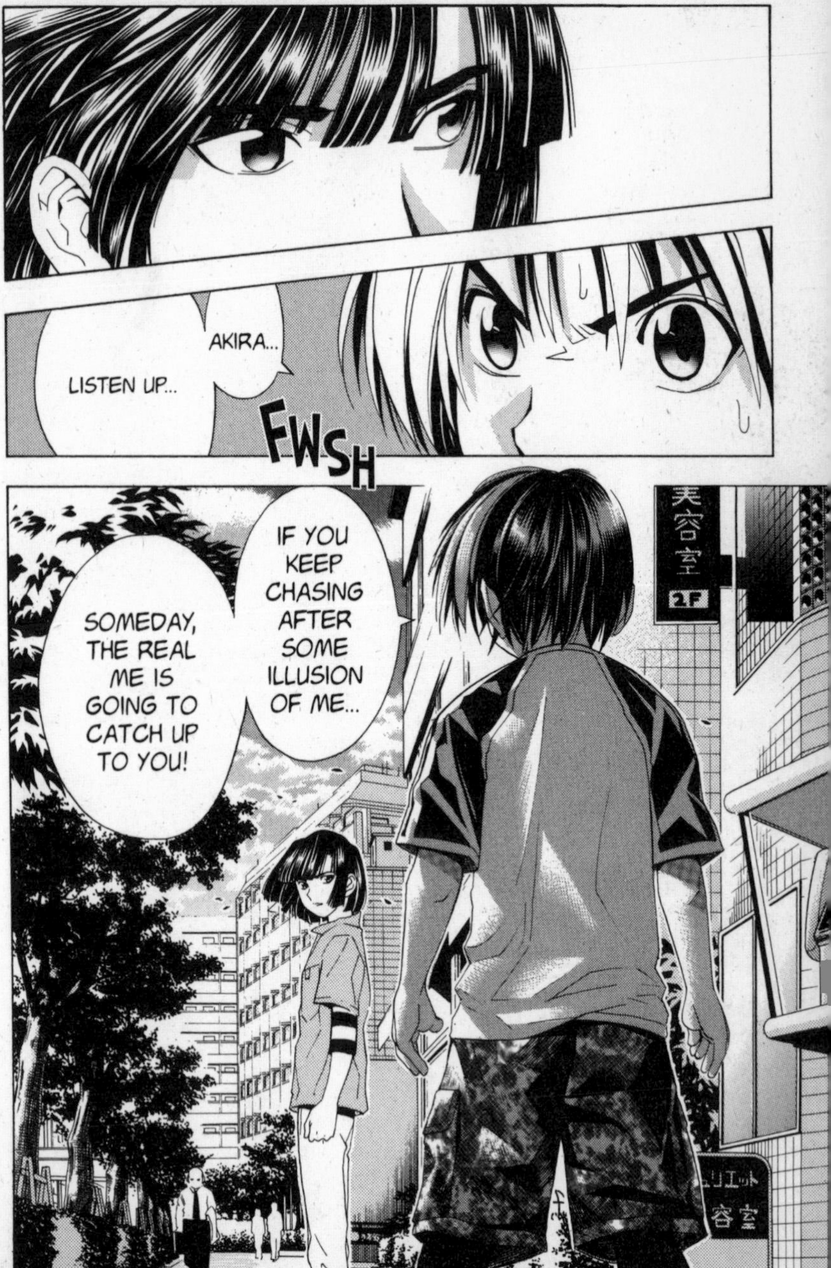
AKIRA...
LISTEN UP...
FWSH
IF YOU KEEP CHASING AFTER SOME ILLUSION OF ME...
SOMEDAY, THE REAL ME IS GOING TO CATCH UP TO YOU!
美容室
2F

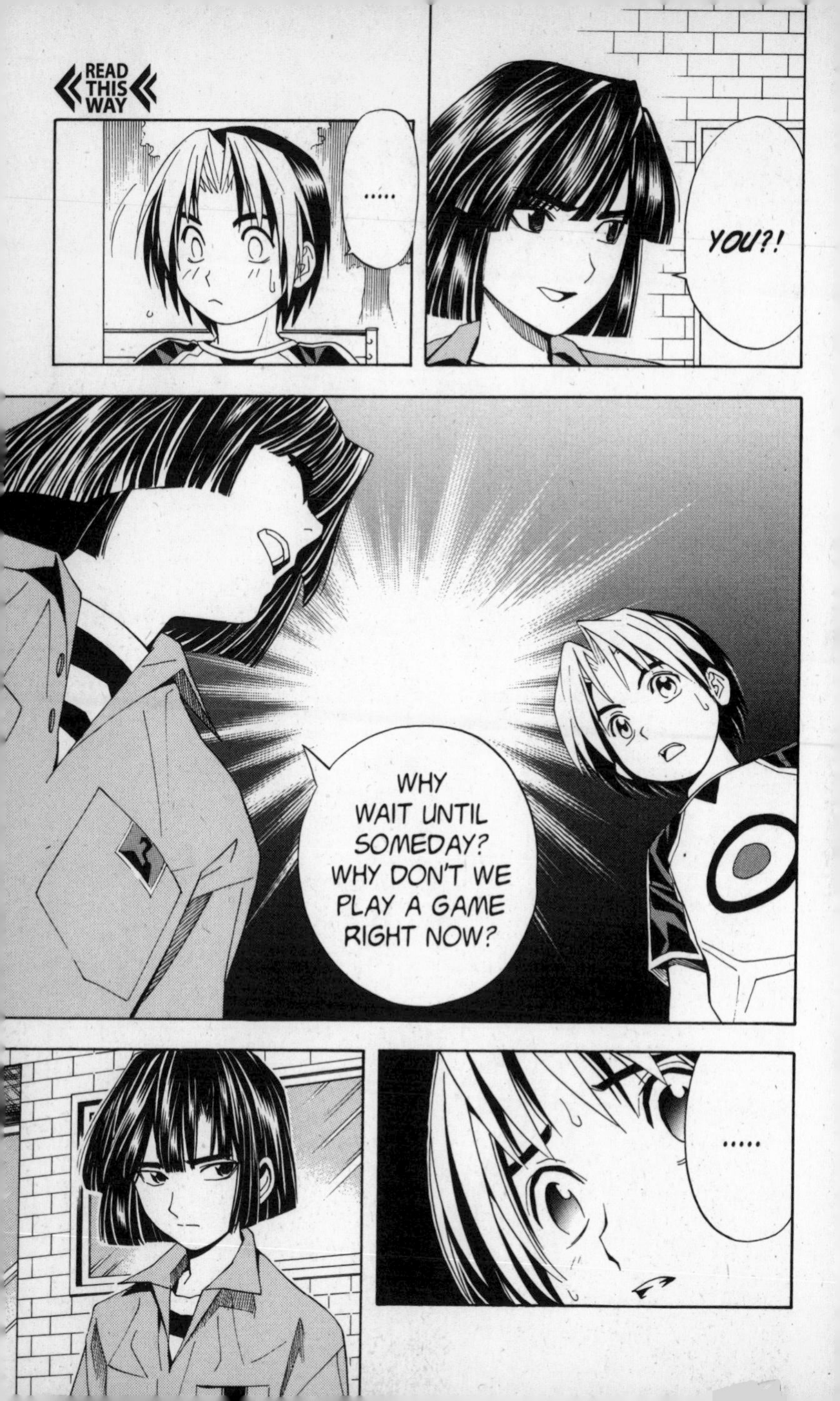

READ THIS WAY
YOU?!
.....
WHY WAIT UNTIL SOMEDAY? WHY DON'T WE PLAY A GAME RIGHT NOW?
.....

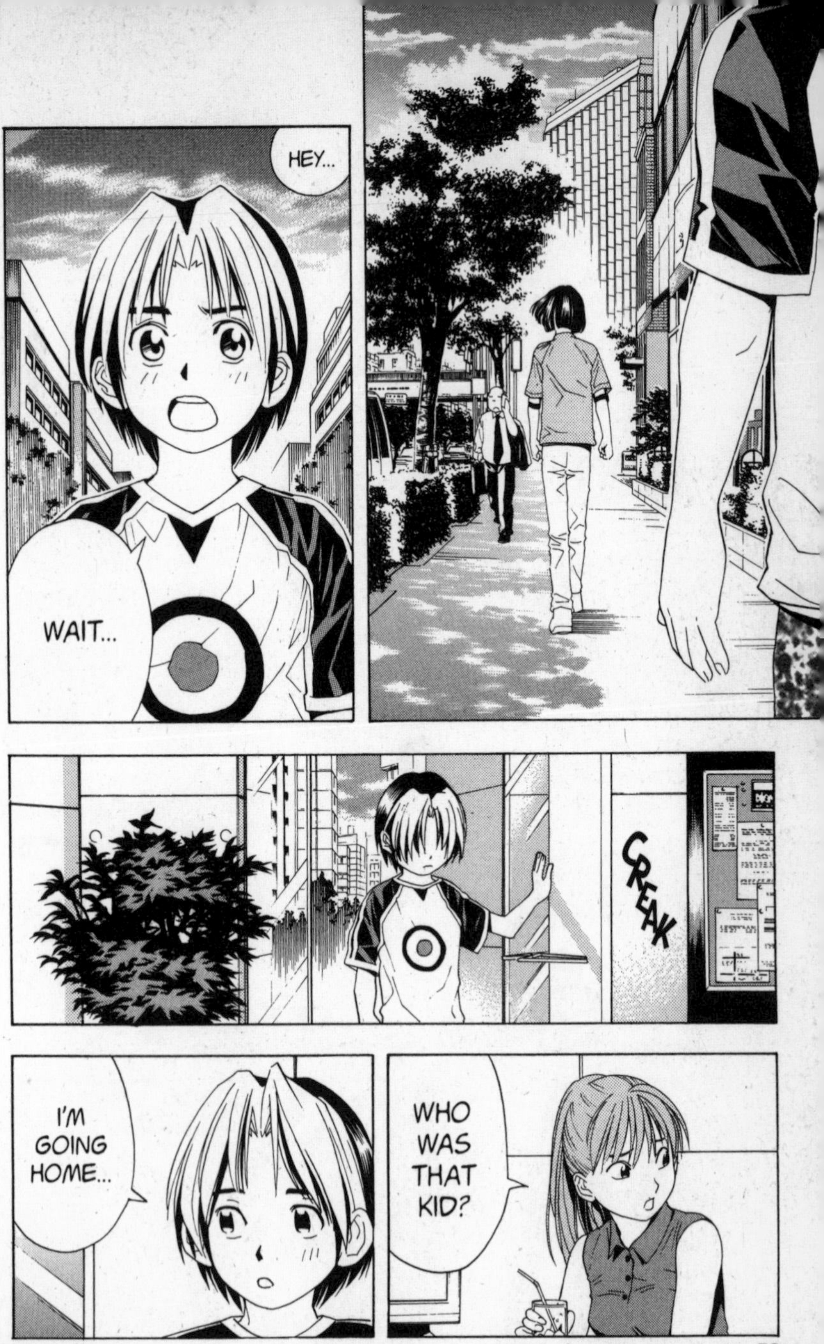
HEY...
WAIT...
CREAK
I'M GOING HOME...
WHO WAS THAT KID?

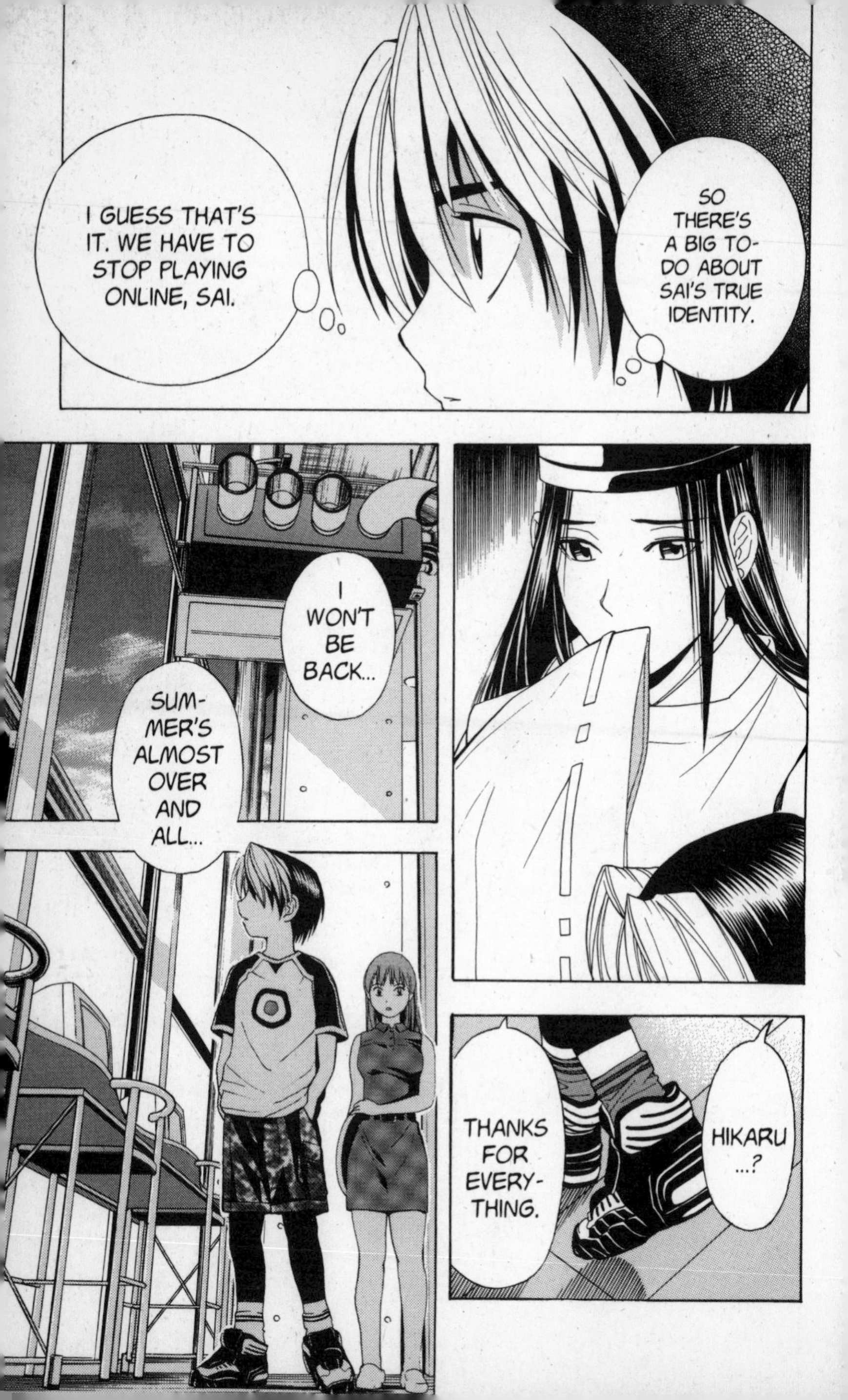
SO THERE'S A BIG TO-DO ABOUT SAI'S TRUE IDENTITY.
I GUESS THAT'S IT. WE HAVE TO STOP PLAYING ONLINE, SAI.
I WON'T BE BACK...
SUMMER'S ALMOST OVER AND ALL...
HIKARU ...?
THANKS FOR EVERYTHING.

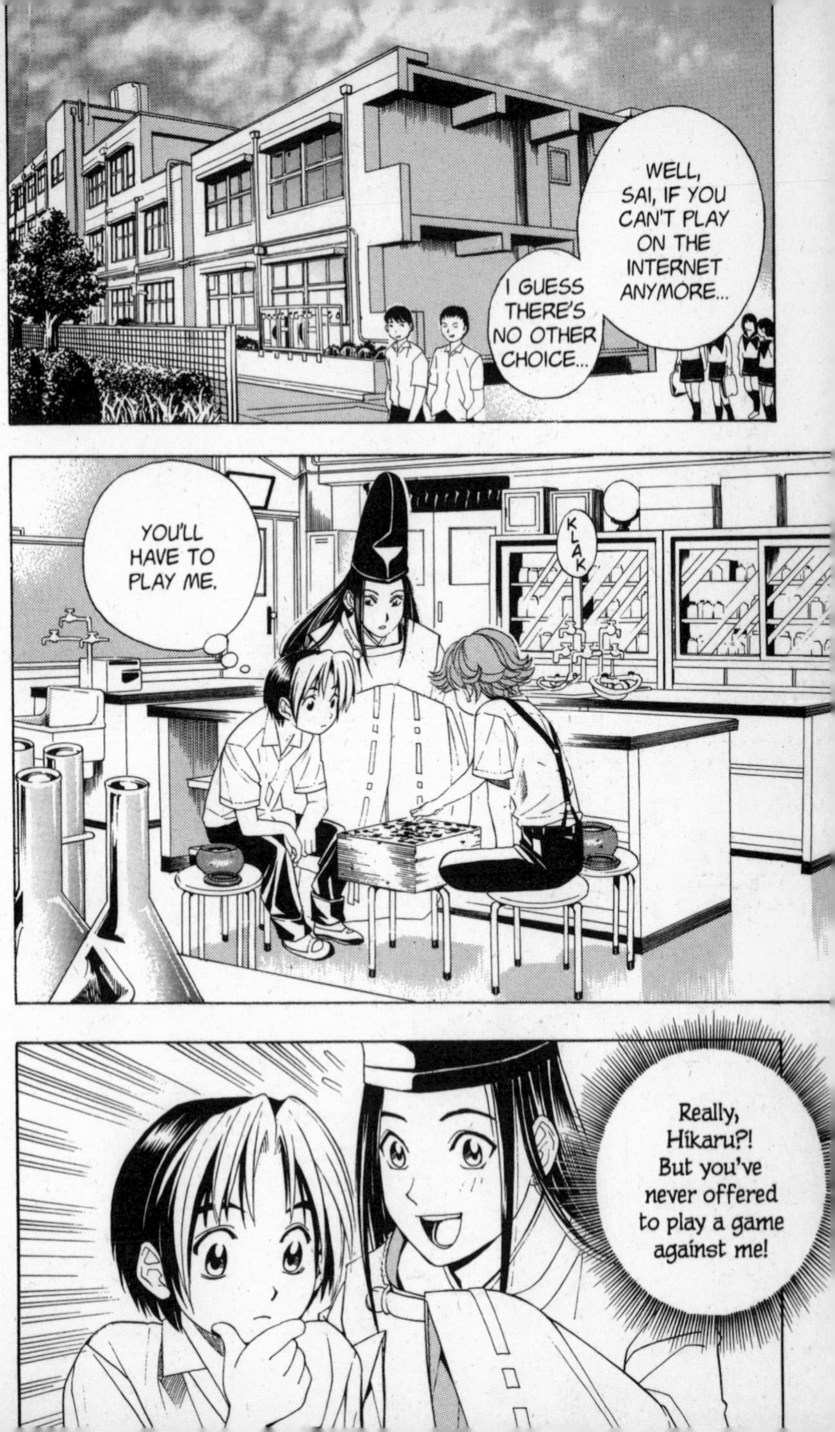
WELL, SAI, IF YOU CAN'T PLAY ON THE INTERNET ANYMORE...
I GUESS THERE'S NO OTHER CHOICE...
KLAK
YOU'LL HAVE TO PLAY ME.
Really, Hikaru?! But you've never offered to play a game against me!

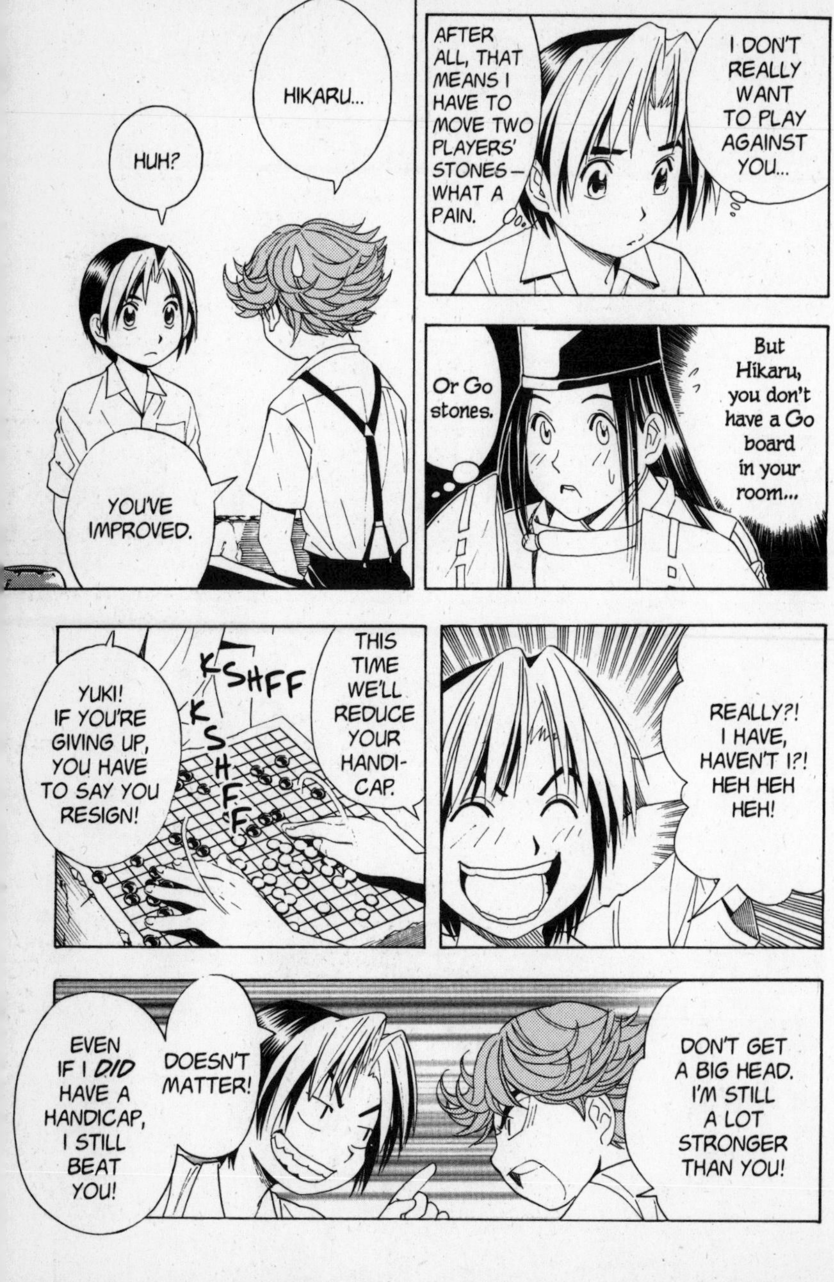
I DON'T REALLY WANT TO PLAY AGAINST YOU...
AFTER ALL, THAT MEANS I HAVE TO MOVE TWO PLAYERS' STONES—WHAT A PAIN.
But Hikaru, you don't have a Go board in your room...
Or Go stones.
HIKARU...
HUH?
YOU'VE IMPROVED.
REALLY?! I HAVE, HAVEN'T I?! HEH HEH HEH!
THIS TIME WE'LL REDUCE YOUR HANDI-CAP.
KSHFF
KSHFF
YUKI! IF YOU'RE GIVING UP, YOU HAVE TO SAY YOU RESIGN!
DON'T GET A BIG HEAD. I'M STILL A LOT STRONGER THAN YOU!
DOESN'T MATTER!
EVEN IF I *DID* HAVE A HANDICAP, I STILL BEAT YOU!

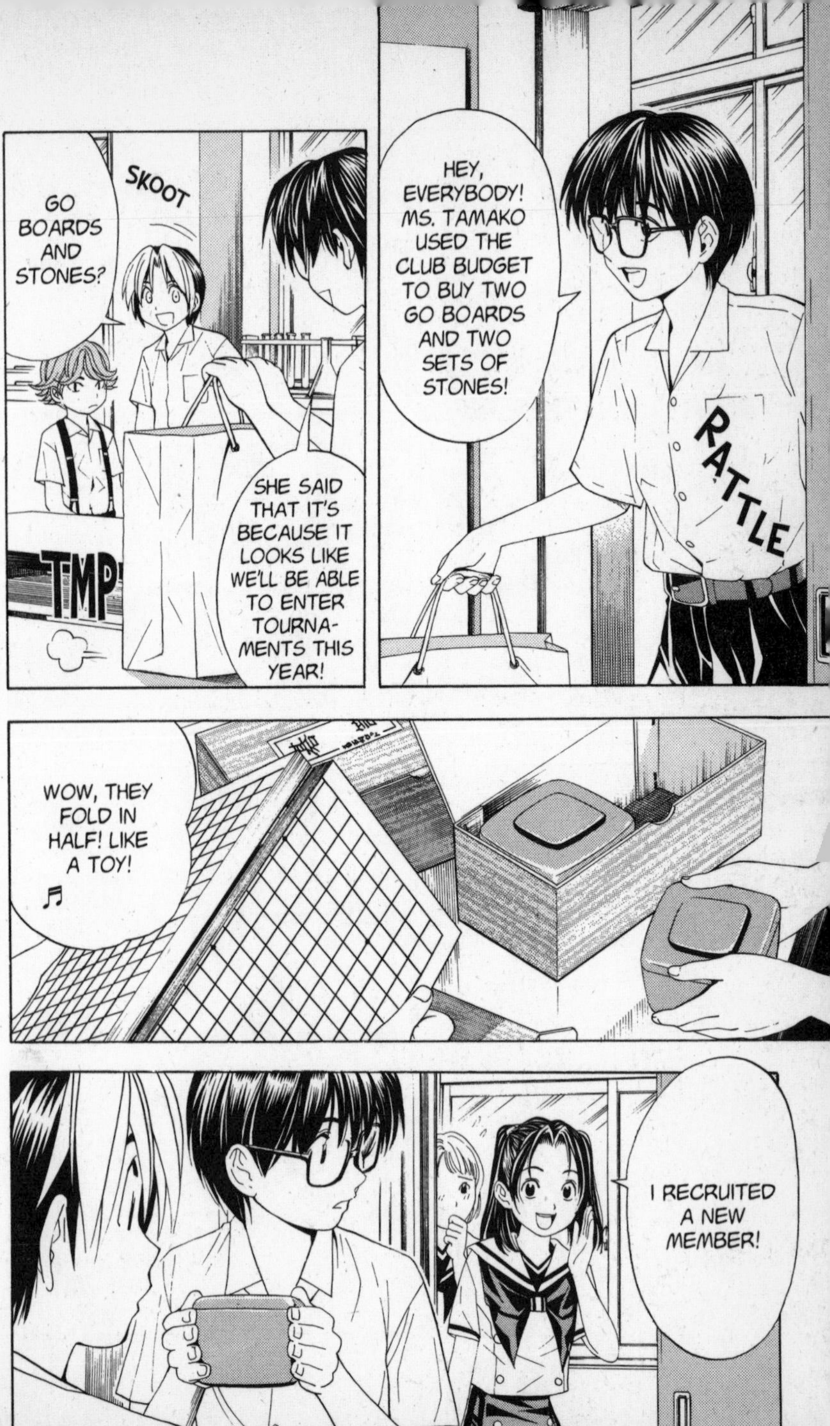
HEY, EVERYBODY! MS. TAMAKO USED THE CLUB BUDGET TO BUY TWO GO BOARDS AND TWO SETS OF STONES!
RATTLE
SHE SAID THAT IT'S BECAUSE IT LOOKS LIKE WE'LL BE ABLE TO ENTER TOURNA-MENTS THIS YEAR!
SKOOT
GO BOARDS AND STONES?
TMP
WOW, THEY FOLD IN HALF! LIKE A TOY! ♪
I RECRUITED A NEW MEMBER!

READ THIS WAY

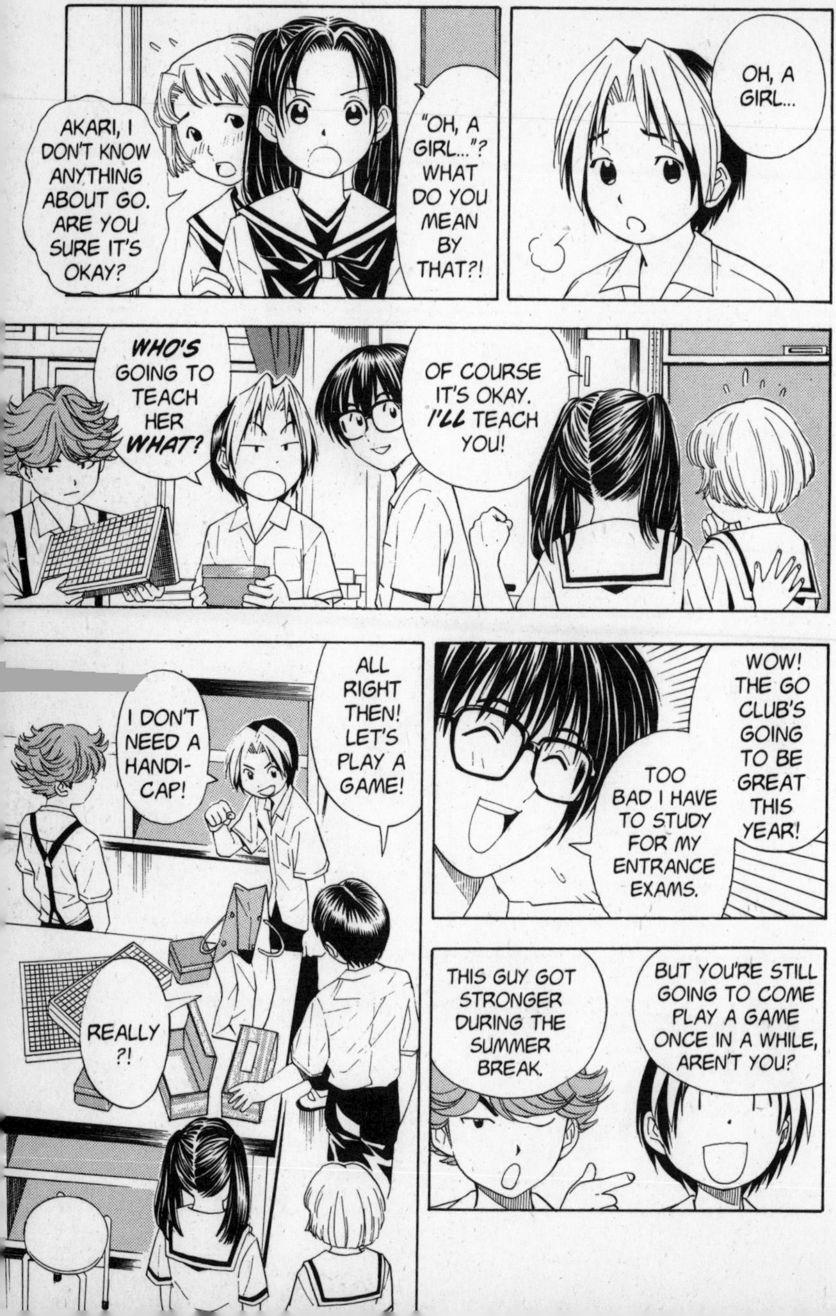
OH, A GIRL...
"OH, A GIRL..."? WHAT DO YOU MEAN BY THAT?!
AKARI, I DON'T KNOW ANYTHING ABOUT GO. ARE YOU SURE IT'S OKAY?
OF COURSE IT'S OKAY. *I'LL* TEACH YOU!
WHO'S GOING TO TEACH HER *WHAT*?
WOW! THE GO CLUB'S GOING TO BE GREAT THIS YEAR!
TOO BAD I HAVE TO STUDY FOR MY ENTRANCE EXAMS.
BUT YOU'RE STILL GOING TO COME PLAY A GAME ONCE IN A WHILE, AREN'T YOU?
THIS GUY GOT STRONGER DURING THE SUMMER BREAK.
ALL RIGHT THEN! LET'S PLAY A GAME!
I DON'T NEED A HANDI-CAP!
REALLY ?!

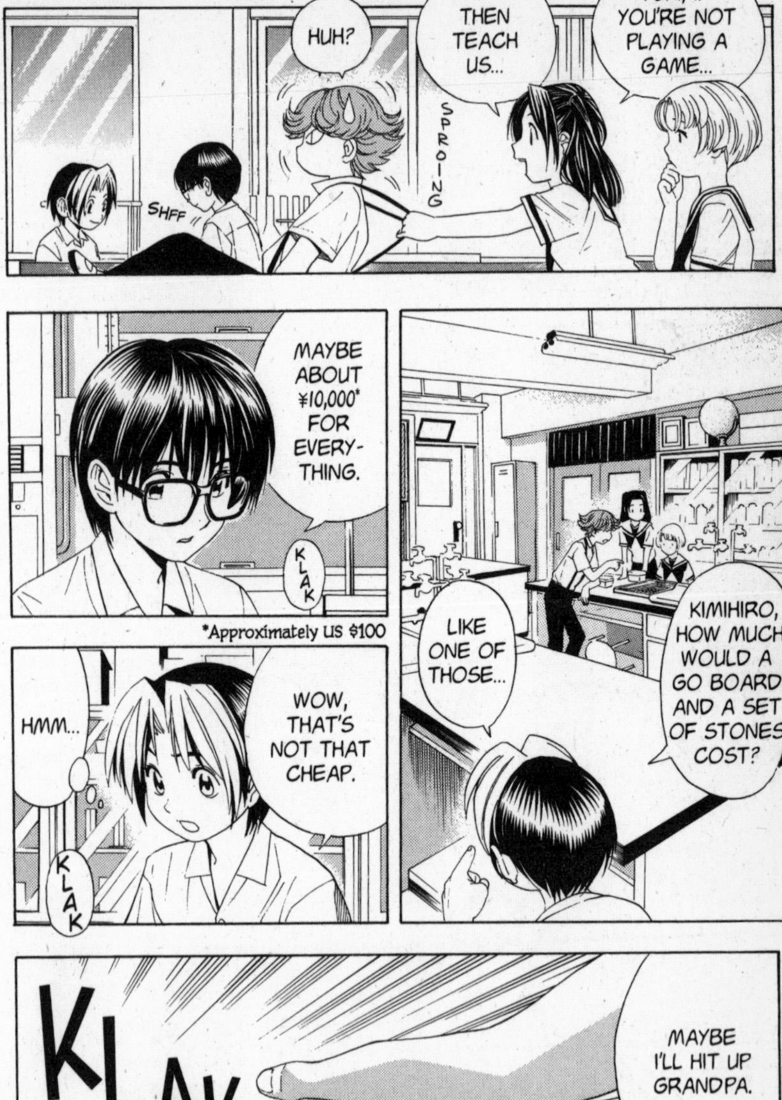
YUKI, IF YOU'RE NOT PLAYING A GAME...
THEN TEACH US...
SPROING
HUH?
SHFF
KIMIHIRO, HOW MUCH WOULD A GO BOARD AND A SET OF STONES COST?
LIKE ONE OF THOSE...
MAYBE ABOUT ¥10,000* FOR EVERYTHING.
KLAK
WOW, THAT'S NOT THAT CHEAP.
HMM...
KLAK
MAYBE I'LL HIT UP GRANDPA.
KLAK

*Approximately US $100

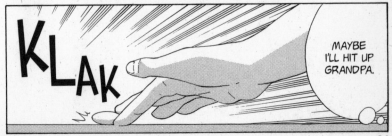

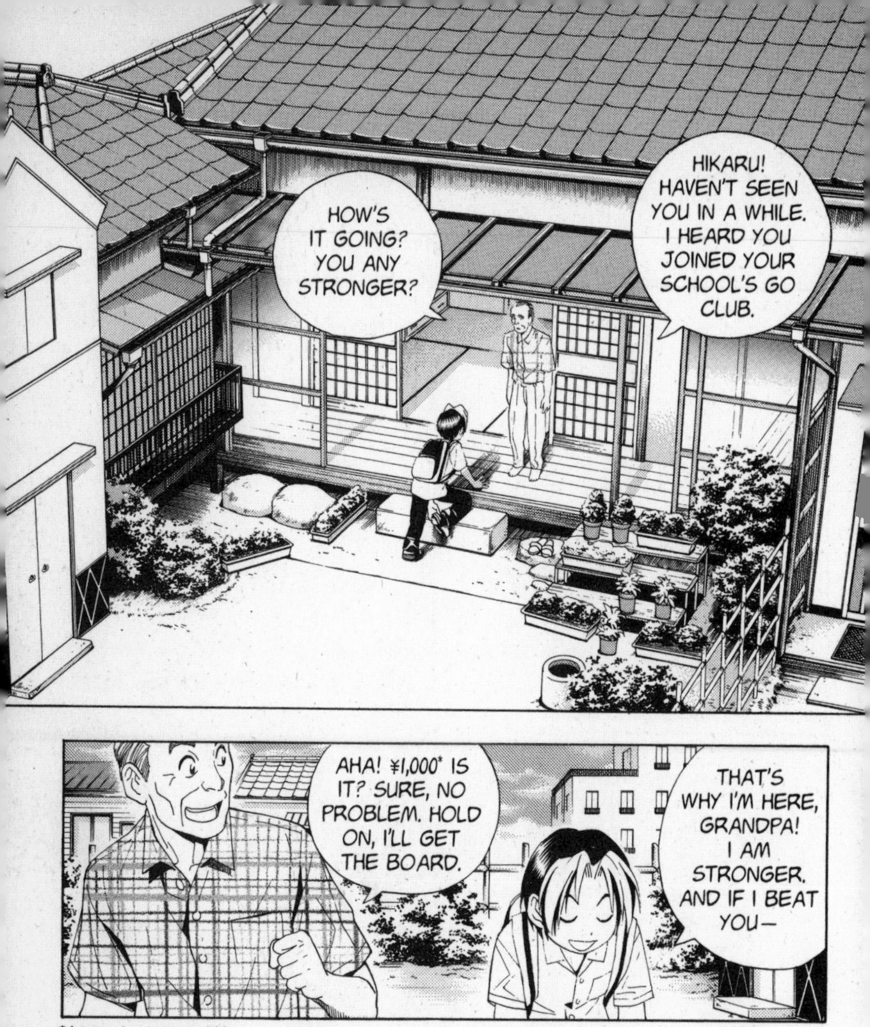
HIKARU! HAVEN'T SEEN YOU IN A WHILE. I HEARD YOU JOINED YOUR SCHOOL'S GO CLUB.
HOW'S IT GOING? YOU ANY STRONGER?
THAT'S WHY I'M HERE, GRANDPA! I AM STRONGER. AND IF I BEAT YOU—
AHA! ¥1,000* IS IT? SURE, NO PROBLEM. HOLD ON, I'LL GET THE BOARD.

*Approximately US $10

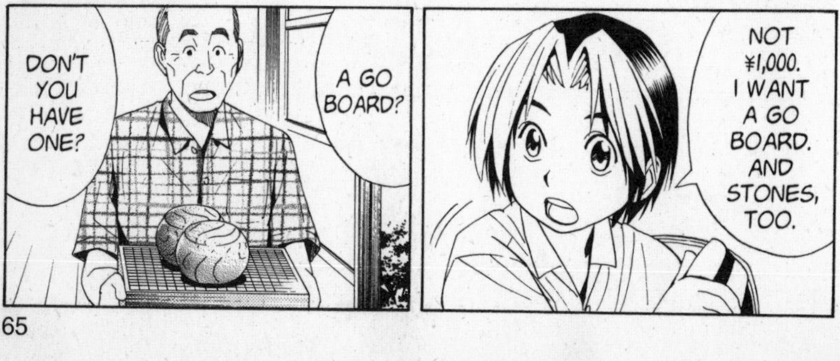
NOT ¥1,000. I WANT A GO BOARD. AND STONES, TOO.
A GO BOARD?
DON'T YOU HAVE ONE?

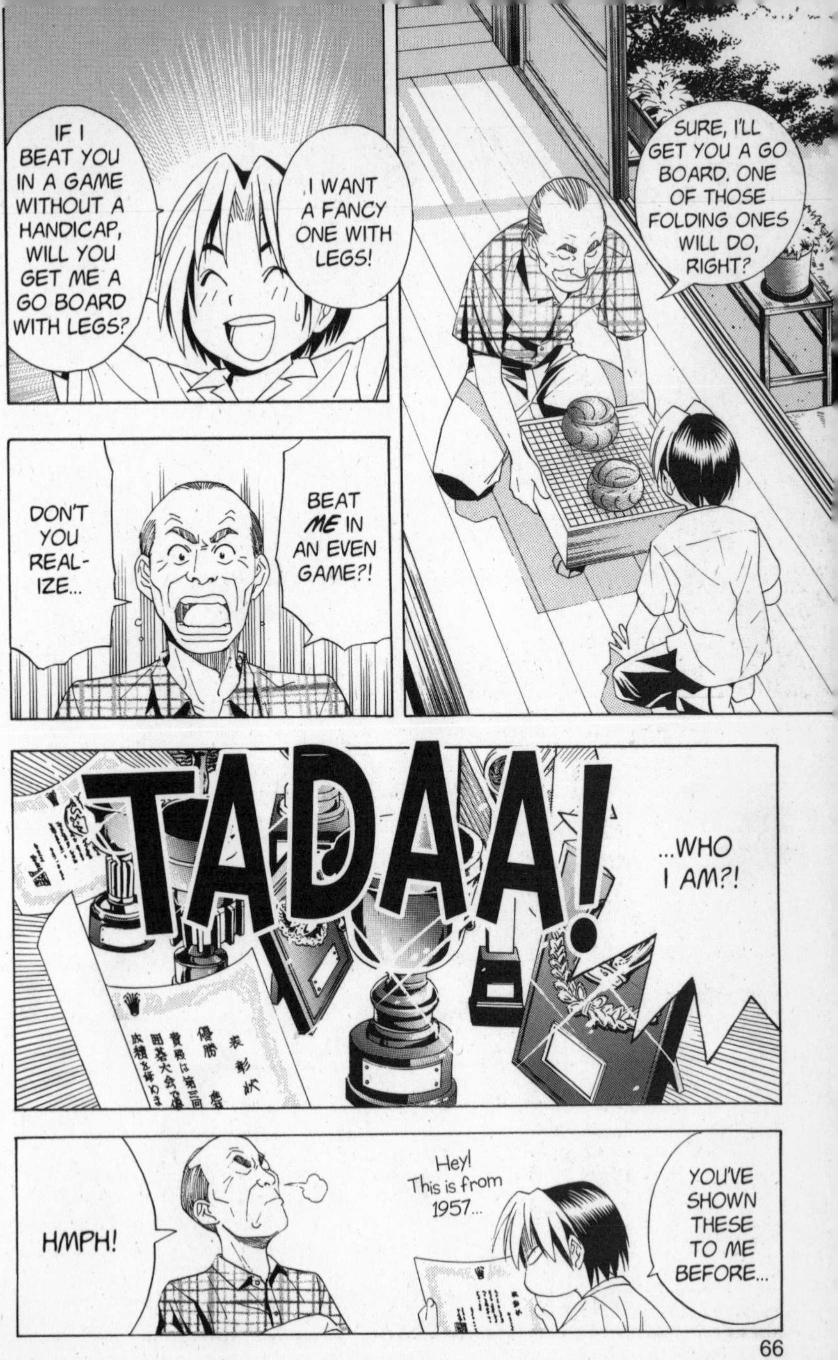
SURE, I'LL GET YOU A GO BOARD. ONE OF THOSE FOLDING ONES WILL DO, RIGHT?
I WANT A FANCY ONE WITH LEGS!
IF I BEAT YOU IN A GAME WITHOUT A HANDICAP, WILL YOU GET ME A GO BOARD WITH LEGS?
BEAT *ME* IN AN EVEN GAME?!
DON'T YOU REAL-IZE...
TADAA!
...WHO I AM?!
表彰状
優勝
YOU'VE SHOWN THESE TO ME BEFORE...
Hey! This is from 1957...
HMPH!

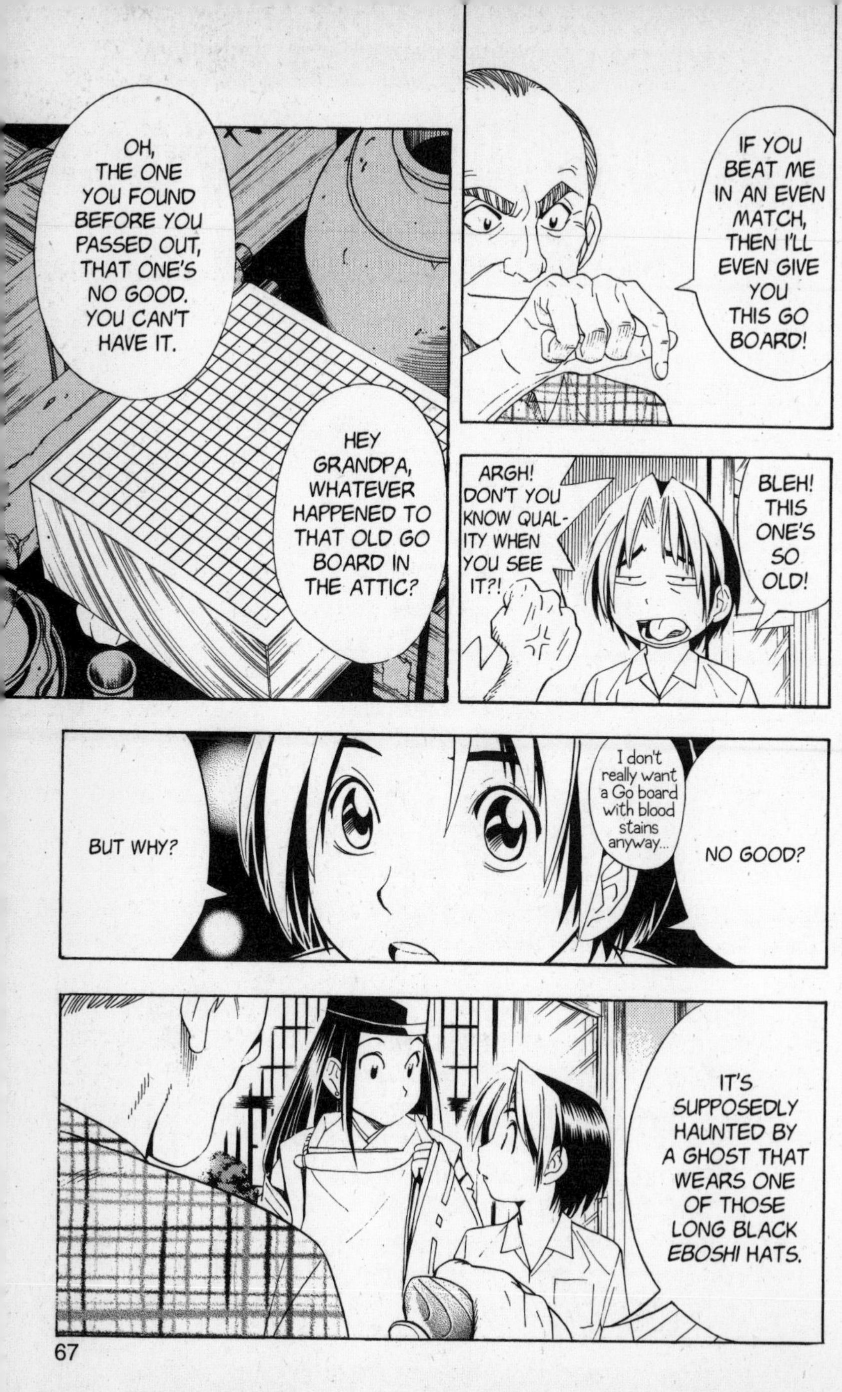
IF YOU BEAT ME IN AN EVEN MATCH, THEN I'LL EVEN GIVE YOU THIS GO BOARD!
BLEH! THIS ONE'S SO OLD!
ARGH! DON'T YOU KNOW QUALITY WHEN YOU SEE IT?!
HEY GRANDPA, WHATEVER HAPPENED TO THAT OLD GO BOARD IN THE ATTIC?
OH, THE ONE YOU FOUND BEFORE YOU PASSED OUT, THAT ONE'S NO GOOD. YOU CAN'T HAVE IT.
NO GOOD?
I don't really want a Go board with blood stains anyway...
BUT WHY?
IT'S SUPPOSEDLY HAUNTED BY A GHOST THAT WEARS ONE OF THOSE LONG BLACK EBOSHI HATS.

A WORD ABOUT HIKARU NO GO

JUMP'S OFFICIAL WEBSITE

AKIRA TOTALLY THOUGHT THAT HIKARU WAS PLAYING GO ONLINE. "WHAT? WHAT *IS* THIS?!" IT SEEMS AKIRA DOESN'T KNOW ABOUT *SHONEN JUMP*.

YOU CAN SEE THE HOME PAGE THAT HIKARU WAS LOOKING AT — JUMP'S OFFICIAL JAPANESE WEBSITE, POP WEB JUMP — AT THE FOLLOWING URL: HTTP://JUMP.SHUEISHA.CO.JP

CHECK OUT THE OFFICIAL WEBSITE FOR THE U.S. VERSION OF *SHONEN JUMP* AT HTTP://WWW.SHONENJUMP.COM

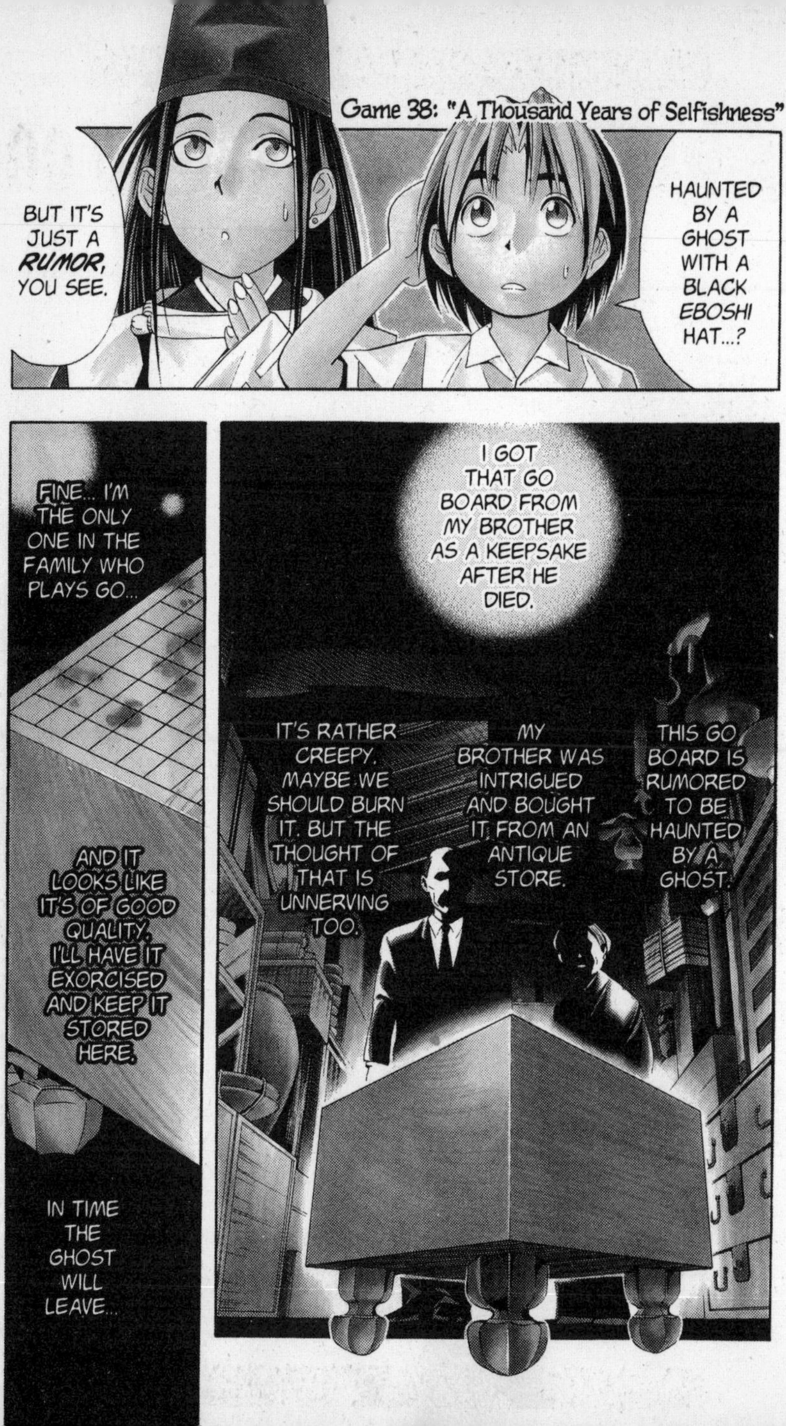
Game 38: "A Thousand Years of Selfishness"
HAUNTED BY A GHOST WITH A BLACK EBOSHI HAT...?
BUT IT'S JUST A RUMOR, YOU SEE.
I GOT THAT GO BOARD FROM MY BROTHER AS A KEEPSAKE AFTER HE DIED.
THIS GO BOARD IS RUMORED TO BE HAUNTED BY A GHOST.
MY BROTHER WAS INTRIGUED AND BOUGHT IT FROM AN ANTIQUE STORE.
IT'S RATHER CREEPY. MAYBE WE SHOULD BURN IT. BUT THE THOUGHT OF THAT IS UNNERVING TOO.
FINE... I'M THE ONLY ONE IN THE FAMILY WHO PLAYS GO...
AND IT LOOKS LIKE IT'S OF GOOD QUALITY. I'LL HAVE IT EXORCISED AND KEEP IT STORED HERE.
IN TIME THE GHOST WILL LEAVE...

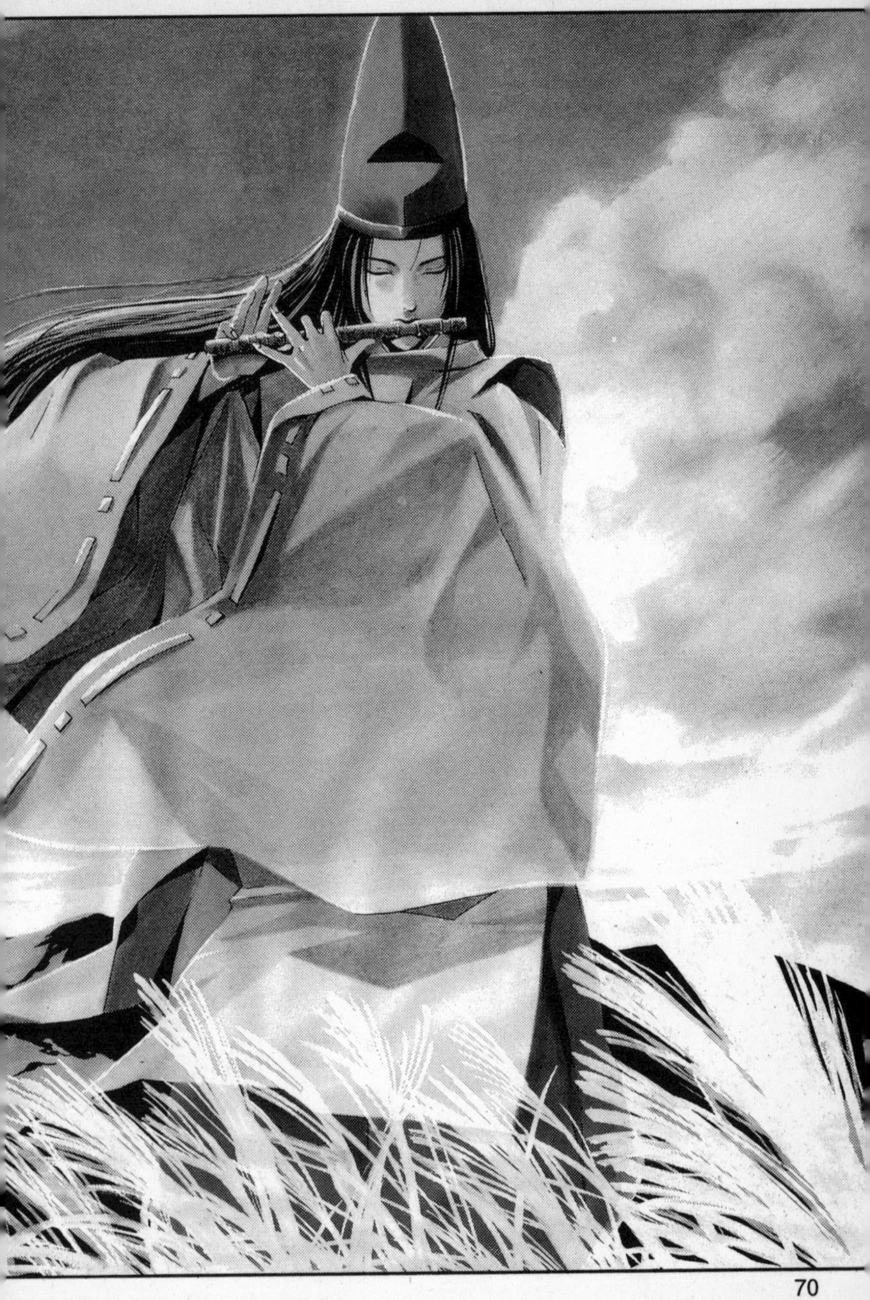

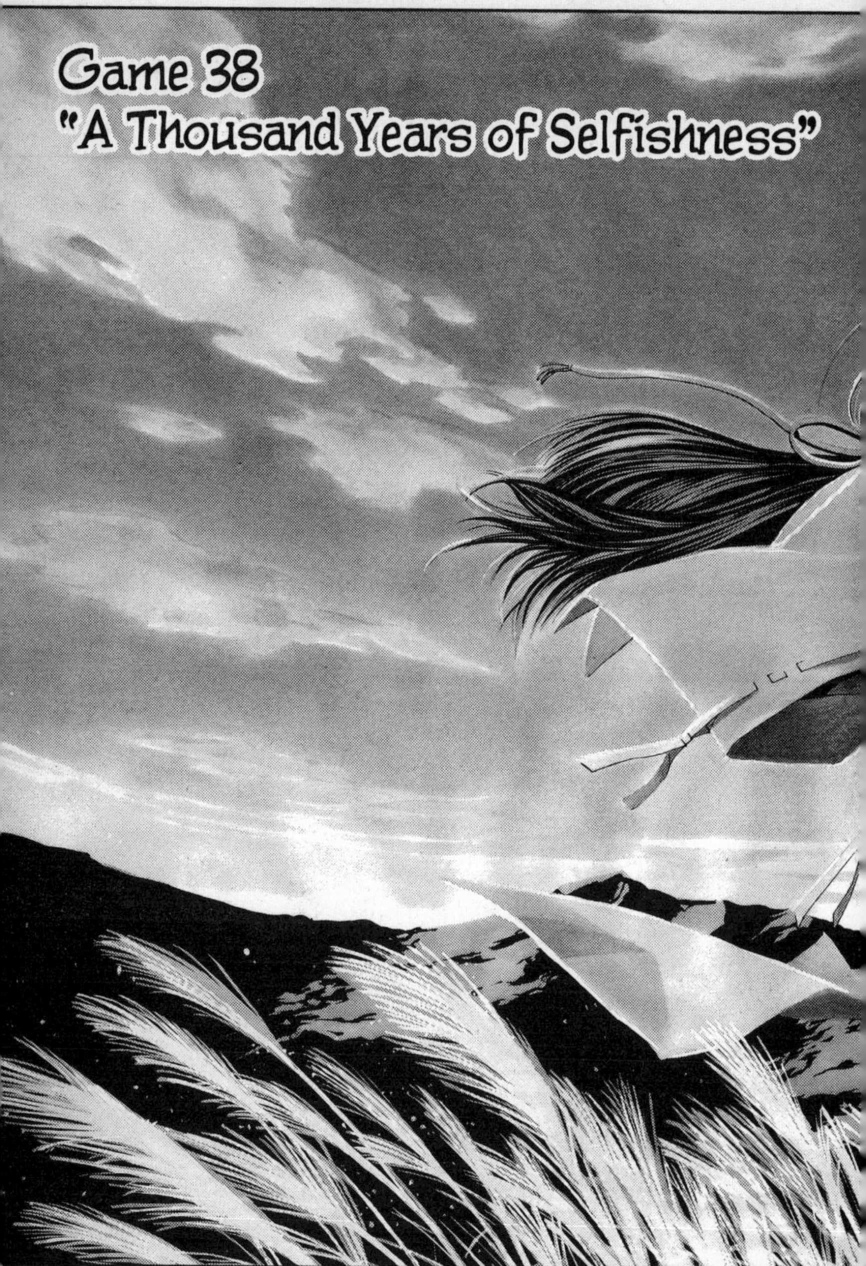
Game 38
"A Thousand Years of Selfishness"

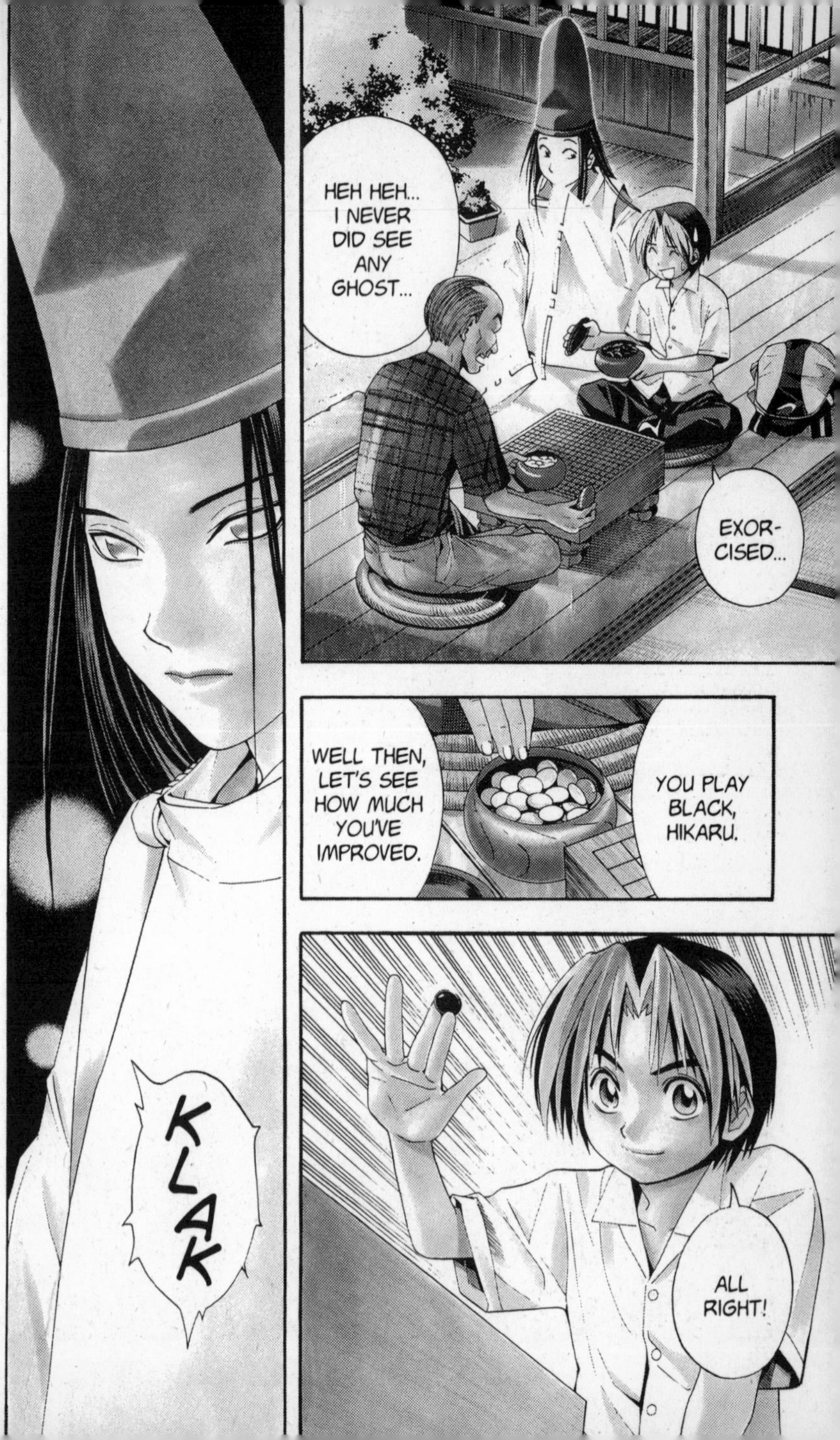

HEH HEH... I NEVER DID SEE ANY GHOST...
EXOR-CISED...
YOU PLAY BLACK, HIKARU.
WELL THEN, LET'S SEE HOW MUCH YOU'VE IMPROVED.
ALL RIGHT!
KLAK

READ THIS WAY

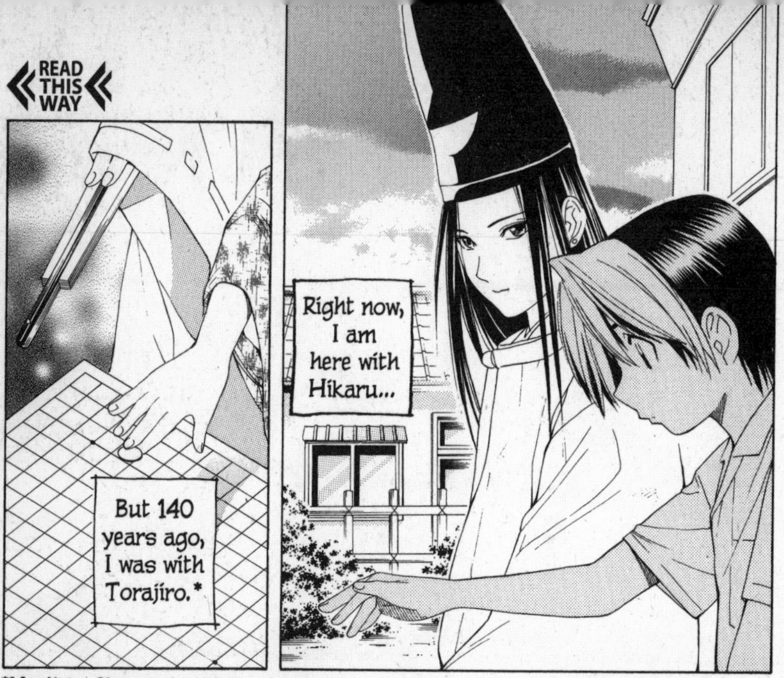
Right now, I am here with Hikaru...
But 140 years ago, I was with Torajiro.*

*Hon'inbo Shusaku's childhood name

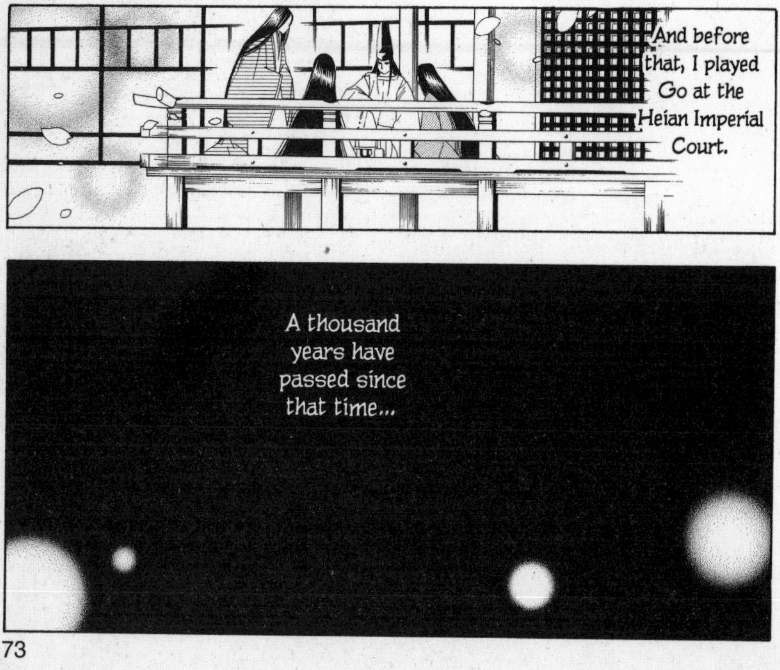
And before that, I played Go at the Heian Imperial Court.
A thousand years have passed since that time...

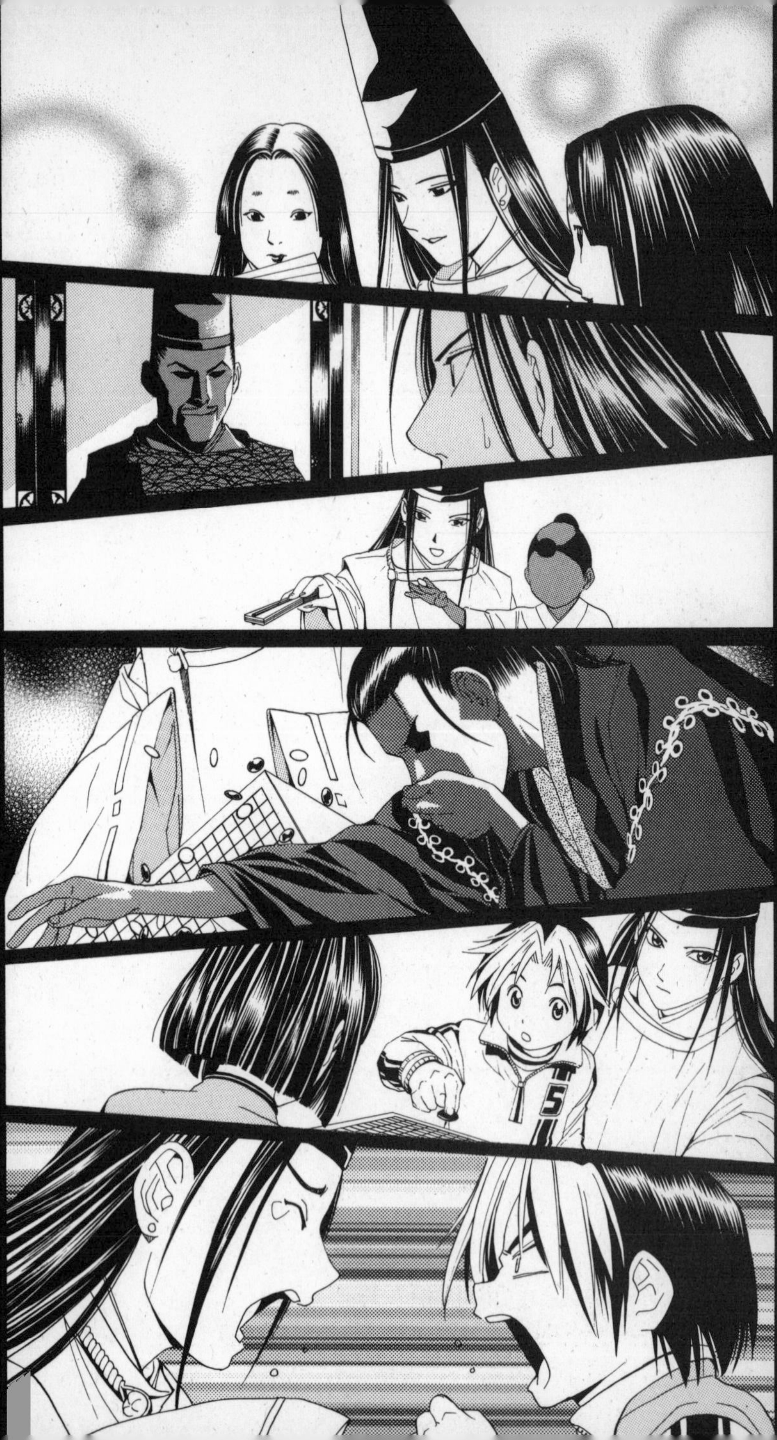

READ THIS WAY

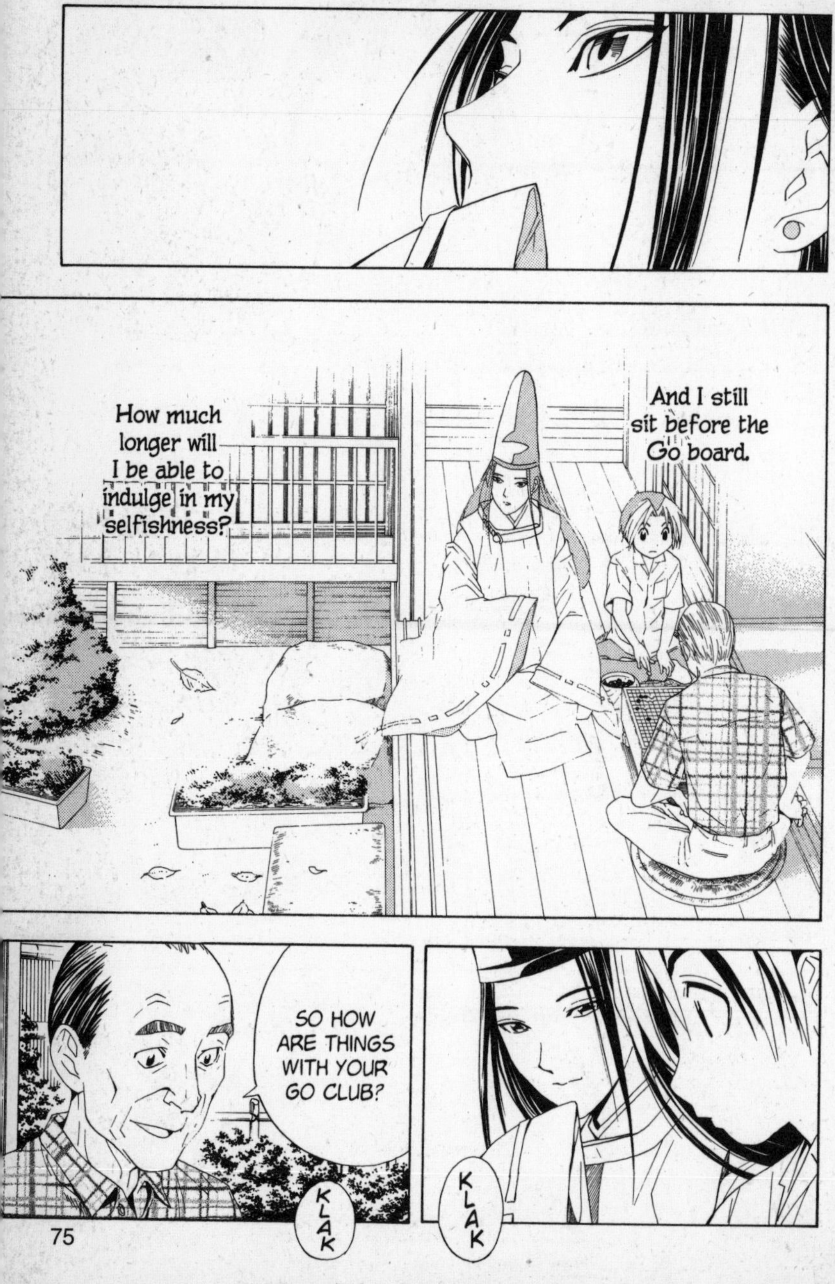
And I still sit before the Go board.
How much longer will I be able to indulge in my selfishness?
KLAK
SO HOW ARE THINGS WITH YOUR GO CLUB?
KLAK

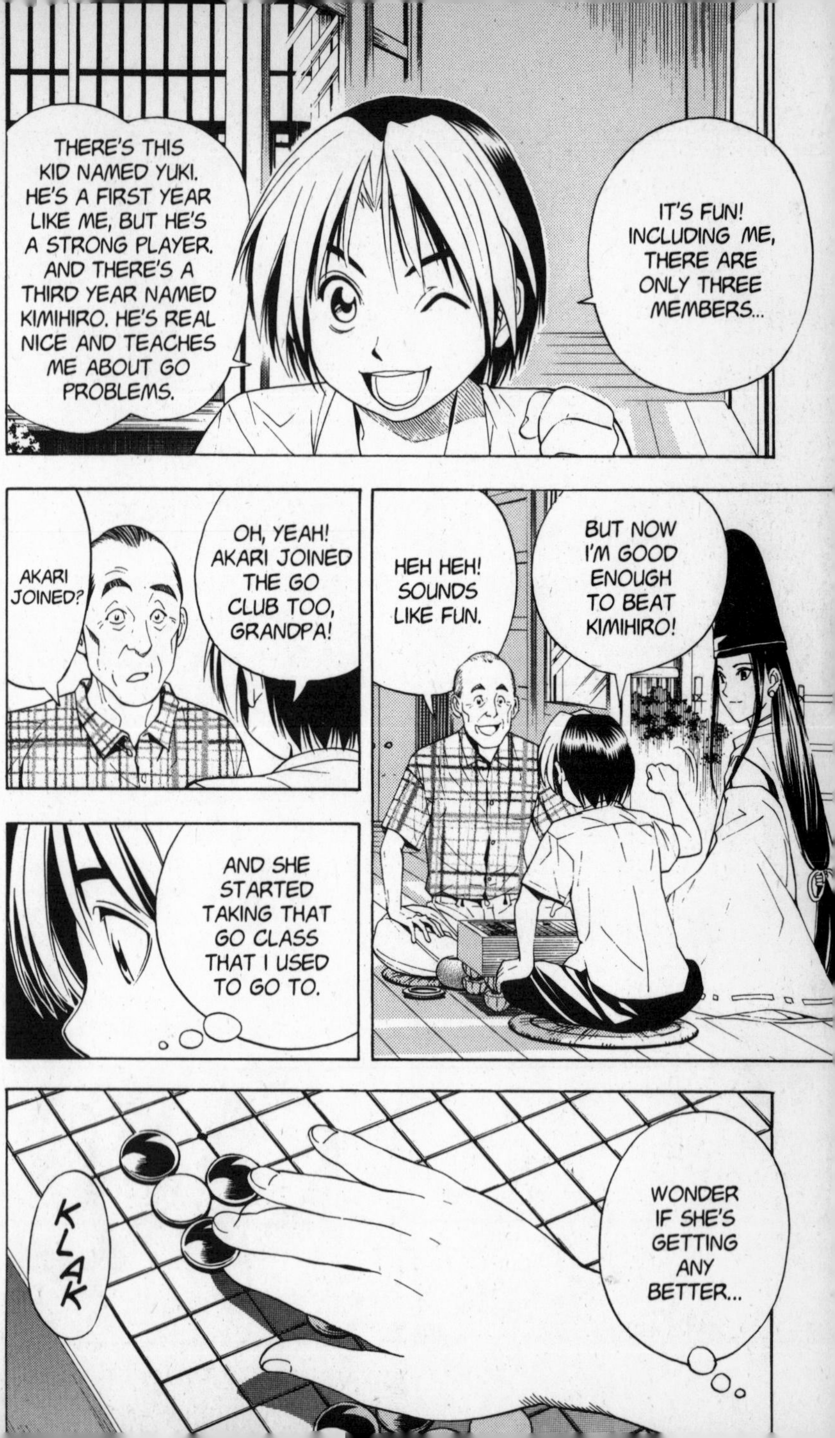
IT'S FUN! INCLUDING ME, THERE ARE ONLY THREE MEMBERS...
THERE'S THIS KID NAMED YUKI. HE'S A FIRST YEAR LIKE ME, BUT HE'S A STRONG PLAYER. AND THERE'S A THIRD YEAR NAMED KIMIHIRO. HE'S REAL NICE AND TEACHES ME ABOUT GO PROBLEMS.
BUT NOW I'M GOOD ENOUGH TO BEAT KIMIHIRO!
HEH HEH! SOUNDS LIKE FUN.
OH, YEAH! AKARI JOINED THE GO CLUB TOO, GRANDPA!
AKARI JOINED?
AND SHE STARTED TAKING THAT GO CLASS THAT I USED TO GO TO.
WONDER IF SHE'S GETTING ANY BETTER...
KLAK

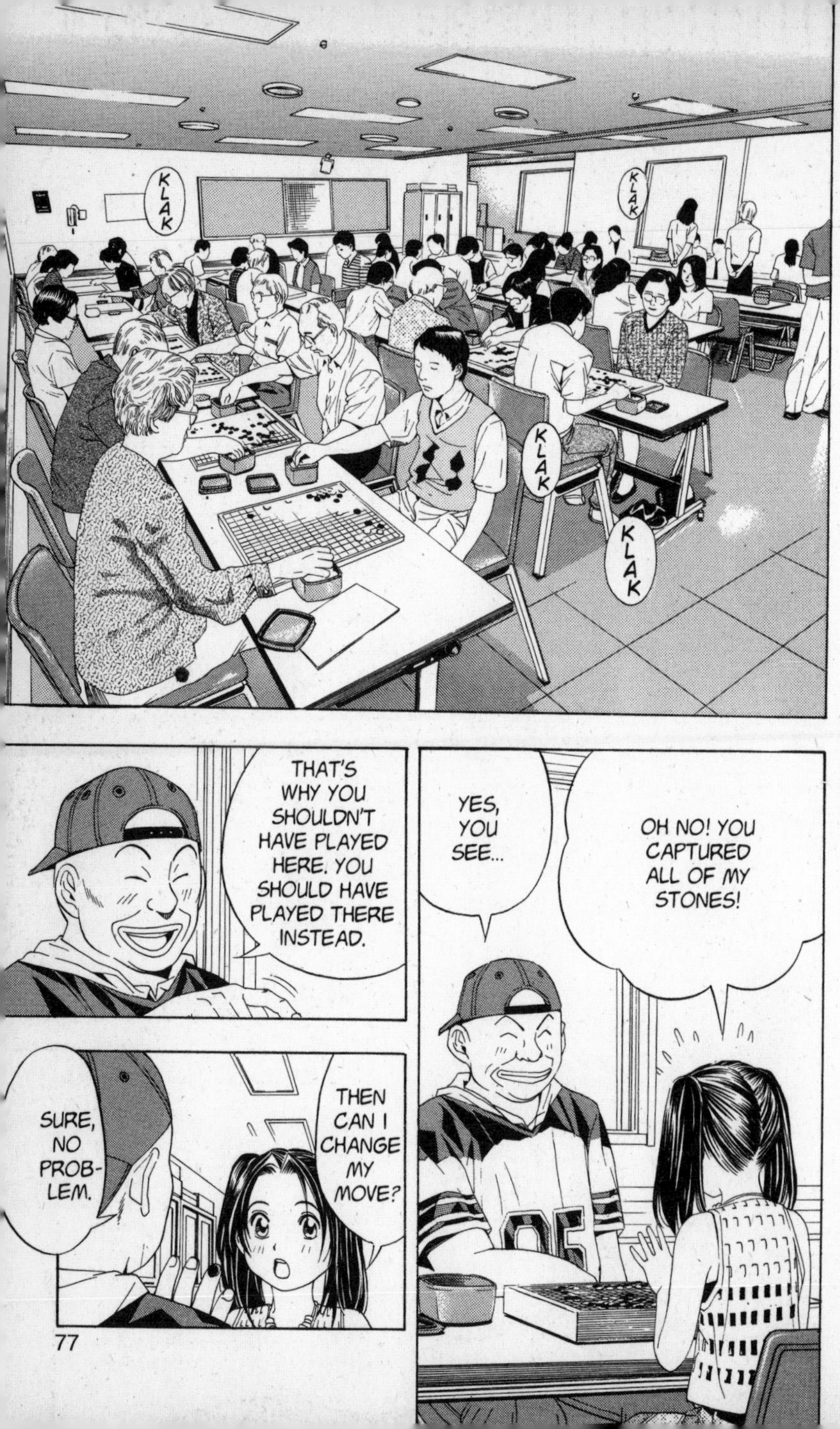
KLAK
KLAK
KLAK
KLAK
OH NO! YOU CAPTURED ALL OF MY STONES!
YES, YOU SEE...
THAT'S WHY YOU SHOULDN'T HAVE PLAYED HERE. YOU SHOULD HAVE PLAYED THERE INSTEAD.
THEN CAN I CHANGE MY MOVE?
SURE, NO PROB-LEM.

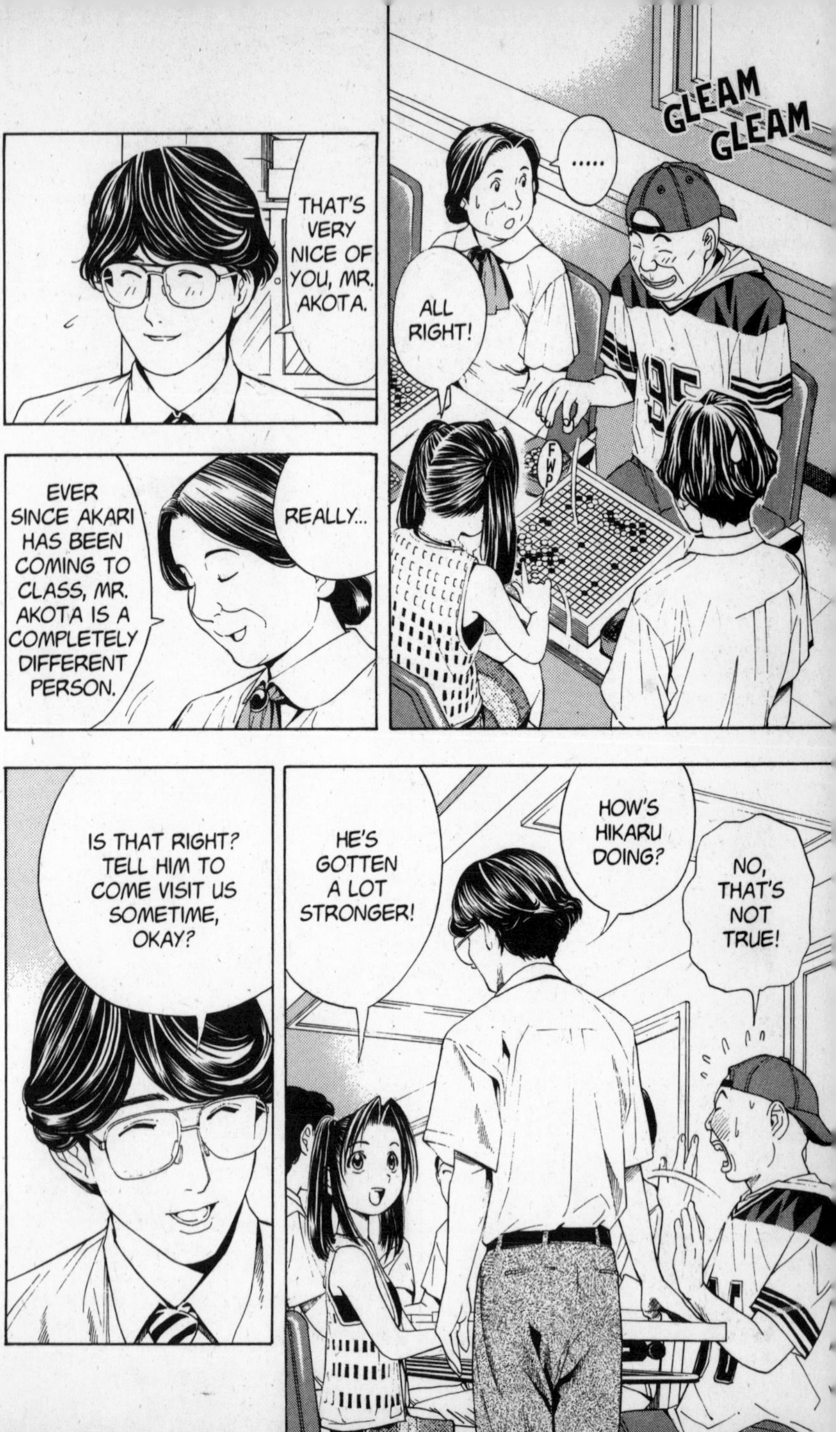
GLEAM
GLEAM
.....
ALL RIGHT!
FWP
THAT'S VERY NICE OF YOU, MR. AKOTA.
REALLY...
EVER SINCE AKARI HAS BEEN COMING TO CLASS, MR. AKOTA IS A COMPLETELY DIFFERENT PERSON.
NO, THAT'S NOT TRUE!
HOW'S HIKARU DOING?
HE'S GOTTEN A LOT STRONGER!
IS THAT RIGHT? TELL HIM TO COME VISIT US SOMETIME, OKAY?

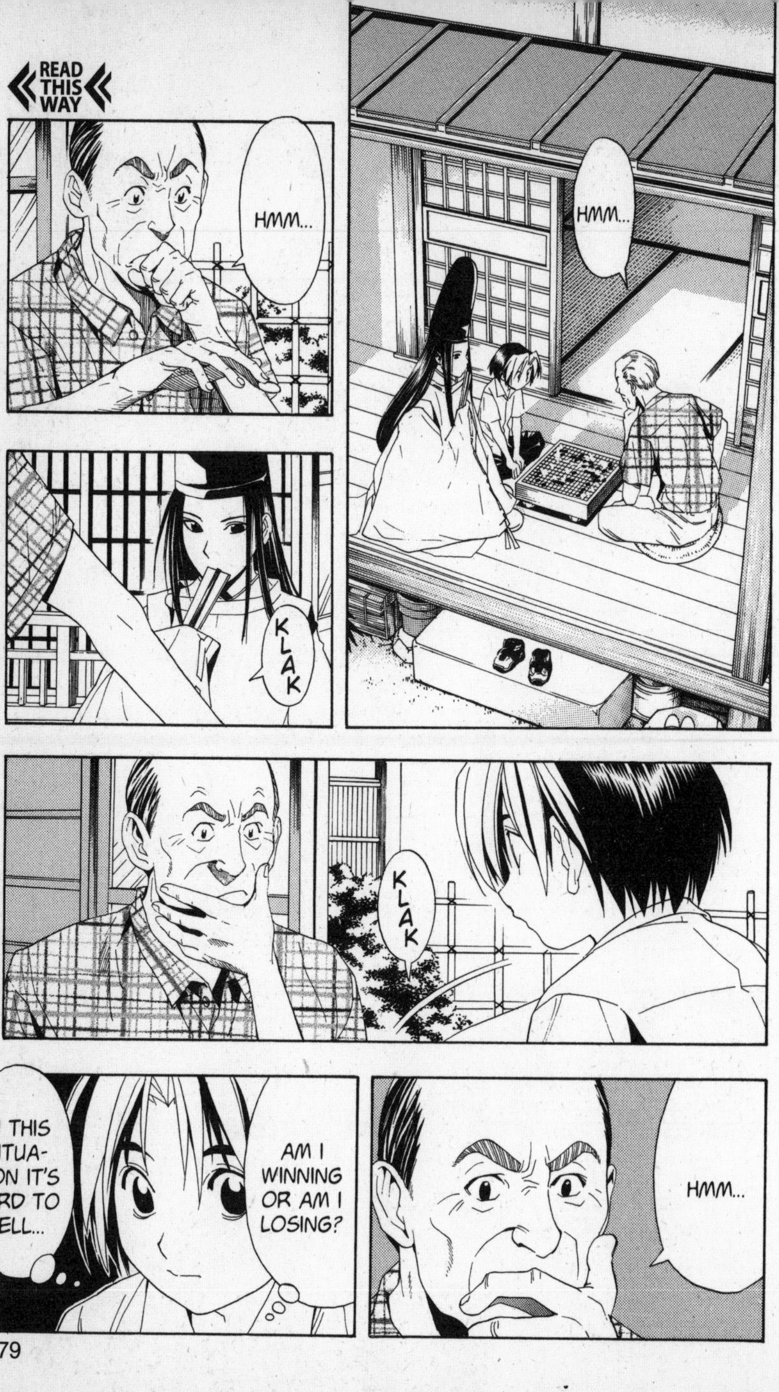
READ THIS WAY
HMM...
HMM...
KLAK
KLAK
HMM...
AM I WINNING OR AM I LOSING?
IN THIS SITUATION IT'S HARD TO TELL...

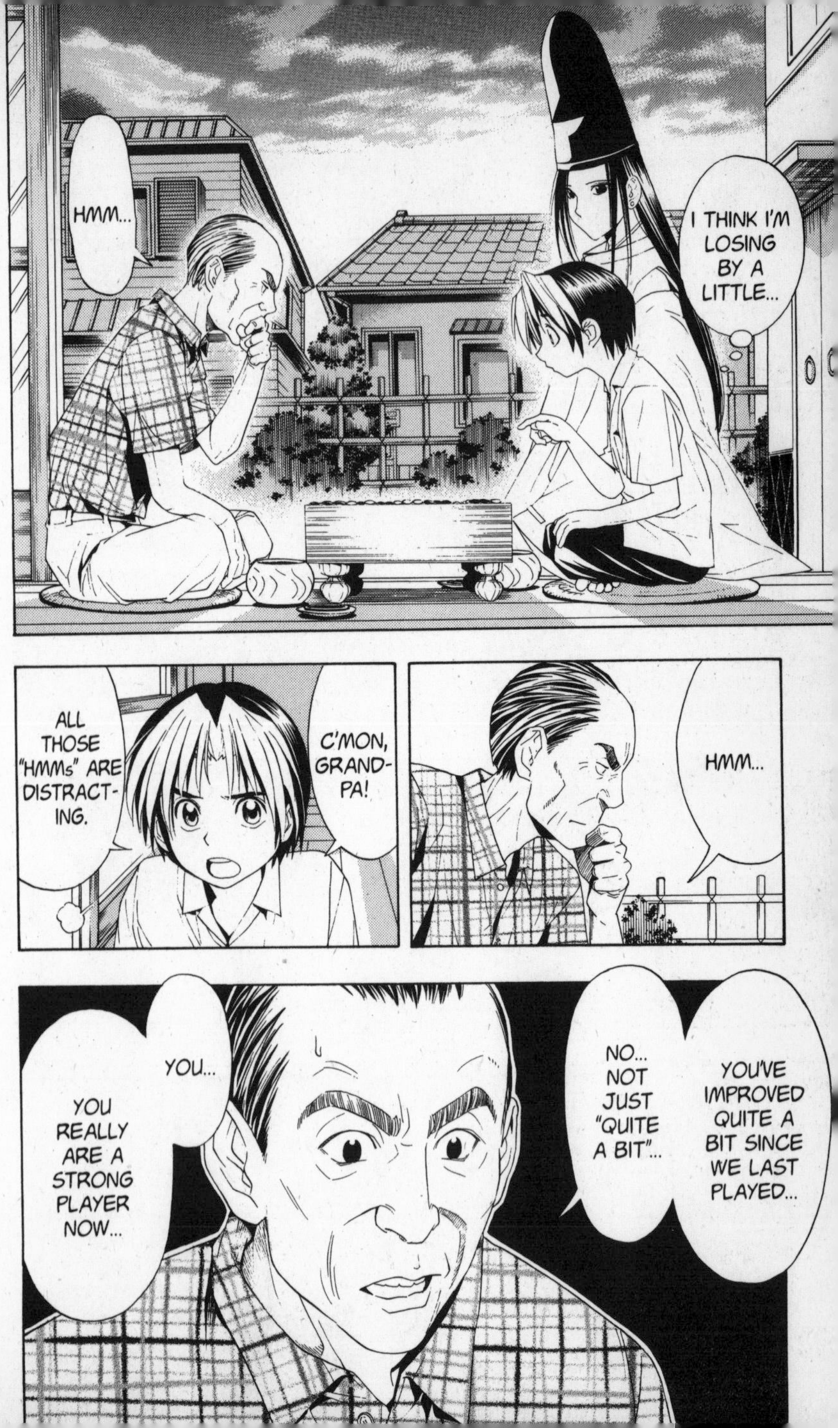
I THINK I'M LOSING BY A LITTLE...
HMM...
HMM...
C'MON, GRAND-PA!
ALL THOSE "HMMs" ARE DISTRACT-ING.
YOU'VE IMPROVED QUITE A BIT SINCE WE LAST PLAYED...
NO... NOT JUST "QUITE A BIT"...
YOU...
YOU REALLY ARE A STRONG PLAYER NOW...

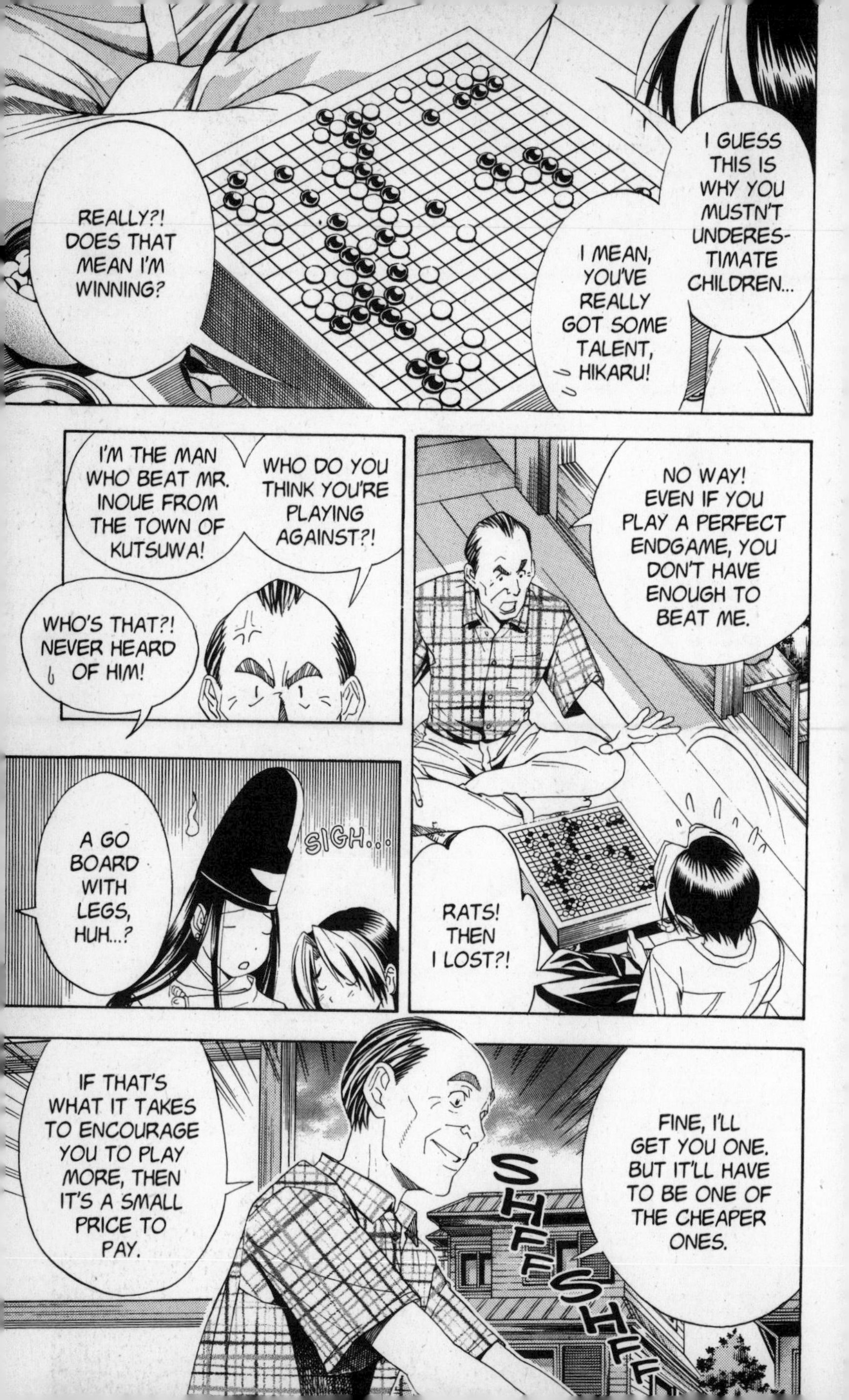
I GUESS THIS IS WHY YOU MUSTN'T UNDERESTIMATE CHILDREN...
I MEAN, YOU'VE REALLY GOT SOME TALENT, HIKARU!
REALLY?! DOES THAT MEAN I'M WINNING?
NO WAY! EVEN IF YOU PLAY A PERFECT ENDGAME, YOU DON'T HAVE ENOUGH TO BEAT ME.
RATS! THEN I LOST?!
WHO DO YOU THINK YOU'RE PLAYING AGAINST?!
I'M THE MAN WHO BEAT MR. INOUE FROM THE TOWN OF KUTSUWA!
WHO'S THAT?! NEVER HEARD OF HIM!
SIGH...
A GO BOARD WITH LEGS, HUH...?
FINE, I'LL GET YOU ONE. BUT IT'LL HAVE TO BE ONE OF THE CHEAPER ONES.
SHFF SHFF
IF THAT'S WHAT IT TAKES TO ENCOURAGE YOU TO PLAY MORE, THEN IT'S A SMALL PRICE TO PAY.

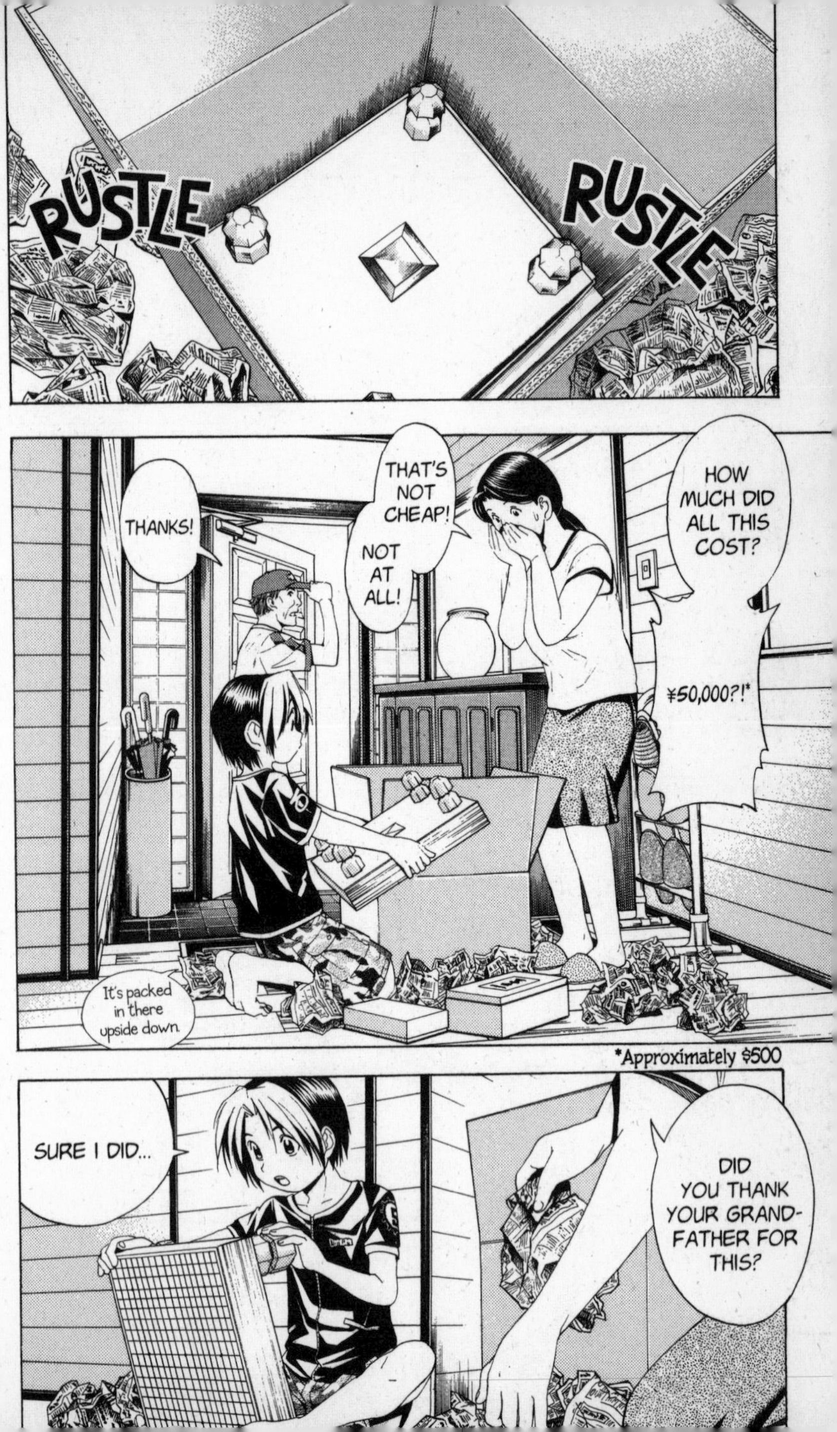
RUSTLE
RUSTLE
HOW MUCH DID ALL THIS COST?
¥50,000?!*
THAT'S NOT CHEAP!
NOT AT ALL!
THANKS!
It's packed in there upside down.
DID YOU THANK YOUR GRAND-FATHER FOR THIS?
SURE I DID...
*Approximately $500

READ THIS WAY

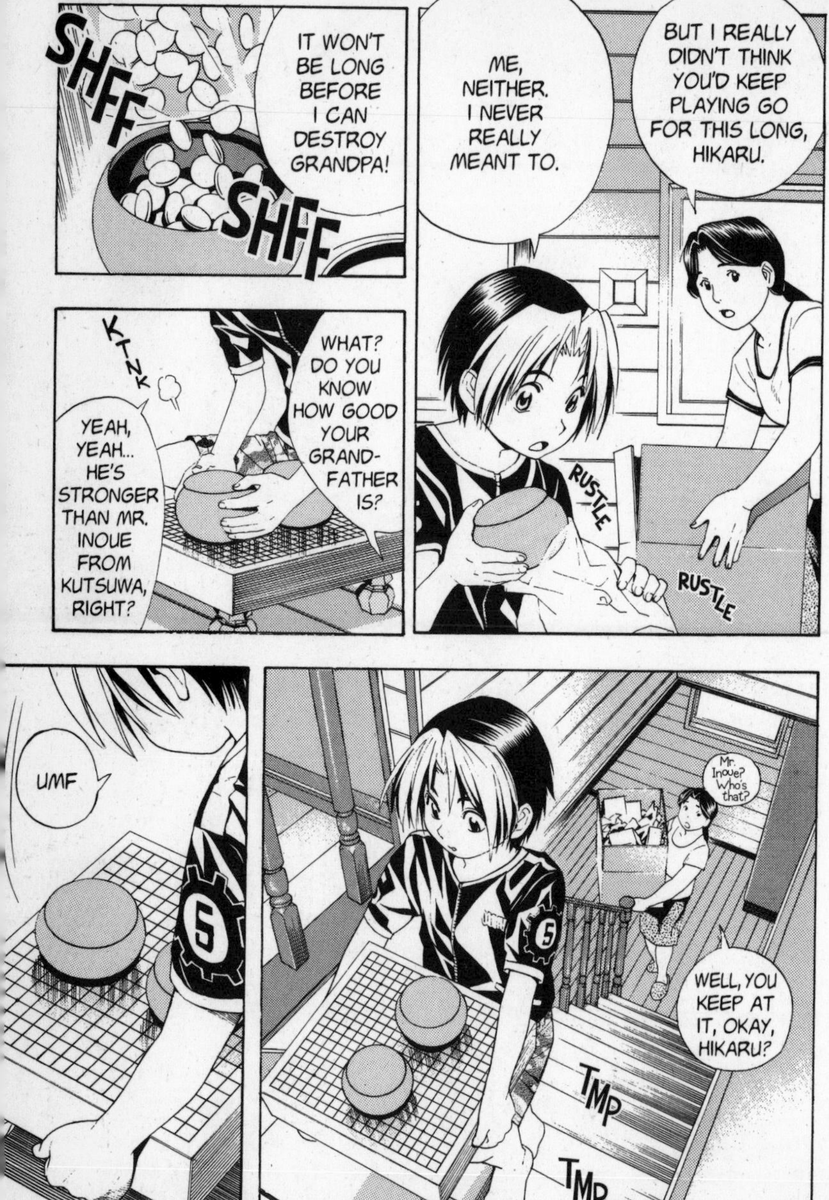
BUT I REALLY DIDN'T THINK YOU'D KEEP PLAYING GO FOR THIS LONG, HIKARU.
ME, NEITHER. I NEVER REALLY MEANT TO.
RUSTLE
RUSTLE
IT WON'T BE LONG BEFORE I CAN DESTROY GRANDPA!
SHFF
SHFF
WHAT? DO YOU KNOW HOW GOOD YOUR GRAND-FATHER IS?
YEAH, YEAH... HE'S STRONGER THAN MR. INOUE FROM KUTSUWA, RIGHT?
KTNK
Mr. Inoue? Who's that?
WELL, YOU KEEP AT IT, OKAY, HIKARU?
TMP
TMP
UMF

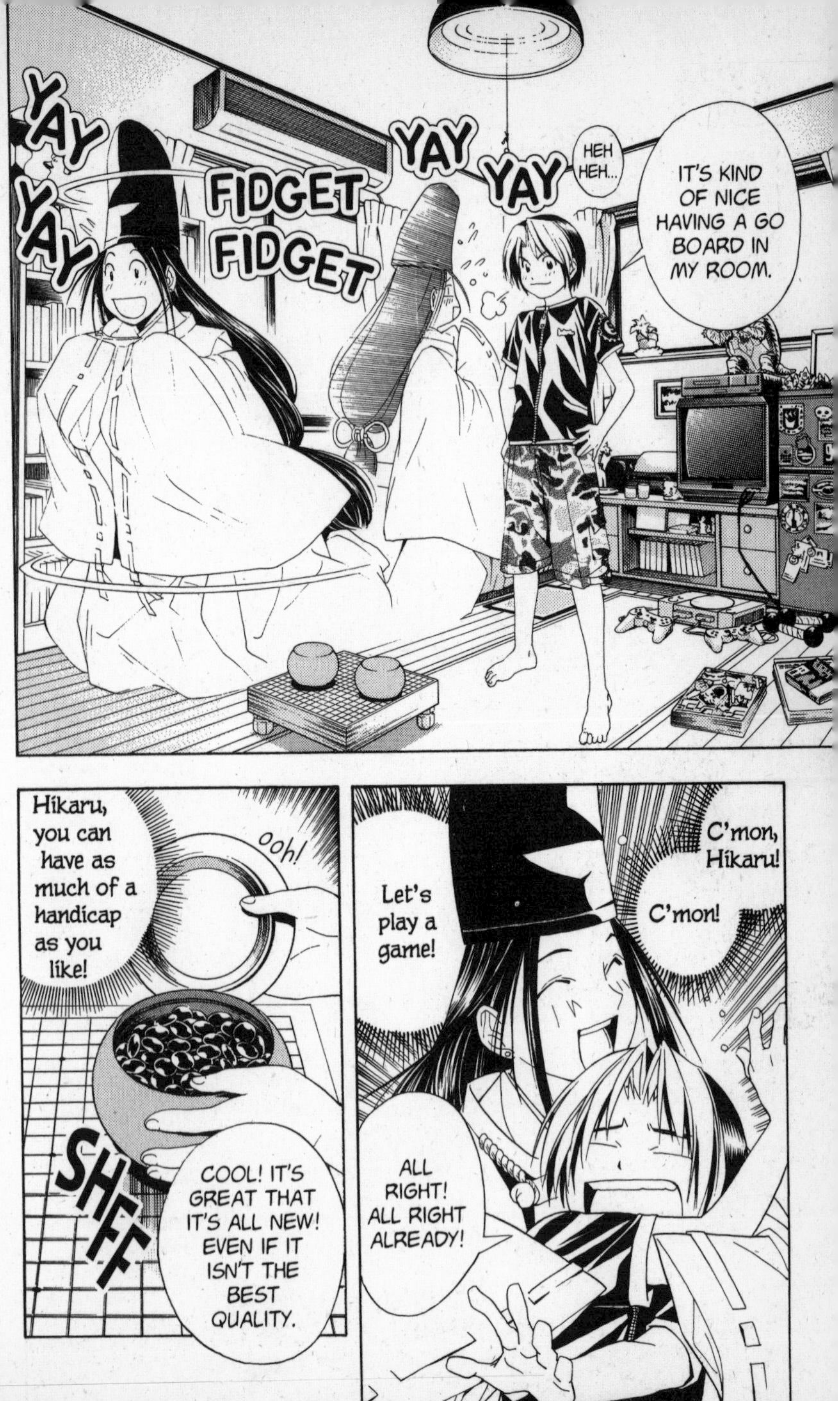
IT'S KIND OF NICE HAVING A GO BOARD IN MY ROOM.
HEH HEH...
YAY YAY
FIDGET FIDGET
YAY YAY
C'mon, Hikaru!
C'mon!
Let's play a game!
ALL RIGHT! ALL RIGHT ALREADY!
Hikaru, you can have as much of a handicap as you like!
ooh!
COOL! IT'S GREAT THAT IT'S ALL NEW! EVEN IF IT ISN'T THE BEST QUALITY.
SHFF

READ THIS WAY

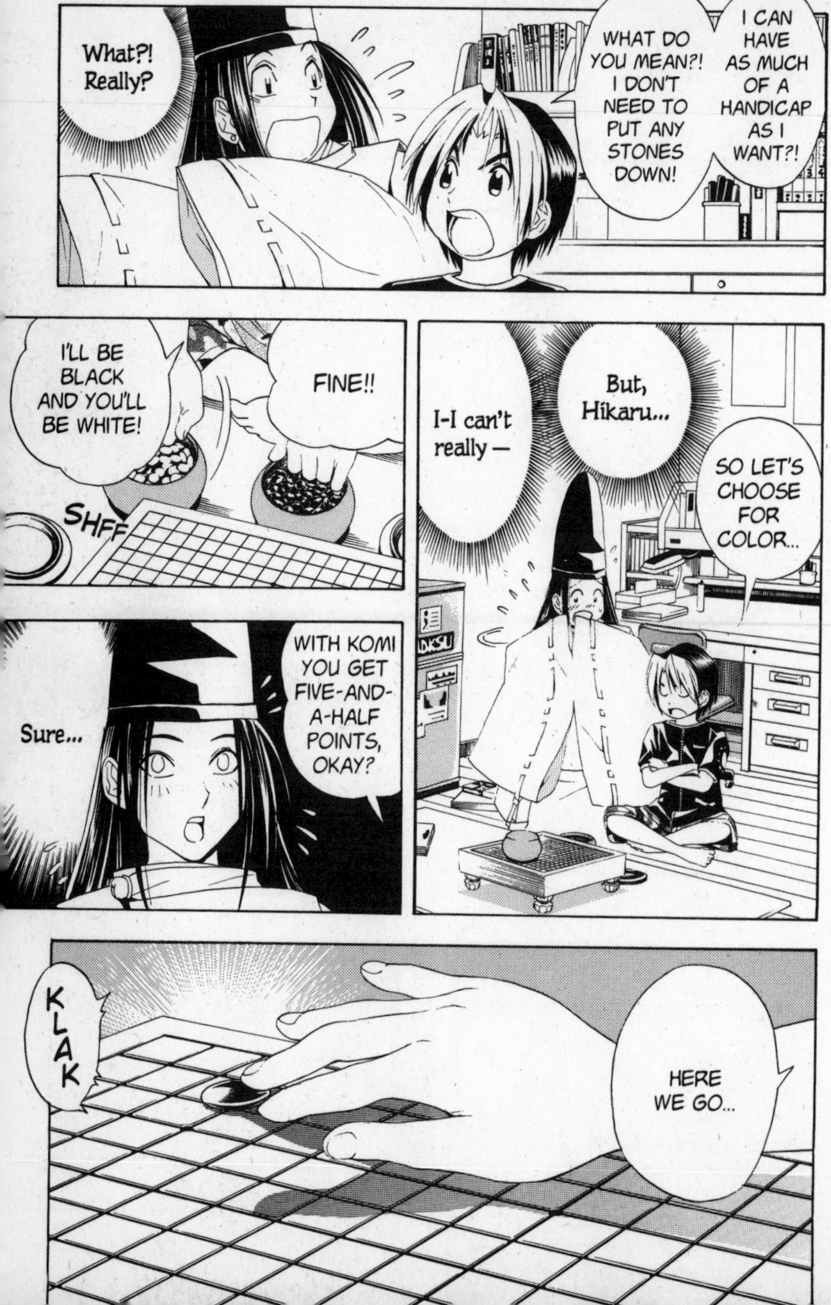
I CAN HAVE AS MUCH OF A HANDICAP AS I WANT?!
WHAT DO YOU MEAN?! I DON'T NEED TO PUT ANY STONES DOWN!
What?! Really?
SO LET'S CHOOSE FOR COLOR...
But, Hikaru...
I-I can't really —
FINE!!
I'LL BE BLACK AND YOU'LL BE WHITE!
SHFF
WITH KOMI YOU GET FIVE-AND-A-HALF POINTS, OKAY?
Sure...
HERE WE GO...
KLAK

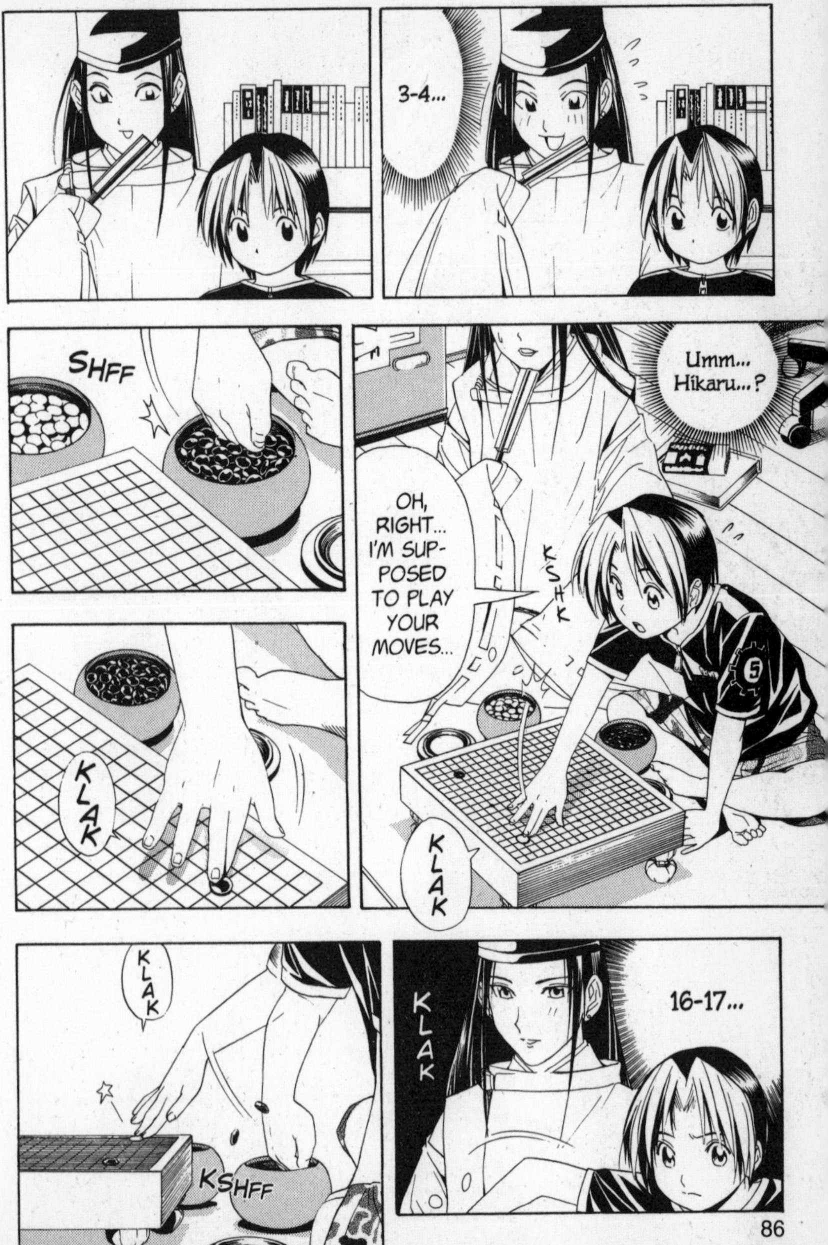
3-4...
Umm... Hikaru...?
OH, RIGHT... I'M SUP-POSED TO PLAY YOUR MOVES...
KSHK
KLAK
SHFF
KLAK
16-17...
KLAK
KLAK
KSHFF

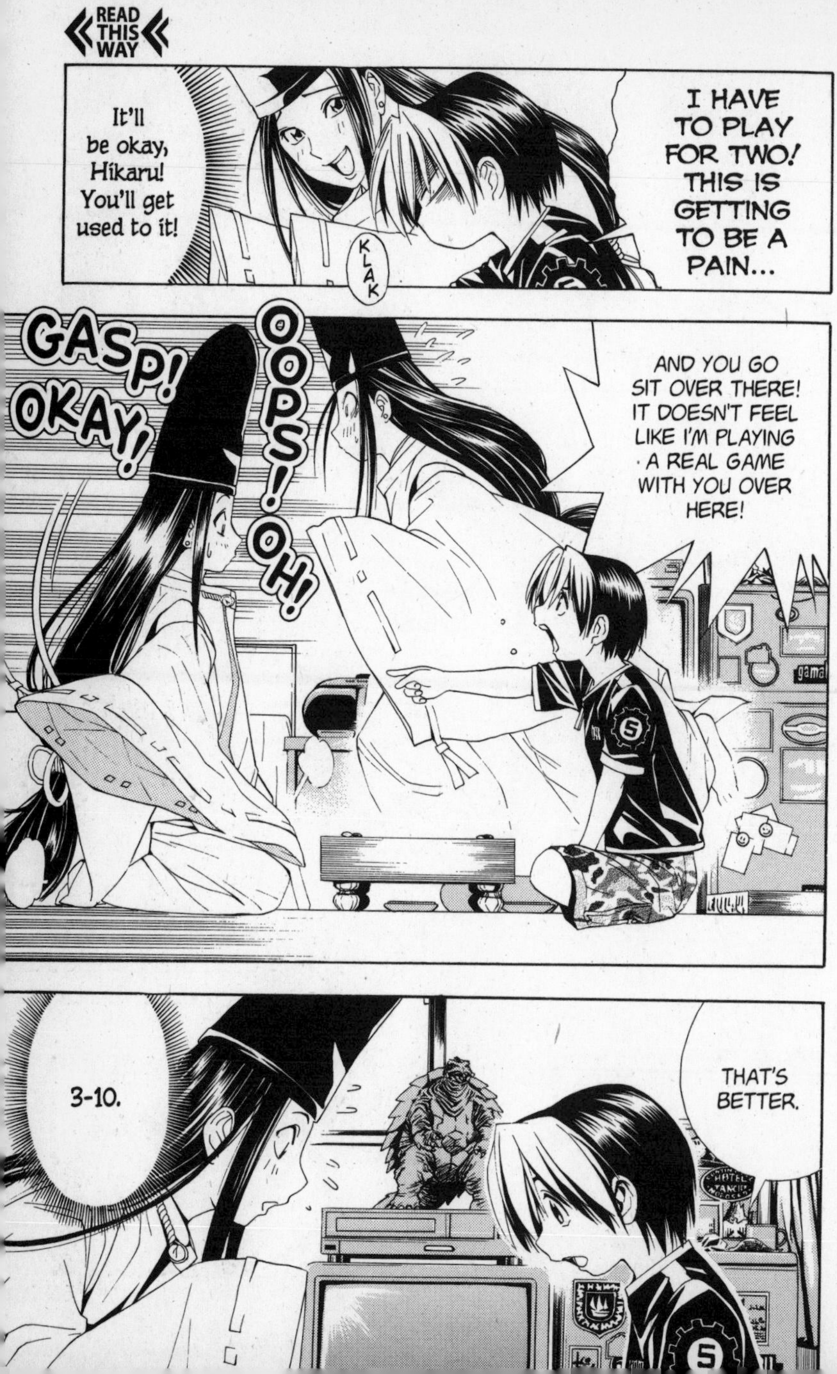
READ THIS WAY
I HAVE TO PLAY FOR TWO! THIS IS GETTING TO BE A PAIN...
KLAK
It'll be okay, Hikaru! You'll get used to it!
AND YOU GO SIT OVER THERE! IT DOESN'T FEEL LIKE I'M PLAYING A REAL GAME WITH YOU OVER HERE!
OOPS! OH!
GASP! OKAY!
THAT'S BETTER.
3-10.

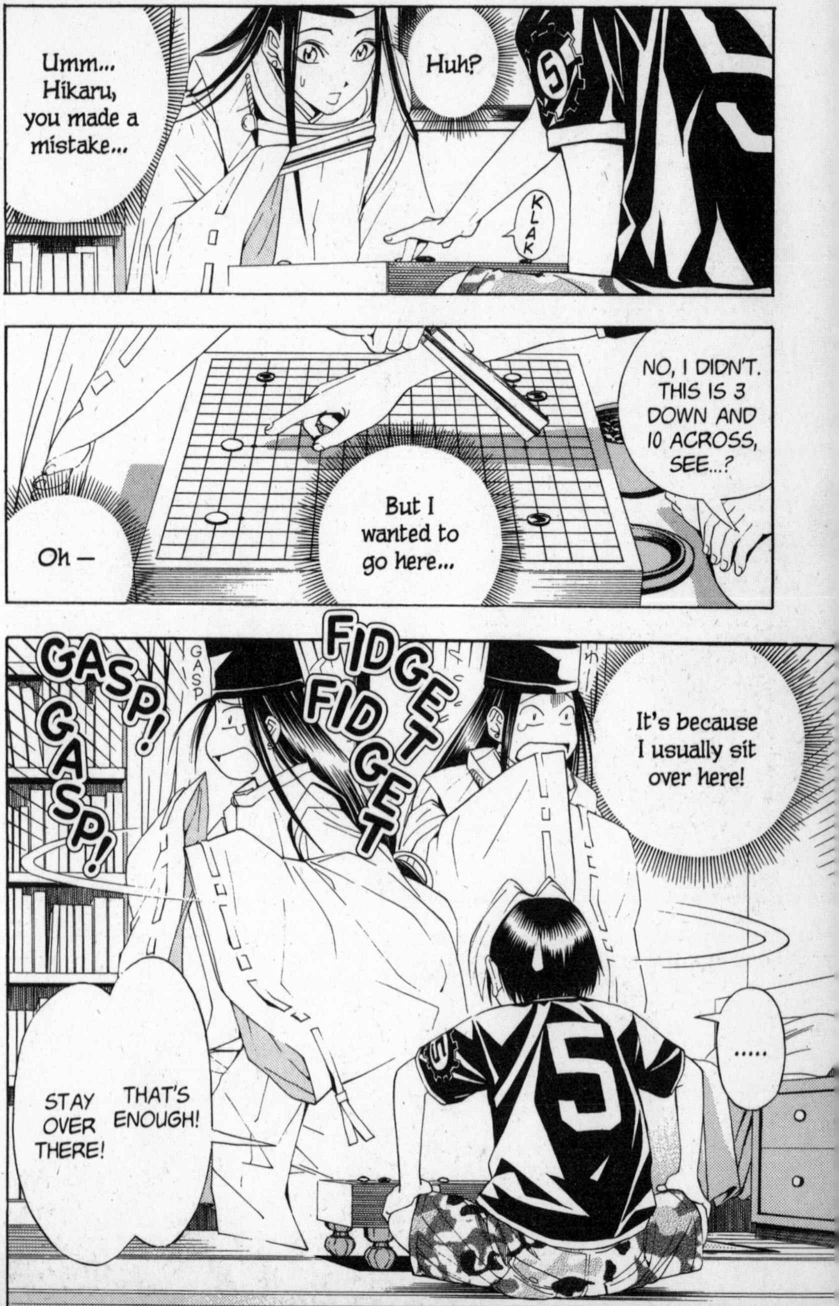
KLAK
Umm... Hikaru, you made a mistake...
Huh?
NO, I DIDN'T. THIS IS 3 DOWN AND 10 ACROSS, SEE...?
But I wanted to go here...
Oh —
It's because I usually sit over here!
FIDGET FIDGET
GASP! GASP!
GASP
.....
THAT'S ENOUGH! STAY OVER THERE!

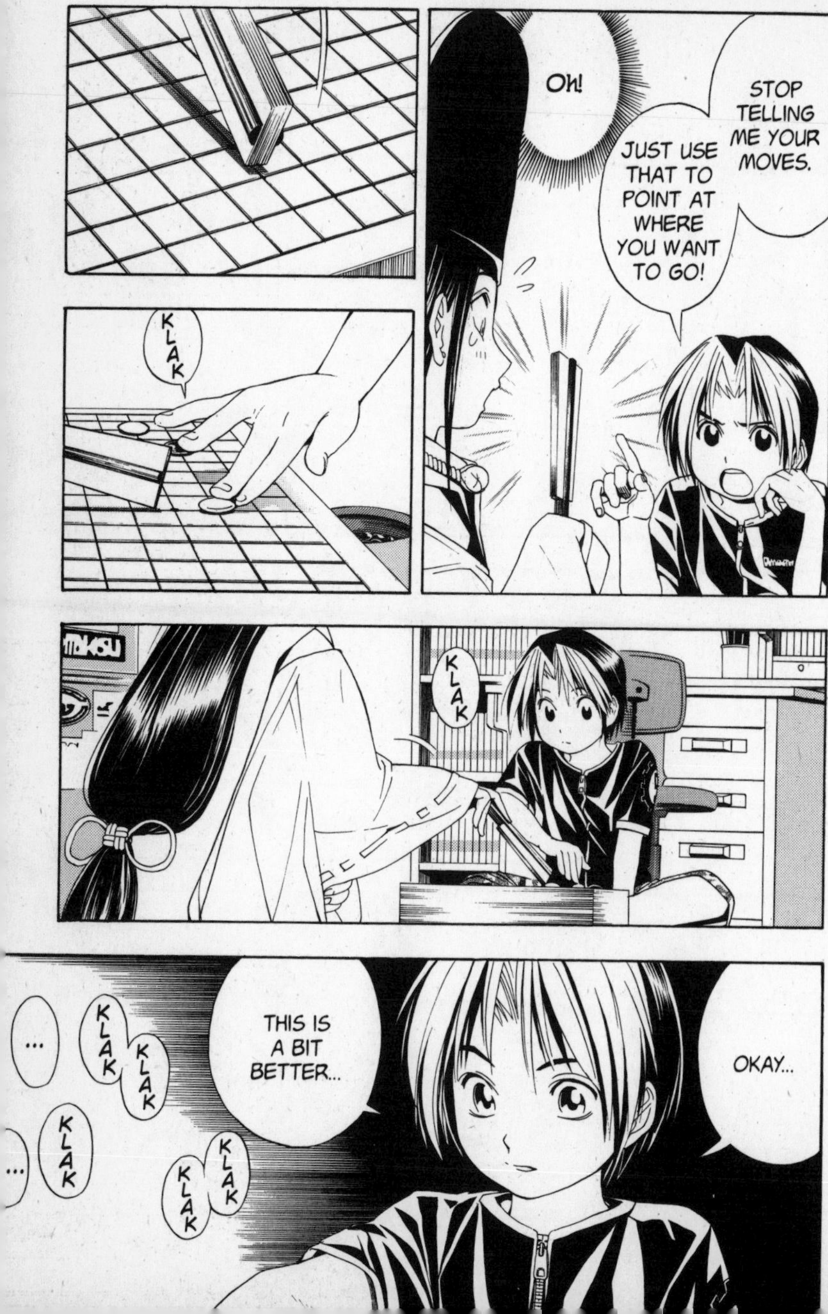

STOP TELLING ME YOUR MOVES.
JUST USE THAT TO POINT AT WHERE YOU WANT TO GO!
Oh!
KLAK
KLAK
OKAY...
THIS IS A BIT BETTER...
KLAK
KLAK
...
KLAK
KLAK
KLAK
...

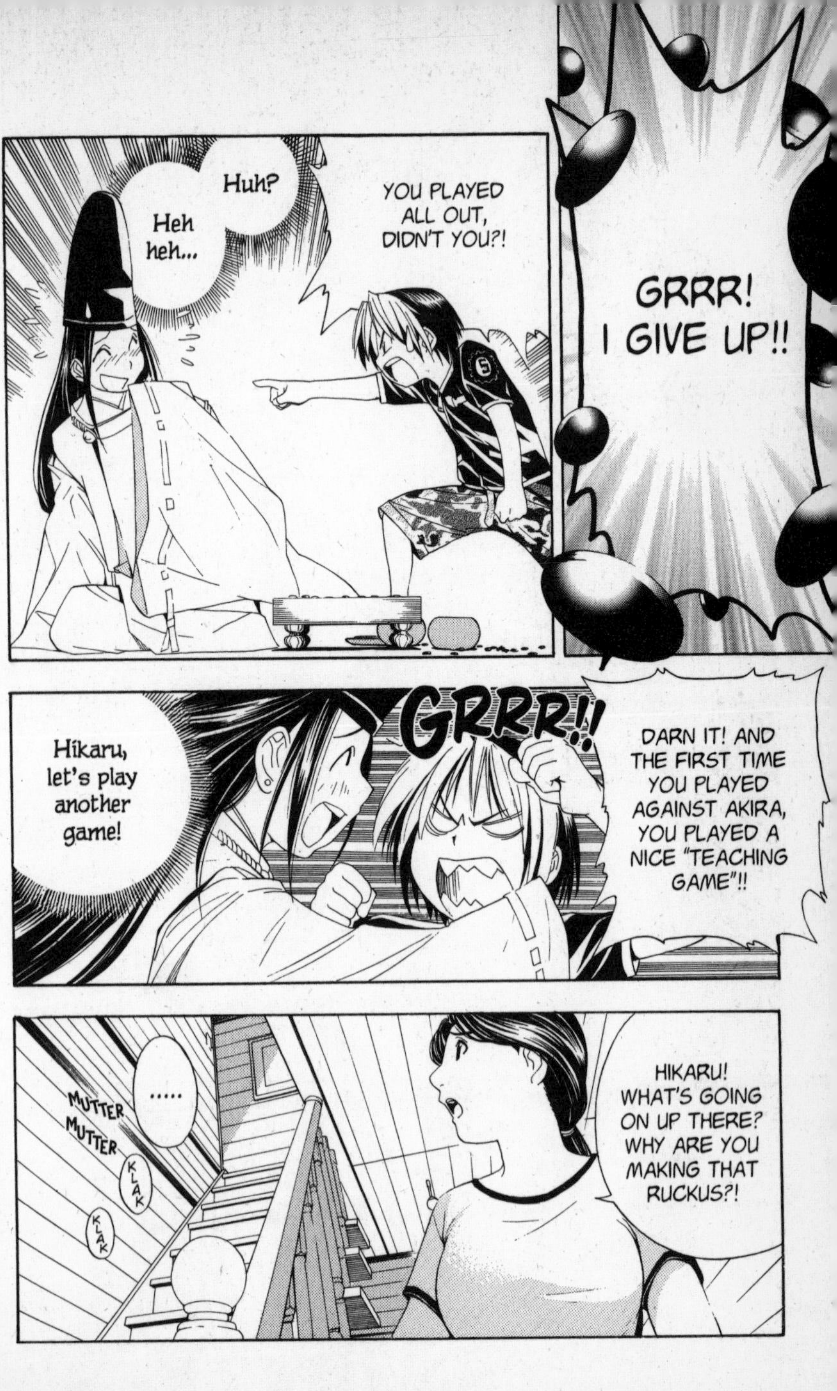
GRRR! I GIVE UP!!
YOU PLAYED ALL OUT, DIDN'T YOU?!
Huh?
Heh heh...
DARN IT! AND THE FIRST TIME YOU PLAYED AGAINST AKIRA, YOU PLAYED A NICE "TEACHING GAME"!!
GRRRR!!
Hikaru, let's play another game!
HIKARU! WHAT'S GOING ON UP THERE? WHY ARE YOU MAKING THAT RUCKUS?!
.....
MUTTER MUTTER
KLAK
KLAK

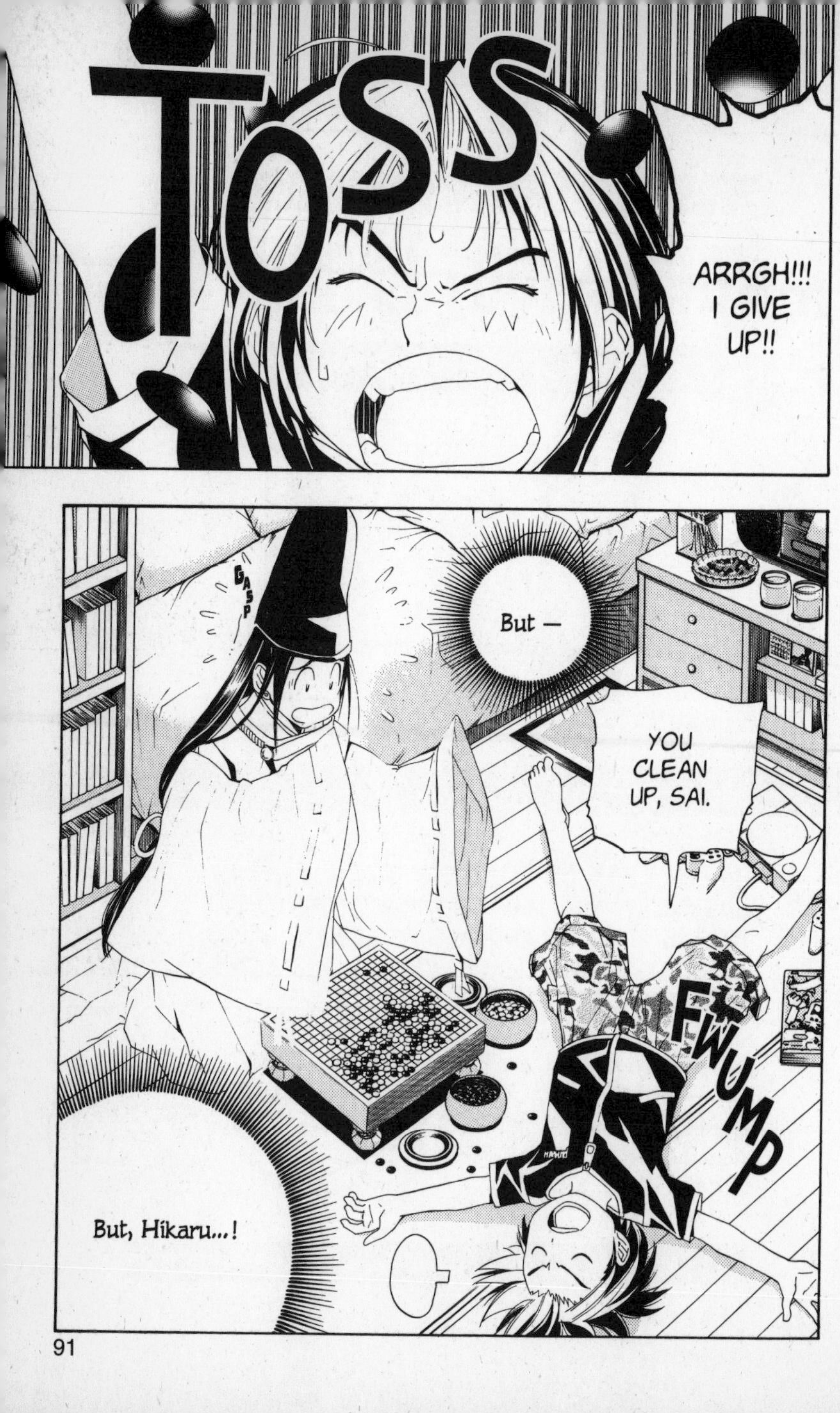
TOSS
ARRGH!!! I GIVE UP!!
But —
GASP
YOU CLEAN UP, SAI.
FWUMP
But, Hikaru...!

A WORD ABOUT HIKARU NO GO

TECHNICAL GO TERMS IN ENGLISH

AM I WINNING OR AM I LOSING?
IN THIS SITUATION IT'S HARD TO TELL...

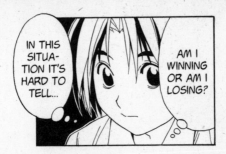

REGARDLESS OF THE SITUATION, A BEGINNER BASICALLY WILL HAVE NO WAY OF KNOWING WHO IS WINNING AND WHO IS LOSING. ALSO, A BEGINNER WILL HAVE NO IDEA HOW LONG TO KEEP PLAYING. SOME GAME, HUH?

THAT'S WHY IT'S HARD TO MAKE SENSE OF THE GAME IF YOU JUST TRY TO LEARN IT FROM A BOOK. YOU MUST PLAY GAMES AND LEARN FROM OTHER PEOPLE. SOME GAME, HUH?

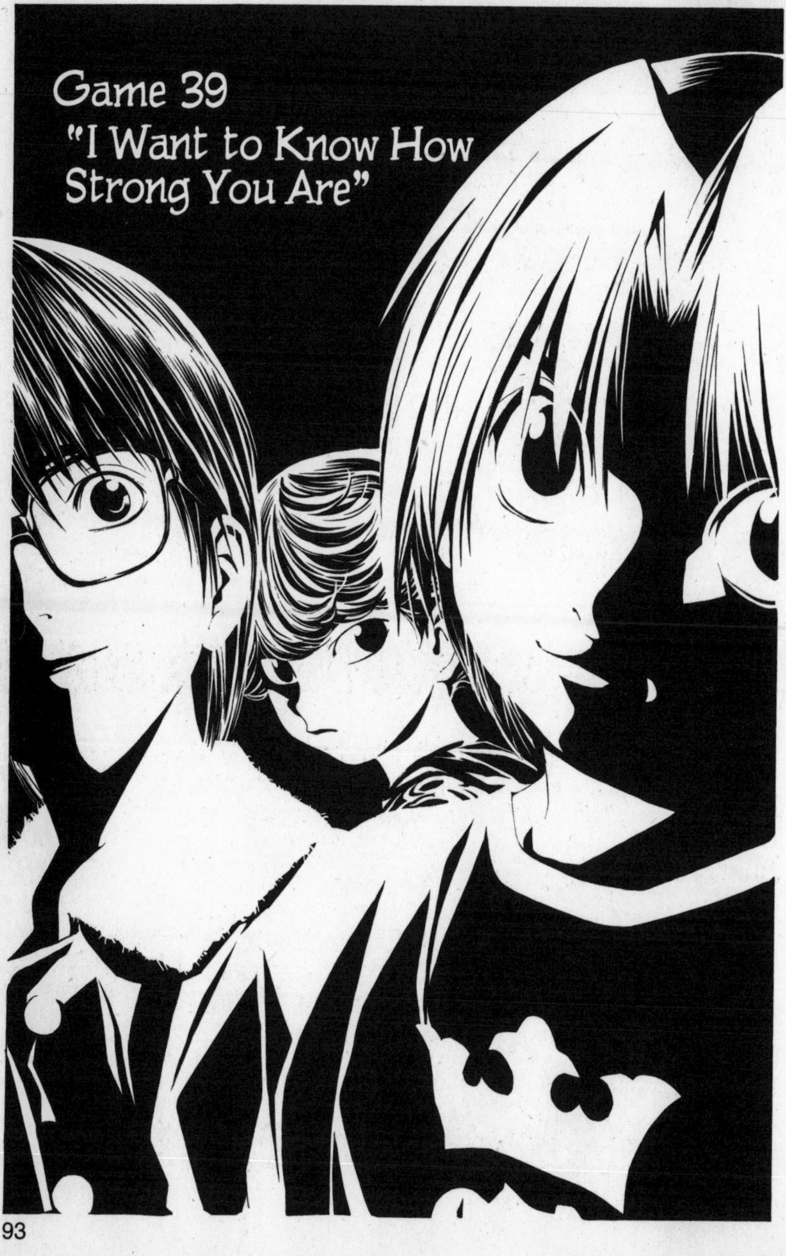
Game 39
"I Want to Know How Strong You Are"

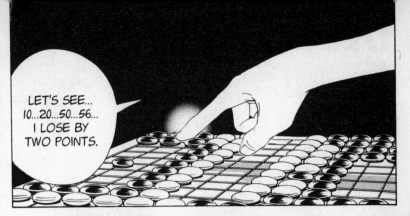

LET'S SEE... 10...20...50...56... I LOSE BY TWO POINTS.

.....

I DID IT! YOU PUT DOWN TWO STONES AND I STILL BEAT YOU!

DARN IT!

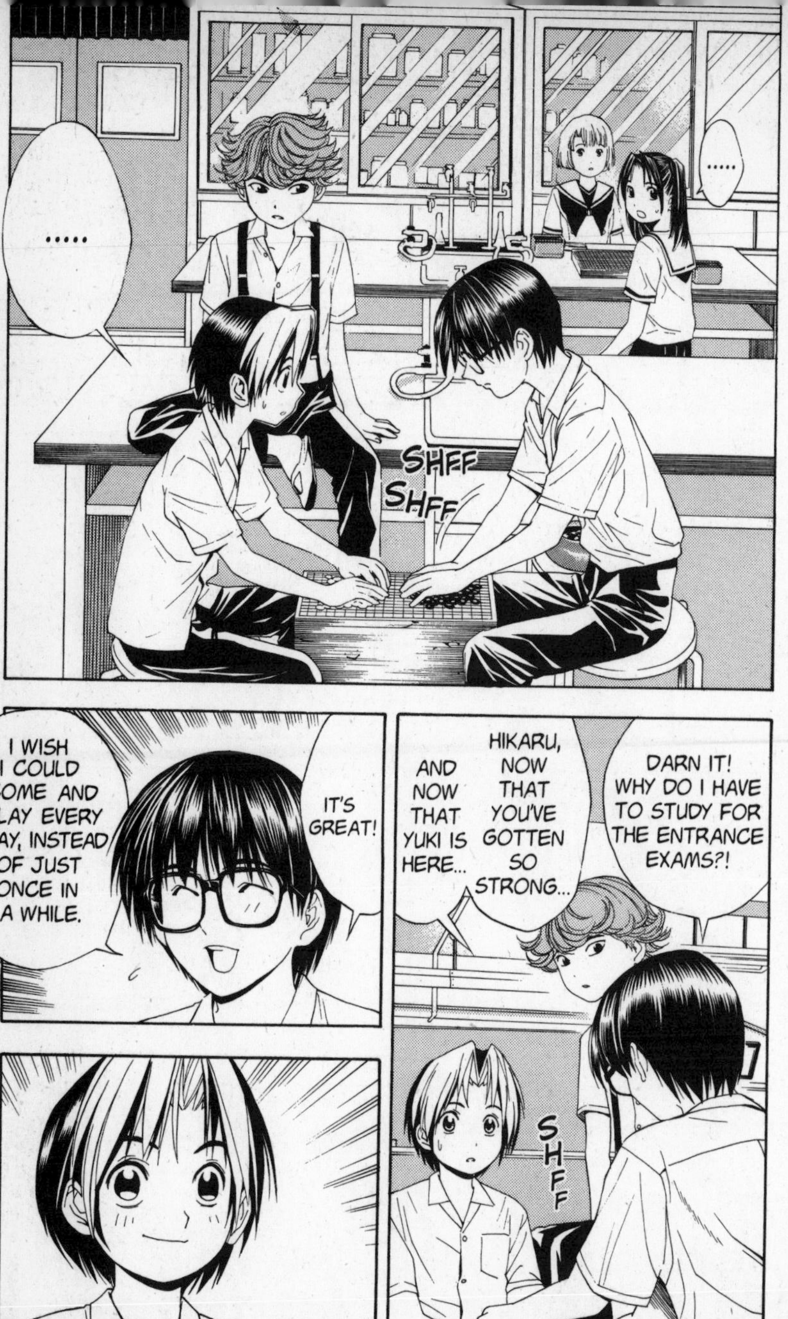
.....
.....
SHFF SHFF
I WISH I COULD COME AND PLAY EVERY DAY, INSTEAD OF JUST ONCE IN A WHILE.
IT'S GREAT!
HIKARU, NOW THAT YOU'VE GOTTEN SO STRONG...
AND NOW THAT YUKI IS HERE...
DARN IT! WHY DO I HAVE TO STUDY FOR THE ENTRANCE EXAMS?!
SHFF

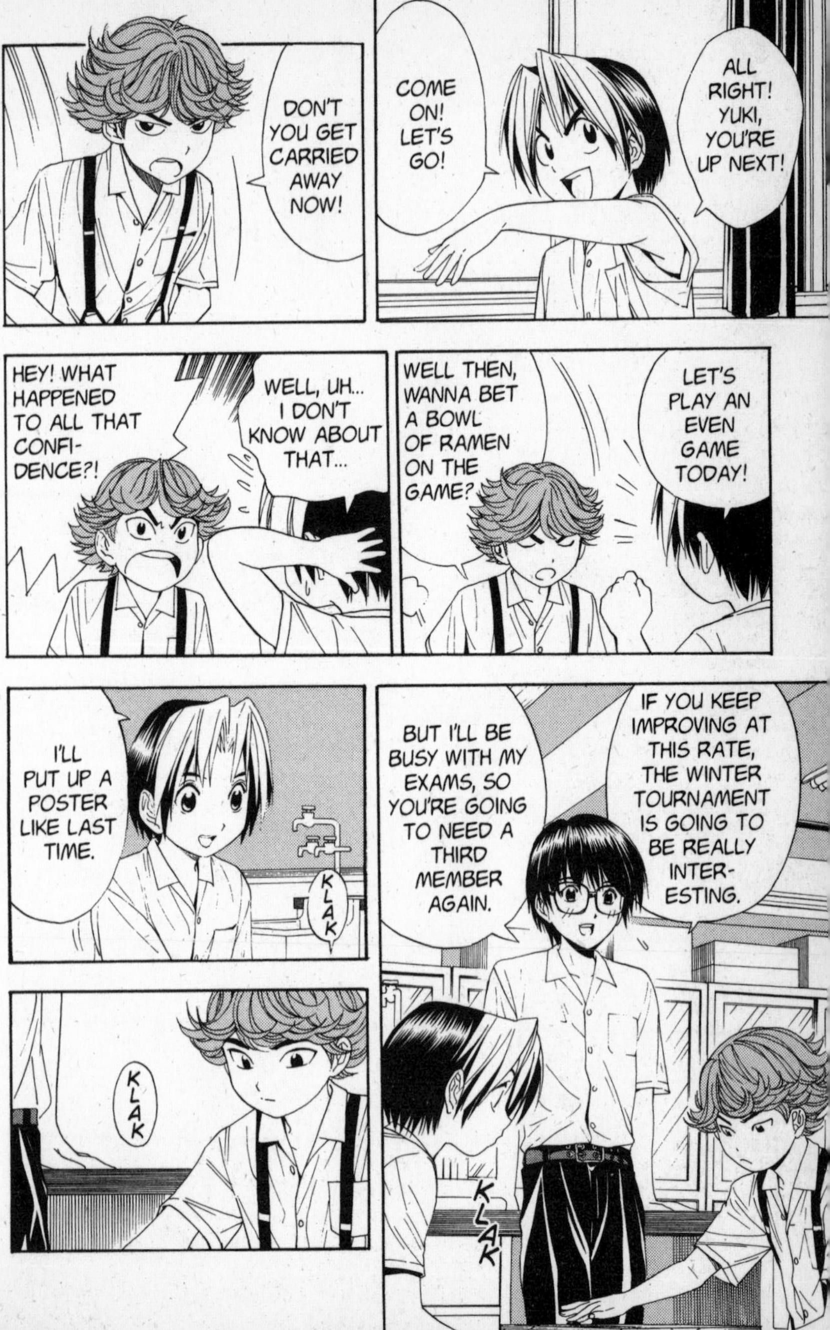
ALL RIGHT! YUKI, YOU'RE UP NEXT!
COME ON! LET'S GO!
DON'T YOU GET CARRIED AWAY NOW!
LET'S PLAY AN EVEN GAME TODAY!
WELL THEN, WANNA BET A BOWL OF RAMEN ON THE GAME?
WELL, UH... I DON'T KNOW ABOUT THAT...
HEY! WHAT HAPPENED TO ALL THAT CONFIDENCE?!
IF YOU KEEP IMPROVING AT THIS RATE, THE WINTER TOURNAMENT IS GOING TO BE REALLY INTER-ESTING.
BUT I'LL BE BUSY WITH MY EXAMS, SO YOU'RE GOING TO NEED A THIRD MEMBER AGAIN.
KLAK
I'LL PUT UP A POSTER LIKE LAST TIME.
KLAK
KLAK

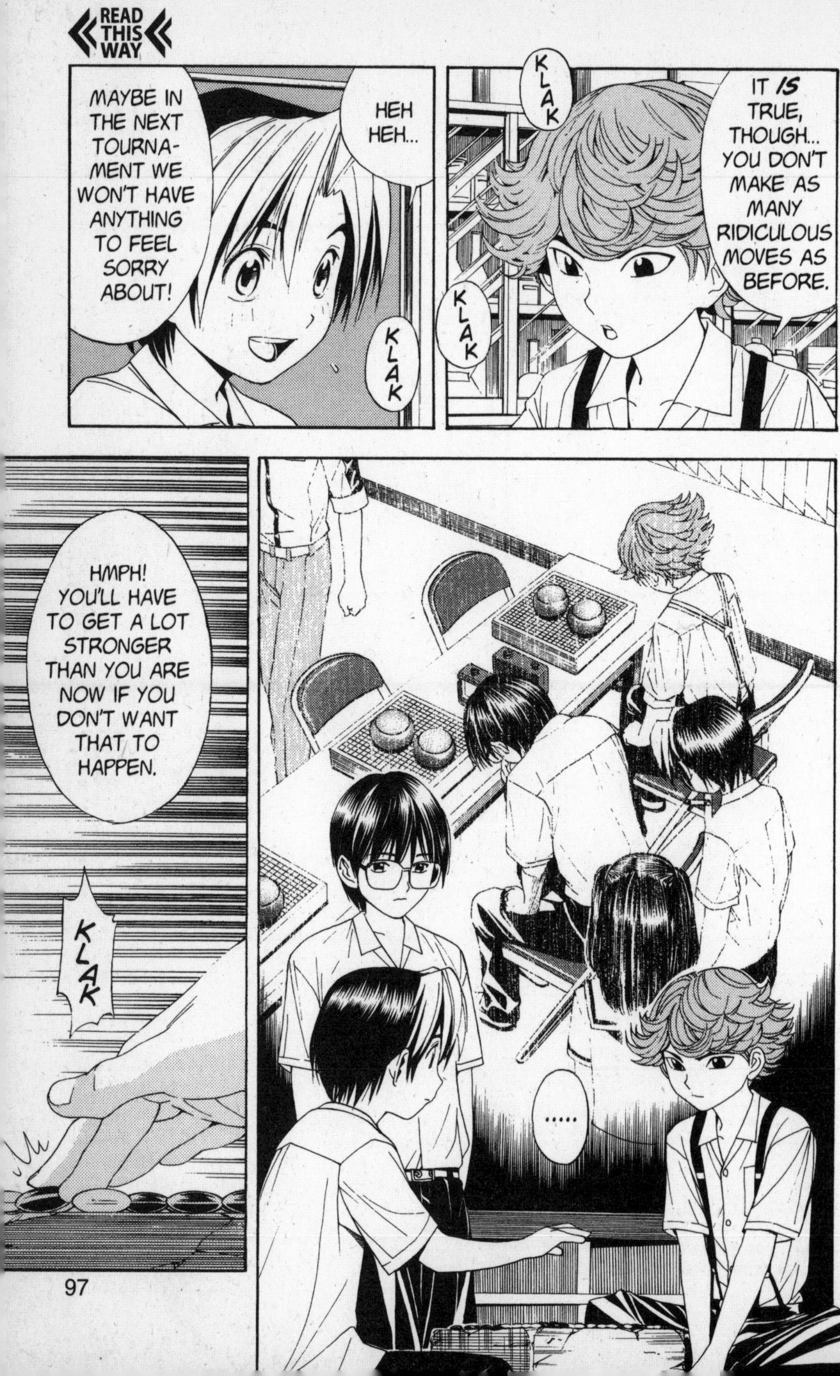
READ THIS WAY
KLAK
IT IS TRUE, THOUGH... YOU DON'T MAKE AS MANY RIDICULOUS MOVES AS BEFORE.
KLAK
KLAK
HEH HEH...
MAYBE IN THE NEXT TOURNA-MENT WE WON'T HAVE ANYTHING TO FEEL SORRY ABOUT!
......
HMPH! YOU'LL HAVE TO GET A LOT STRONGER THAN YOU ARE NOW IF YOU DON'T WANT THAT TO HAPPEN.
KLAK

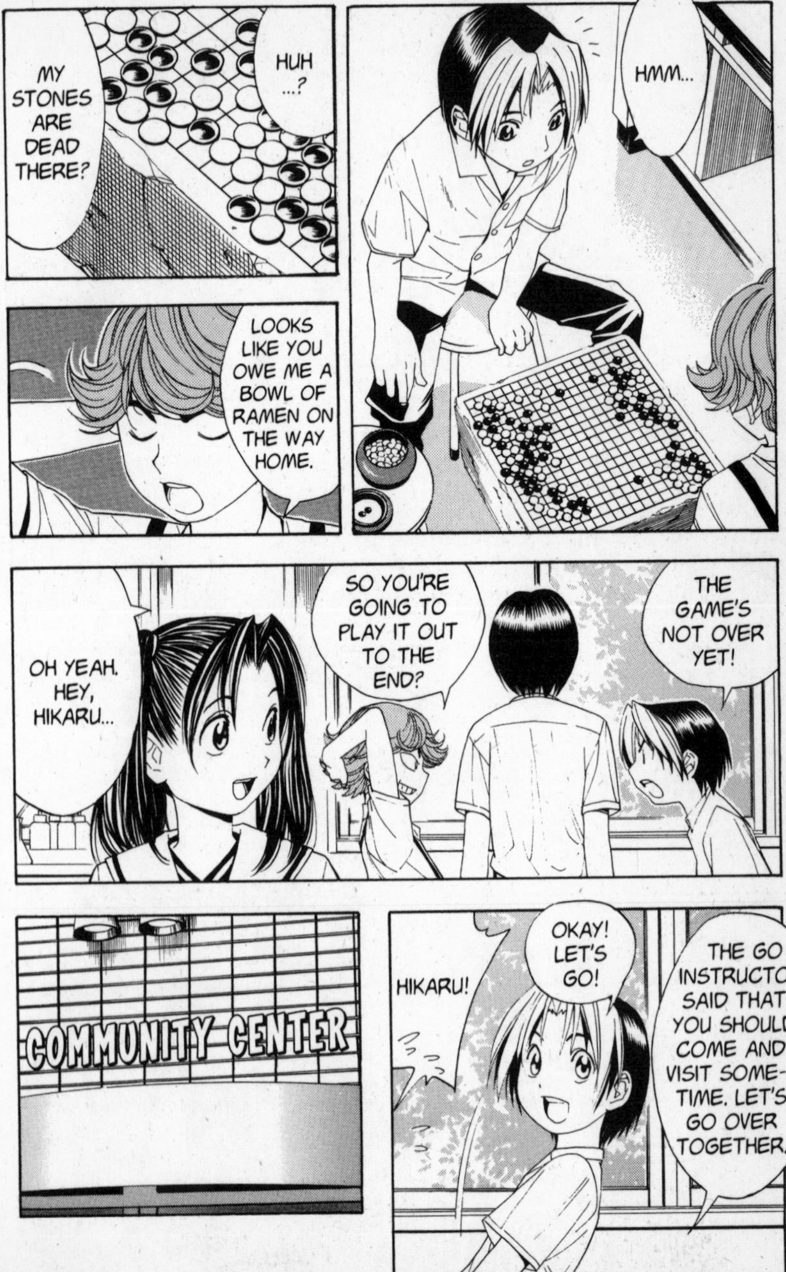
HMM...
HUH ...?
MY STONES ARE DEAD THERE?
LOOKS LIKE YOU OWE ME A BOWL OF RAMEN ON THE WAY HOME.
THE GAME'S NOT OVER YET!
SO YOU'RE GOING TO PLAY IT OUT TO THE END?
OH YEAH. HEY, HIKARU...
THE GO INSTRUCTOR SAID THAT YOU SHOULD COME AND VISIT SOME-TIME. LET'S GO OVER TOGETHER.
OKAY! LET'S GO!
HIKARU!
COMMUNITY CENTER

READ THIS WAY

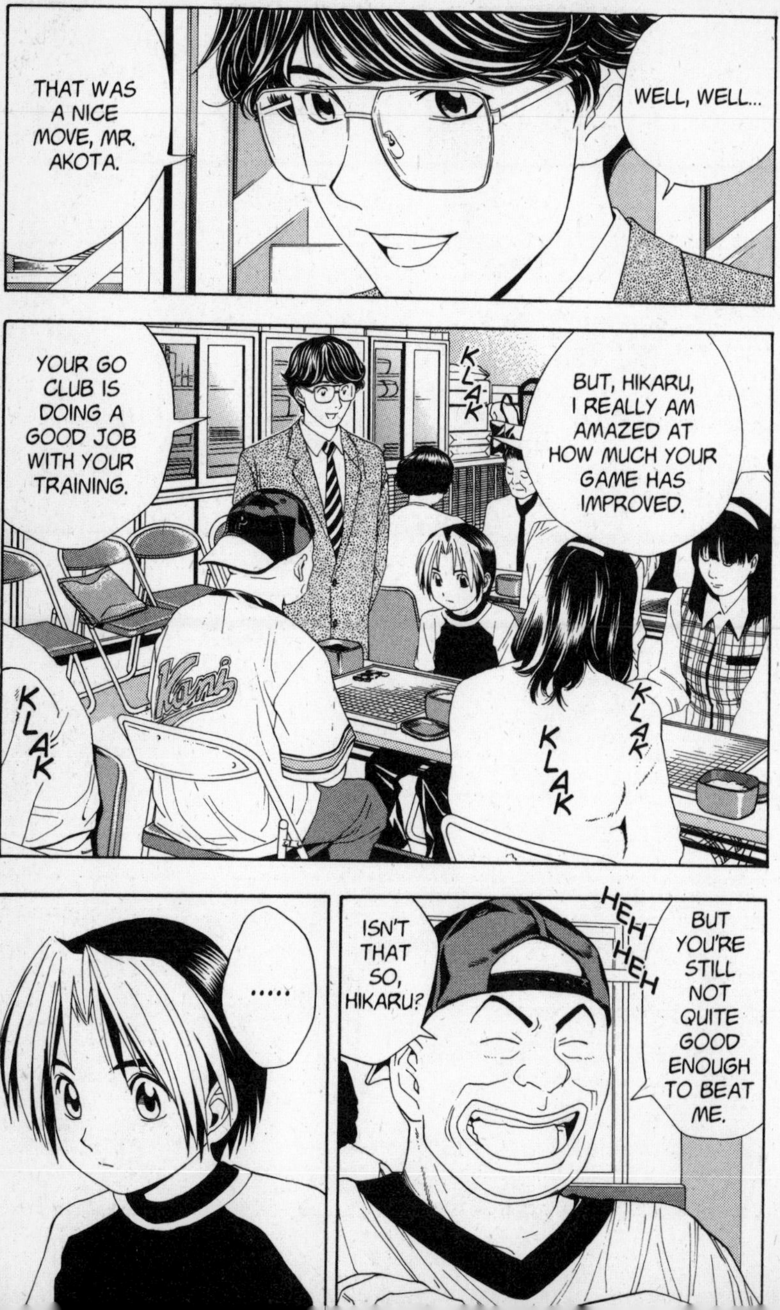
WELL, WELL...
THAT WAS A NICE MOVE, MR. AKOTA.
BUT, HIKARU, I REALLY AM AMAZED AT HOW MUCH YOUR GAME HAS IMPROVED.
KLAK
KLAK KLAK
YOUR GO CLUB IS DOING A GOOD JOB WITH YOUR TRAINING.
KLAK
HEH HEH HEH
BUT YOU'RE STILL NOT QUITE GOOD ENOUGH TO BEAT ME.
ISN'T THAT SO, HIKARU?
.....

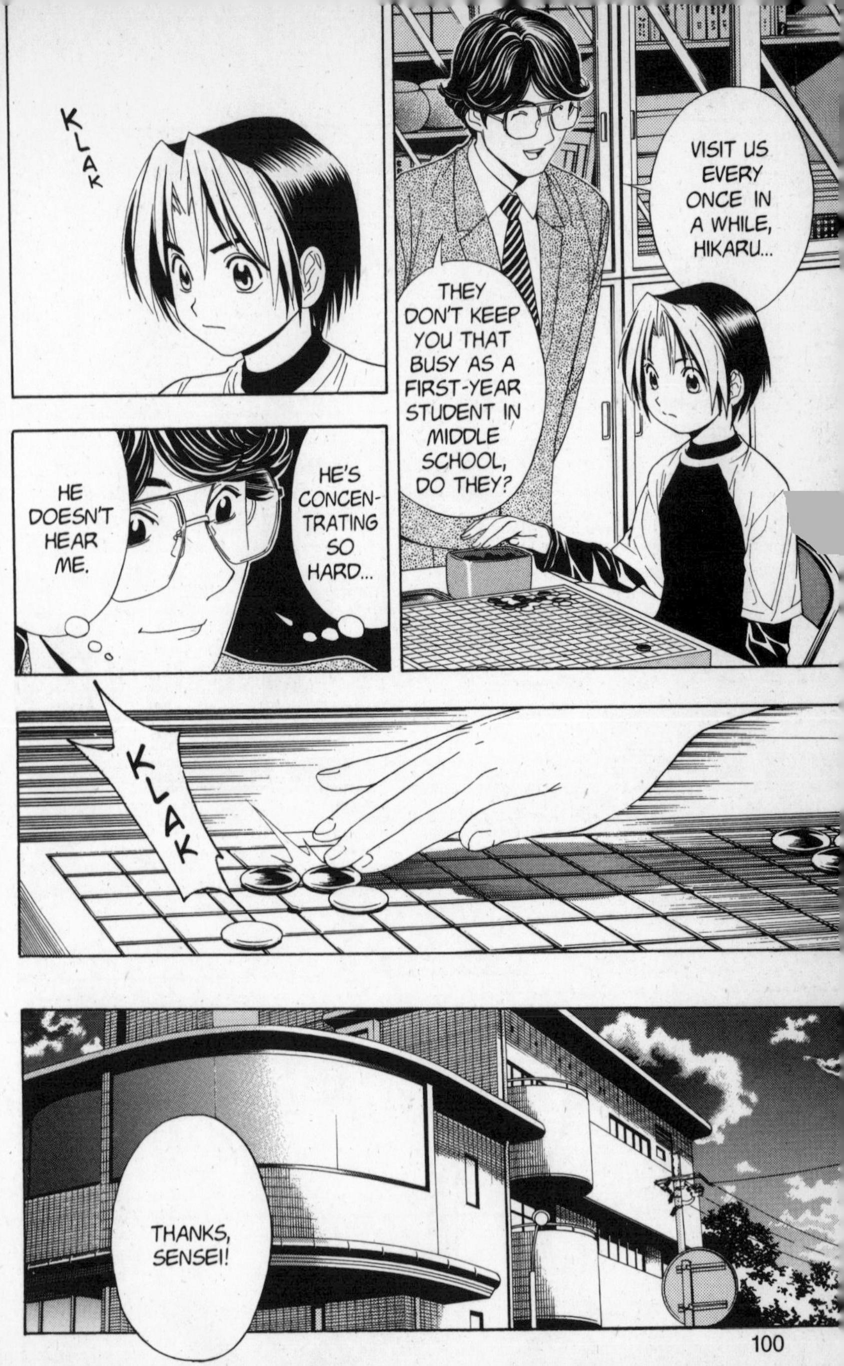
VISIT US EVERY ONCE IN A WHILE, HIKARU...
THEY DON'T KEEP YOU THAT BUSY AS A FIRST-YEAR STUDENT IN MIDDLE SCHOOL, DO THEY?
KLAK
HE'S CONCEN-TRATING SO HARD...
HE DOESN'T HEAR ME.
KLAK
THANKS, SENSEI!

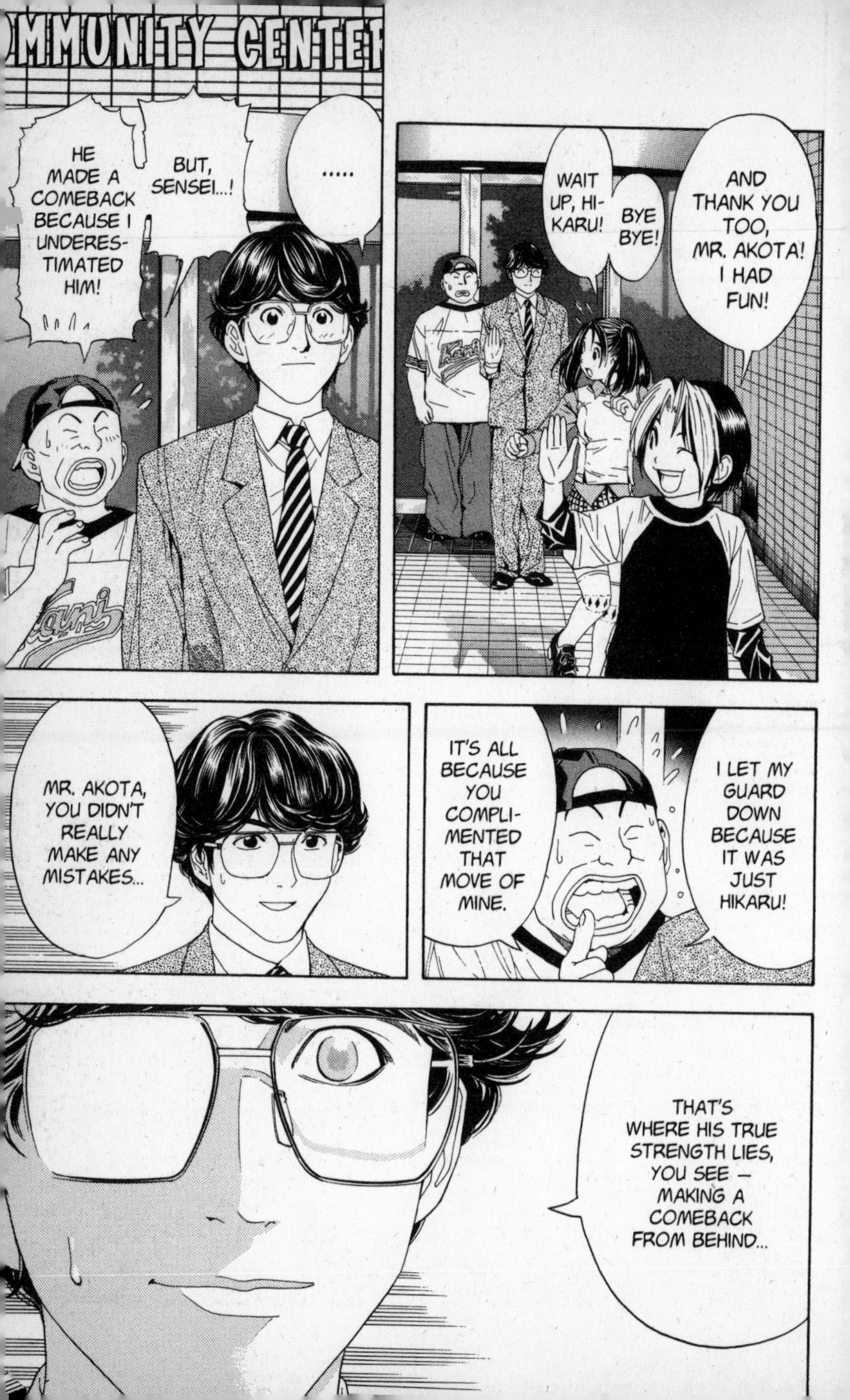
AND THANK YOU TOO, MR. AKOTA! I HAD FUN!
BYE BYE!
WAIT UP, HI-KARU!
COMMUNITY CENTER
.....
BUT, SENSEI...!
HE MADE A COMEBACK BECAUSE I UNDERES-TIMATED HIM!
I LET MY GUARD DOWN BECAUSE IT WAS JUST HIKARU!
IT'S ALL BECAUSE YOU COMPLI-MENTED THAT MOVE OF MINE.
MR. AKOTA, YOU DIDN'T REALLY MAKE ANY MISTAKES...
THAT'S WHERE HIS TRUE STRENGTH LIES, YOU SEE — MAKING A COMEBACK FROM BEHIND...

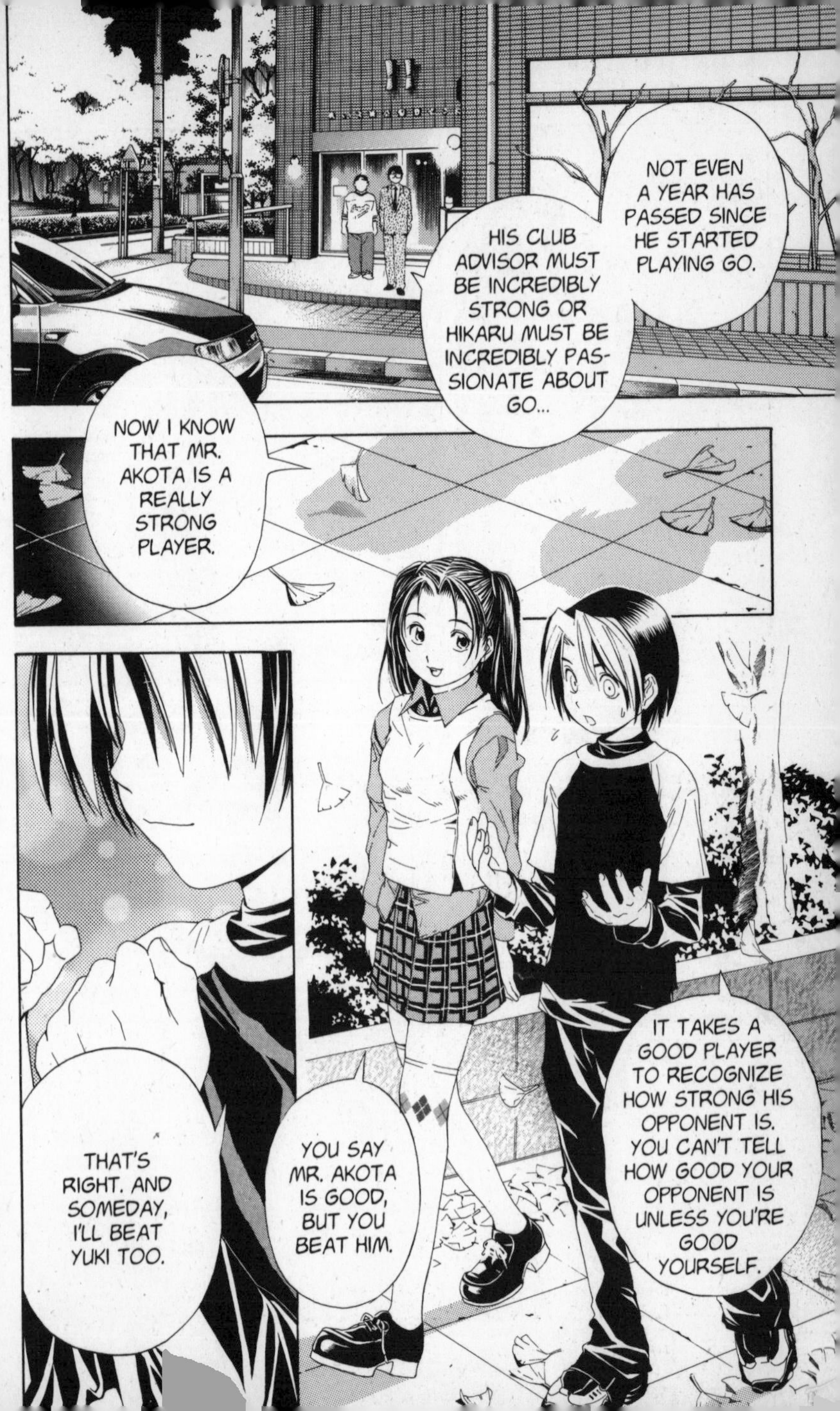
NOT EVEN A YEAR HAS PASSED SINCE HE STARTED PLAYING GO.
HIS CLUB ADVISOR MUST BE INCREDIBLY STRONG OR HIKARU MUST BE INCREDIBLY PAS-SIONATE ABOUT GO...
NOW I KNOW THAT MR. AKOTA IS A REALLY STRONG PLAYER.
IT TAKES A GOOD PLAYER TO RECOGNIZE HOW STRONG HIS OPPONENT IS. YOU CAN'T TELL HOW GOOD YOUR OPPONENT IS UNLESS YOU'RE GOOD YOURSELF.
YOU SAY MR. AKOTA IS GOOD, BUT YOU BEAT HIM.
THAT'S RIGHT. AND SOMEDAY, I'LL BEAT YUKI TOO.

READ THIS WAY

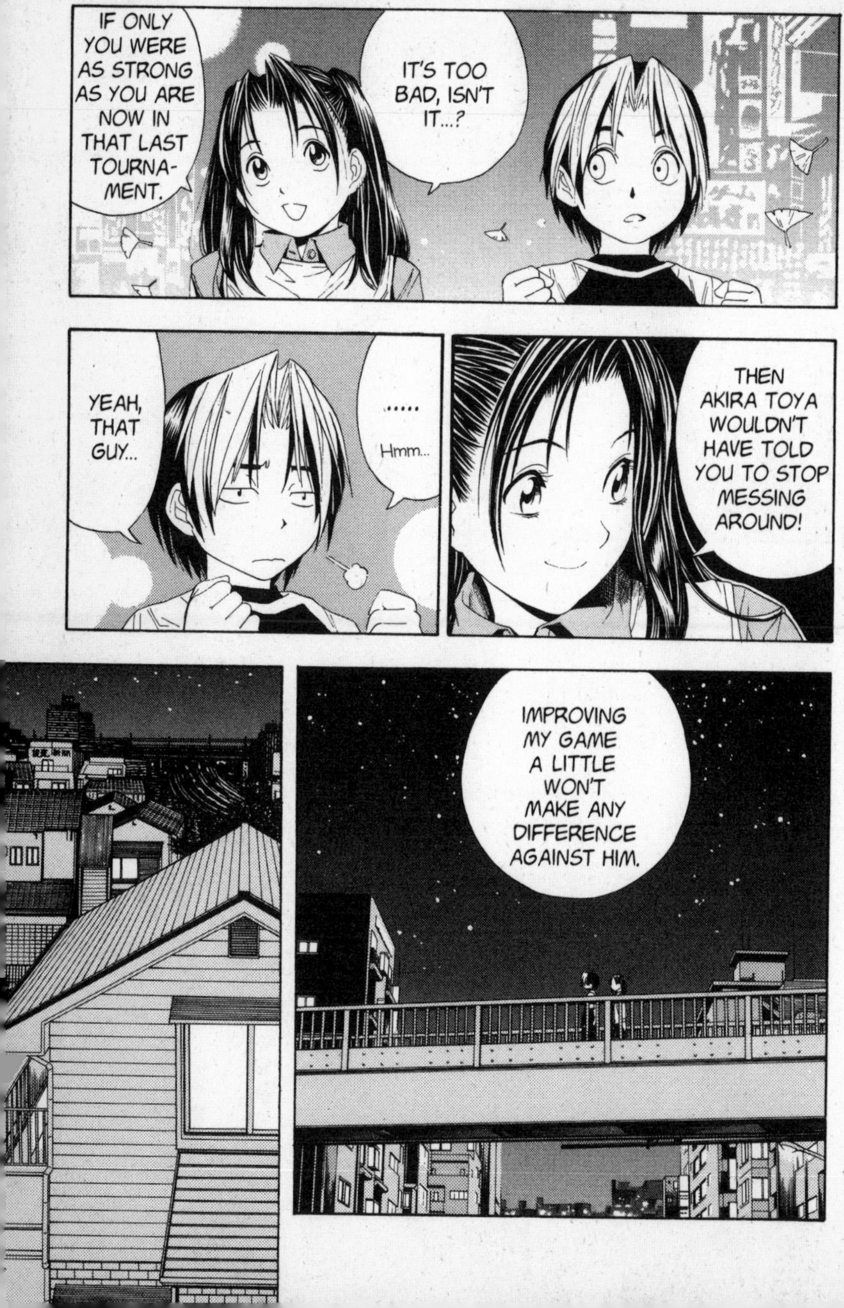
IT'S TOO BAD, ISN'T IT...?
IF ONLY YOU WERE AS STRONG AS YOU ARE NOW IN THAT LAST TOURNAMENT.
THEN AKIRA TOYA WOULDN'T HAVE TOLD YOU TO STOP MESSING AROUND!
...... Hmm...
YEAH, THAT GUY...
IMPROVING MY GAME A LITTLE WON'T MAKE ANY DIFFERENCE AGAINST HIM.

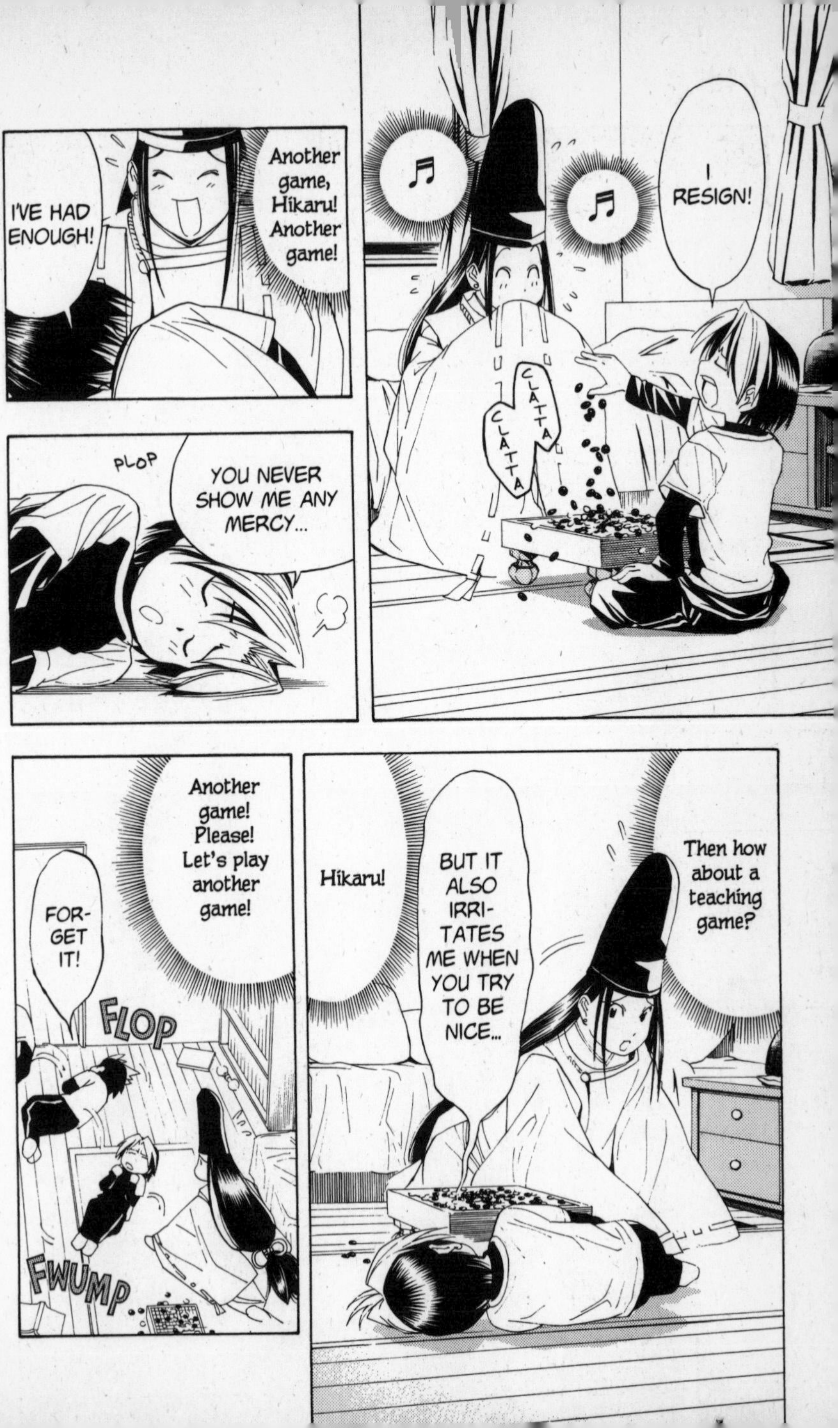
I RESIGN!
CLATTA
CLATTA
Another game, Hikaru! Another game!
I'VE HAD ENOUGH!
PLOP
YOU NEVER SHOW ME ANY MERCY...
Then how about a teaching game?
BUT IT ALSO IRRITATES ME WHEN YOU TRY TO BE NICE...
Hikaru!
Another game! Please! Let's play another game!
FORGET IT!
FLOP
FWUMP

READ THIS WAY

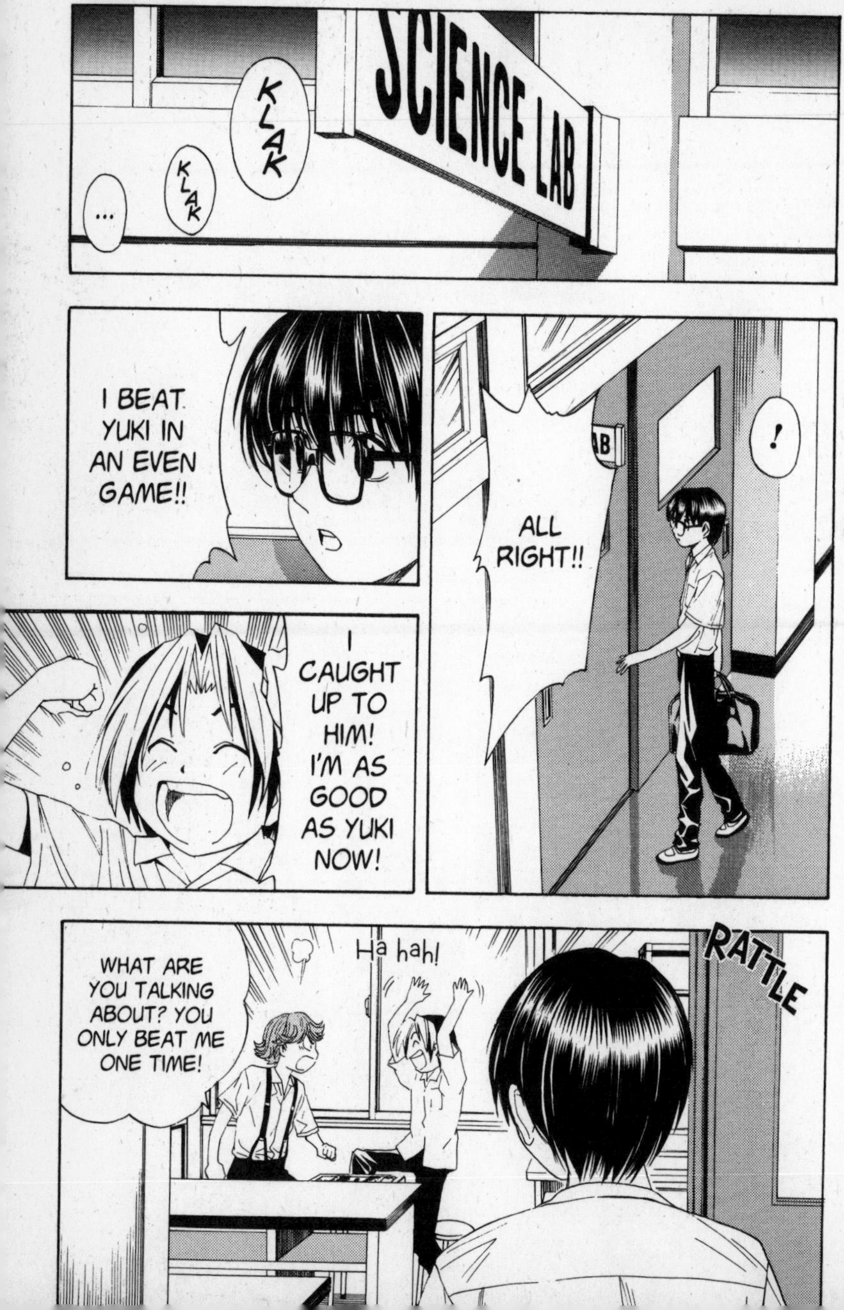
SCIENCE LAB
KLAK
KLAK
...
!
LAB
ALL RIGHT!!
I BEAT YUKI IN AN EVEN GAME!!
I CAUGHT UP TO HIM! I'M AS GOOD AS YUKI NOW!
RATTLE
Ha hah!
WHAT ARE YOU TALKING ABOUT? YOU ONLY BEAT ME ONE TIME!

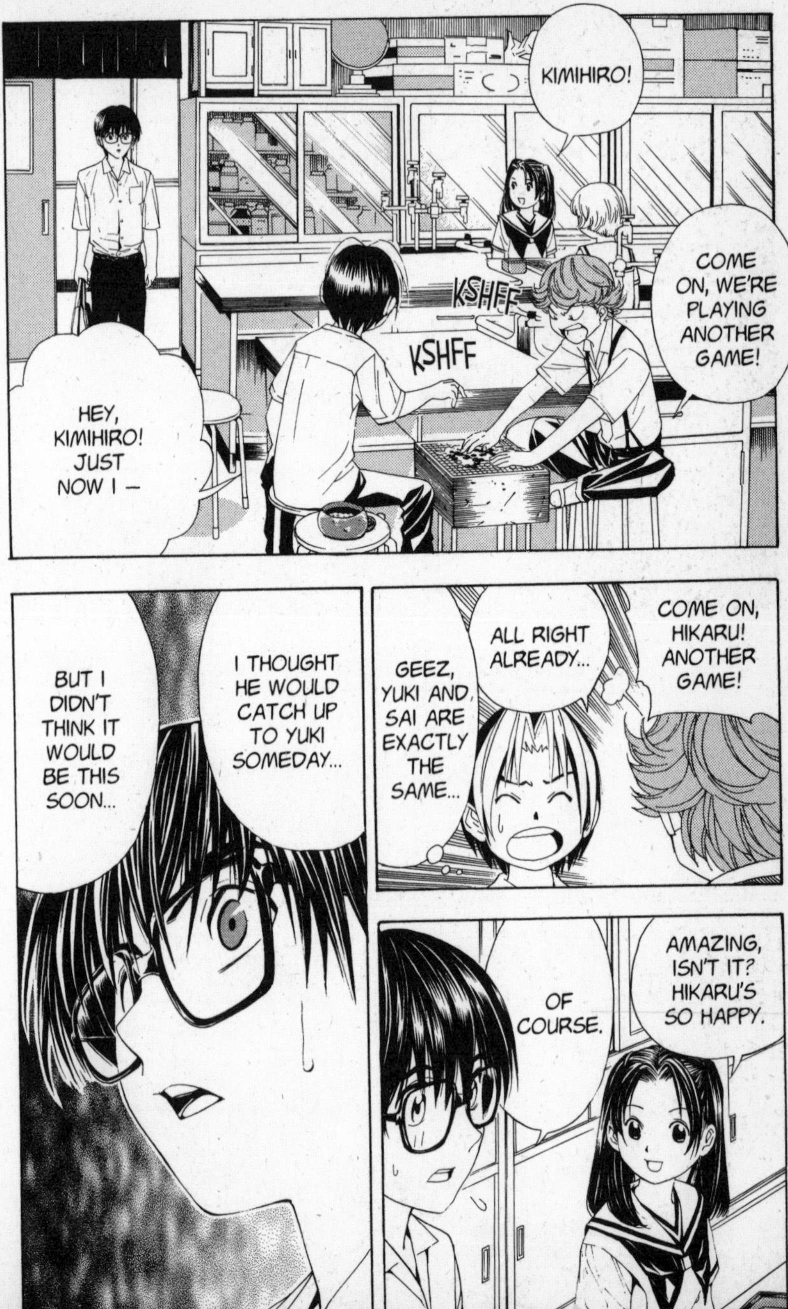
KIMIHIRO!
COME ON, WE'RE PLAYING ANOTHER GAME!
KSHFF
KSHFF
HEY, KIMIHIRO! JUST NOW I –
COME ON, HIKARU! ANOTHER GAME!
ALL RIGHT ALREADY...
GEEZ, YUKI AND SAI ARE EXACTLY THE SAME...
AMAZING, ISN'T IT? HIKARU'S SO HAPPY.
OF COURSE.
I THOUGHT HE WOULD CATCH UP TO YUKI SOMEDAY...
BUT I DIDN'T THINK IT WOULD BE THIS SOON...

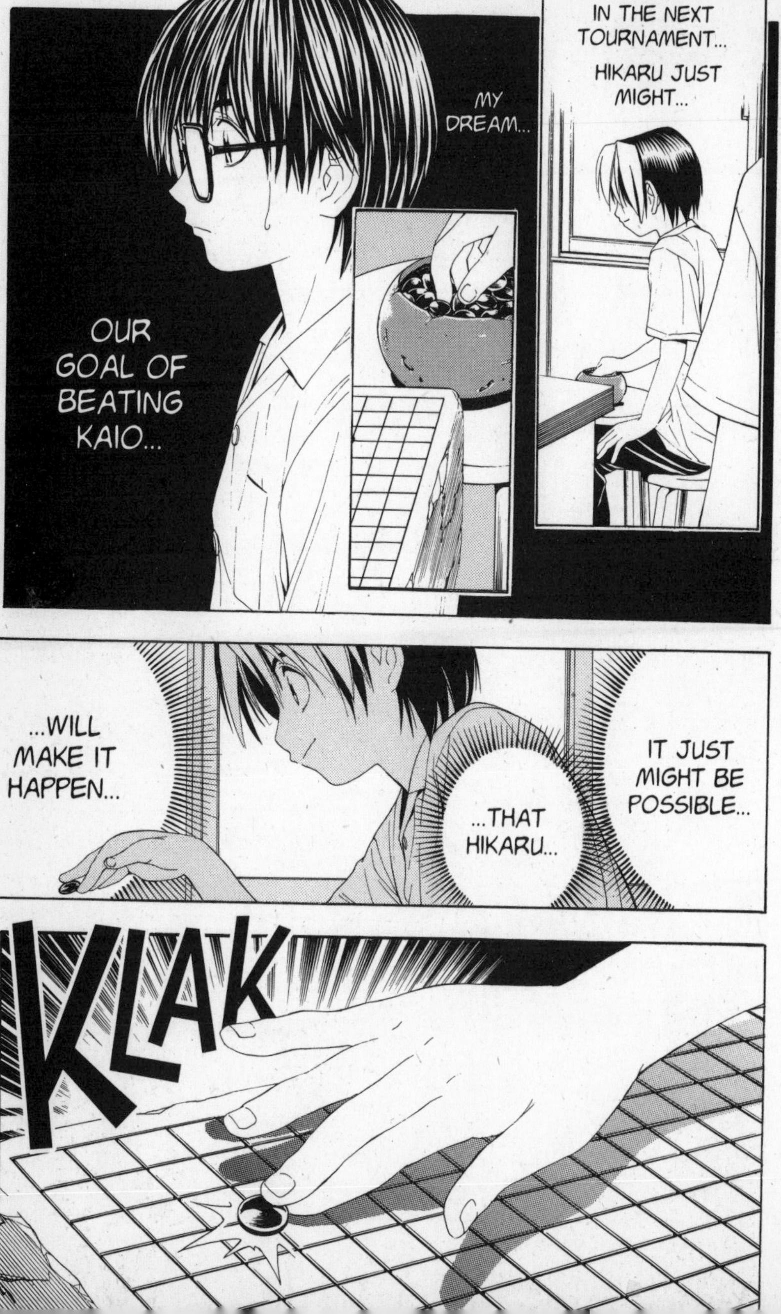
MAYBE IN THE NEXT TOURNAMENT...
HIKARU JUST MIGHT...
MY DREAM...
OUR GOAL OF BEATING KAIO...
IT JUST MIGHT BE POSSIBLE...
...THAT HIKARU...
...WILL MAKE IT HAPPEN...
KLAK

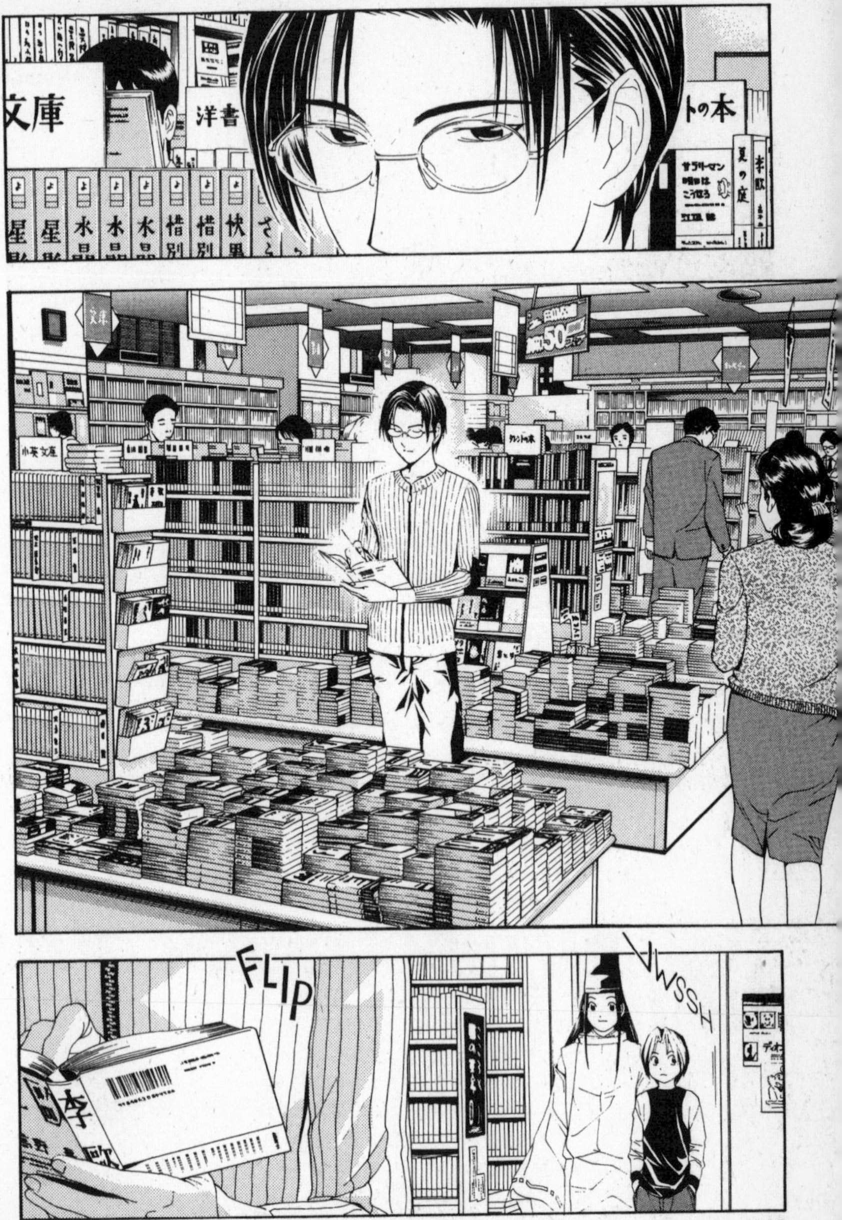
文庫
洋書
トの本
夏の庭
李歐
FLIP

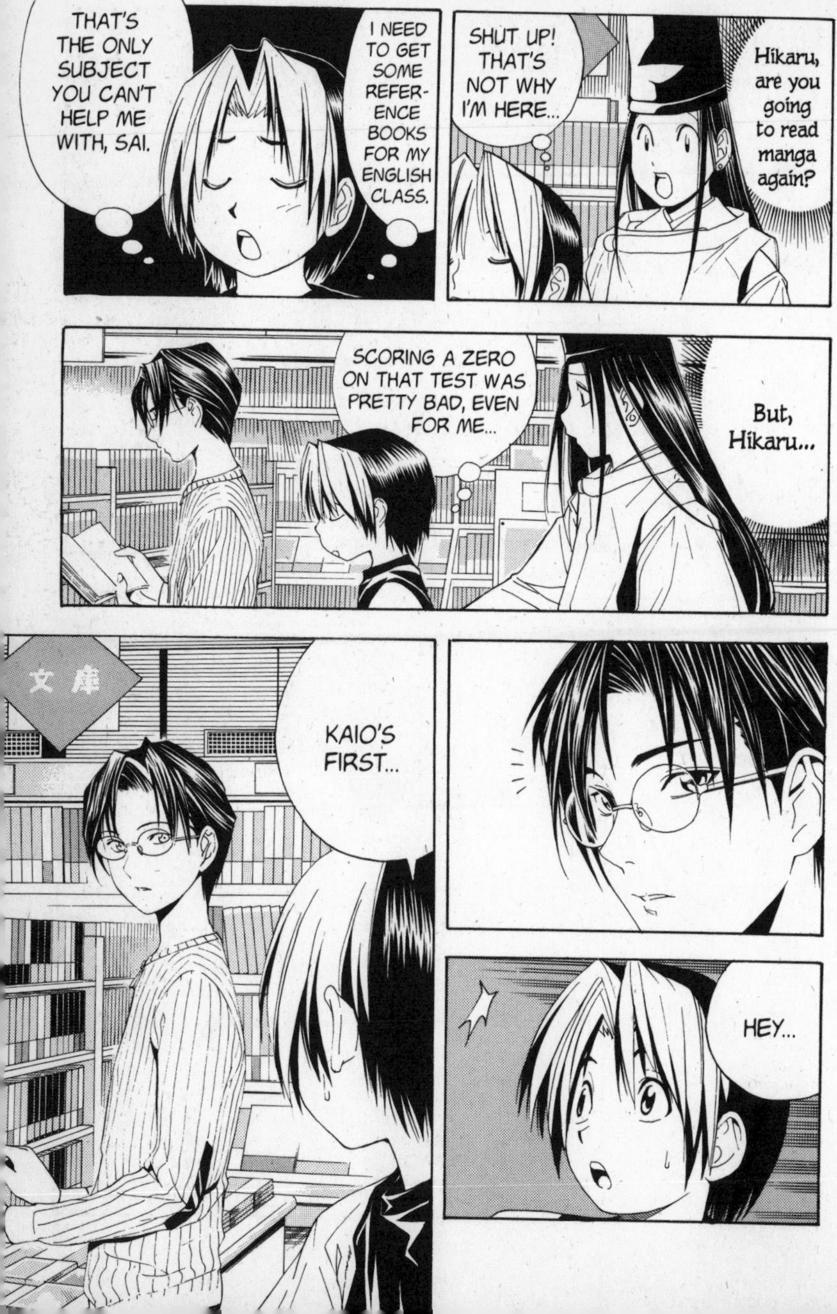
Hikaru, are you going to read manga again?
SHUT UP! THAT'S NOT WHY I'M HERE...
I NEED TO GET SOME REFER-ENCE BOOKS FOR MY ENGLISH CLASS.
THAT'S THE ONLY SUBJECT YOU CAN'T HELP ME WITH, SAI.
But, Hikaru...
SCORING A ZERO ON THAT TEST WAS PRETTY BAD, EVEN FOR ME...
HEY...
KAIO'S FIRST...
文庫

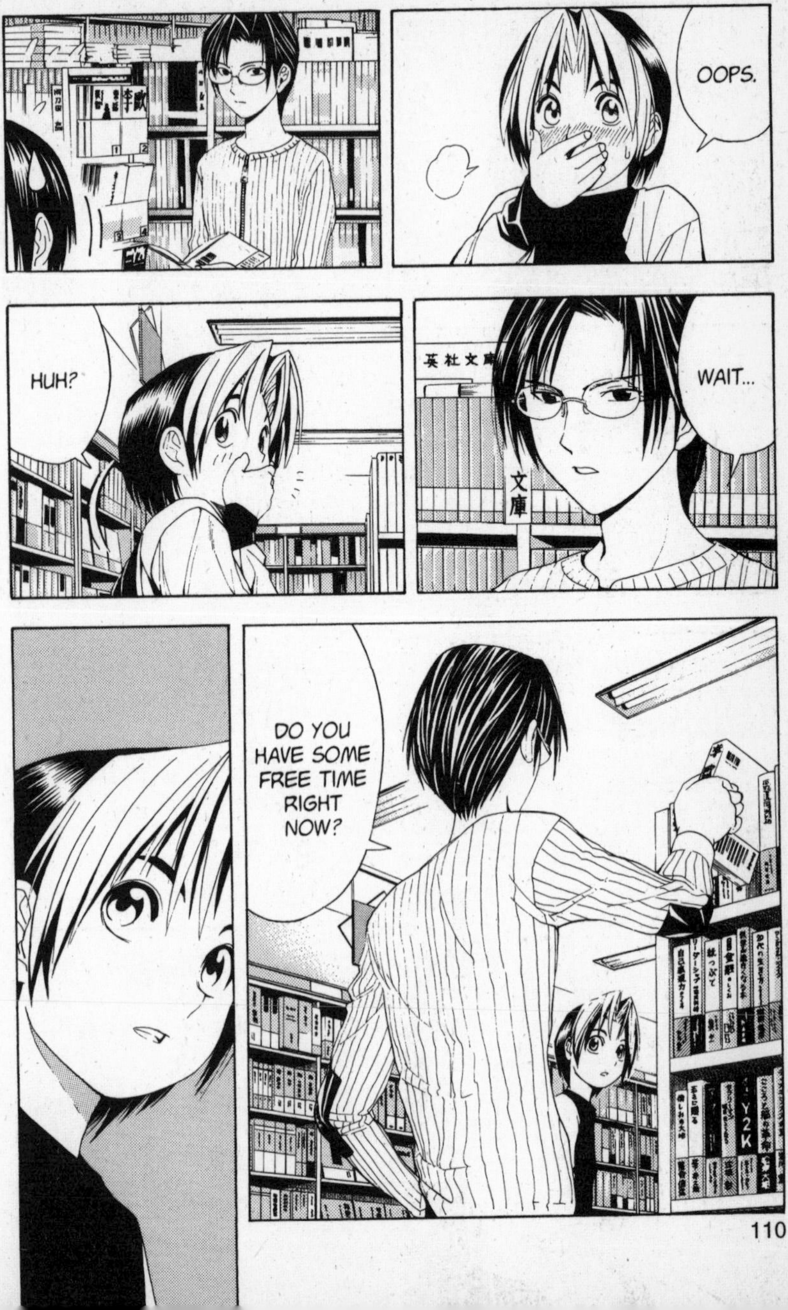
OOPS.
WAIT...
HUH?
DO YOU HAVE SOME FREE TIME RIGHT NOW?

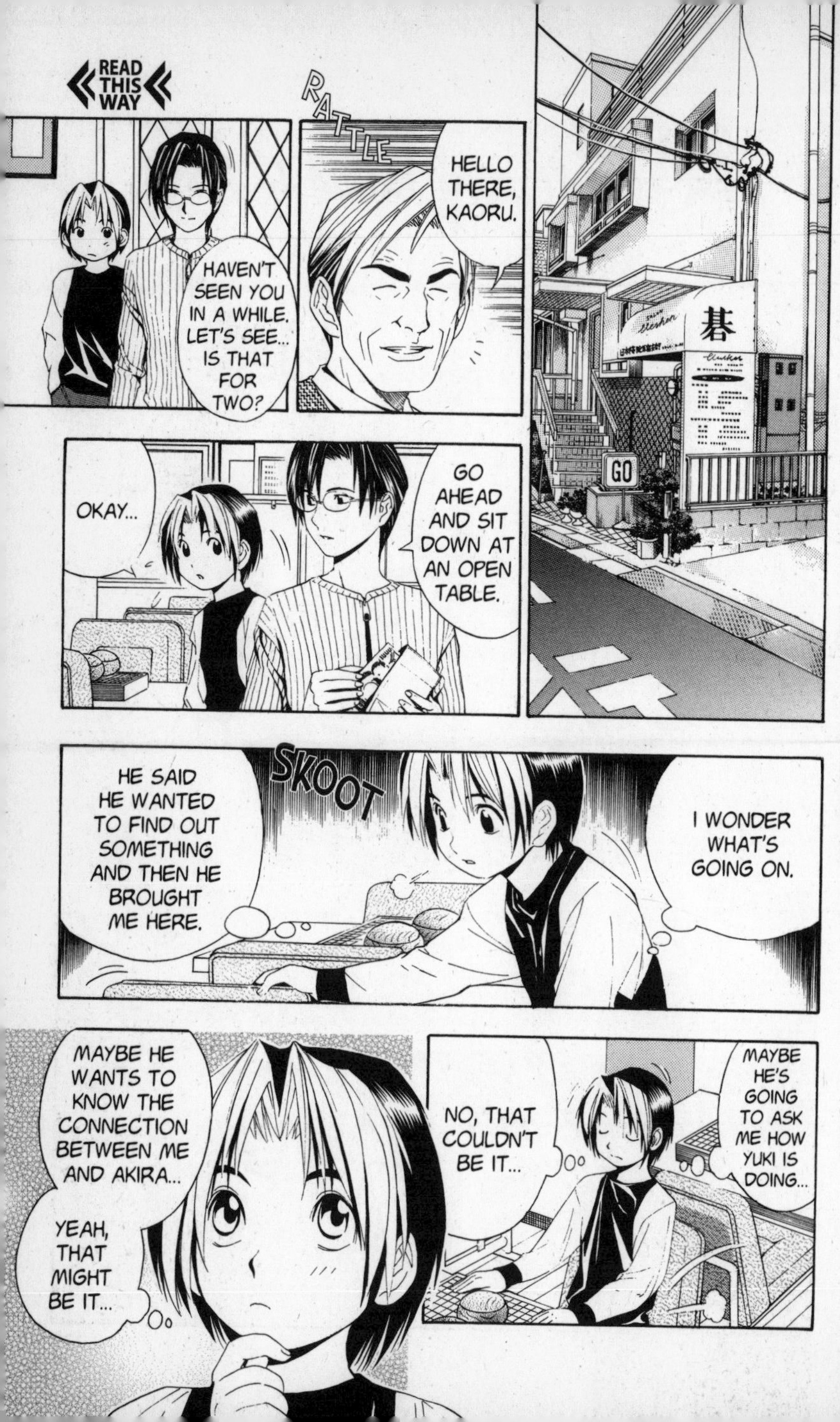
READ THIS WAY
碁
GO
RATTLE
HELLO THERE, KAORU.
HAVEN'T SEEN YOU IN A WHILE. LET'S SEE... IS THAT FOR TWO?
GO AHEAD AND SIT DOWN AT AN OPEN TABLE.
OKAY...
SKOOT
I WONDER WHAT'S GOING ON.
HE SAID HE WANTED TO FIND OUT SOMETHING AND THEN HE BROUGHT ME HERE.
MAYBE HE'S GOING TO ASK ME HOW YUKI IS DOING...
NO, THAT COULDN'T BE IT...
MAYBE HE WANTS TO KNOW THE CONNECTION BETWEEN ME AND AKIRA...
YEAH, THAT MIGHT BE IT...

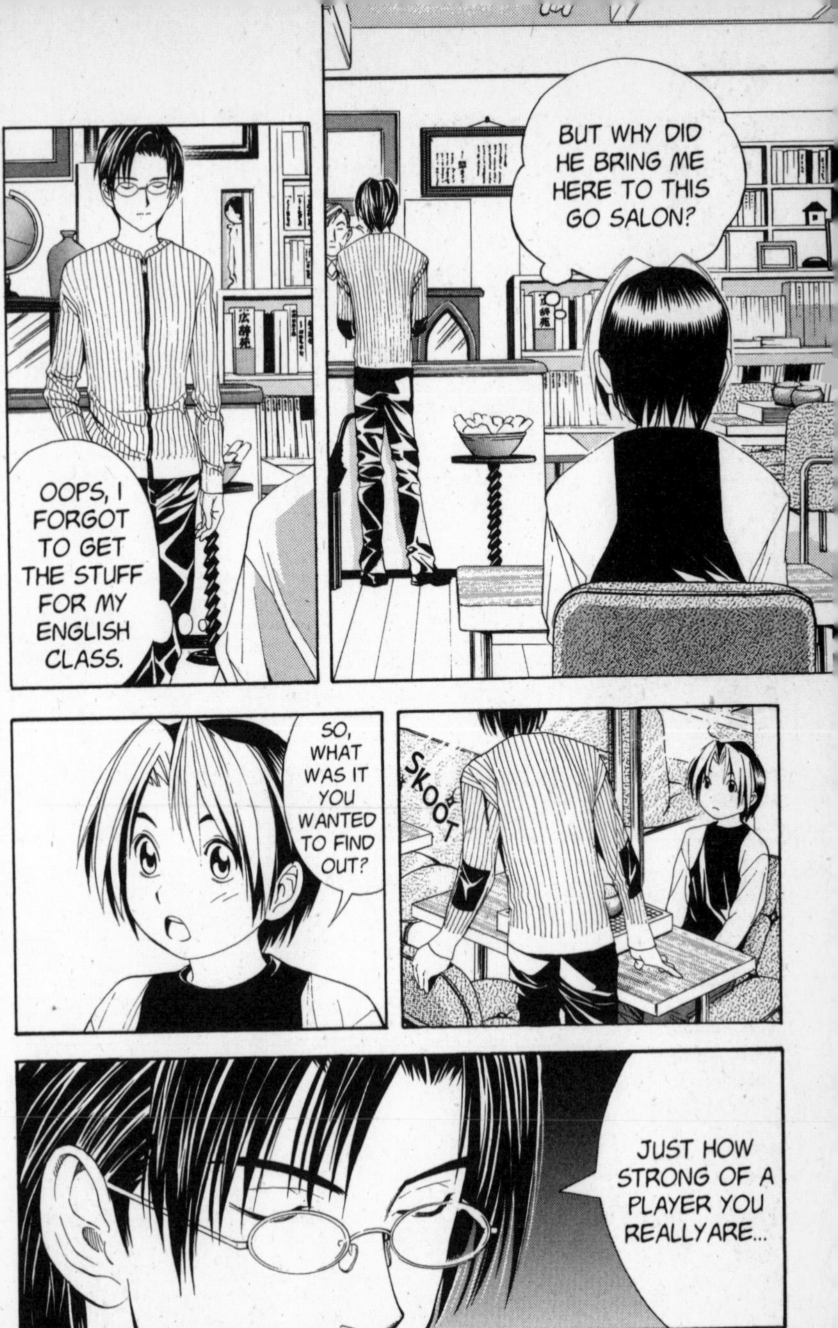
OOPS, I FORGOT TO GET THE STUFF FOR MY ENGLISH CLASS.
BUT WHY DID HE BRING ME HERE TO THIS GO SALON?
SO, WHAT WAS IT YOU WANTED TO FIND OUT?
SKOOT
JUST HOW STRONG OF A PLAYER YOU REALLYARE...

READ THIS WAY

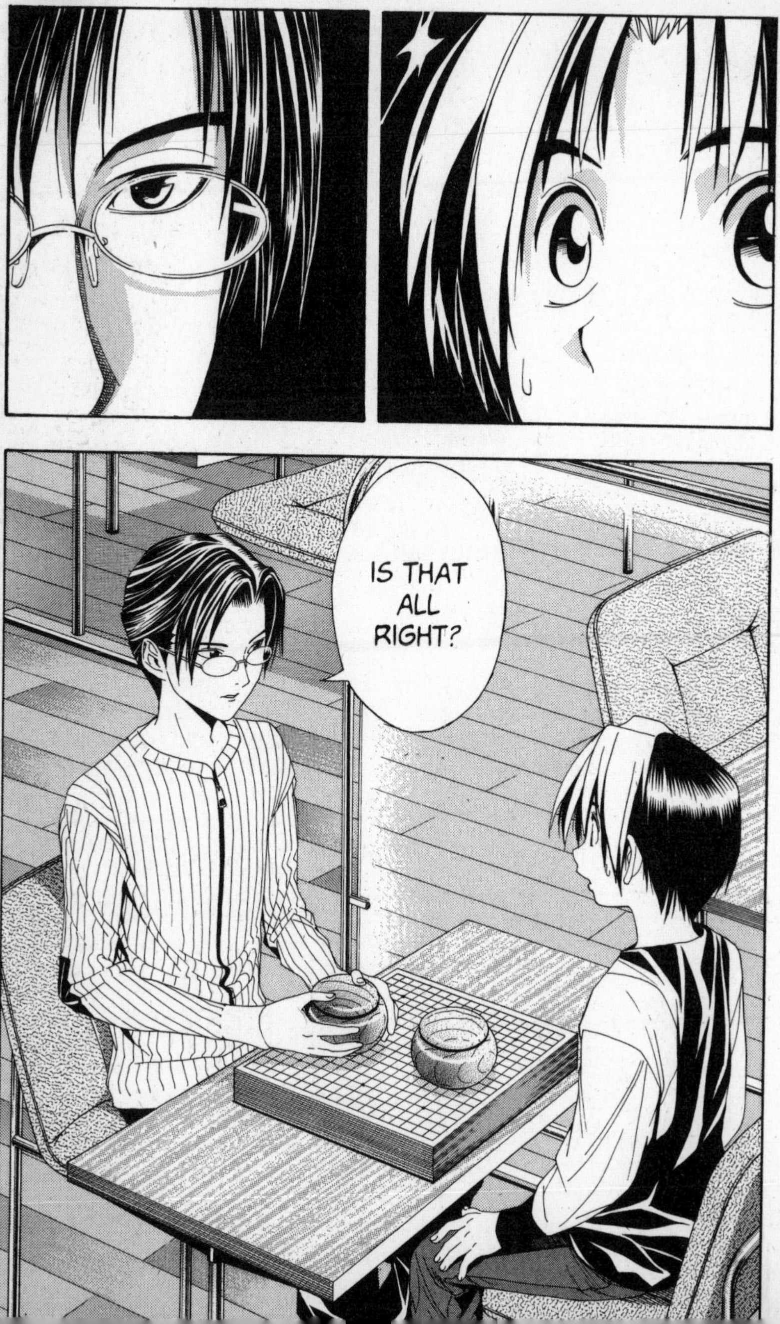
IS THAT ALL RIGHT?

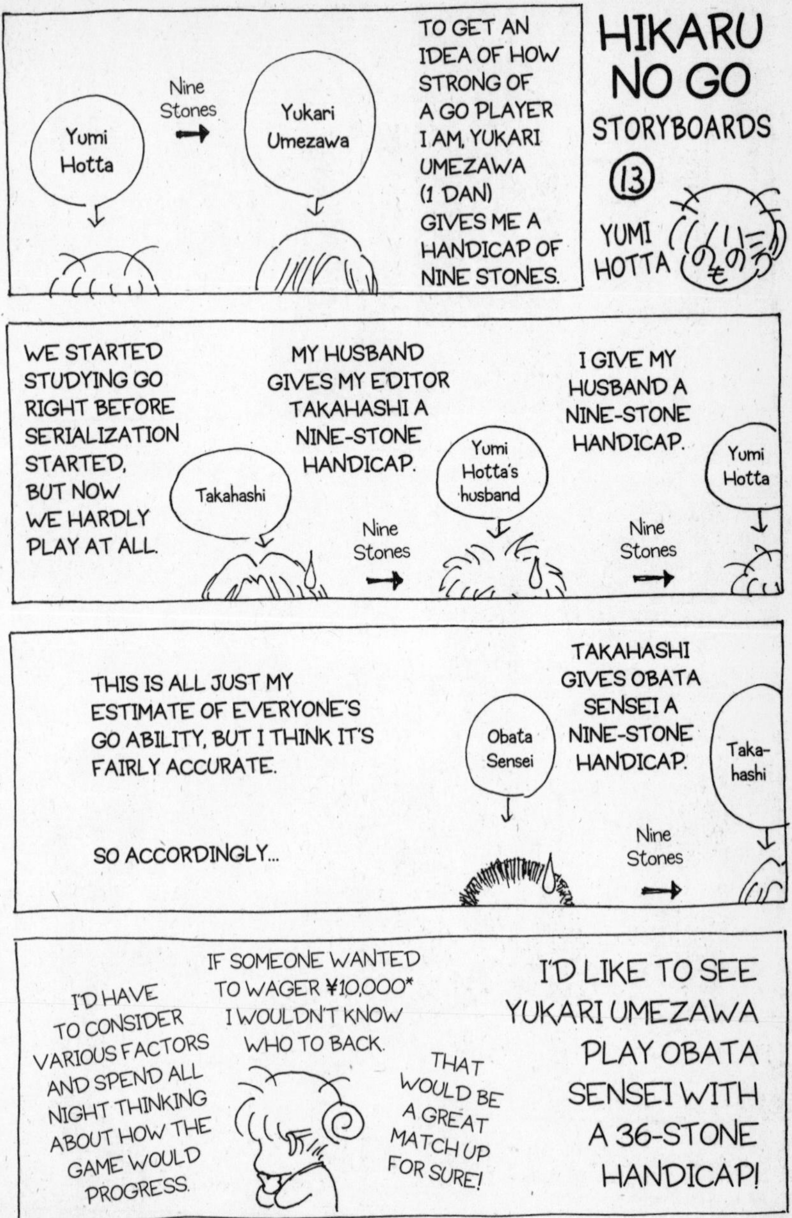
HIKARU NO GO STORYBOARDS
13
YUMI HOTTA
Yumi Hotta
Nine Stones
Yukari Umezawa
TO GET AN IDEA OF HOW STRONG OF A GO PLAYER I AM, YUKARI UMEZAWA (1 DAN) GIVES ME A HANDICAP OF NINE STONES.
WE STARTED STUDYING GO RIGHT BEFORE SERIALIZATION STARTED, BUT NOW WE HARDLY PLAY AT ALL.
Takahashi
MY HUSBAND GIVES MY EDITOR TAKAHASHI A NINE-STONE HANDICAP.
Nine Stones
Yumi Hotta's husband
I GIVE MY HUSBAND A NINE-STONE HANDICAP.
Nine Stones
Yumi Hotta
THIS IS ALL JUST MY ESTIMATE OF EVERYONE'S GO ABILITY, BUT I THINK IT'S FAIRLY ACCURATE.
SO ACCORDINGLY...
Obata Sensei
TAKAHASHI GIVES OBATA SENSEI A NINE-STONE HANDICAP.
Nine Stones
Taka-hashi
I'D HAVE TO CONSIDER VARIOUS FACTORS AND SPEND ALL NIGHT THINKING ABOUT HOW THE GAME WOULD PROGRESS.
IF SOMEONE WANTED TO WAGER ¥10,000* I WOULDN'T KNOW WHO TO BACK.
THAT WOULD BE A GREAT MATCH UP FOR SURE!
I'D LIKE TO SEE YUKARI UMEZAWA PLAY OBATA SENSEI WITH A 36-STONE HANDICAP!

*ABOUT US $100

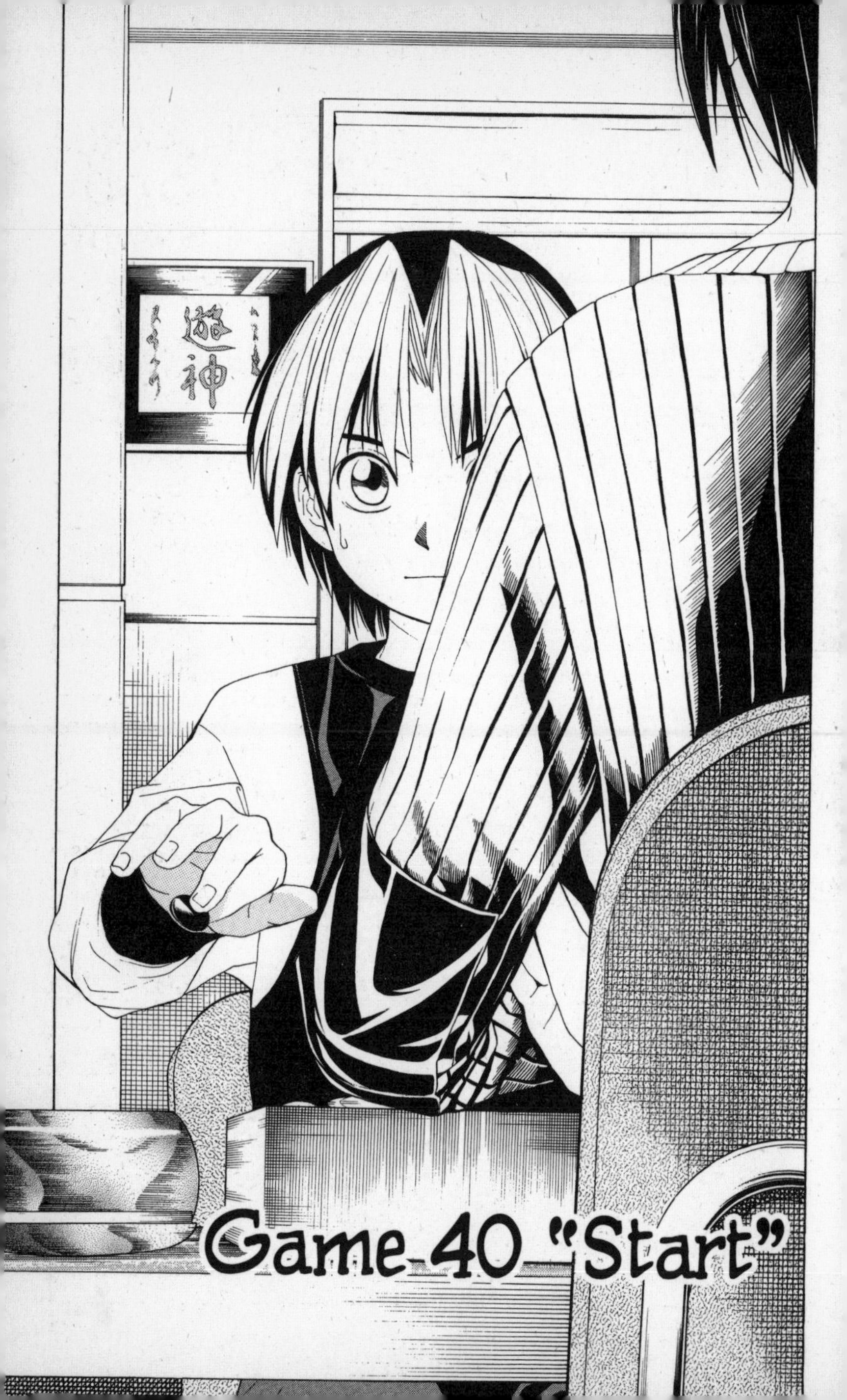
遊神
Game 40 "Start"

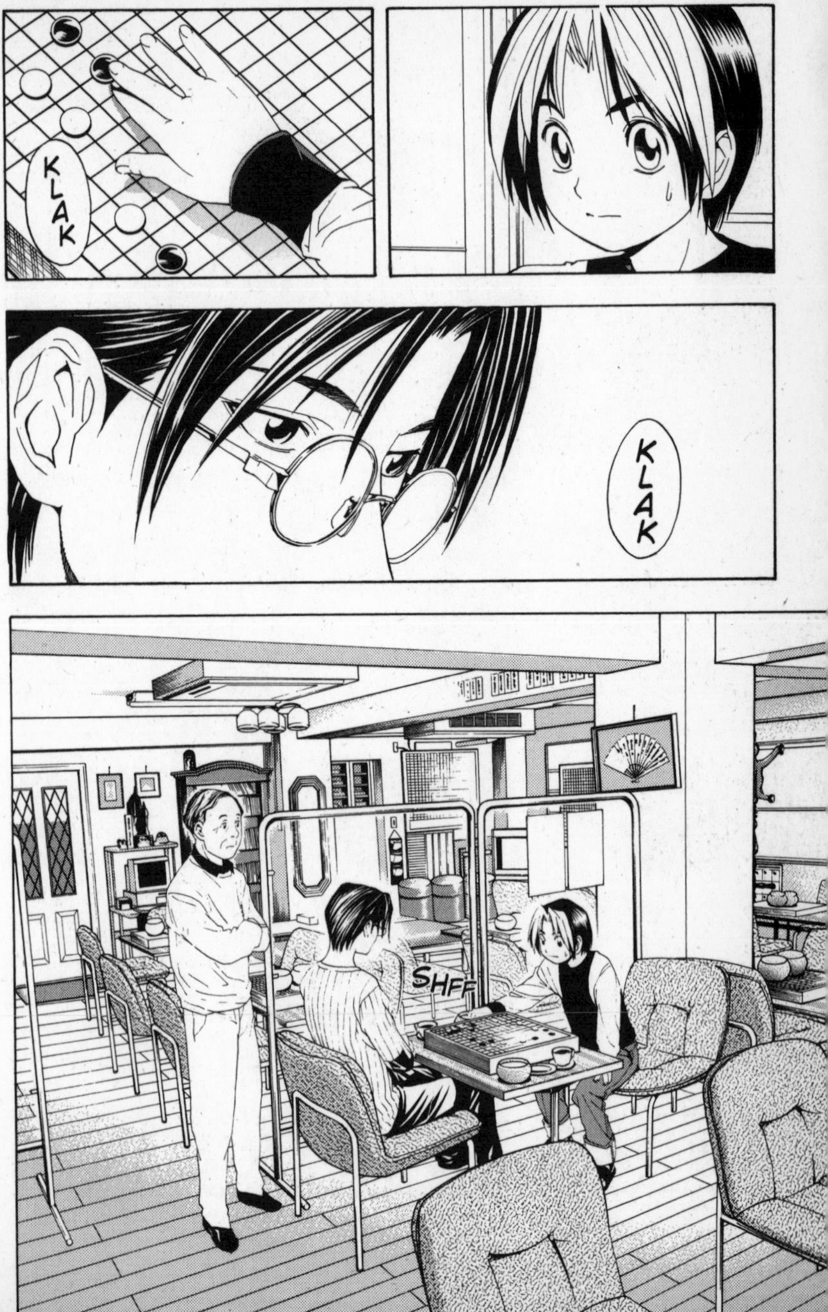
KLAK
KLAK
SHFF

READ THIS WAY

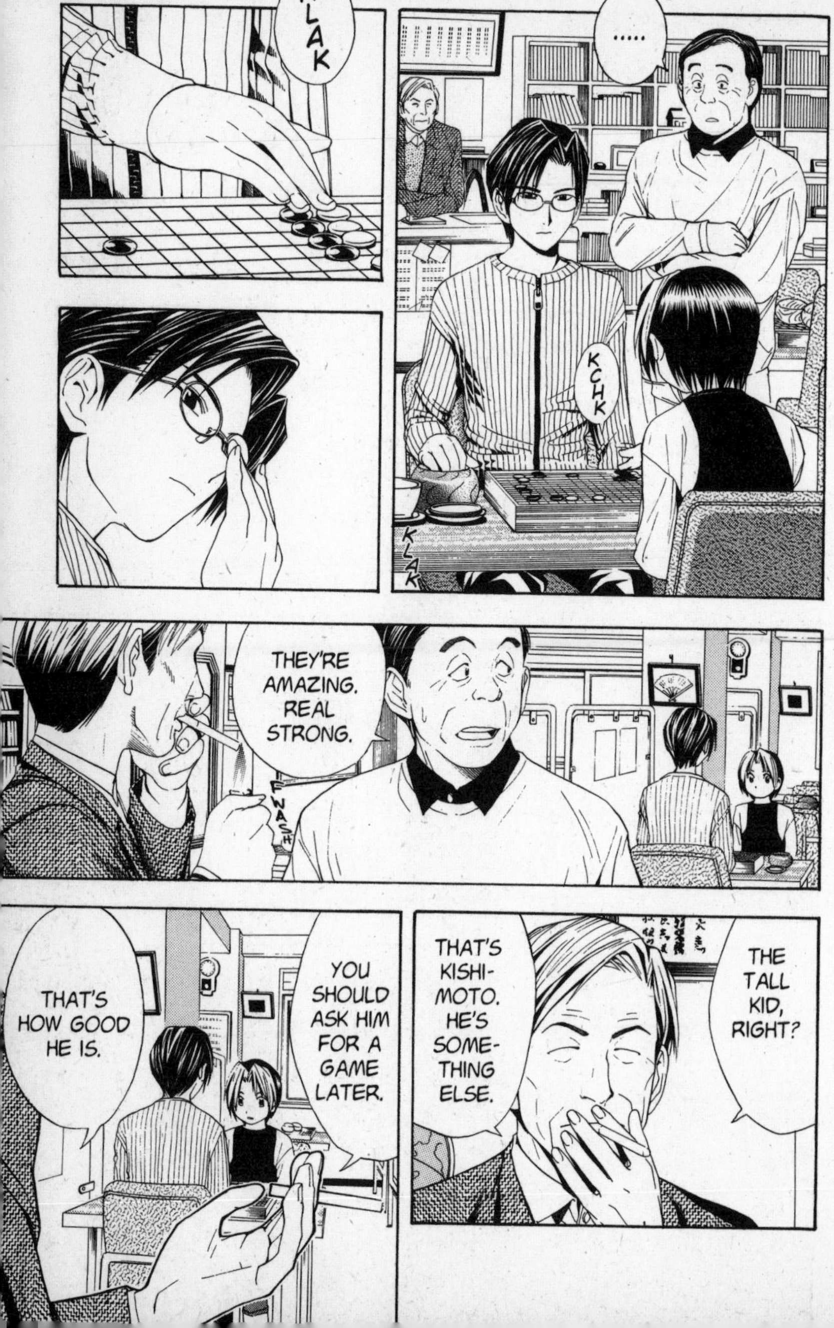

......
KCHK
KLAK
KLAK
THEY'RE AMAZING. REAL STRONG.
FWASH
THE TALL KID, RIGHT?
THAT'S KISHI-MOTO. HE'S SOME-THING ELSE.
YOU SHOULD ASK HIM FOR A GAME LATER.
THAT'S HOW GOOD HE IS.

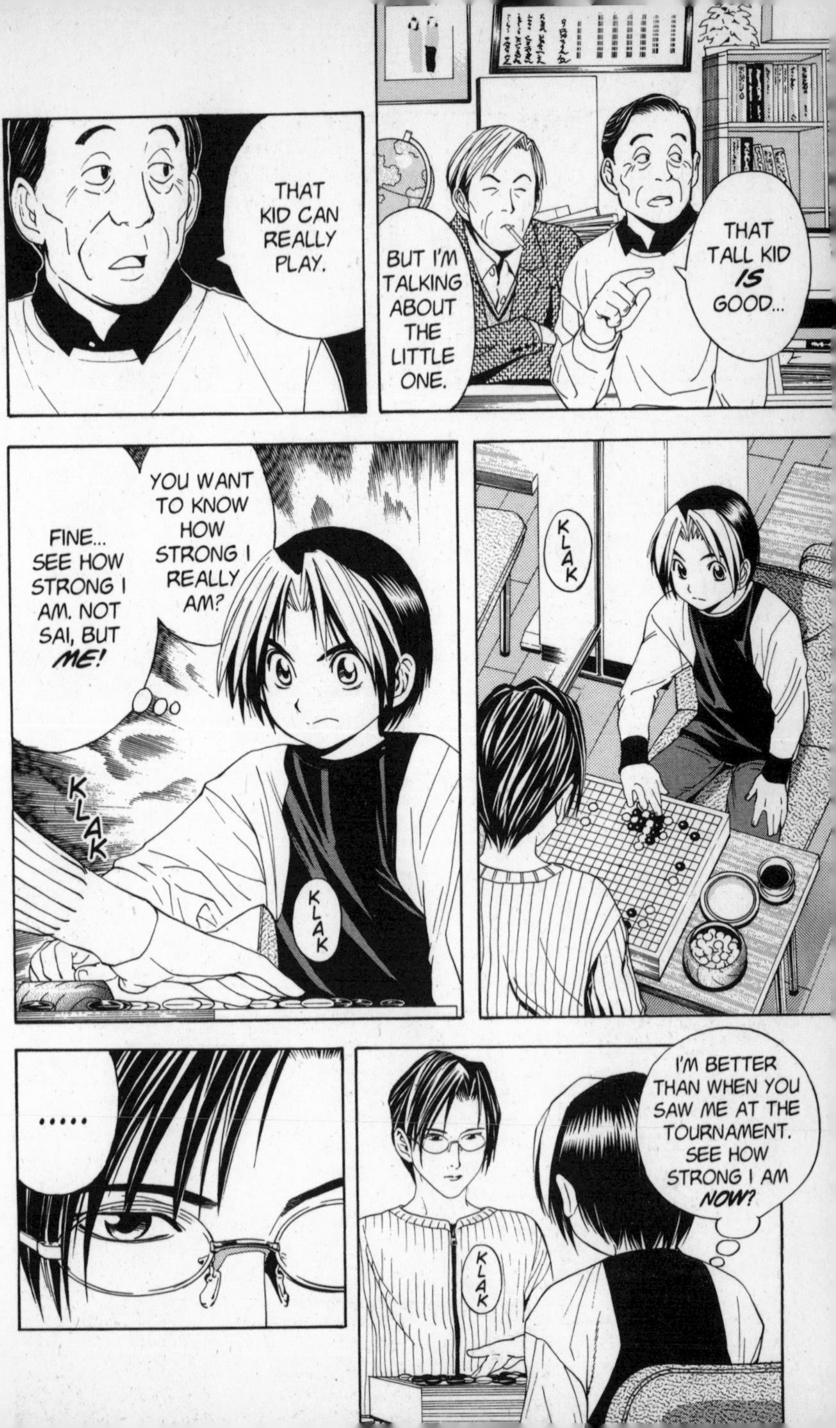
THAT TALL KID IS GOOD...
BUT I'M TALKING ABOUT THE LITTLE ONE.
THAT KID CAN REALLY PLAY.
KLAK
YOU WANT TO KNOW HOW STRONG I REALLY AM?
FINE... SEE HOW STRONG I AM. NOT SAI, BUT ME!
KLAK
KLAK
I'M BETTER THAN WHEN YOU SAW ME AT THE TOURNAMENT. SEE HOW STRONG I AM NOW?
KLAK
.....

READ THIS WAY

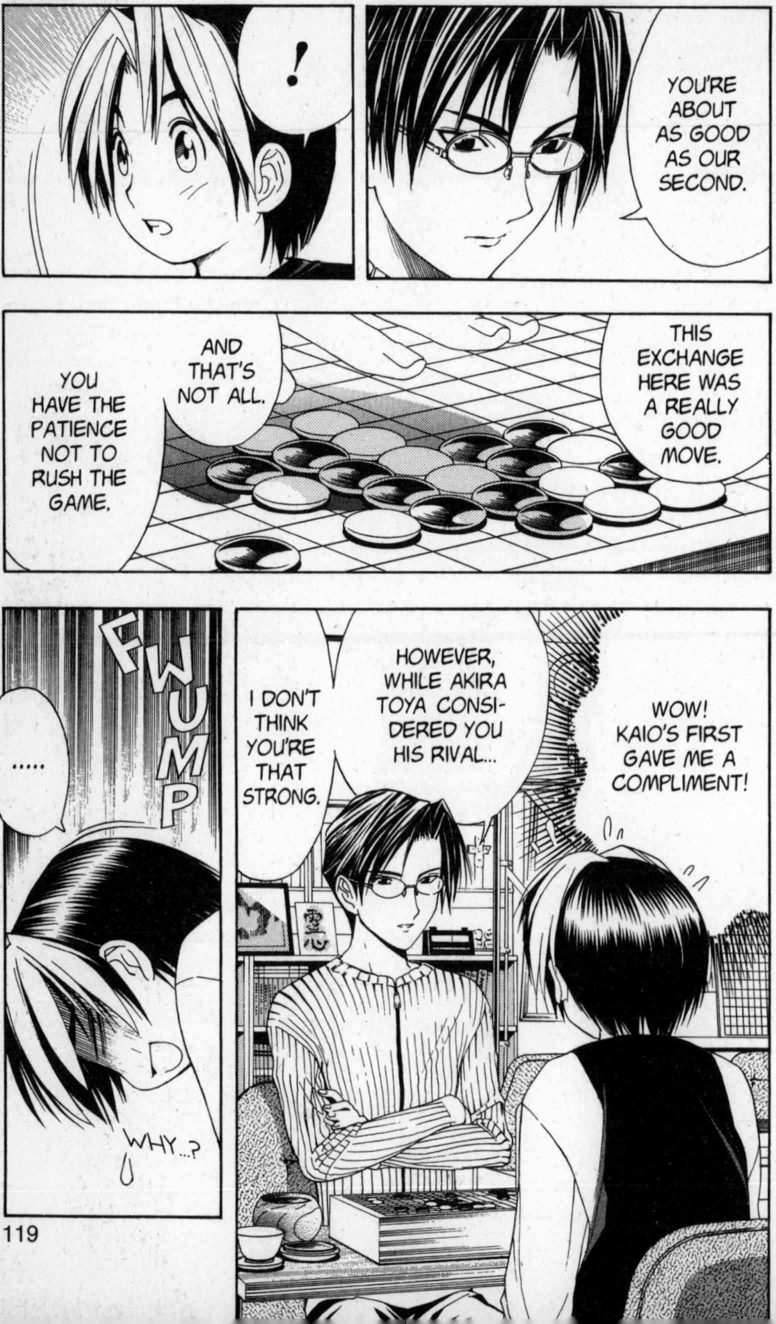
YOU'RE ABOUT AS GOOD AS OUR SECOND.
!
THIS EXCHANGE HERE WAS A REALLY GOOD MOVE.
AND THAT'S NOT ALL.
YOU HAVE THE PATIENCE NOT TO RUSH THE GAME.
WOW! KAIO'S FIRST GAVE ME A COMPLIMENT!
HOWEVER, WHILE AKIRA TOYA CONSI-DERED YOU HIS RIVAL...
I DON'T THINK YOU'RE THAT STRONG.
FWUMP
.....
WHY...?

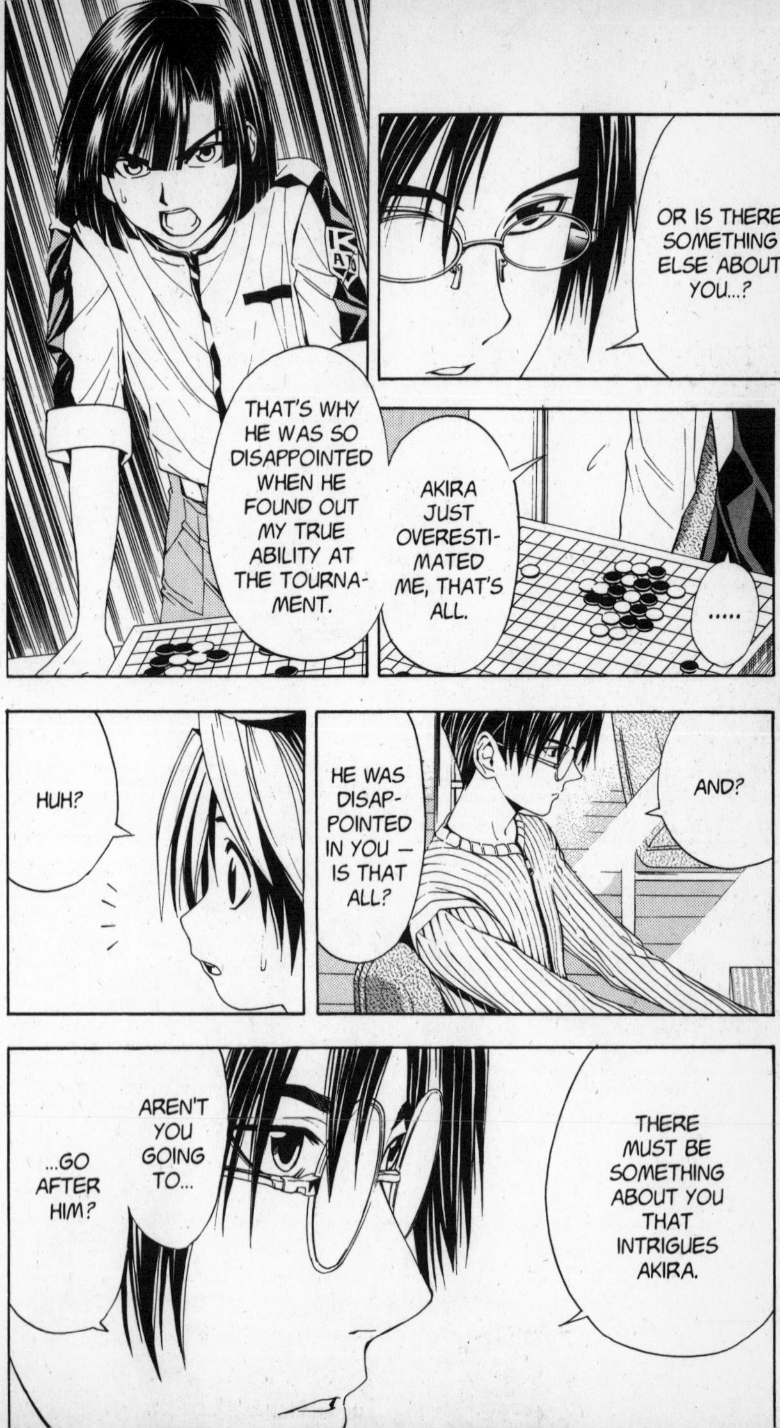
OR IS THERE SOMETHING ELSE ABOUT YOU...?
.....
AKIRA JUST OVERESTIMATED ME, THAT'S ALL.
THAT'S WHY HE WAS SO DISAPPOINTED WHEN HE FOUND OUT MY TRUE ABILITY AT THE TOURNAMENT.
AND?
HE WAS DISAPPOINTED IN YOU — IS THAT ALL?
HUH?
THERE MUST BE SOMETHING ABOUT YOU THAT INTRIGUES AKIRA.
AREN'T YOU GOING TO...
...GO AFTER HIM?

READ THIS WAY

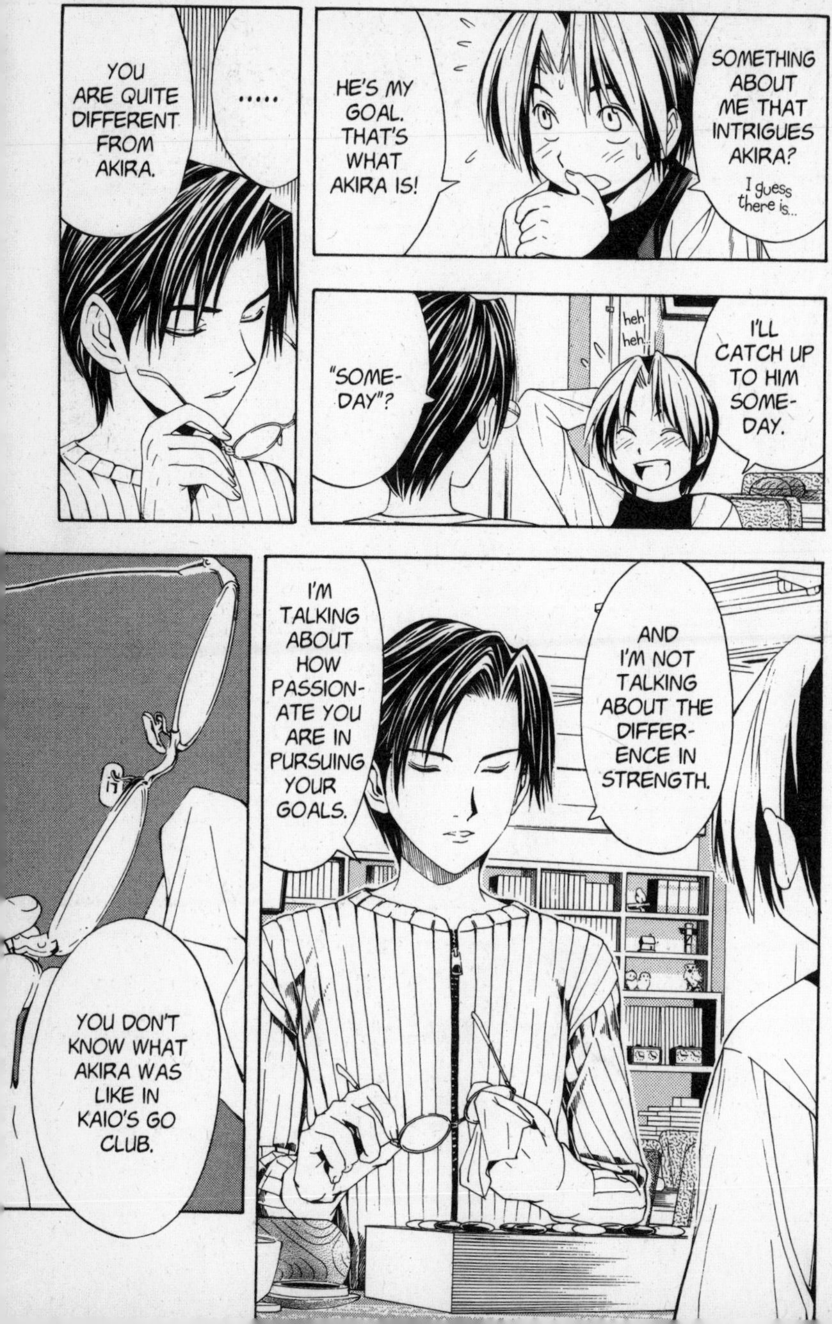
SOMETHING ABOUT ME THAT INTRIGUES AKIRA?
I guess there is...
HE'S MY GOAL. THAT'S WHAT AKIRA IS!
I'LL CATCH UP TO HIM SOME-DAY.
heh heh
"SOME-DAY"?
.....
YOU ARE QUITE DIFFERENT FROM AKIRA.
AND I'M NOT TALKING ABOUT THE DIFFER-ENCE IN STRENGTH.
I'M TALKING ABOUT HOW PASSION-ATE YOU ARE IN PURSUING YOUR GOALS.
YOU DON'T KNOW WHAT AKIRA WAS LIKE IN KAIO'S GO CLUB.

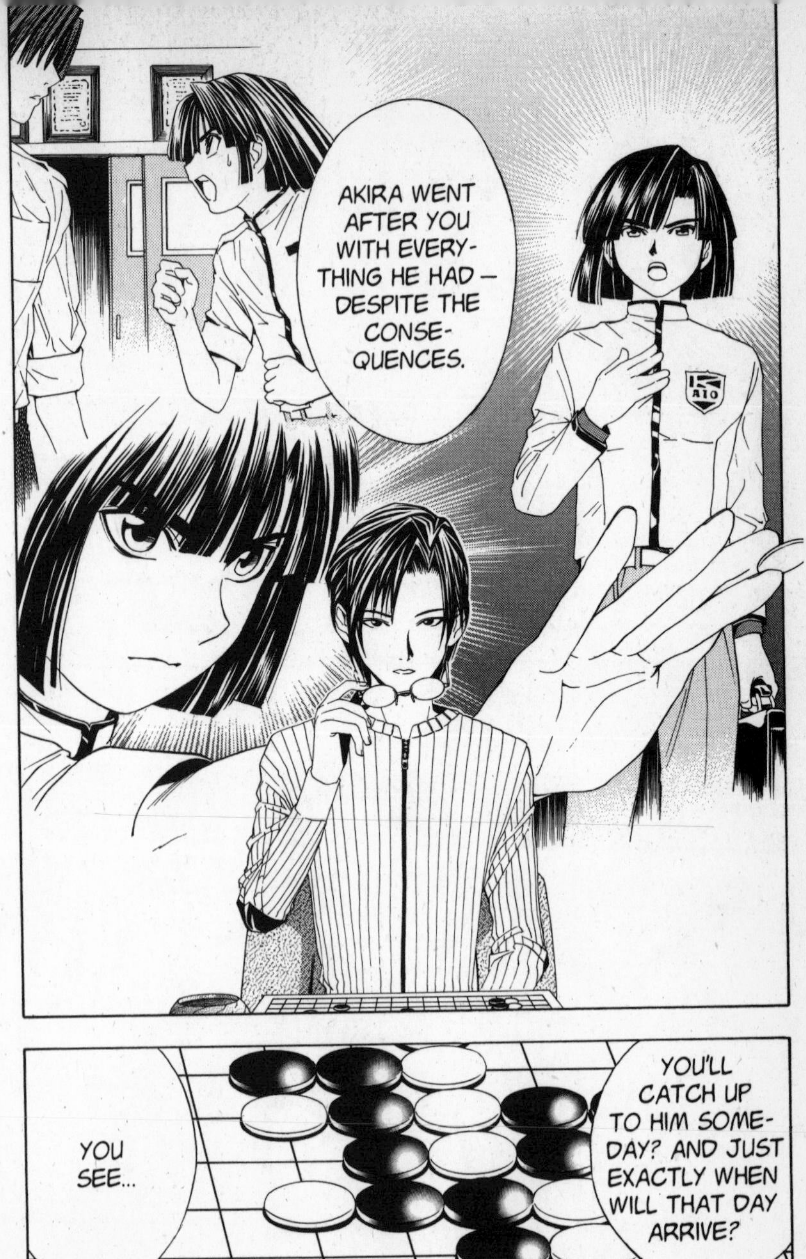
AKIRA WENT AFTER YOU WITH EVERY-THING HE HAD – DESPITE THE CONSE-QUENCES.
YOU'LL CATCH UP TO HIM SOME-DAY? AND JUST EXACTLY WHEN WILL THAT DAY ARRIVE?
YOU SEE...

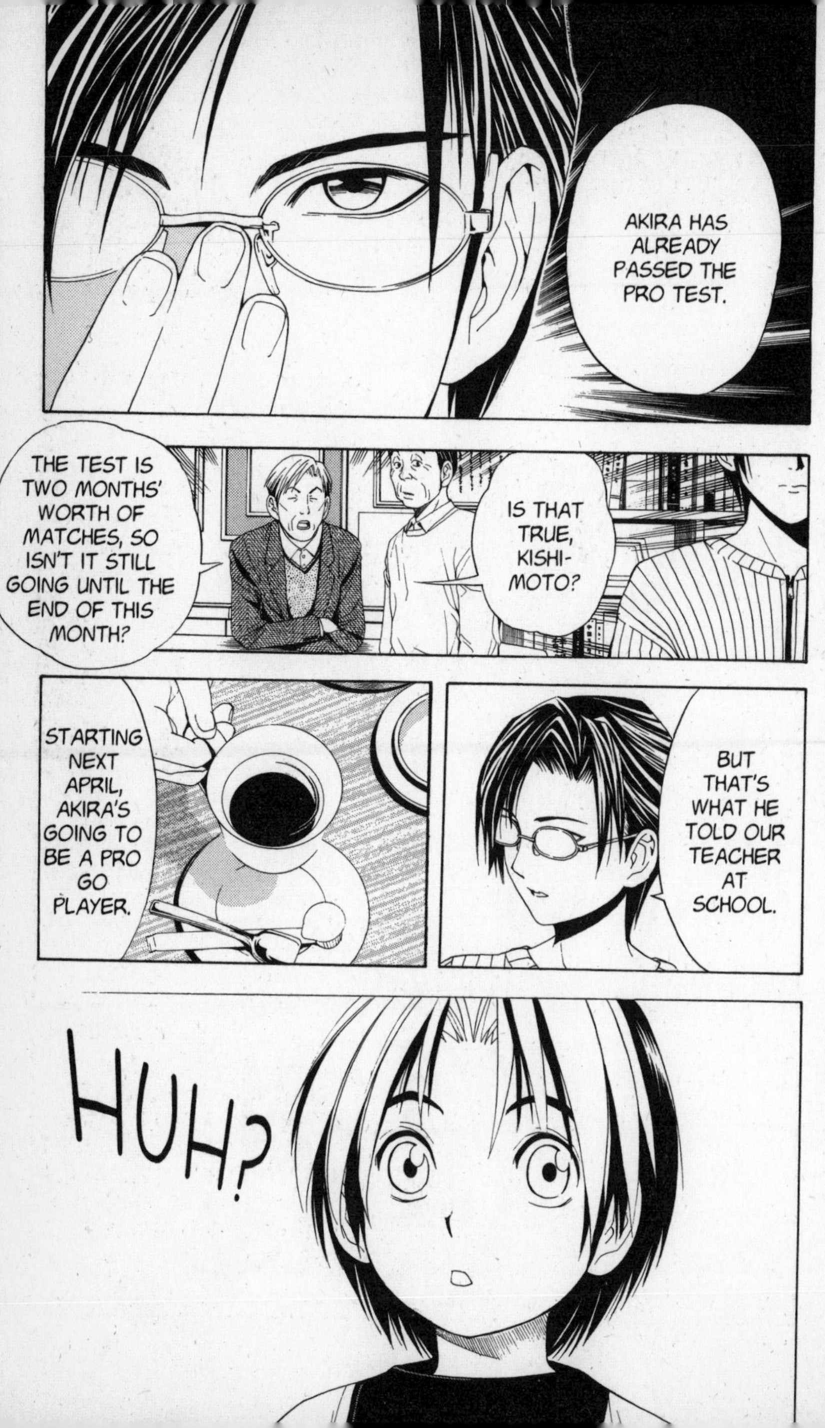
AKIRA HAS ALREADY PASSED THE PRO TEST.
IS THAT TRUE, KISHI- MOTO?
THE TEST IS TWO MONTHS' WORTH OF MATCHES, SO ISN'T IT STILL GOING UNTIL THE END OF THIS MONTH?
BUT THAT'S WHAT HE TOLD OUR TEACHER AT SCHOOL.
STARTING NEXT APRIL, AKIRA'S GOING TO BE A PRO GO PLAYER.
HUH?

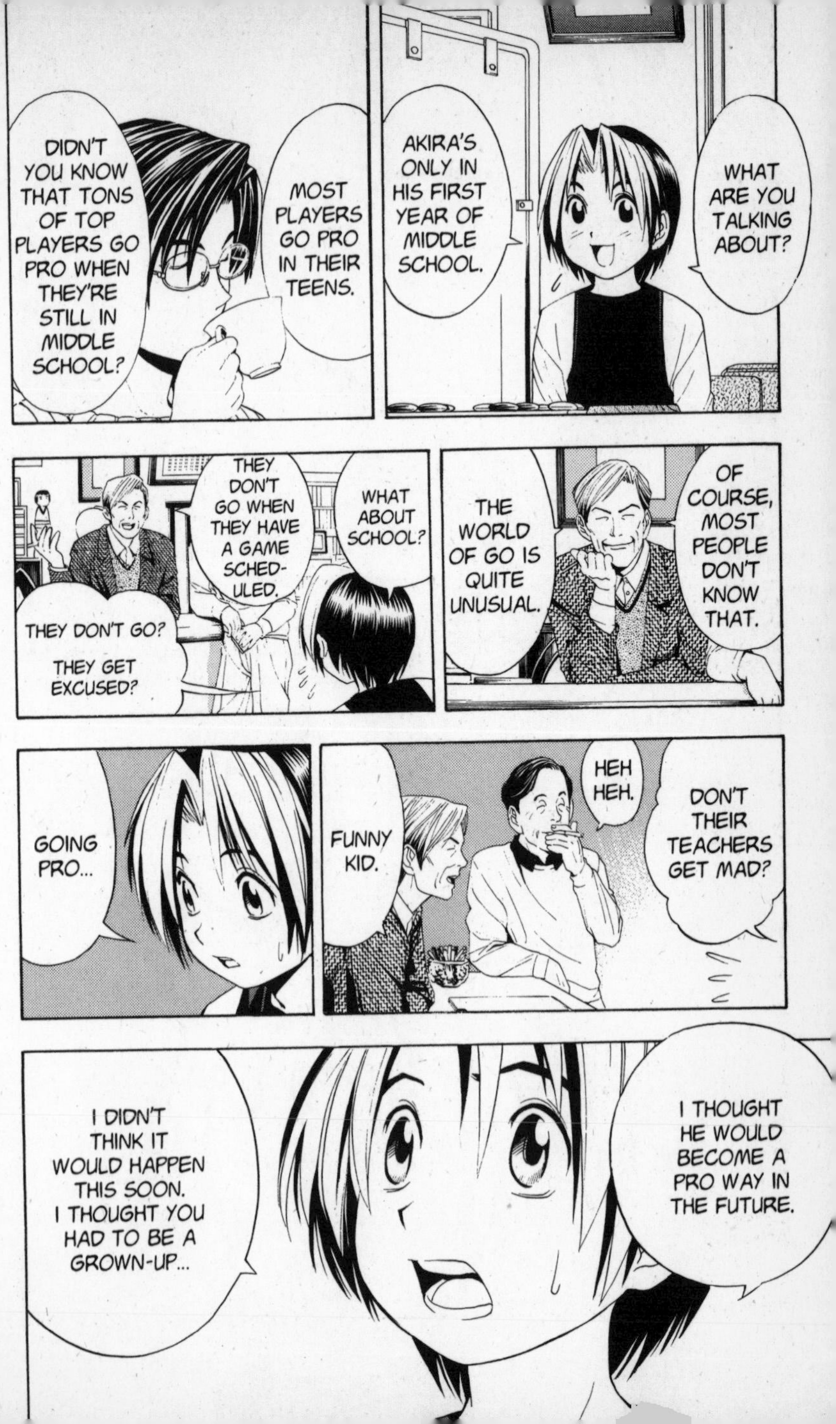
WHAT ARE YOU TALKING ABOUT?
AKIRA'S ONLY IN HIS FIRST YEAR OF MIDDLE SCHOOL.
MOST PLAYERS GO PRO IN THEIR TEENS.
DIDN'T YOU KNOW THAT TONS OF TOP PLAYERS GO PRO WHEN THEY'RE STILL IN MIDDLE SCHOOL?
OF COURSE, MOST PEOPLE DON'T KNOW THAT.
THE WORLD OF GO IS QUITE UNUSUAL.
WHAT ABOUT SCHOOL?
THEY DON'T GO WHEN THEY HAVE A GAME SCHED-ULED.
THEY DON'T GO?
THEY GET EXCUSED?
DON'T THEIR TEACHERS GET MAD?
HEH HEH.
FUNNY KID.
GOING PRO...
I THOUGHT HE WOULD BECOME A PRO WAY IN THE FUTURE.
I DIDN'T THINK IT WOULD HAPPEN THIS SOON. I THOUGHT YOU HAD TO BE A GROWN-UP...

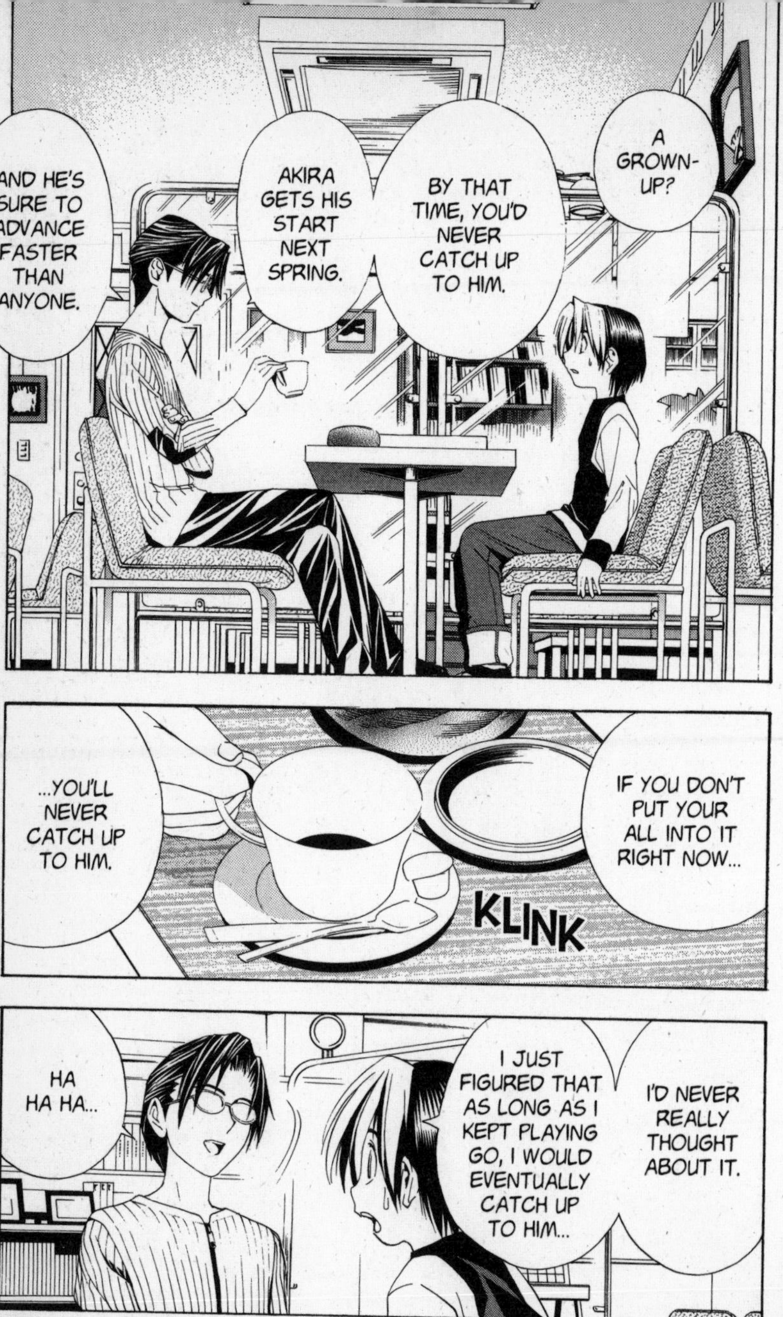
A GROWN-UP?
BY THAT TIME, YOU'D NEVER CATCH UP TO HIM.
AKIRA GETS HIS START NEXT SPRING.
AND HE'S SURE TO ADVANCE FASTER THAN ANYONE.
IF YOU DON'T PUT YOUR ALL INTO IT RIGHT NOW...
KLINK
...YOU'LL NEVER CATCH UP TO HIM.
I'D NEVER REALLY THOUGHT ABOUT IT.
I JUST FIGURED THAT AS LONG AS I KEPT PLAYING GO, I WOULD EVENTUALLY CATCH UP TO HIM...
HA HA HA...

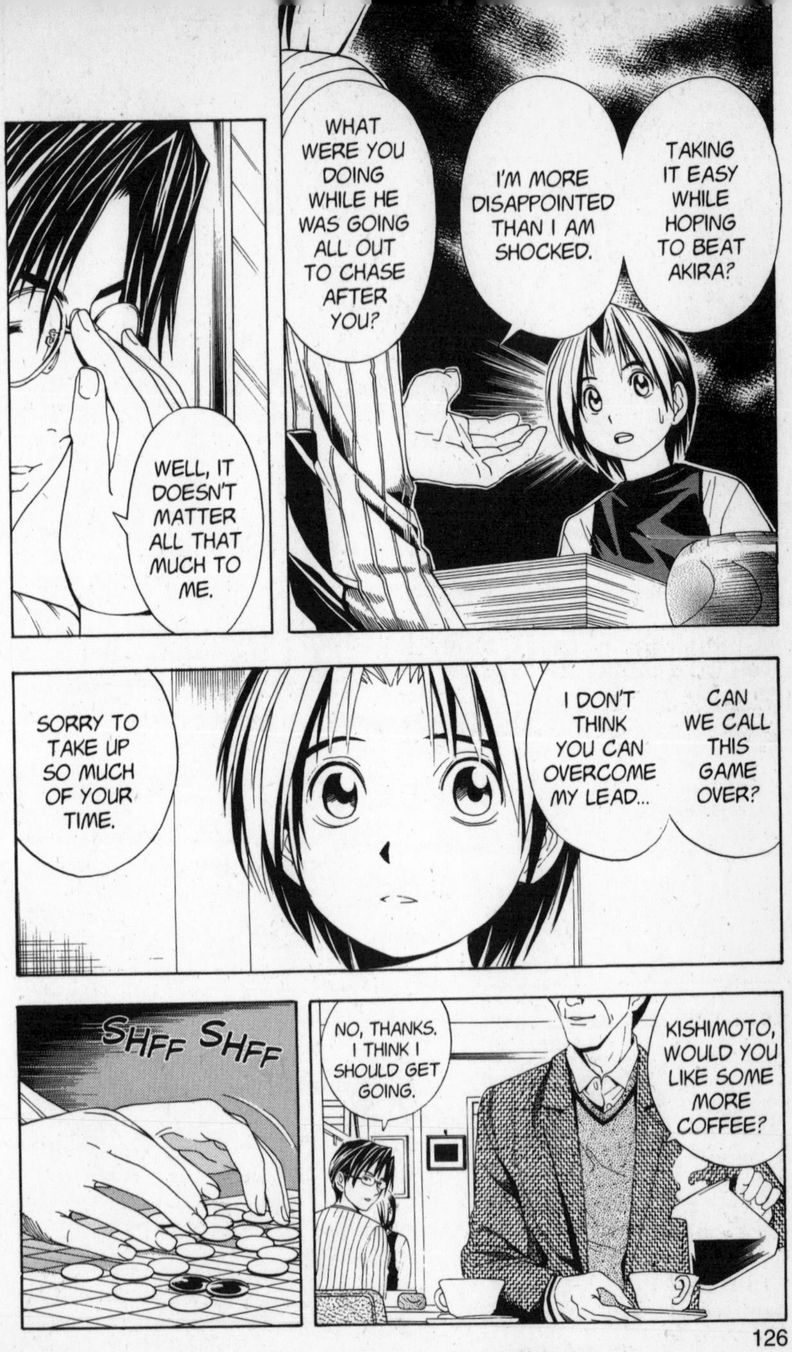
TAKING IT EASY WHILE HOPING TO BEAT AKIRA?
I'M MORE DISAPPOINTED THAN I AM SHOCKED.
WHAT WERE YOU DOING WHILE HE WAS GOING ALL OUT TO CHASE AFTER YOU?
WELL, IT DOESN'T MATTER ALL THAT MUCH TO ME.
CAN WE CALL THIS GAME OVER?
I DON'T THINK YOU CAN OVERCOME MY LEAD...
SORRY TO TAKE UP SO MUCH OF YOUR TIME.
KISHIMOTO, WOULD YOU LIKE SOME MORE COFFEE?
NO, THANKS. I THINK I SHOULD GET GOING.
SHFF SHFF

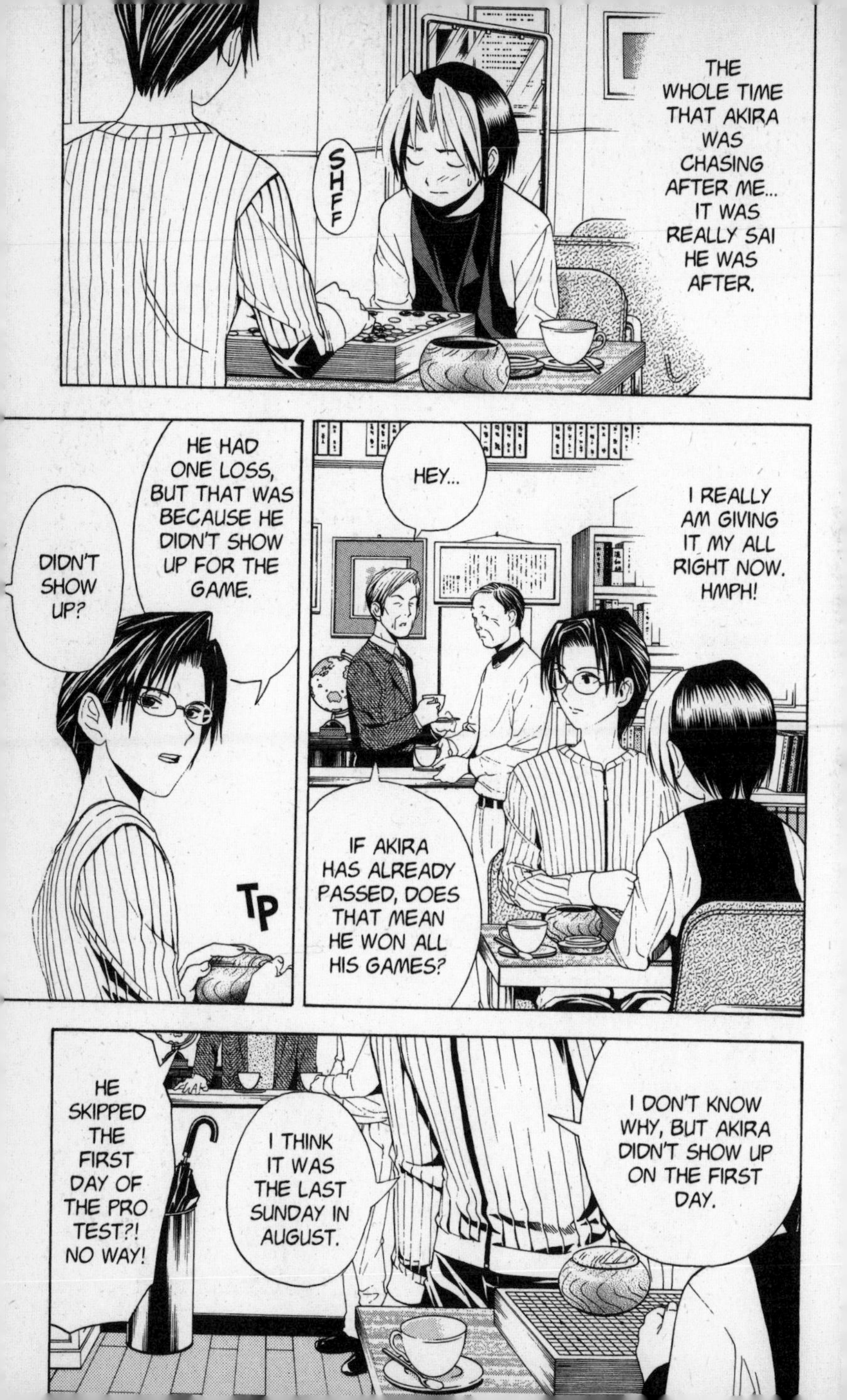
THE WHOLE TIME THAT AKIRA WAS CHASING AFTER ME... IT WAS REALLY SAI HE WAS AFTER.
SHFF
I REALLY AM GIVING IT MY ALL RIGHT NOW. HMPH!
HEY...
IF AKIRA HAS ALREADY PASSED, DOES THAT MEAN HE WON ALL HIS GAMES?
HE HAD ONE LOSS, BUT THAT WAS BECAUSE HE DIDN'T SHOW UP FOR THE GAME.
DIDN'T SHOW UP?
TP
I DON'T KNOW WHY, BUT AKIRA DIDN'T SHOW UP ON THE FIRST DAY.
I THINK IT WAS THE LAST SUNDAY IN AUGUST.
HE SKIPPED THE FIRST DAY OF THE PRO TEST?! NO WAY!

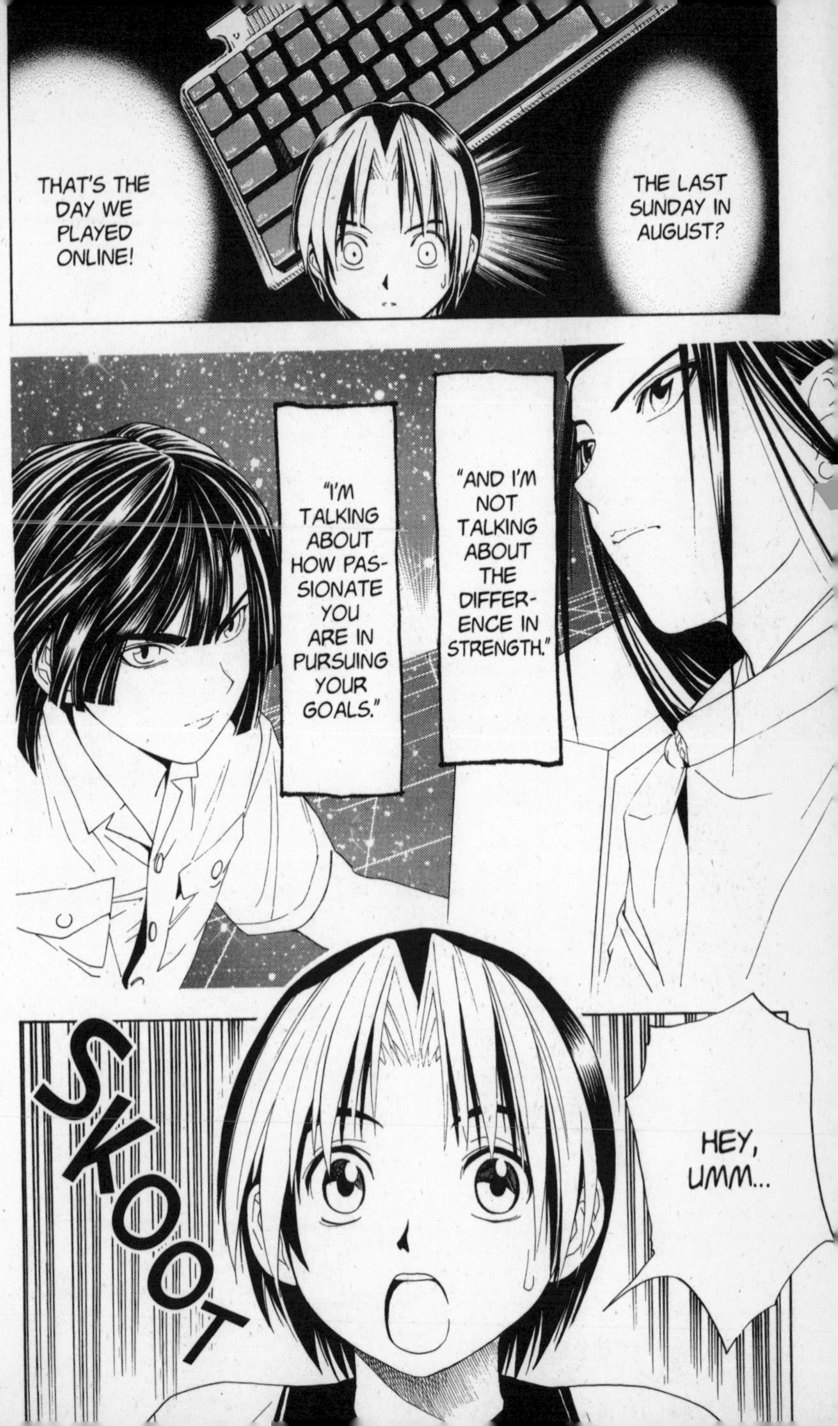
THE LAST SUNDAY IN AUGUST?
THAT'S THE DAY WE PLAYED ONLINE!
"AND I'M NOT TALKING ABOUT THE DIFFERENCE IN STRENGTH."
"I'M TALKING ABOUT HOW PASSIONATE YOU ARE IN PURSUING YOUR GOALS."
HEY, UMM...
SKOOT

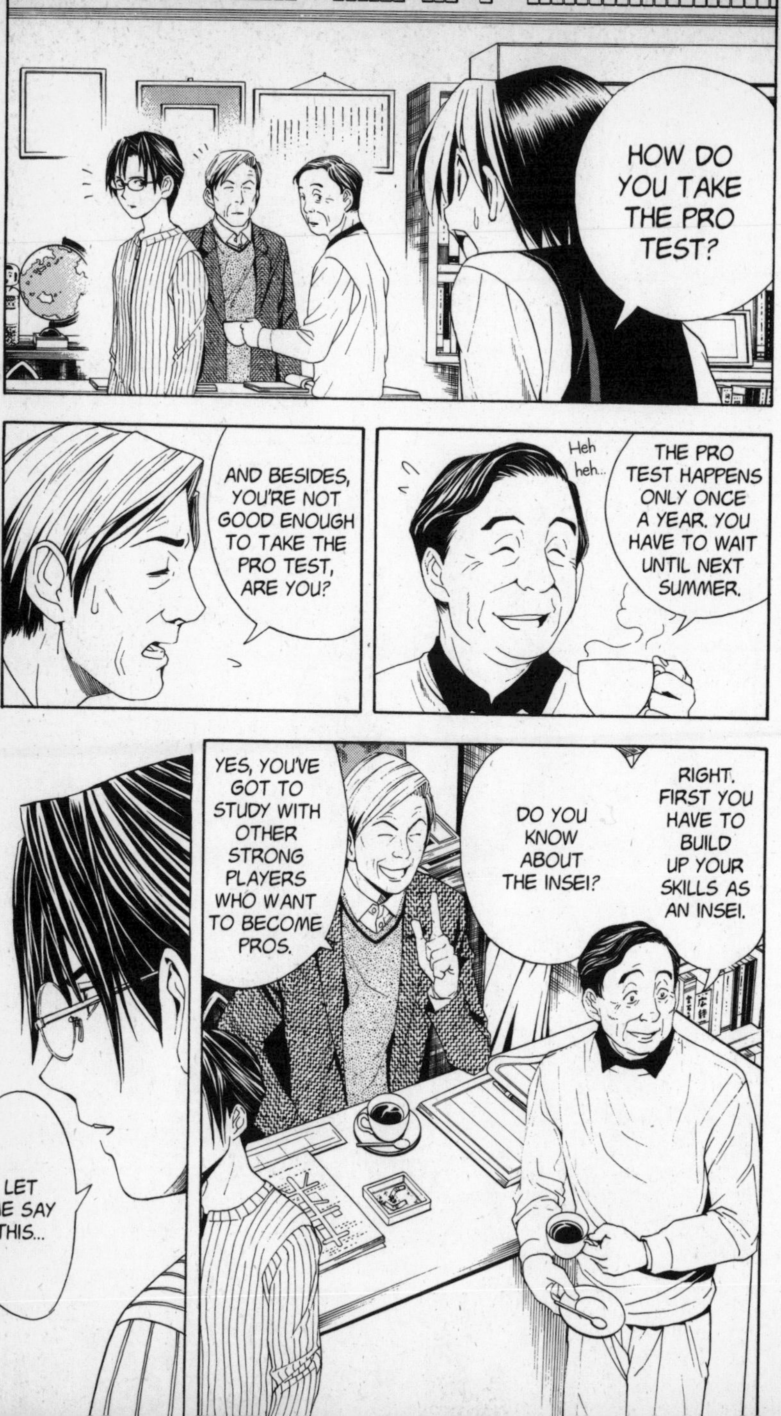
HOW DO YOU TAKE THE PRO TEST?
Heh heh...
THE PRO TEST HAPPENS ONLY ONCE A YEAR. YOU HAVE TO WAIT UNTIL NEXT SUMMER.
AND BESIDES, YOU'RE NOT GOOD ENOUGH TO TAKE THE PRO TEST, ARE YOU?
RIGHT. FIRST YOU HAVE TO BUILD UP YOUR SKILLS AS AN INSEI.
DO YOU KNOW ABOUT THE INSEI?
YES, YOU'VE GOT TO STUDY WITH OTHER STRONG PLAYERS WHO WANT TO BECOME PROS.
LET ME SAY THIS...

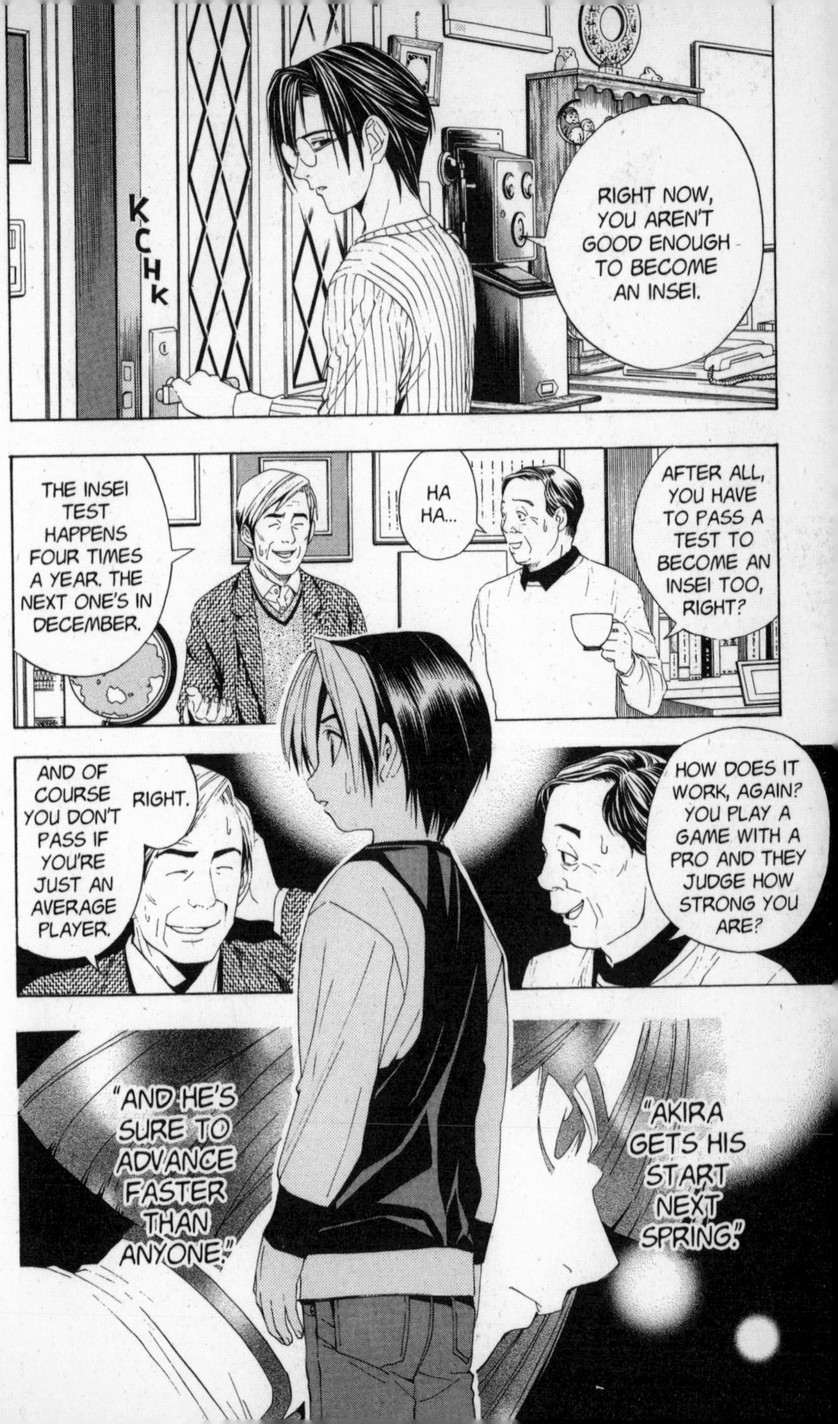
RIGHT NOW, YOU AREN'T GOOD ENOUGH TO BECOME AN INSEI.
KCHK
AFTER ALL, YOU HAVE TO PASS A TEST TO BECOME AN INSEI TOO, RIGHT?
HA HA...
THE INSEI TEST HAPPENS FOUR TIMES A YEAR. THE NEXT ONE'S IN DECEMBER.
HOW DOES IT WORK, AGAIN? YOU PLAY A GAME WITH A PRO AND THEY JUDGE HOW STRONG YOU ARE?
RIGHT.
AND OF COURSE YOU DON'T PASS IF YOU'RE JUST AN AVERAGE PLAYER.
"AKIRA GETS HIS START NEXT SPRING."
"AND HE'S SURE TO ADVANCE FASTER THAN ANYONE."

READ THIS WAY

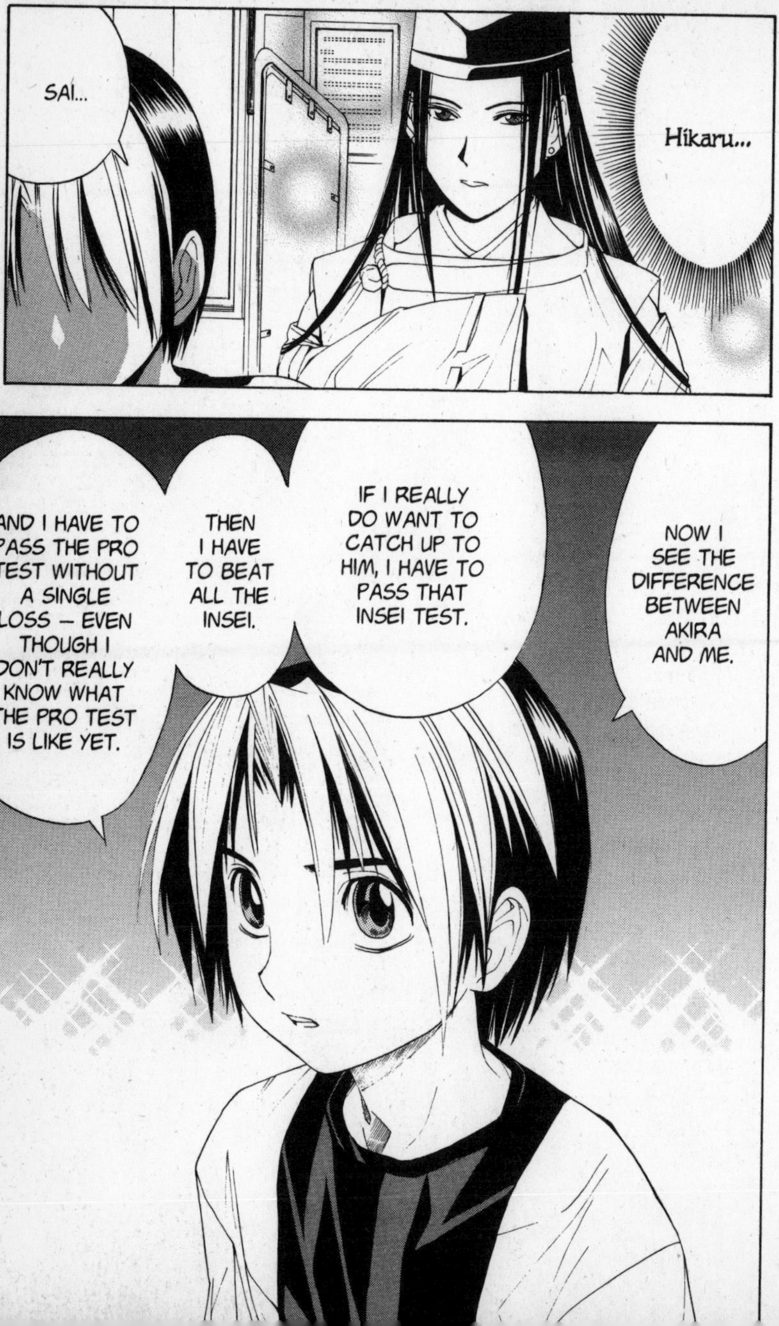

Hikaru...
SAI...
NOW I SEE THE DIFFERENCE BETWEEN AKIRA AND ME.
IF I REALLY DO WANT TO CATCH UP TO HIM, I HAVE TO PASS THAT INSEI TEST.
THEN I HAVE TO BEAT ALL THE INSEI.
AND I HAVE TO PASS THE PRO TEST WITHOUT A SINGLE LOSS – EVEN THOUGH I DON'T REALLY KNOW WHAT THE PRO TEST IS LIKE YET.

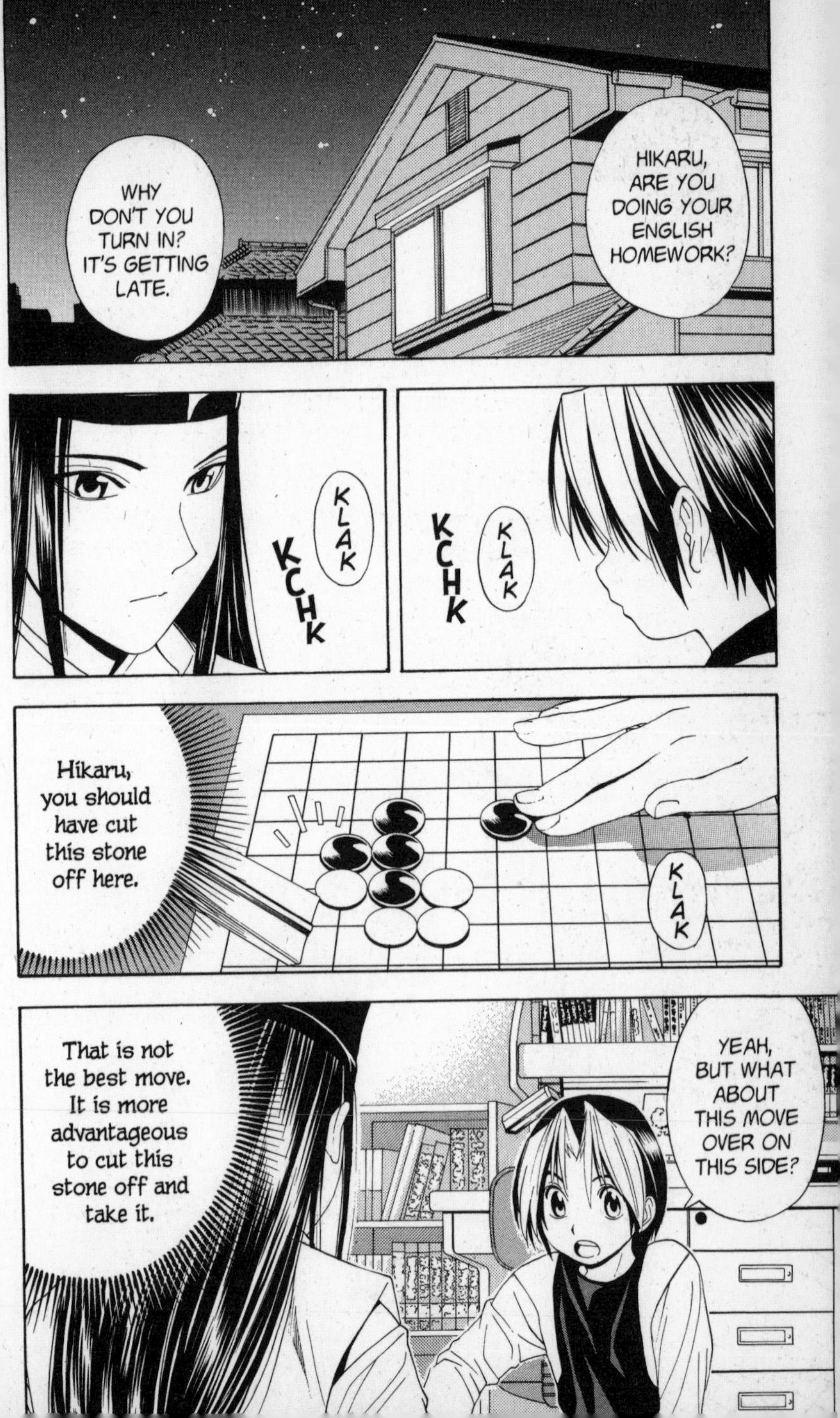
HIKARU, ARE YOU DOING YOUR ENGLISH HOMEWORK?
WHY DON'T YOU TURN IN? IT'S GETTING LATE.
KLAK
KCHK
KLAK
KCHK
KLAK
Hikaru, you should have cut this stone off here.
YEAH, BUT WHAT ABOUT THIS MOVE OVER ON THIS SIDE?
That is not the best move. It is more advantageous to cut this stone off and take it.

READ THIS WAY

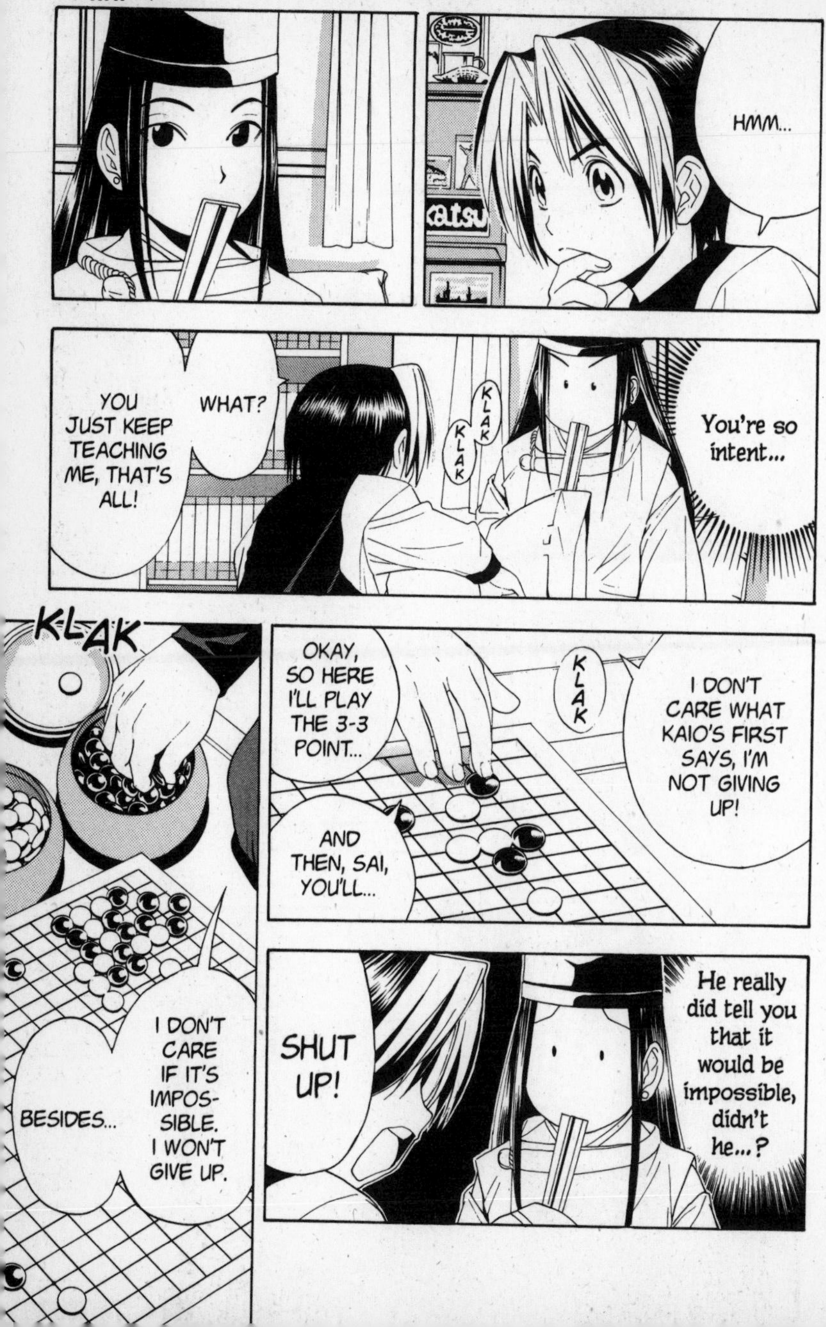
HMM...
You're so intent...
KLAK
KLAK
WHAT?
YOU JUST KEEP TEACHING ME, THAT'S ALL!
I DON'T CARE WHAT KAIO'S FIRST SAYS, I'M NOT GIVING UP!
KLAK
OKAY, SO HERE I'LL PLAY THE 3-3 POINT...
AND THEN, SAI, YOU'LL...
He really did tell you that it would be impossible, didn't he...?
SHUT UP!
KLAK
I DON'T CARE IF IT'S IMPOS-SIBLE. I WON'T GIVE UP.
BESIDES...

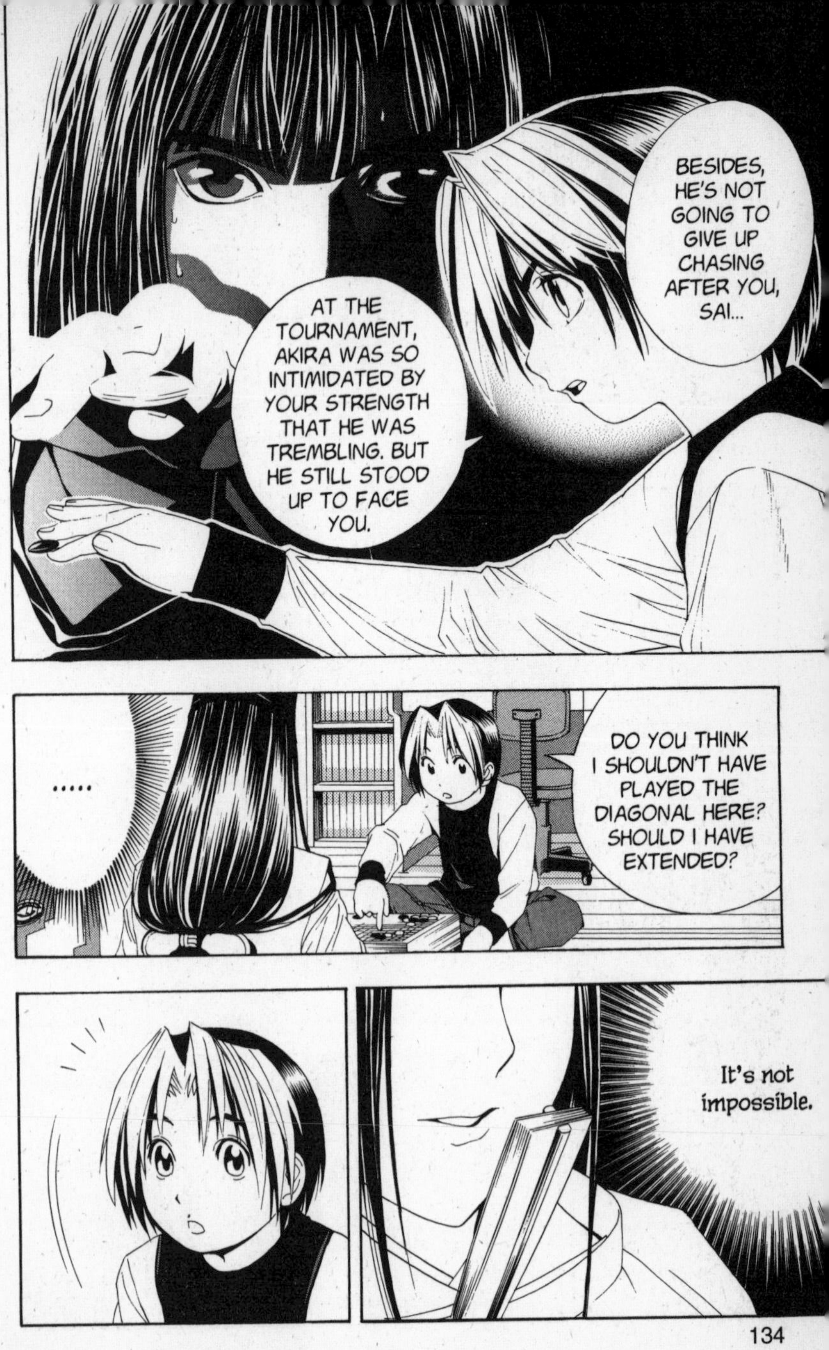
AT THE TOURNAMENT, AKIRA WAS SO INTIMIDATED BY YOUR STRENGTH THAT HE WAS TREMBLING. BUT HE STILL STOOD UP TO FACE YOU.
BESIDES, HE'S NOT GOING TO GIVE UP CHASING AFTER YOU, SAI...
DO YOU THINK I SHOULDN'T HAVE PLAYED THE DIAGONAL HERE? SHOULD I HAVE EXTENDED?
.....
It's not impossible.

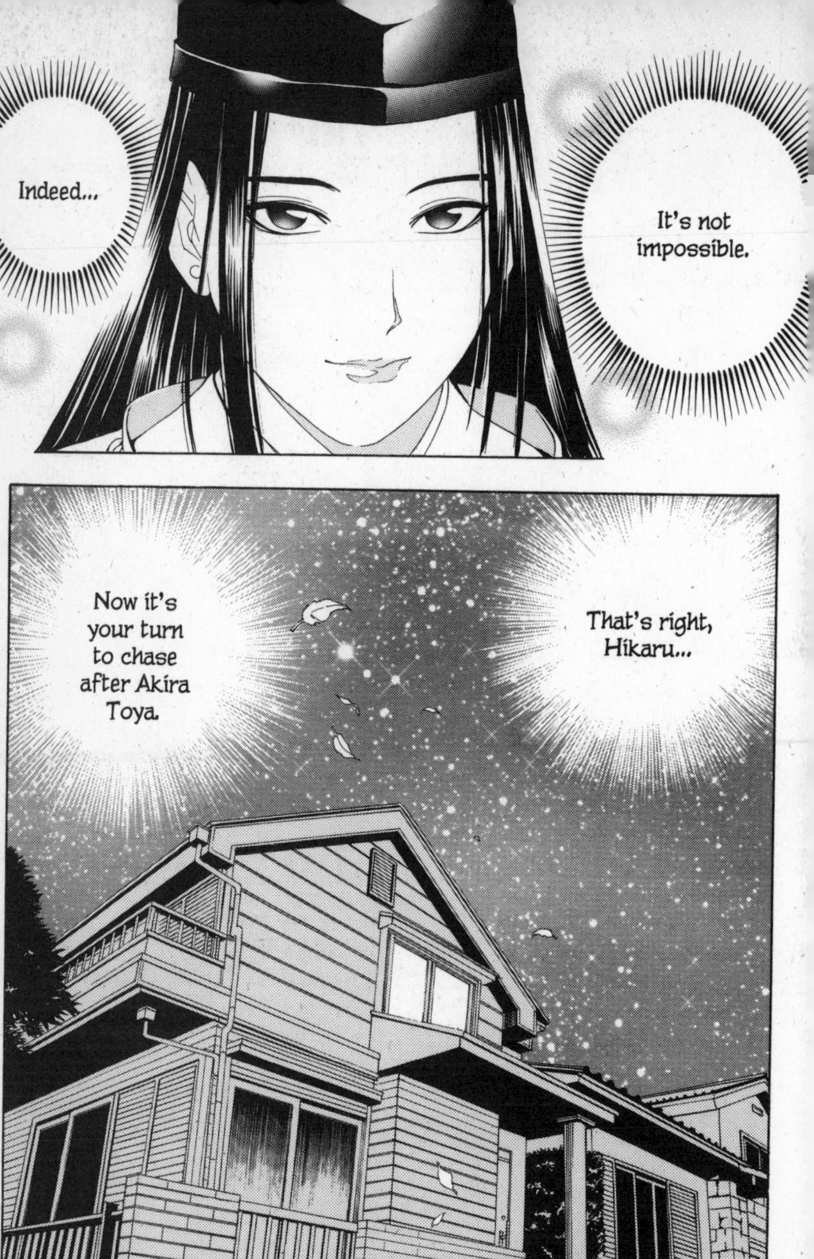
It's not impossible.
Indeed...
That's right, Hikaru...
Now it's your turn to chase after Akira Toya.

A WORD ABOUT HIKARU NO GO

THE VALUE OF GO BOARDS

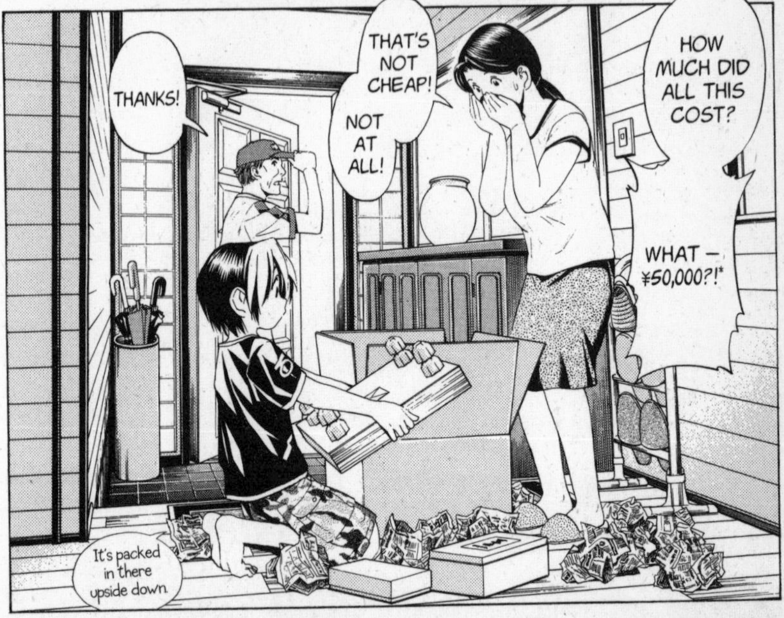
HOW MUCH DID ALL THIS COST?
WHAT — ¥50,000?!*
THAT'S NOT CHEAP!
NOT AT ALL!
THANKS!
It's packed in there upside down.

THE BOARD ALONE WOULD COST ABOUT ¥35,000.*

THE HIGHEST-QUALITY GO BOARD WOULD COST MILLIONS OF YEN. EVEN PROFESSIONAL GO PLAYERS CAN'T AFFORD ONE. SO WHO CAN?

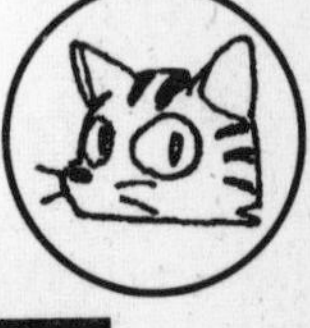

*ABOUT US $340

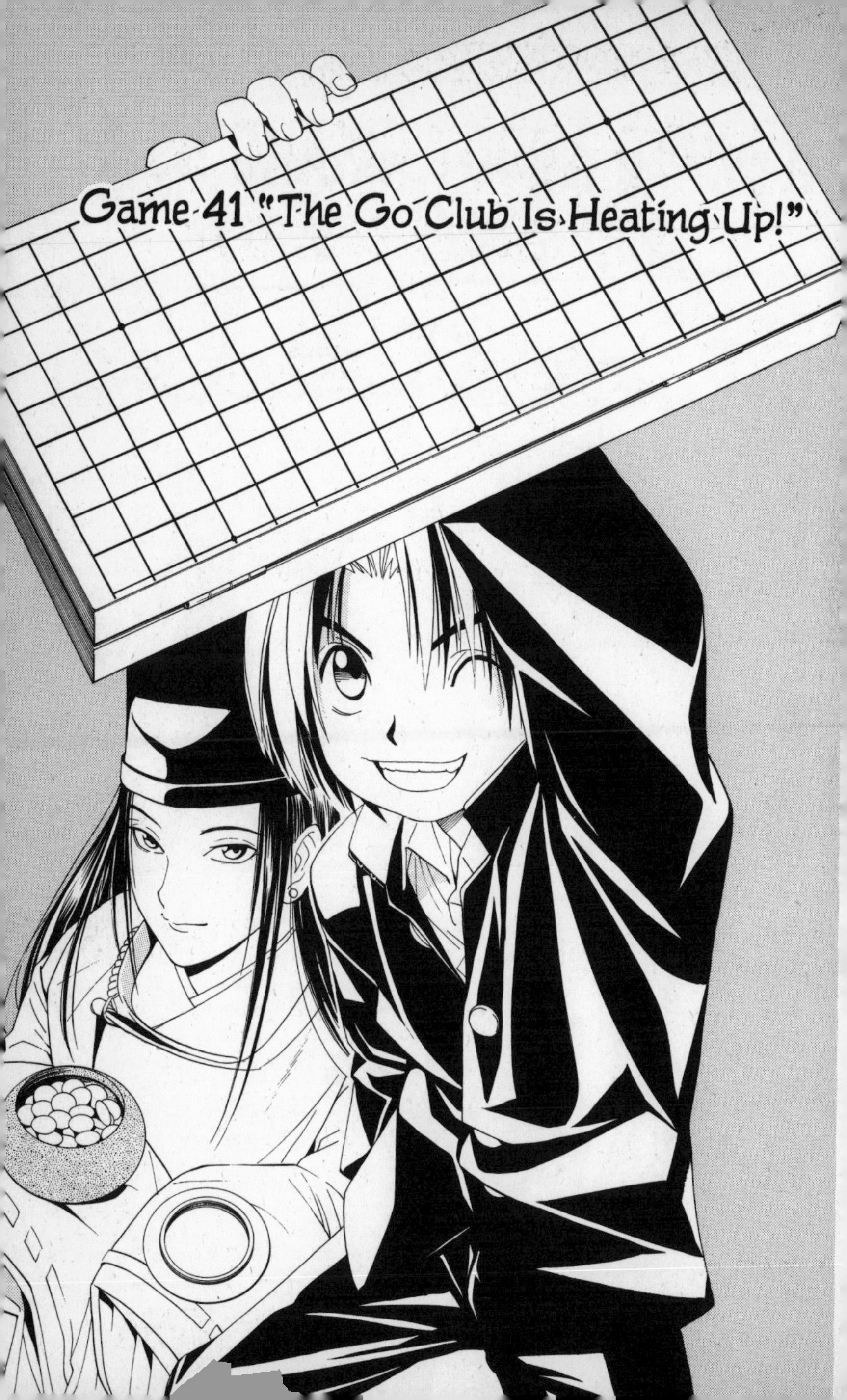
Game 41 "The Go Club Is Heating Up!"

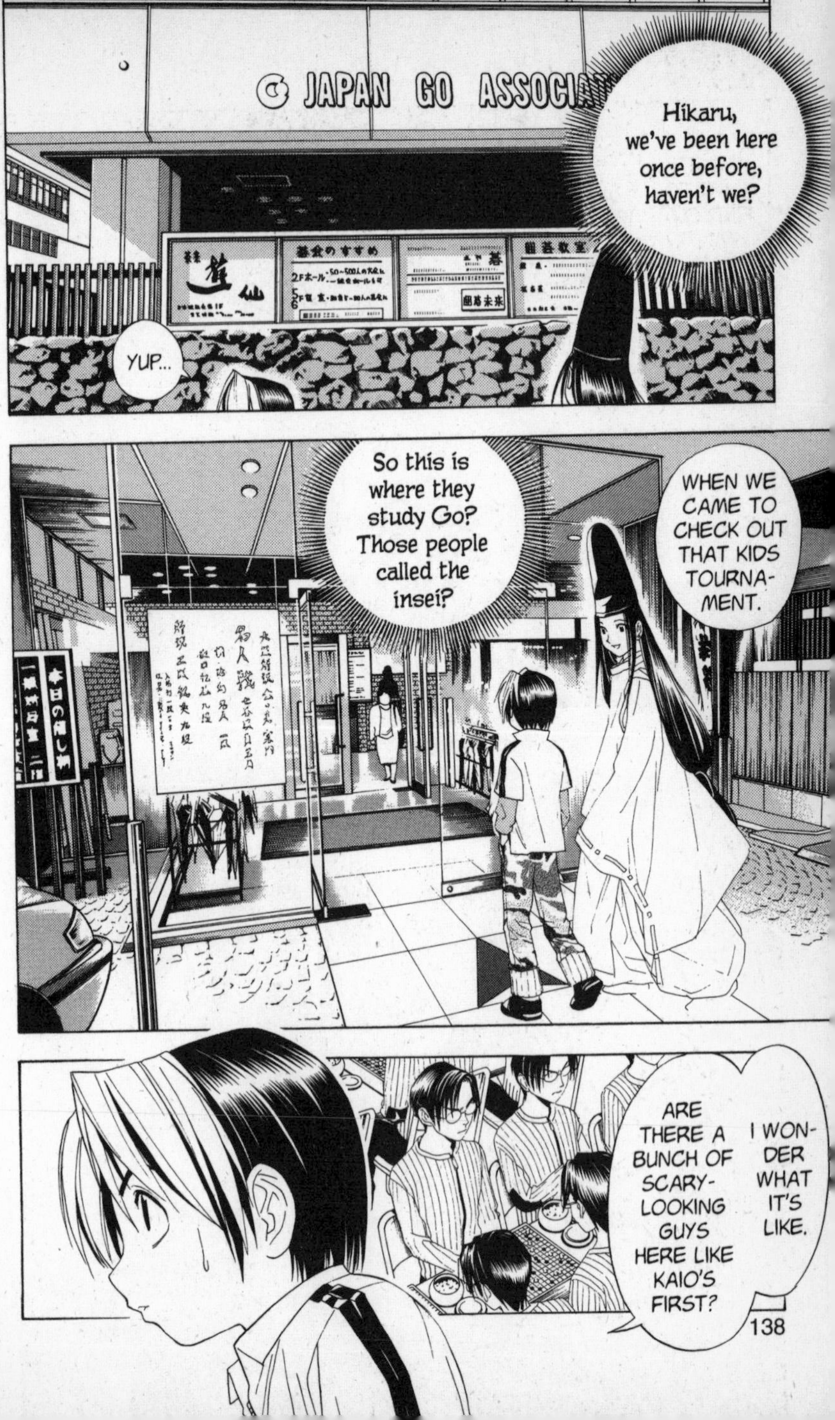
JAPAN GO ASSOCIAT
Hikaru, we've been here once before, haven't we?
YUP...
WHEN WE CAME TO CHECK OUT THAT KIDS TOURNA-MENT.
So this is where they study Go? Those people called the insei?
I WONDER WHAT IT'S LIKE.
ARE THERE A BUNCH OF SCARY-LOOKING GUYS HERE LIKE KAIO'S FIRST?

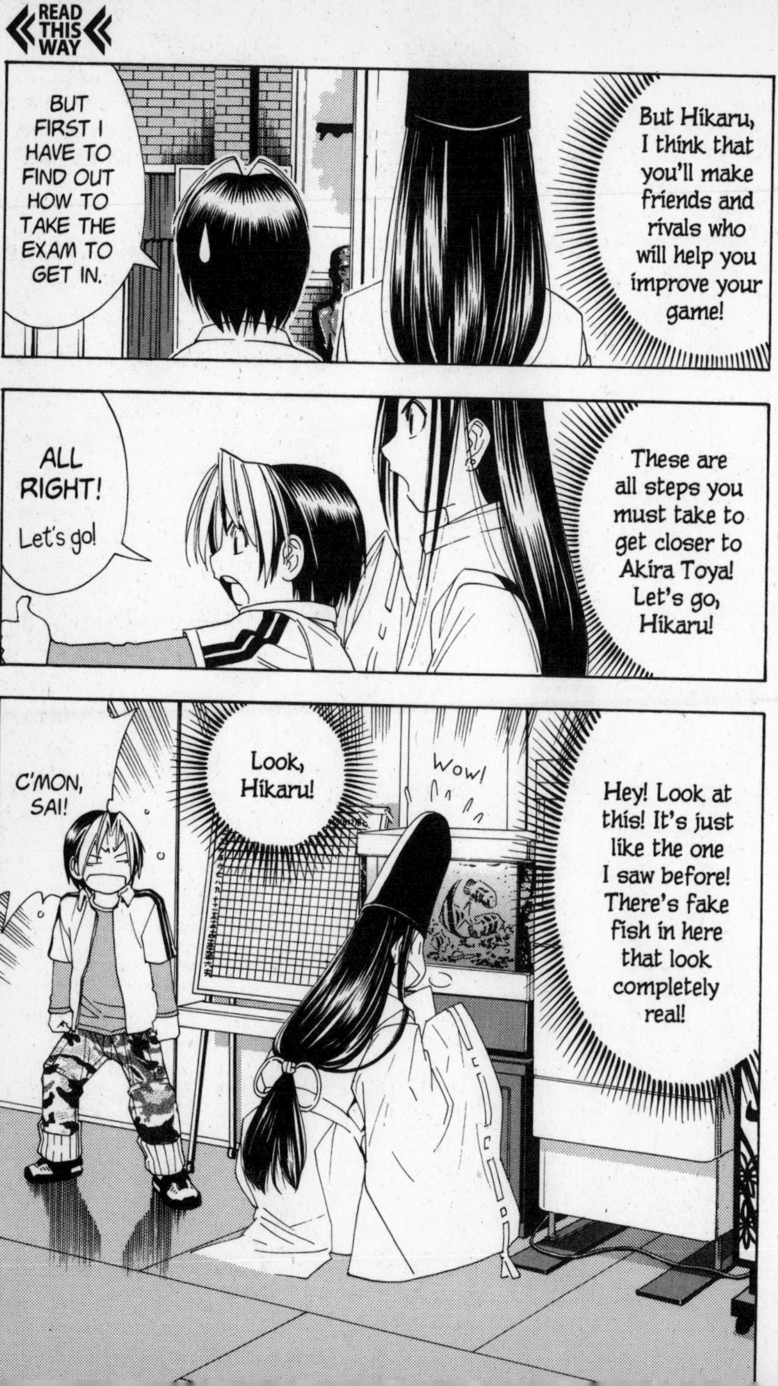
READ THIS WAY
But Hikaru, I think that you'll make friends and rivals who will help you improve your game!
BUT FIRST I HAVE TO FIND OUT HOW TO TAKE THE EXAM TO GET IN.
These are all steps you must take to get closer to Akira Toya! Let's go, Hikaru!
ALL RIGHT! Let's go!
Hey! Look at this! It's just like the one I saw before! There's fake fish in here that look completely real!
Wow!
Look, Hikaru!
C'MON, SAI!

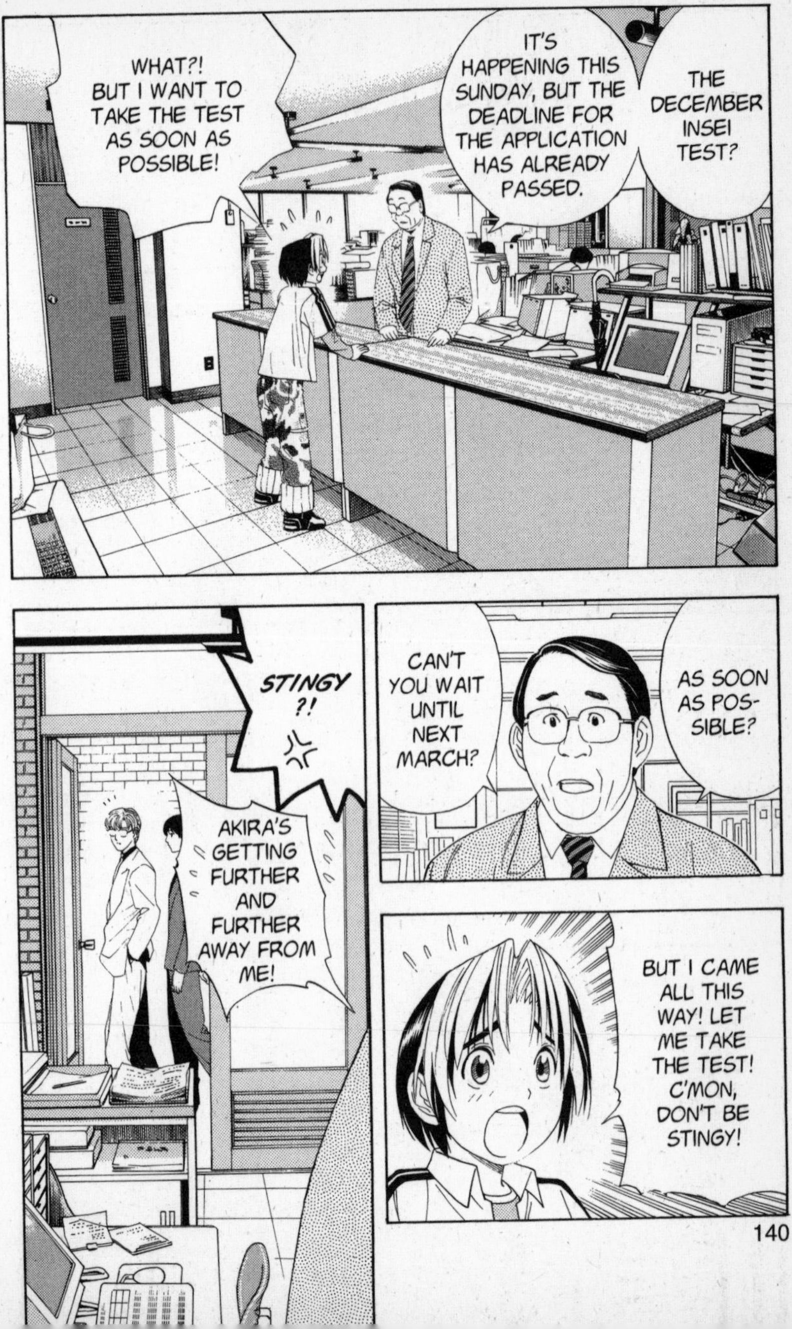
THE DECEMBER INSEI TEST?
IT'S HAPPENING THIS SUNDAY, BUT THE DEADLINE FOR THE APPLICATION HAS ALREADY PASSED.
WHAT?! BUT I WANT TO TAKE THE TEST AS SOON AS POSSIBLE!
AS SOON AS POS-SIBLE?
CAN'T YOU WAIT UNTIL NEXT MARCH?
BUT I CAME ALL THIS WAY! LET ME TAKE THE TEST! C'MON, DON'T BE STINGY!
STINGY?!
AKIRA'S GETTING FURTHER AND FURTHER AWAY FROM ME!

READ THIS WAY

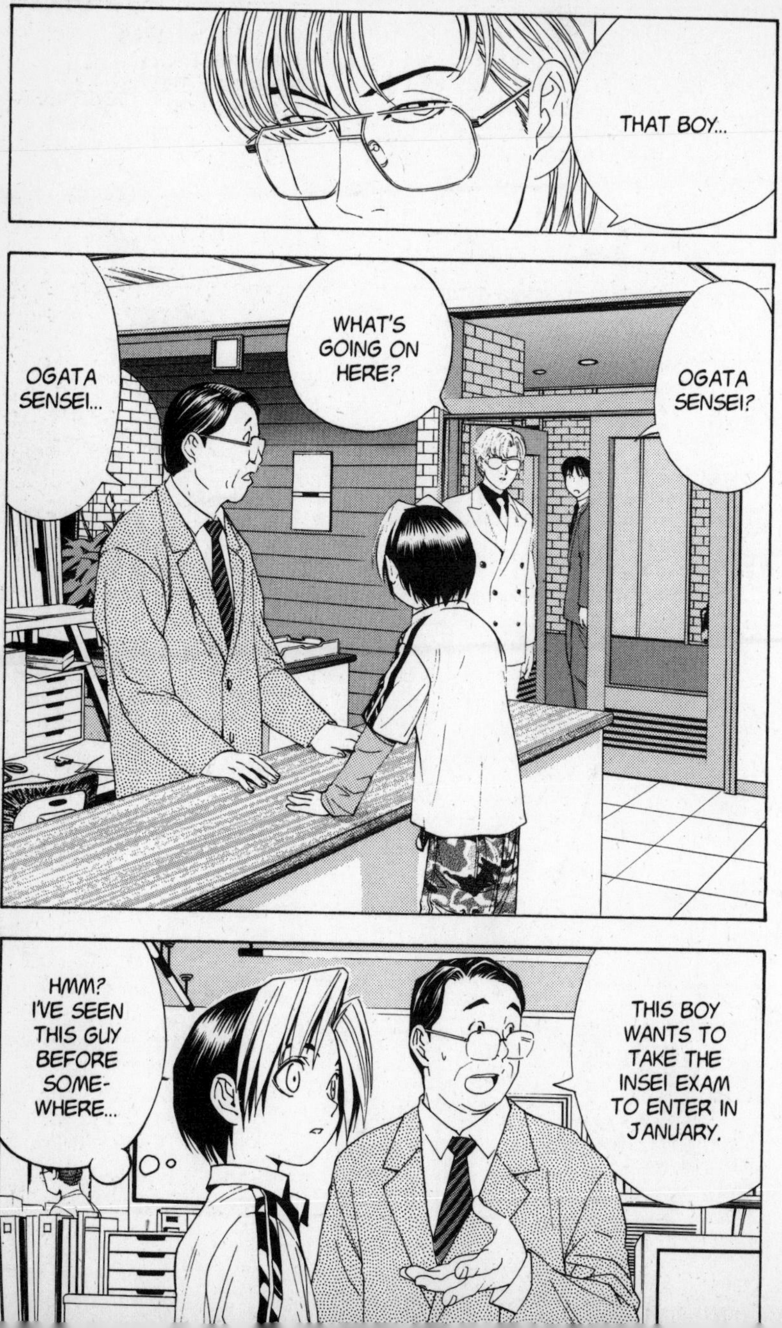
THAT BOY...
OGATA SENSEI?
WHAT'S GOING ON HERE?
OGATA SENSEI...
THIS BOY WANTS TO TAKE THE INSEI EXAM TO ENTER IN JANUARY.
HMM? I'VE SEEN THIS GUY BEFORE SOME-WHERE...

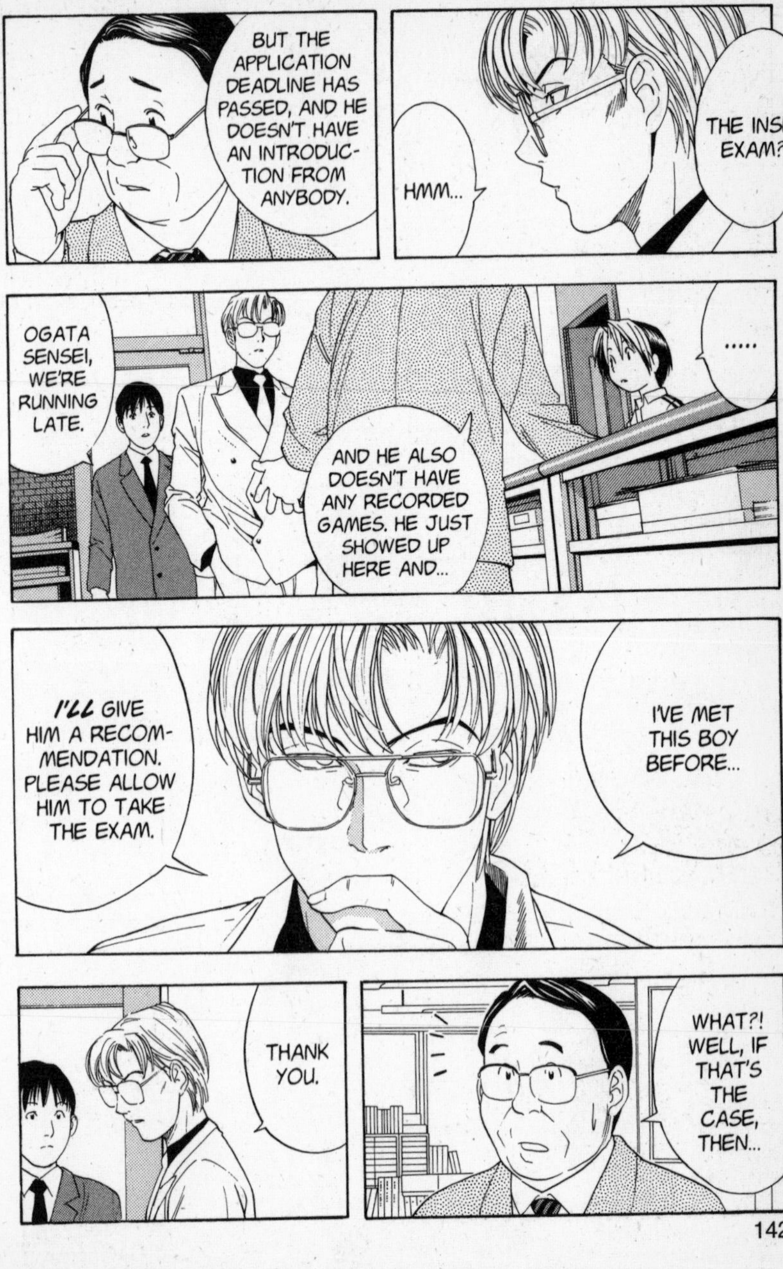

THE INSEI EXAM?
HMM...
BUT THE APPLICATION DEADLINE HAS PASSED, AND HE DOESN'T HAVE AN INTRODUCTION FROM ANYBODY.
.....
AND HE ALSO DOESN'T HAVE ANY RECORDED GAMES. HE JUST SHOWED UP HERE AND...
OGATA SENSEI, WE'RE RUNNING LATE.
I'VE MET THIS BOY BEFORE...
I'LL GIVE HIM A RECOMMENDATION. PLEASE ALLOW HIM TO TAKE THE EXAM.
WHAT?! WELL, IF THAT'S THE CASE, THEN...
THANK YOU.

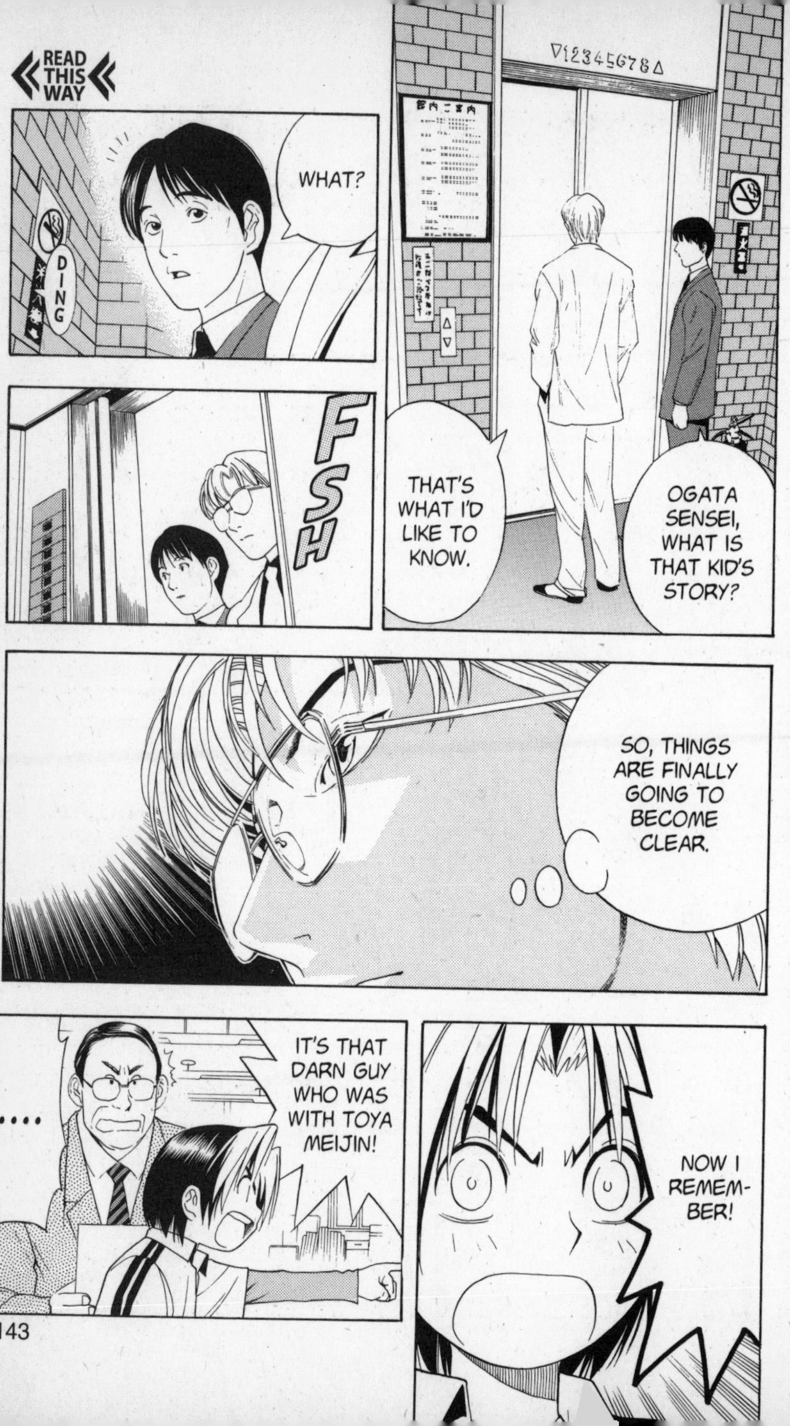
READ THIS WAY
OGATA SENSEI, WHAT IS THAT KID'S STORY?
THAT'S WHAT I'D LIKE TO KNOW.
WHAT?
DING
FSH
SO, THINGS ARE FINALLY GOING TO BECOME CLEAR.
NOW I REMEMBER!
IT'S THAT DARN GUY WHO WAS WITH TOYA MEIJIN!
.....

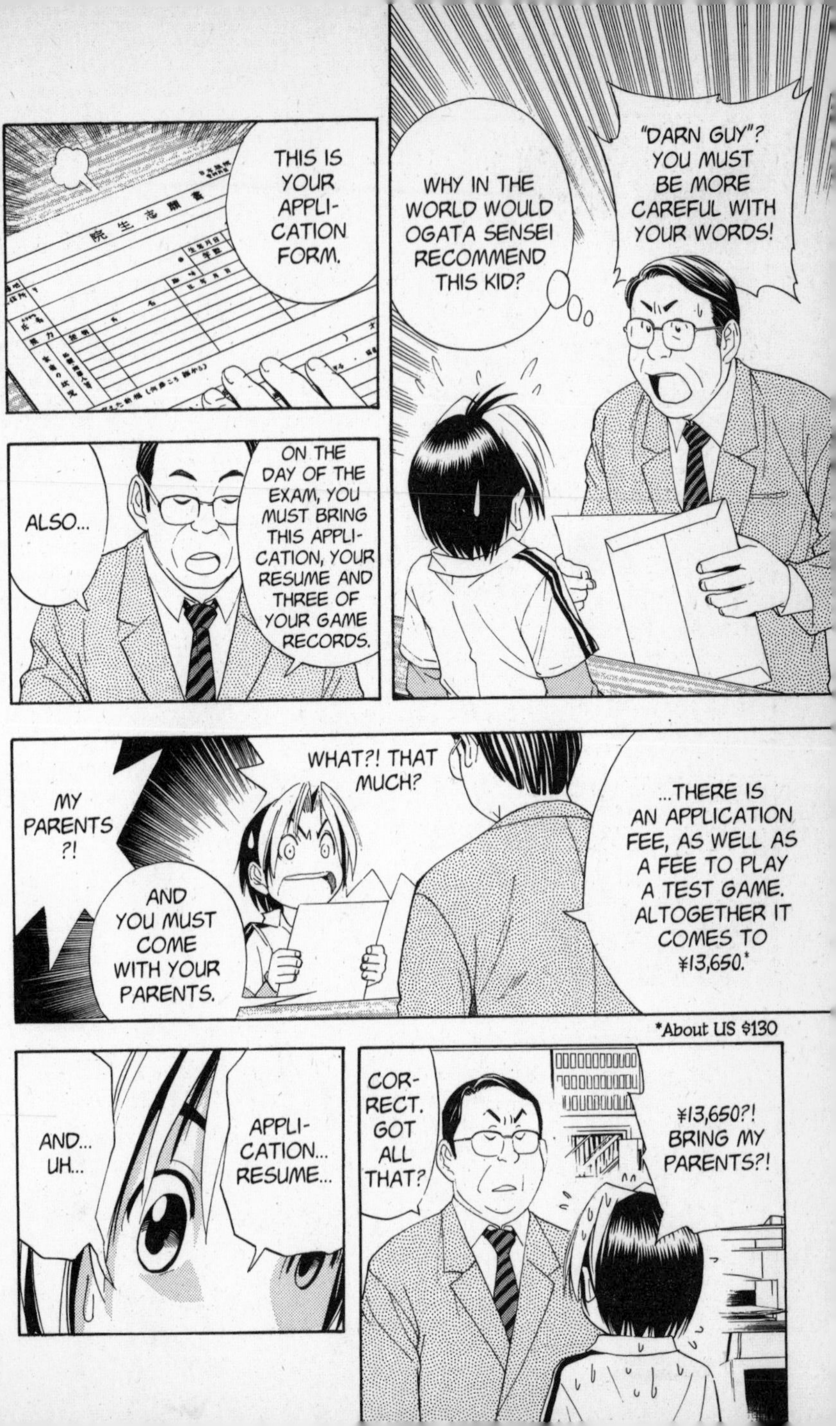
"DARN GUY"? YOU MUST BE MORE CAREFUL WITH YOUR WORDS!
WHY IN THE WORLD WOULD OGATA SENSEI RECOMMEND THIS KID?
THIS IS YOUR APPLICATION FORM.
ON THE DAY OF THE EXAM, YOU MUST BRING THIS APPLICATION, YOUR RESUME AND THREE OF YOUR GAME RECORDS.
ALSO...
...THERE IS AN APPLICATION FEE, AS WELL AS A FEE TO PLAY A TEST GAME. ALTOGETHER IT COMES TO ¥13,650.*
WHAT?! THAT MUCH?
AND YOU MUST COME WITH YOUR PARENTS.
MY PARENTS ?!
*About US $130
¥13,650?! BRING MY PARENTS?!
CORRECT. GOT ALL THAT?
APPLICATION... RESUME...
AND... UH...

READ THIS WAY

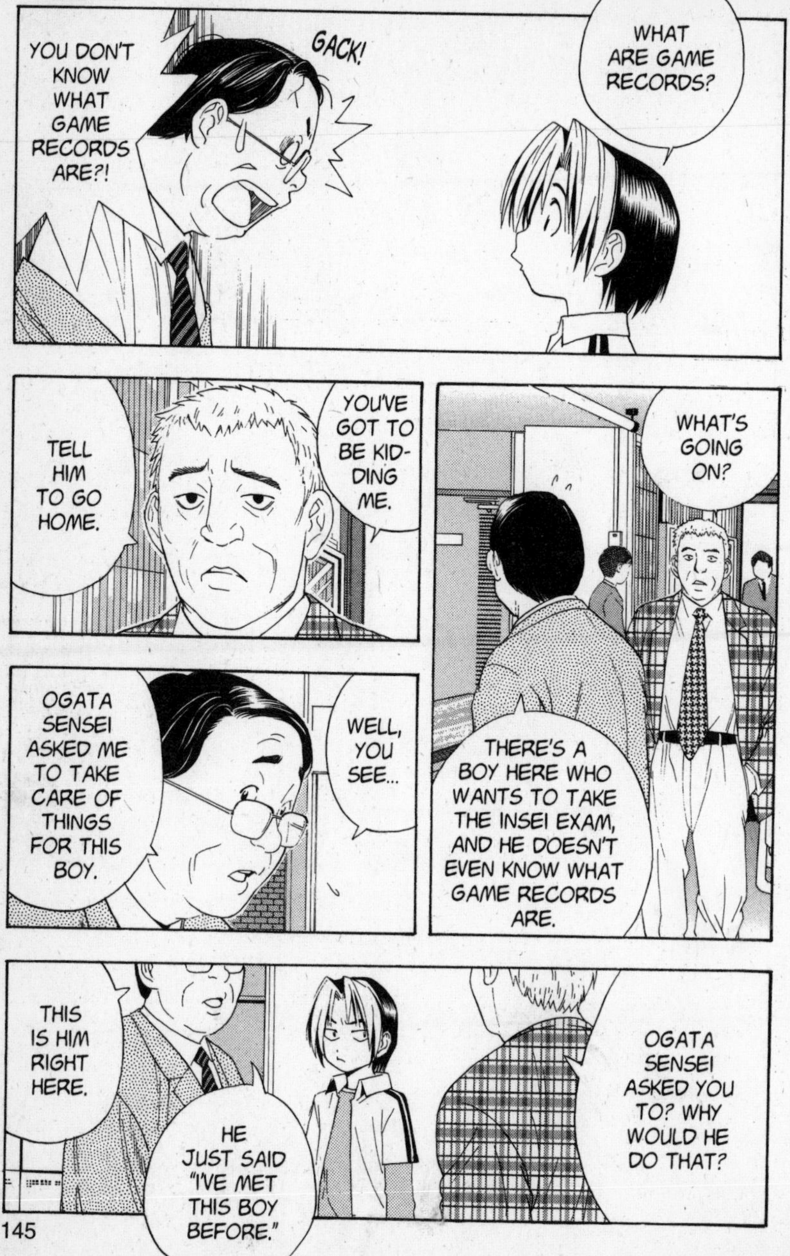
WHAT ARE GAME RECORDS?
GACK!
YOU DON'T KNOW WHAT GAME RECORDS ARE?!
WHAT'S GOING ON?
THERE'S A BOY HERE WHO WANTS TO TAKE THE INSEI EXAM, AND HE DOESN'T EVEN KNOW WHAT GAME RECORDS ARE.
YOU'VE GOT TO BE KID-DING ME.
TELL HIM TO GO HOME.
WELL, YOU SEE...
OGATA SENSEI ASKED ME TO TAKE CARE OF THINGS FOR THIS BOY.
OGATA SENSEI ASKED YOU TO? WHY WOULD HE DO THAT?
HE JUST SAID "I'VE MET THIS BOY BEFORE."
THIS IS HIM RIGHT HERE.

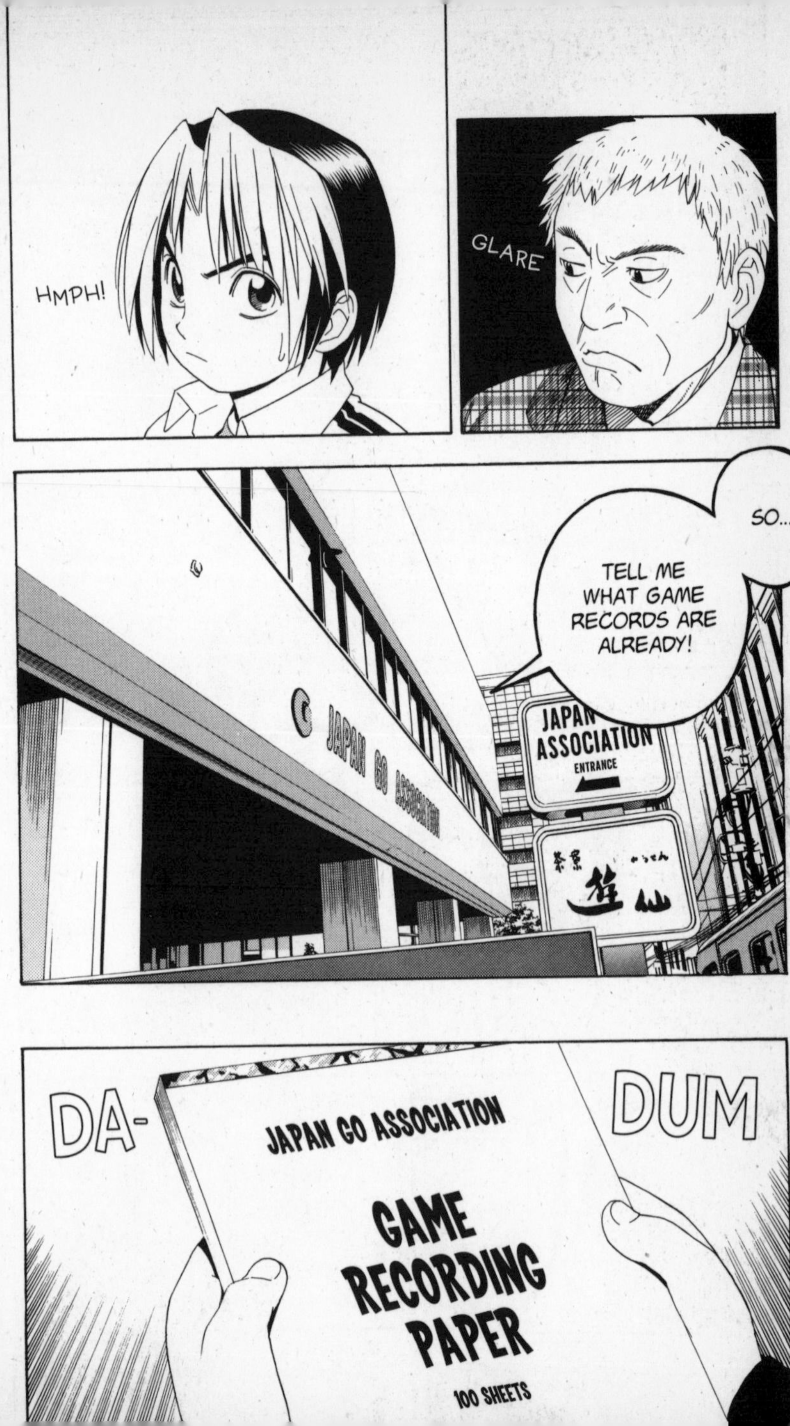
GLARE
HMPH!
SO...
TELL ME WHAT GAME RECORDS ARE ALREADY!
JAPAN GO ASSOCIATION
JAPAN ASSOCIATION
ENTRANCE
DA-
DUM
JAPAN GO ASSOCIATION
GAME RECORDING PAPER
100 SHEETS

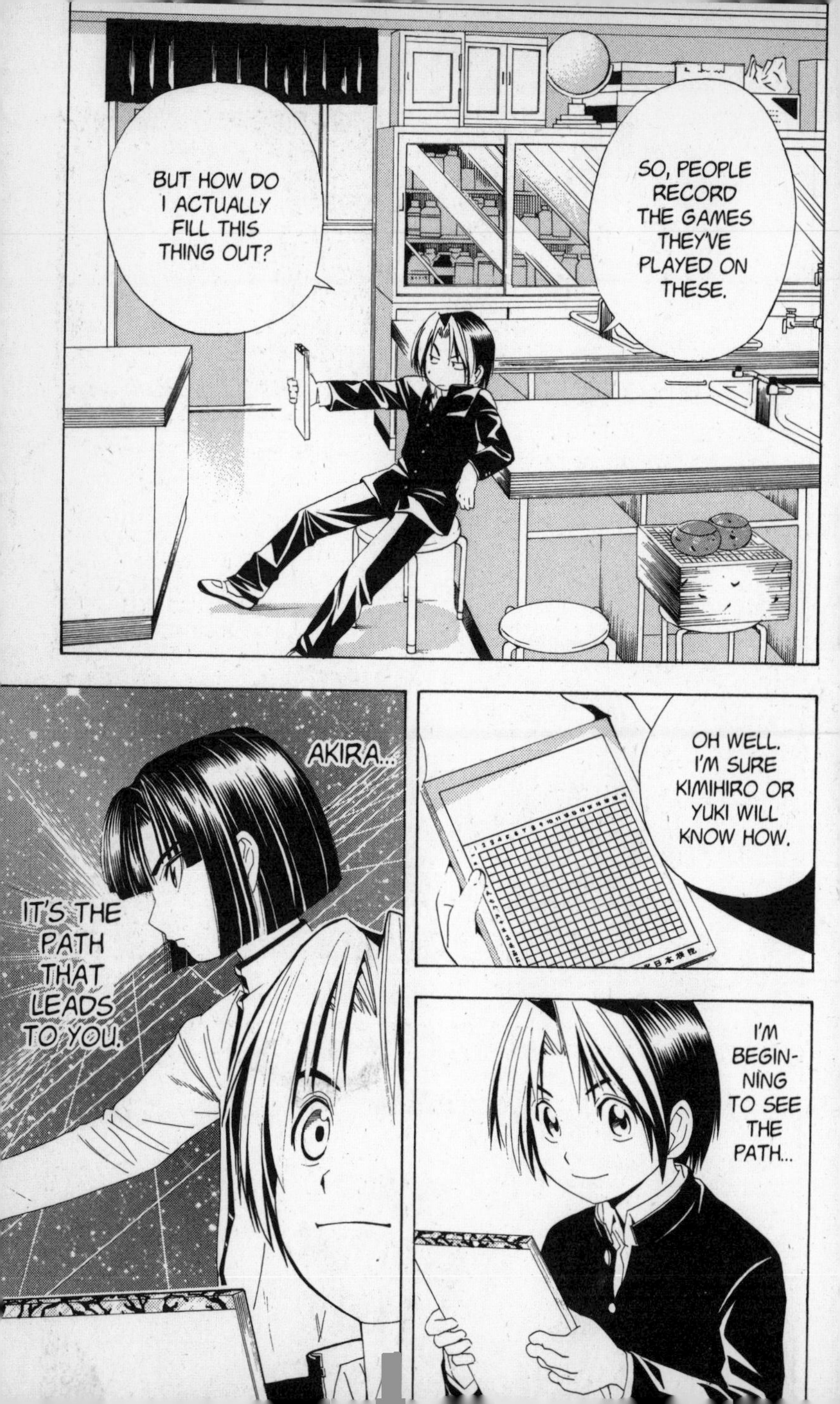
SO, PEOPLE RECORD THE GAMES THEY'VE PLAYED ON THESE.
BUT HOW DO I ACTUALLY FILL THIS THING OUT?
OH WELL. I'M SURE KIMIHIRO OR YUKI WILL KNOW HOW.
I'M BEGIN-NING TO SEE THE PATH...
AKIRA...
IT'S THE PATH THAT LEADS TO YOU.

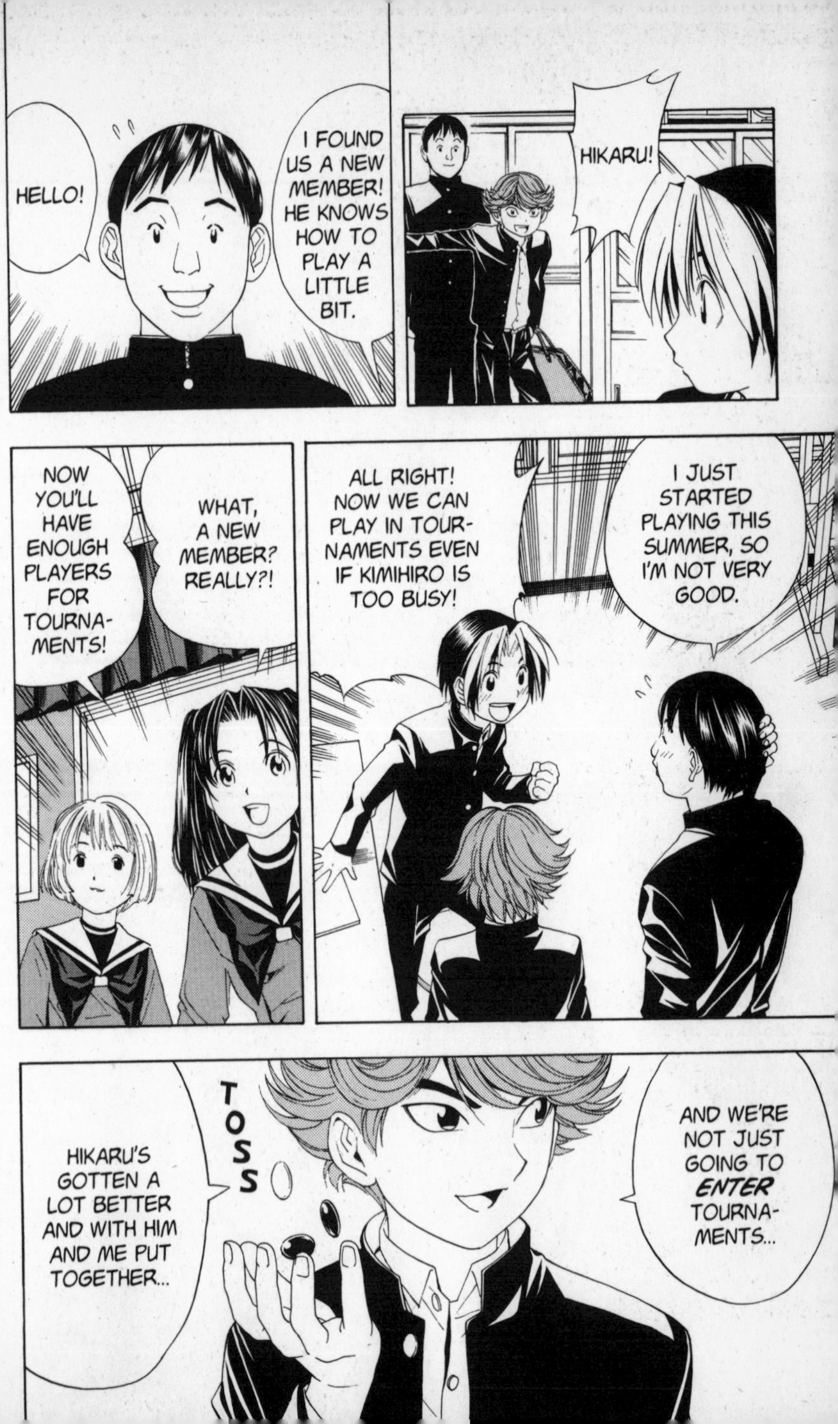
HIKARU!
I FOUND US A NEW MEMBER! HE KNOWS HOW TO PLAY A LITTLE BIT.
HELLO!
I JUST STARTED PLAYING THIS SUMMER, SO I'M NOT VERY GOOD.
ALL RIGHT! NOW WE CAN PLAY IN TOURNAMENTS EVEN IF KIMIHIRO IS TOO BUSY!
WHAT, A NEW MEMBER? REALLY?!
NOW YOU'LL HAVE ENOUGH PLAYERS FOR TOURNAMENTS!
AND WE'RE NOT JUST GOING TO *ENTER* TOURNAMENTS...
TOSS
HIKARU'S GOTTEN A LOT BETTER AND WITH HIM AND ME PUT TOGETHER...

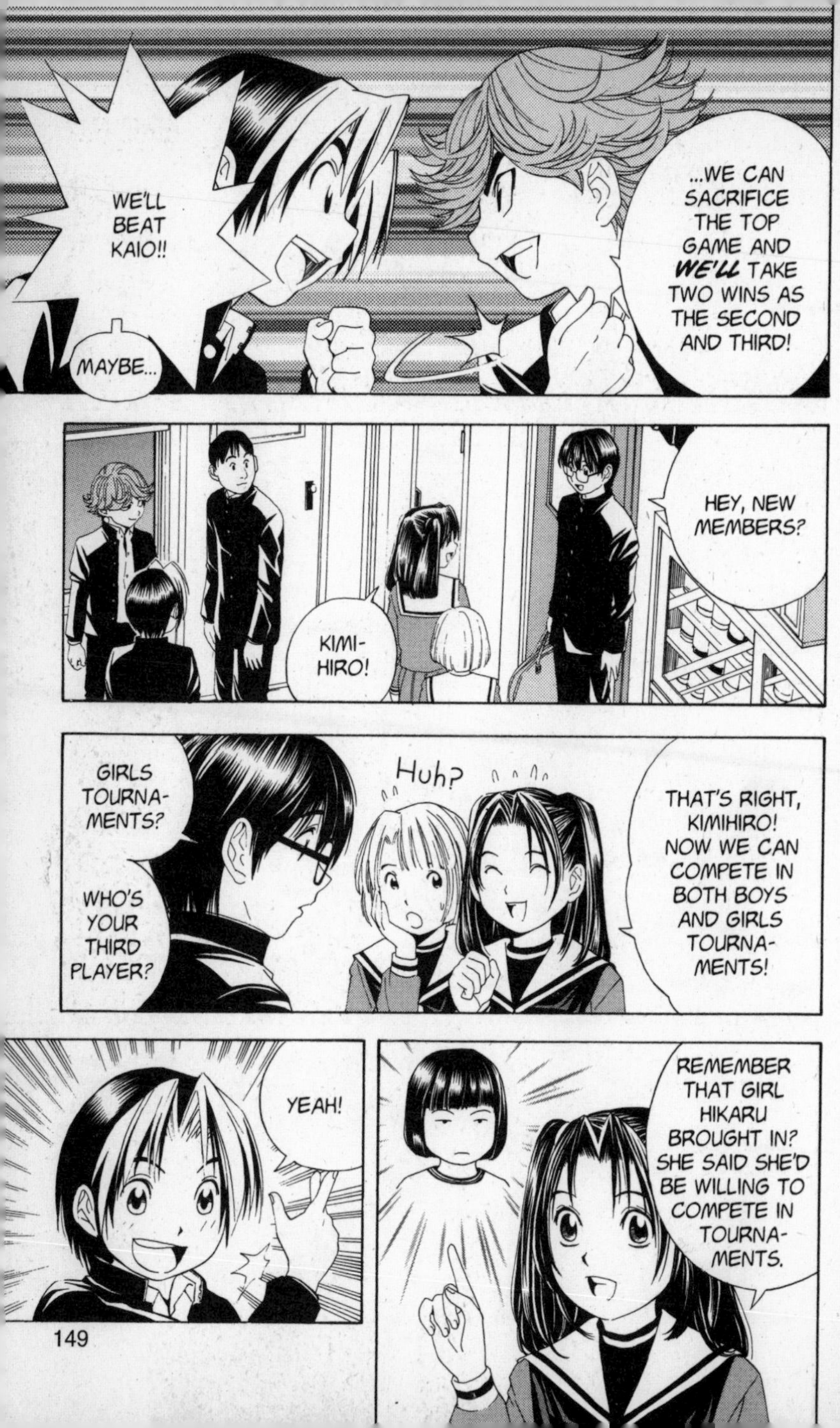
...WE CAN SACRIFICE THE TOP GAME AND **WE'LL** TAKE TWO WINS AS THE SECOND AND THIRD!
WE'LL BEAT KAIO!!
MAYBE...
HEY, NEW MEMBERS?
KIMI-HIRO!
THAT'S RIGHT, KIMIHIRO! NOW WE CAN COMPETE IN BOTH BOYS AND GIRLS TOURNA-MENTS!
Huh?
GIRLS TOURNA-MENTS?
WHO'S YOUR THIRD PLAYER?
REMEMBER THAT GIRL HIKARU BROUGHT IN? SHE SAID SHE'D BE WILLING TO COMPETE IN TOURNA-MENTS.
YEAH!

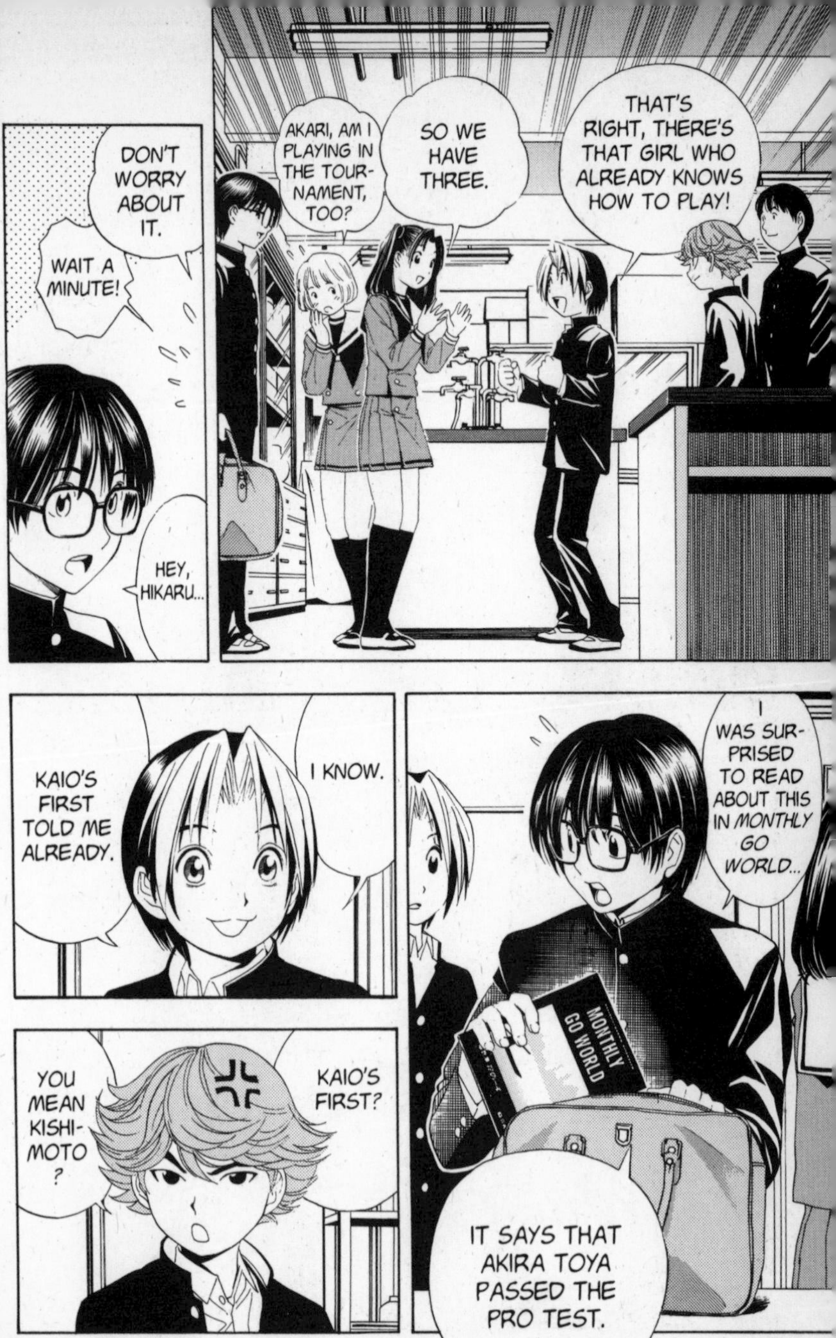

THAT'S RIGHT, THERE'S THAT GIRL WHO ALREADY KNOWS HOW TO PLAY!
SO WE HAVE THREE.
AKARI, AM I PLAYING IN THE TOURNAMENT, TOO?
DON'T WORRY ABOUT IT.
WAIT A MINUTE!
HEY, HIKARU...
I WAS SURPRISED TO READ ABOUT THIS IN *MONTHLY GO WORLD*...
MONTHLY GO WORLD
IT SAYS THAT AKIRA TOYA PASSED THE PRO TEST.
I KNOW.
KAIO'S FIRST TOLD ME ALREADY.
KAIO'S FIRST?
YOU MEAN KISHIMOTO?

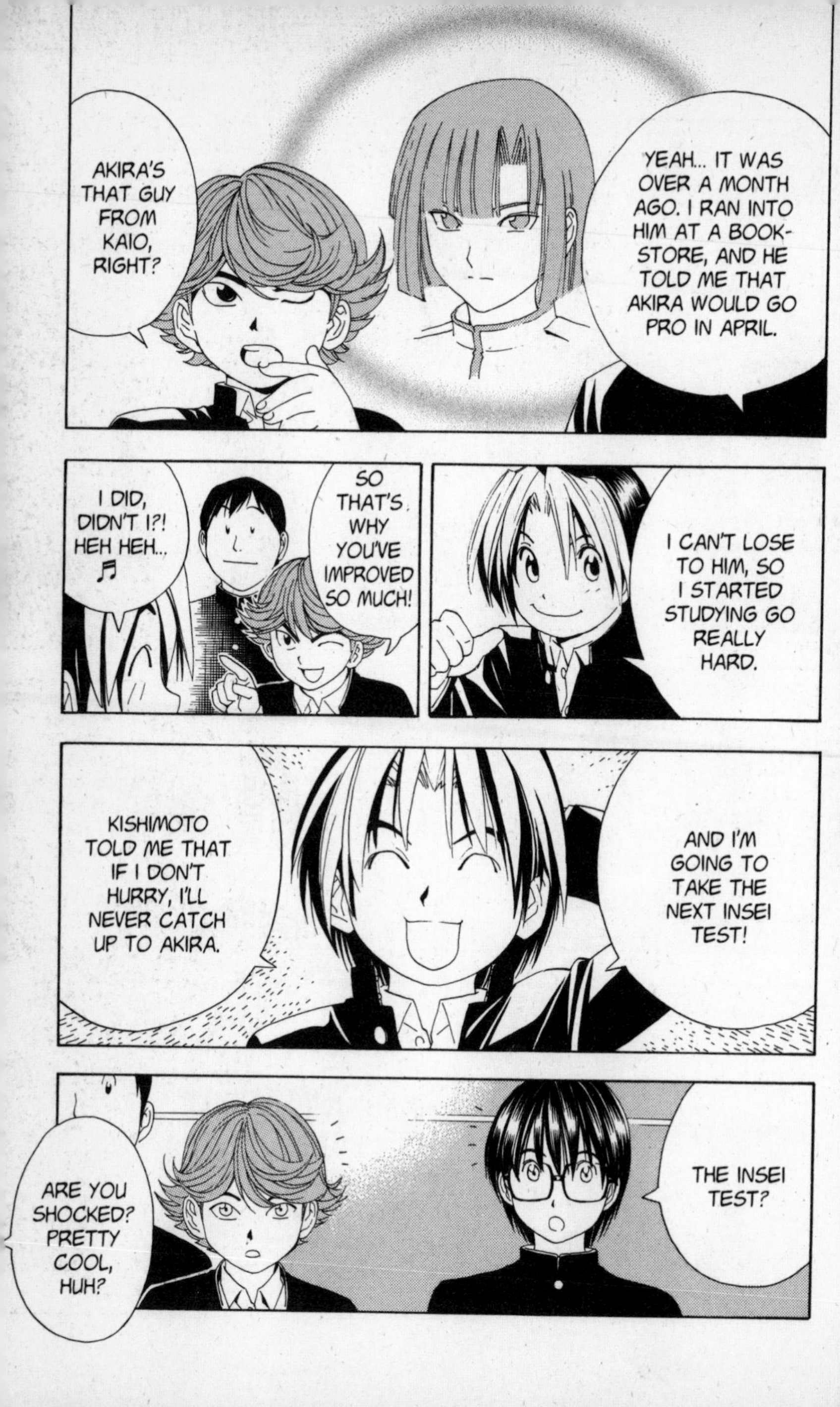

AKIRA'S THAT GUY FROM KAIO, RIGHT?
YEAH... IT WAS OVER A MONTH AGO. I RAN INTO HIM AT A BOOK-STORE, AND HE TOLD ME THAT AKIRA WOULD GO PRO IN APRIL.
I CAN'T LOSE TO HIM, SO I STARTED STUDYING GO REALLY HARD.
SO THAT'S WHY YOU'VE IMPROVED SO MUCH!
I DID, DIDN'T I?! HEH HEH... ♬
KISHIMOTO TOLD ME THAT IF I DON'T HURRY, I'LL NEVER CATCH UP TO AKIRA.
AND I'M GOING TO TAKE THE NEXT INSEI TEST!
THE INSEI TEST?
ARE YOU SHOCKED? PRETTY COOL, HUH?

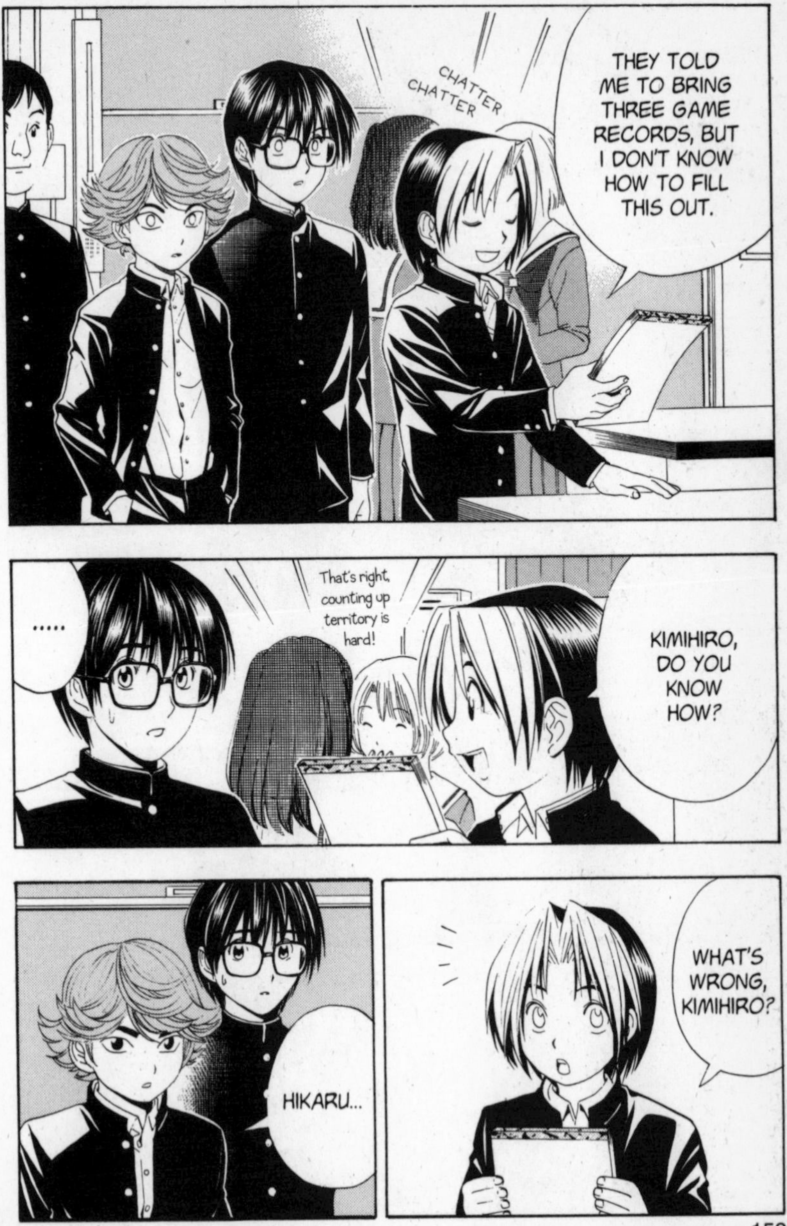
CHATTER CHATTER
THEY TOLD ME TO BRING THREE GAME RECORDS, BUT I DON'T KNOW HOW TO FILL THIS OUT.
KIMIHIRO, DO YOU KNOW HOW?
That's right, counting up territory is hard!
......
WHAT'S WRONG, KIMIHIRO?
HIKARU...

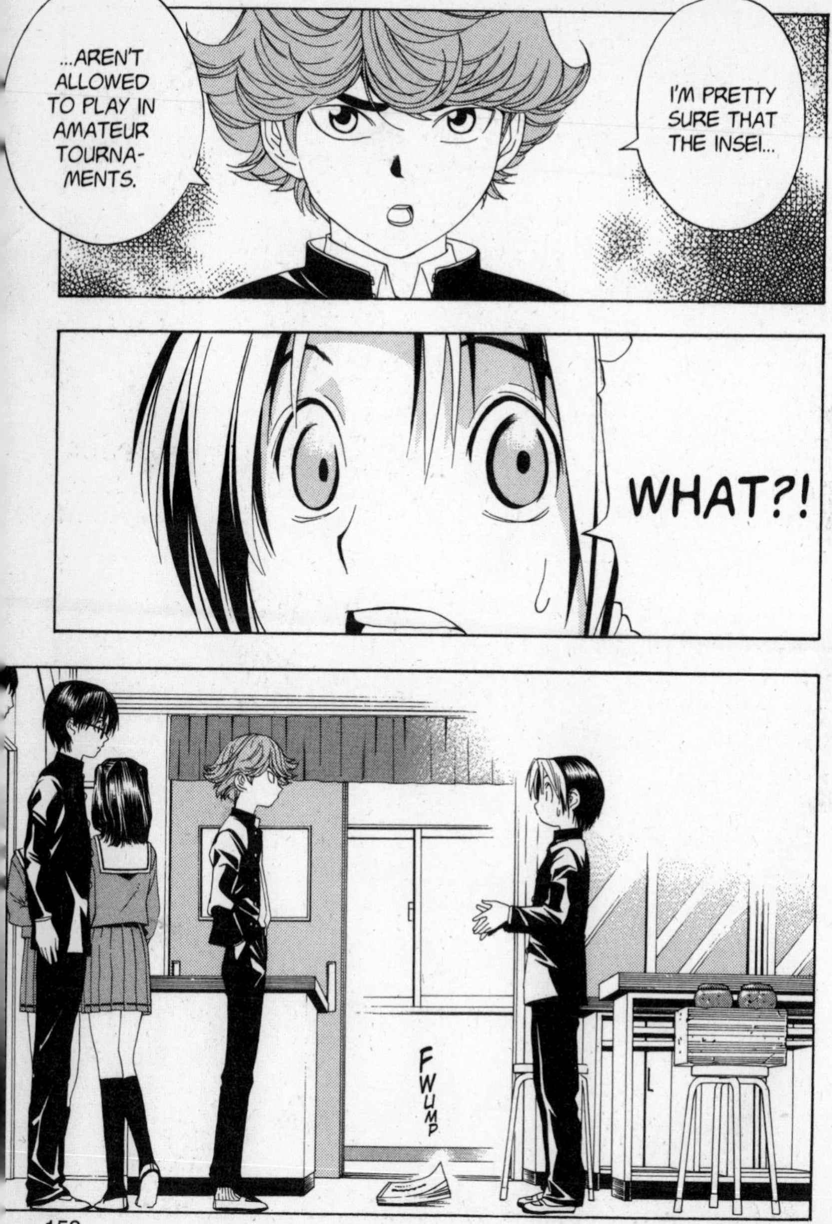
I'M PRETTY SURE THAT THE INSEI...
...AREN'T ALLOWED TO PLAY IN AMATEUR TOURNA-MENTS.
WHAT?!
FWUMP

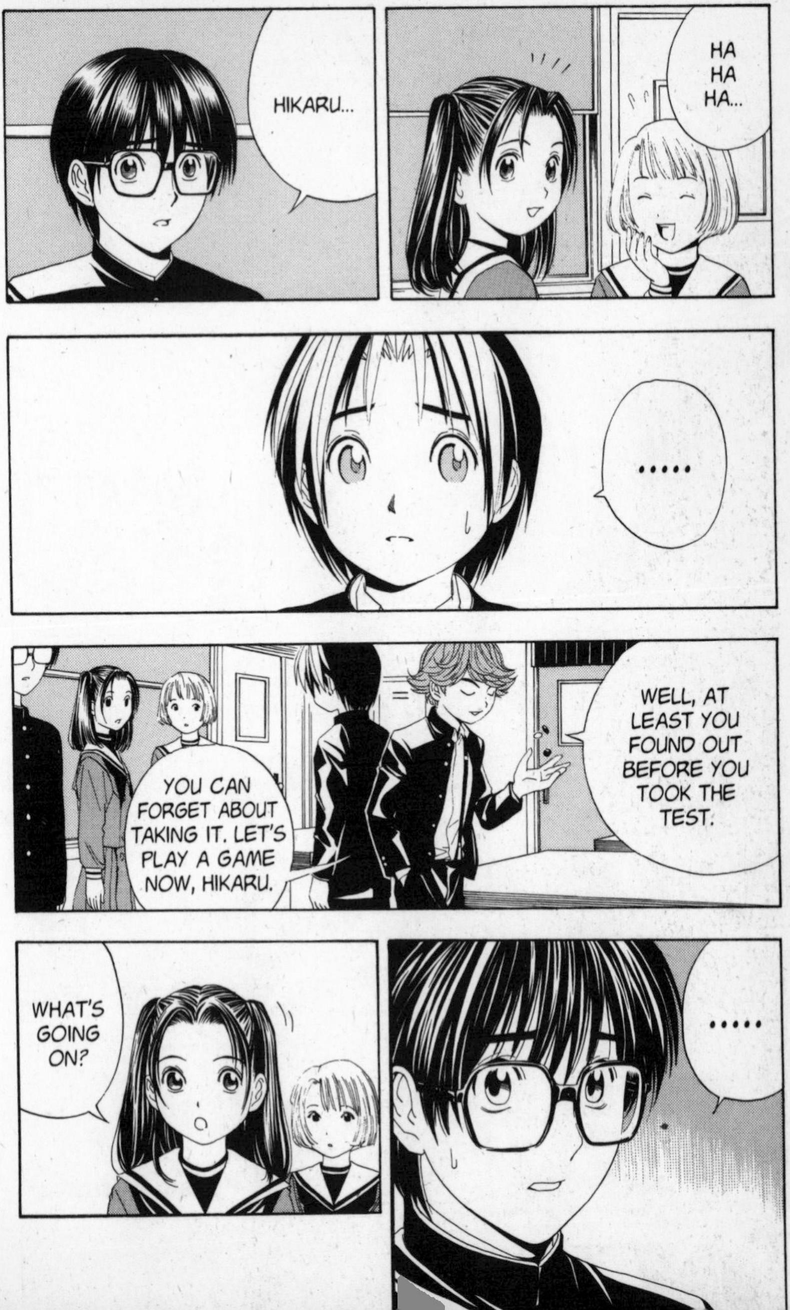
HA HA HA...
HIKARU...
.....
WELL, AT LEAST YOU FOUND OUT BEFORE YOU TOOK THE TEST.
YOU CAN FORGET ABOUT TAKING IT. LET'S PLAY A GAME NOW, HIKARU.
.....
WHAT'S GOING ON?

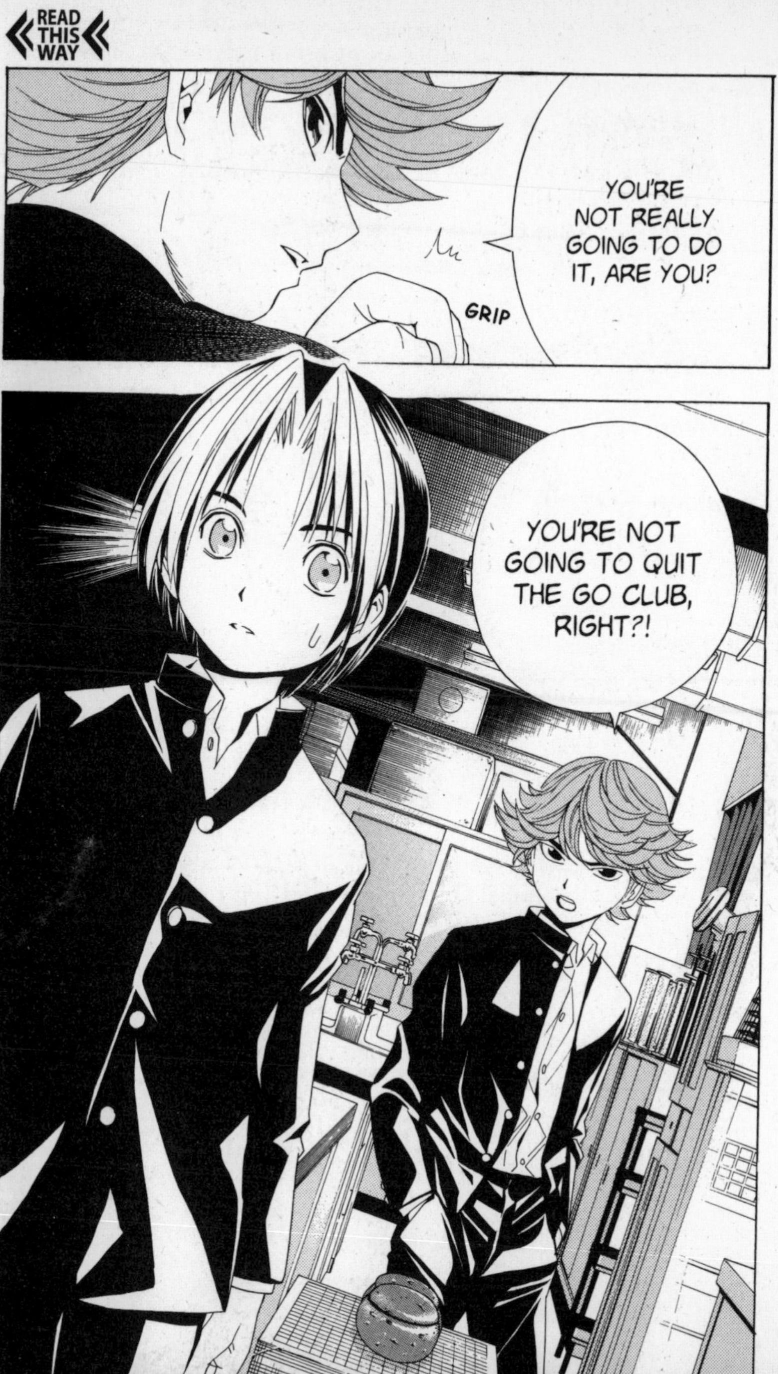
READ THIS WAY
YOU'RE NOT REALLY GOING TO DO IT, ARE YOU?
GRIP
YOU'RE NOT GOING TO QUIT THE GO CLUB, RIGHT?!

A WORD ABOUT HIKARU NO GO

MANGA PRINT TYPES

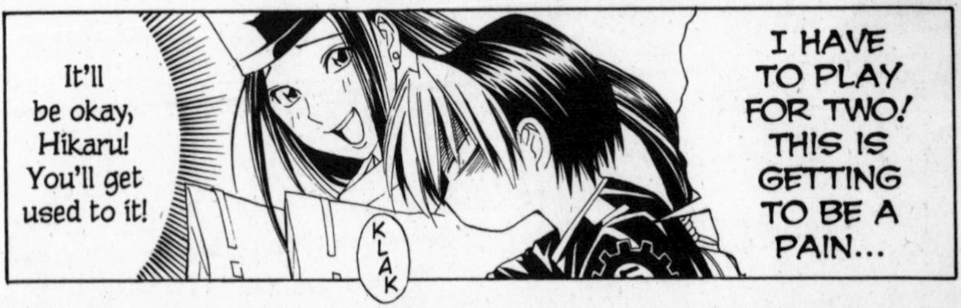
I HAVE TO PLAY FOR TWO! THIS IS GETTING TO BE A PAIN...
KLAK
It'll be okay, Hikaru! You'll get used to it!

THE ABOVE PANEL SHOWS THREE DIFFERENT KINDS OF PRINT TYPES (OR FONTS).

THE EDITOR OF A GIVEN TITLE DECIDES ON THE STYLE AND SIZE OF THE FONTS. THEY MUST CHOOSE FROM OVER 2,000 DIFFERENT STYLES.

THE FONT IS A PART OF THE MANGA.

HIKARU'S LINE, "THIS IS GETTING TO BE A PAIN!" IS SET IN AN EXASPERATED STYLE. SAI'S LINES ARE ALWAYS DONE IN A SLIGHTLY GHOSTLY (?) TYPE. IT'S FUN TO COMPARE THE DIFFERENT FONT STYLES.

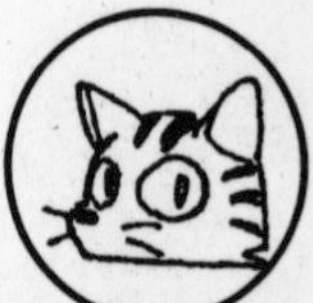

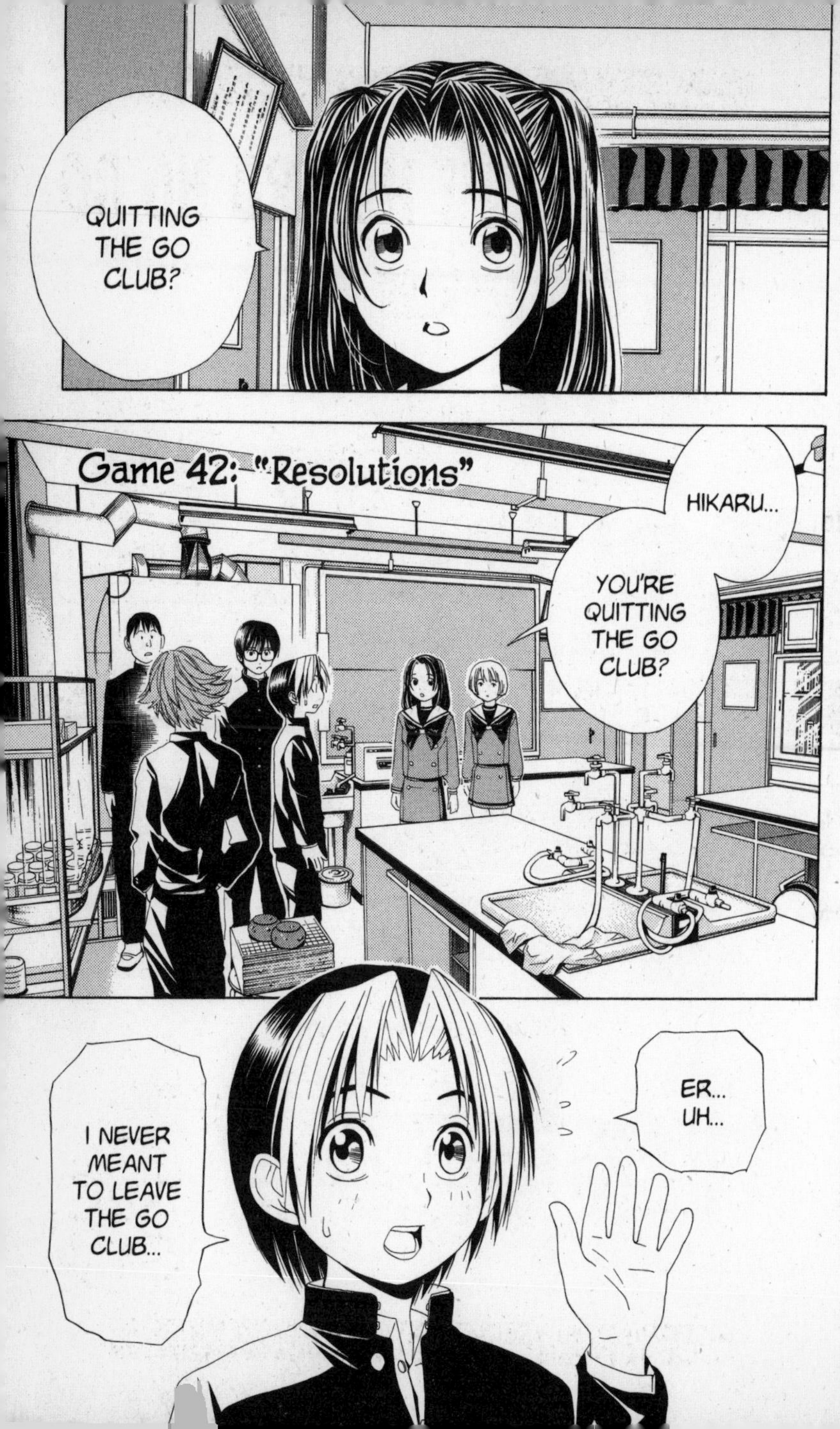
QUITTING THE GO CLUB?
Game 42: "Resolutions"
HIKARU...
YOU'RE QUITTING THE GO CLUB?
ER... UH...
I NEVER MEANT TO LEAVE THE GO CLUB...

Game 42

"Resolutions"

READ THIS WAY

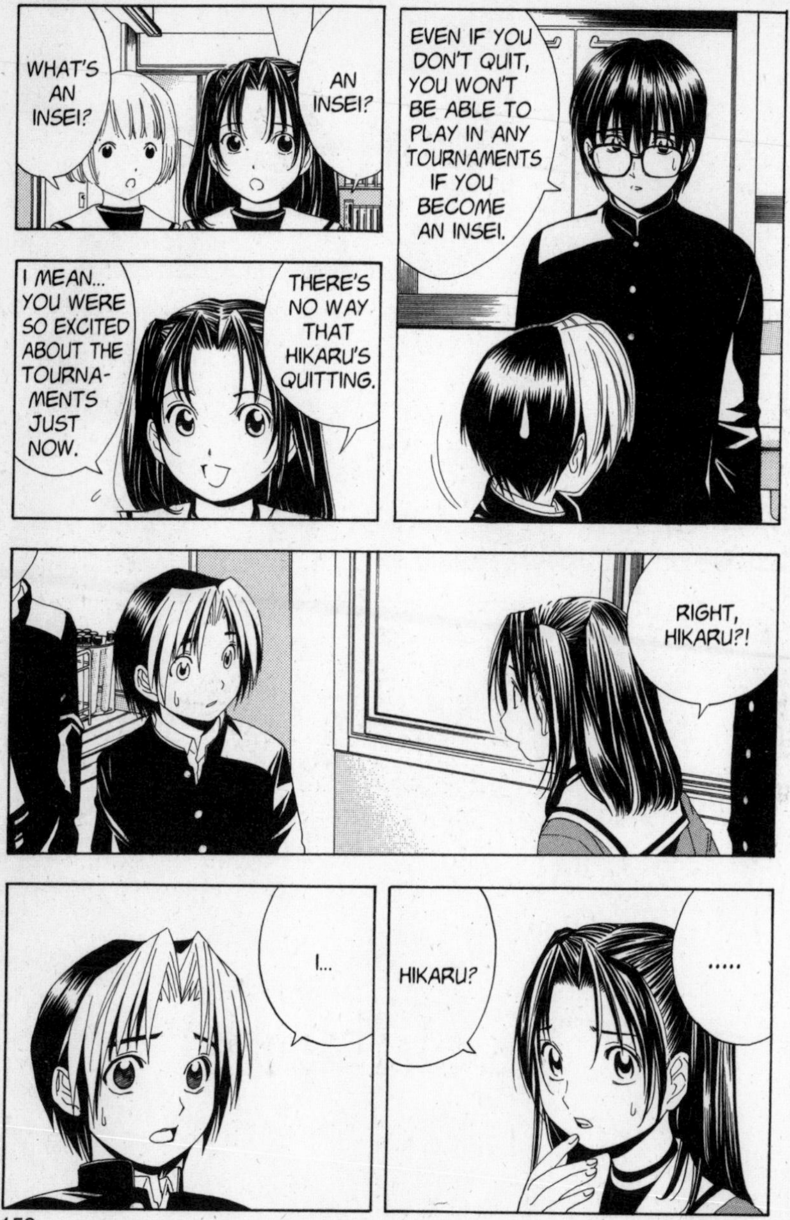
EVEN IF YOU DON'T QUIT, YOU WON'T BE ABLE TO PLAY IN ANY TOURNAMENTS IF YOU BECOME AN INSEI.
AN INSEI?
WHAT'S AN INSEI?
THERE'S NO WAY THAT HIKARU'S QUITTING.
I MEAN... YOU WERE SO EXCITED ABOUT THE TOURNA-MENTS JUST NOW.
RIGHT, HIKARU?!
.....
HIKARU?
I...

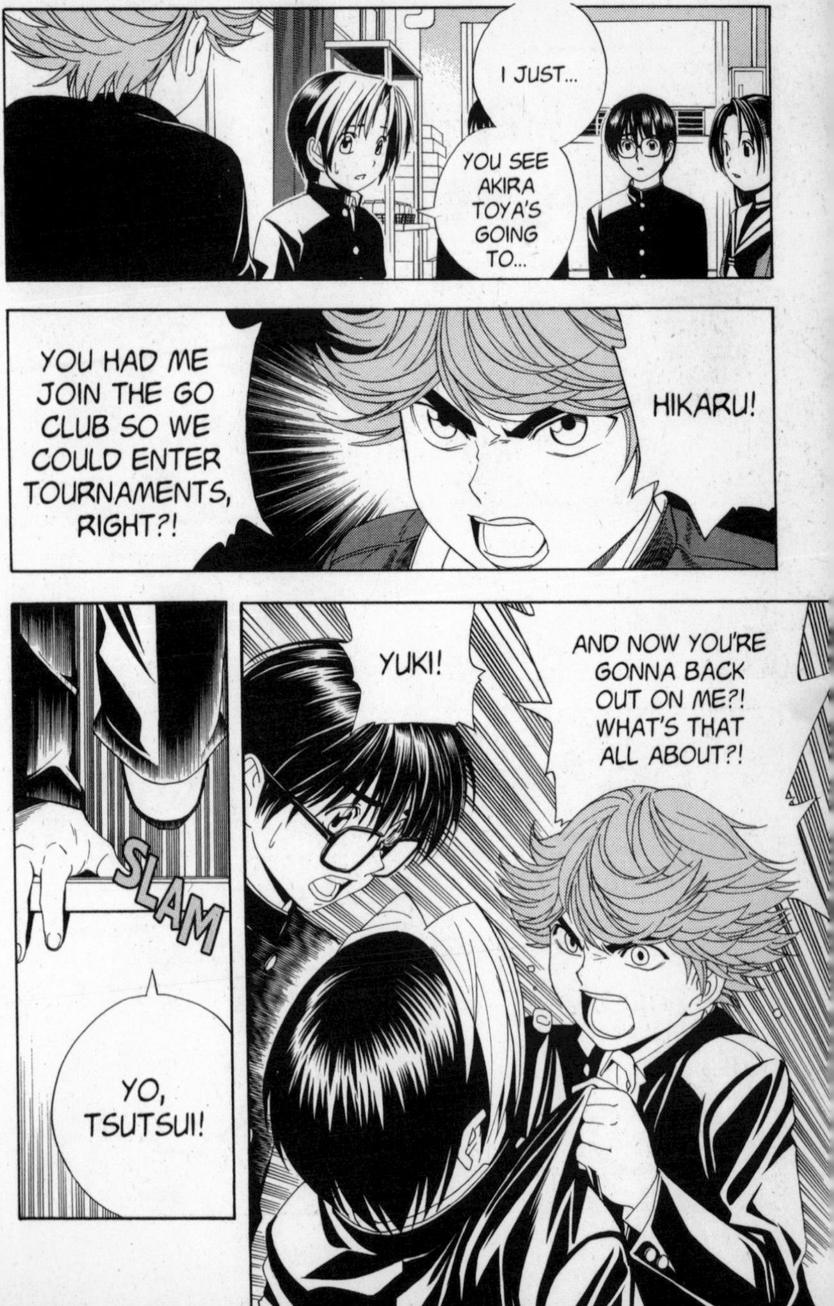
I JUST...
YOU SEE AKIRA TOYA'S GOING TO...
HIKARU!
YOU HAD ME JOIN THE GO CLUB SO WE COULD ENTER TOURNAMENTS, RIGHT?!
AND NOW YOU'RE GONNA BACK OUT ON ME?! WHAT'S THAT ALL ABOUT?!
YUKI!
SLAM
YO, TSUTSUI!

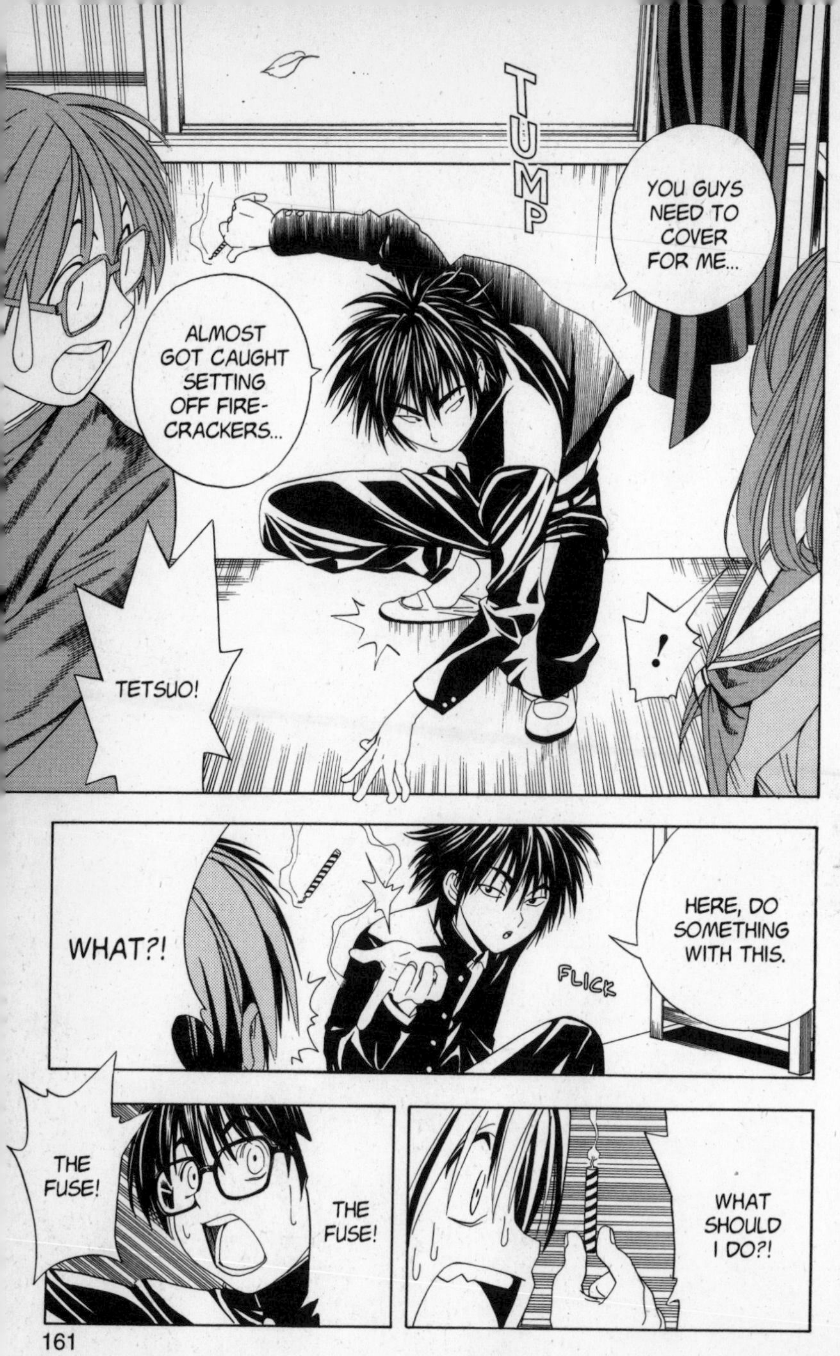
YOU GUYS NEED TO COVER FOR ME...
TUMP
ALMOST GOT CAUGHT SETTING OFF FIRE-CRACKERS...
!
TETSUO!
HERE, DO SOMETHING WITH THIS.
FLICK
WHAT?!
WHAT SHOULD I DO?!
THE FUSE!
THE FUSE!

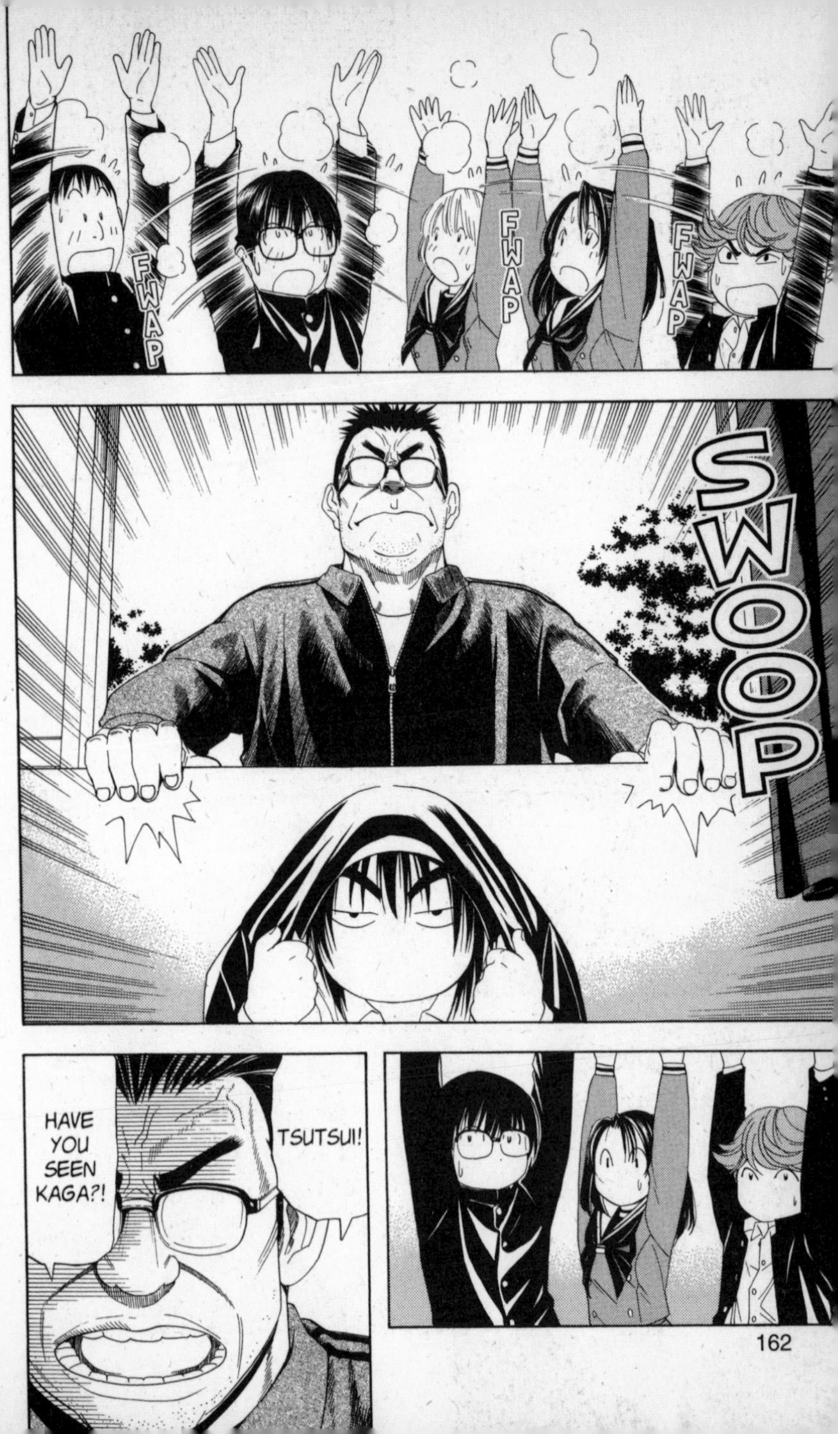
FWAP
FWAP
FWAP
SWOOP
TSUTSUI!
HAVE YOU SEEN KAGA?!

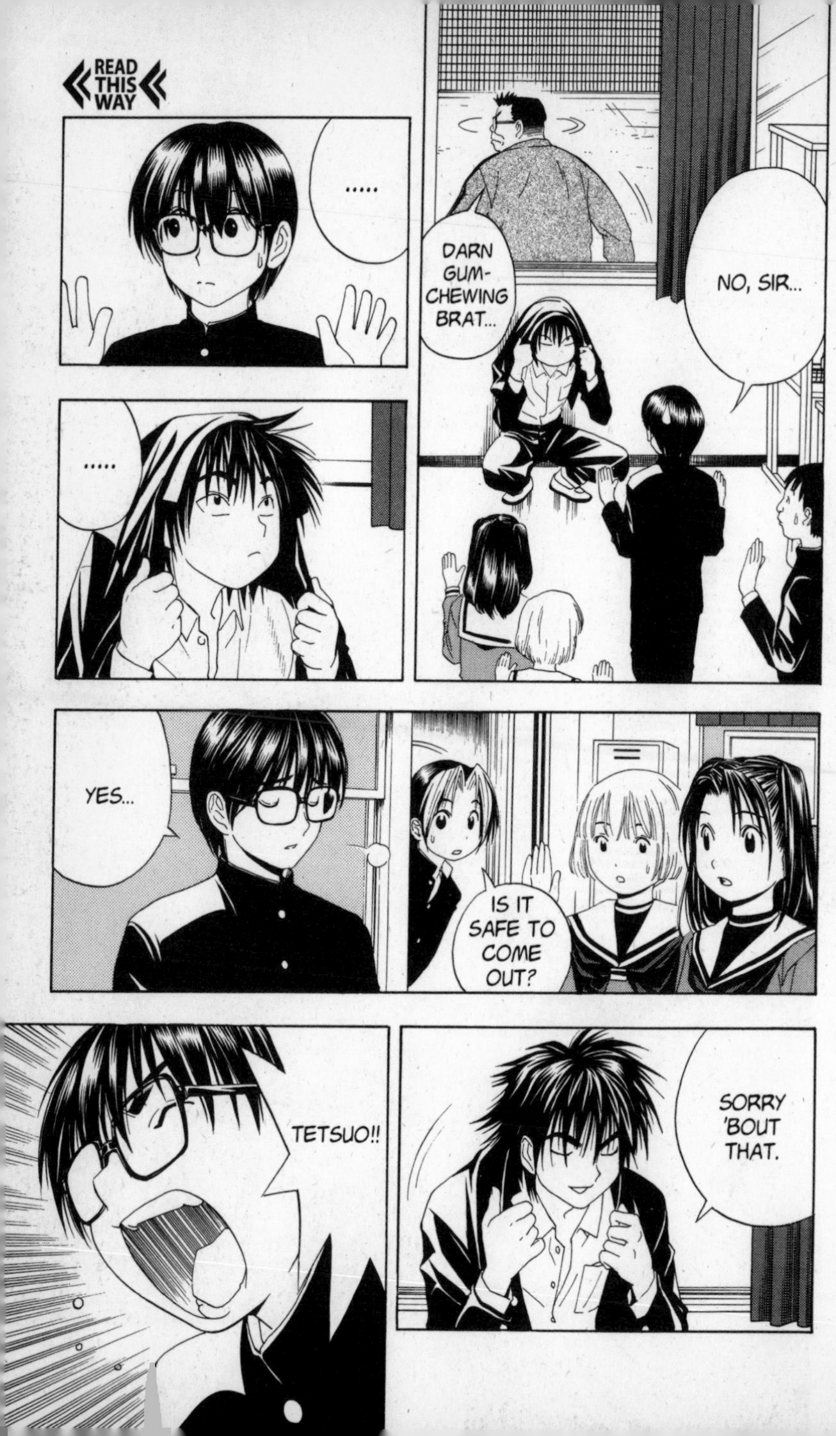
READ THIS WAY
NO, SIR...
DARN GUM-CHEWING BRAT...
.....
.....
IS IT SAFE TO COME OUT?
YES...
SORRY 'BOUT THAT.
TETSUO!!

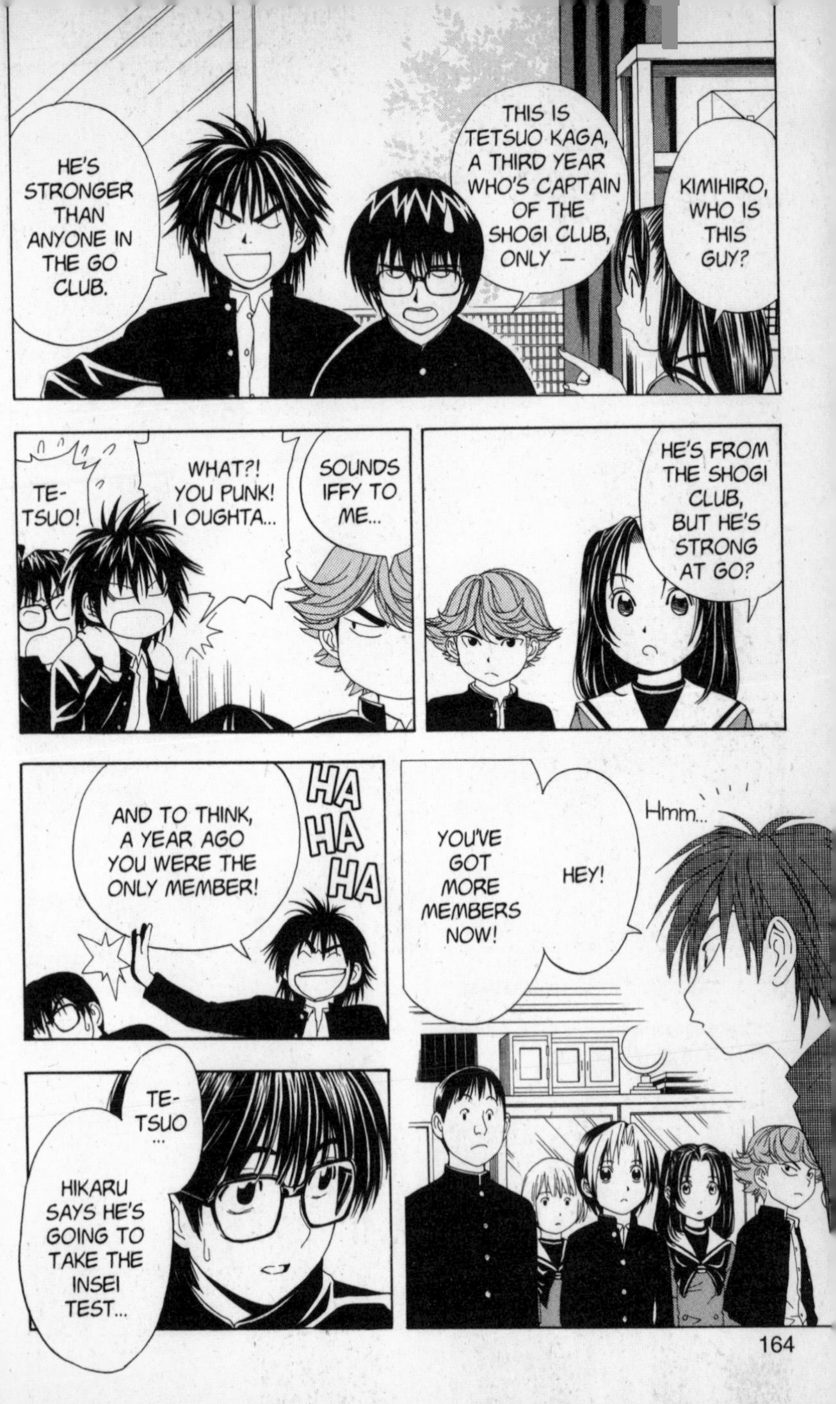
KIMIHIRO, WHO IS THIS GUY?
THIS IS TETSUO KAGA, A THIRD YEAR WHO'S CAPTAIN OF THE SHOGI CLUB, ONLY —
HE'S STRONGER THAN ANYONE IN THE GO CLUB.
HE'S FROM THE SHOGI CLUB, BUT HE'S STRONG AT GO?
SOUNDS IFFY TO ME...
WHAT?! YOU PUNK! I OUGHTA...
TE-TSUO!
Hmm...
HEY!
YOU'VE GOT MORE MEMBERS NOW!
HA HA HA
AND TO THINK, A YEAR AGO YOU WERE THE ONLY MEMBER!
TE-TSUO ...
HIKARU SAYS HE'S GOING TO TAKE THE INSEI TEST...

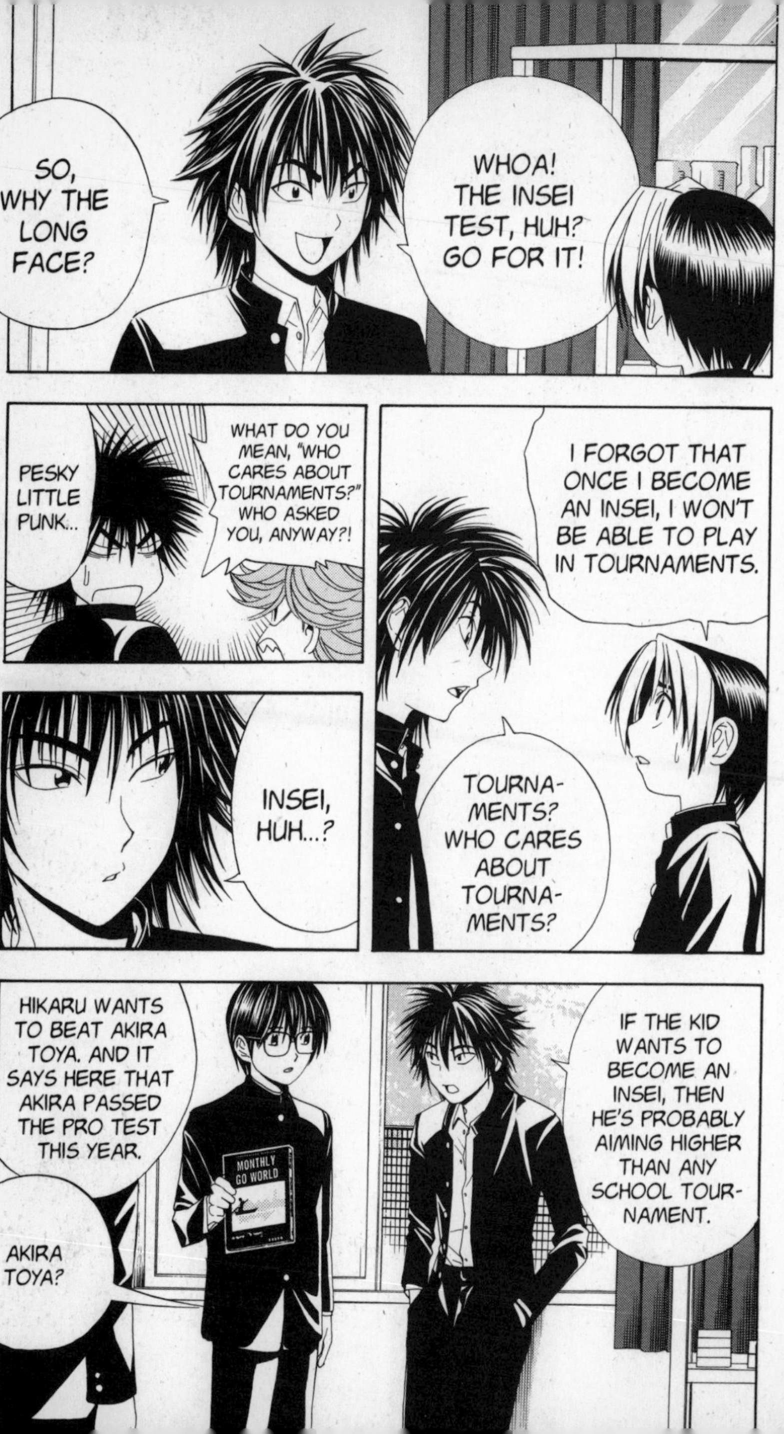

WHOA! THE INSEI TEST, HUH? GO FOR IT!
SO, WHY THE LONG FACE?
I FORGOT THAT ONCE I BECOME AN INSEI, I WON'T BE ABLE TO PLAY IN TOURNAMENTS.
TOURNA-MENTS? WHO CARES ABOUT TOURNA-MENTS?
WHAT DO YOU MEAN, "WHO CARES ABOUT TOURNAMENTS?" WHO ASKED YOU, ANYWAY?!
PESKY LITTLE PUNK...
INSEI, HUH...?
IF THE KID WANTS TO BECOME AN INSEI, THEN HE'S PROBABLY AIMING HIGHER THAN ANY SCHOOL TOUR-NAMENT.
HIKARU WANTS TO BEAT AKIRA TOYA. AND IT SAYS HERE THAT AKIRA PASSED THE PRO TEST THIS YEAR.
MONTHLY GO WORLD
AKIRA TOYA?

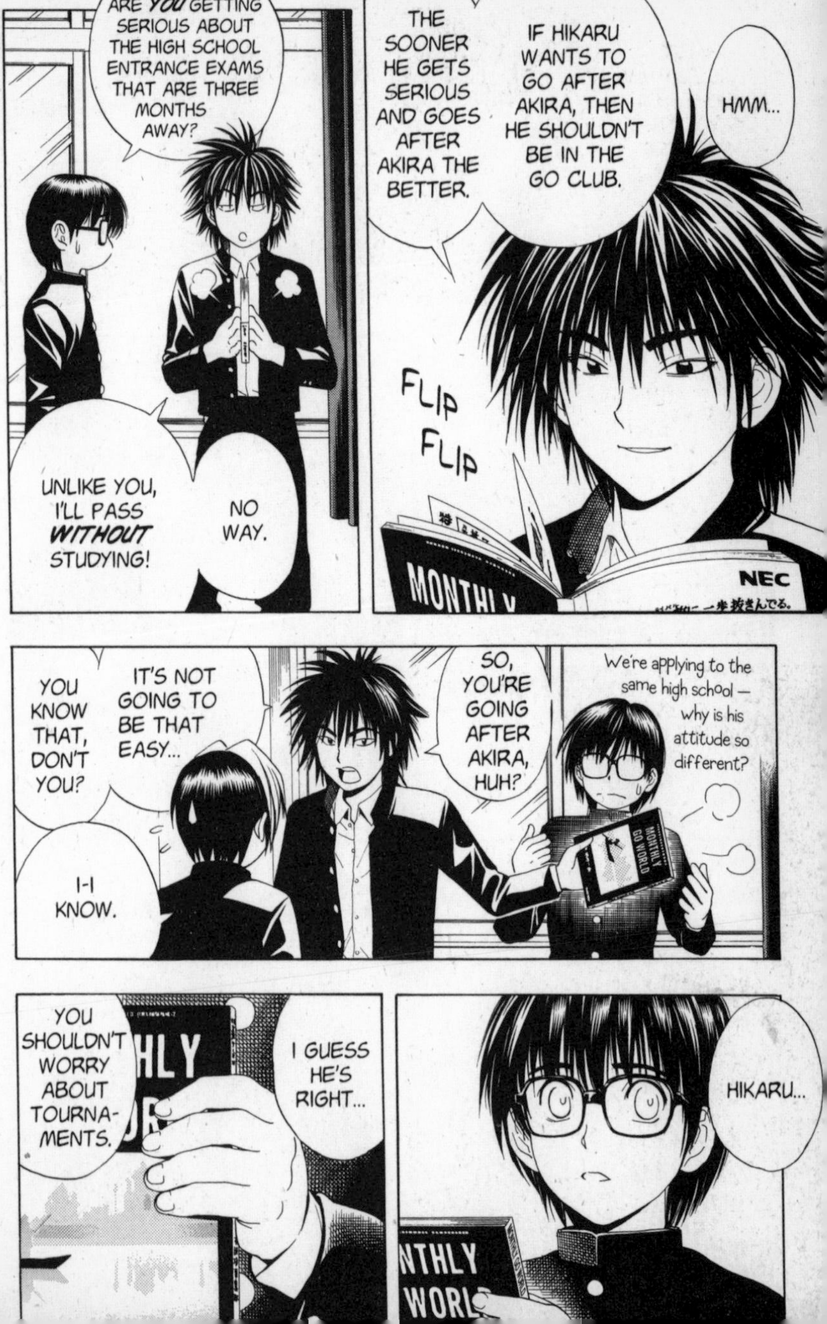
HMM...
IF HIKARU WANTS TO GO AFTER AKIRA, THEN HE SHOULDN'T BE IN THE GO CLUB.
THE SOONER HE GETS SERIOUS AND GOES AFTER AKIRA THE BETTER.
FLIP FLIP
MONTHLY
NEC
TETSUO, ARE *YOU* GETTING SERIOUS ABOUT THE HIGH SCHOOL ENTRANCE EXAMS THAT ARE THREE MONTHS AWAY?
NO WAY.
UNLIKE YOU, I'LL PASS ***WITHOUT*** STUDYING!
We're applying to the same high school — why is his attitude so different?
SO, YOU'RE GOING AFTER AKIRA, HUH?
MONTHLY GO WORLD
IT'S NOT GOING TO BE THAT EASY...
YOU KNOW THAT, DON'T YOU?
I-I KNOW.
HIKARU...
I GUESS HE'S RIGHT...
YOU SHOULDN'T WORRY ABOUT TOURNAMENTS.

READ THIS WAY

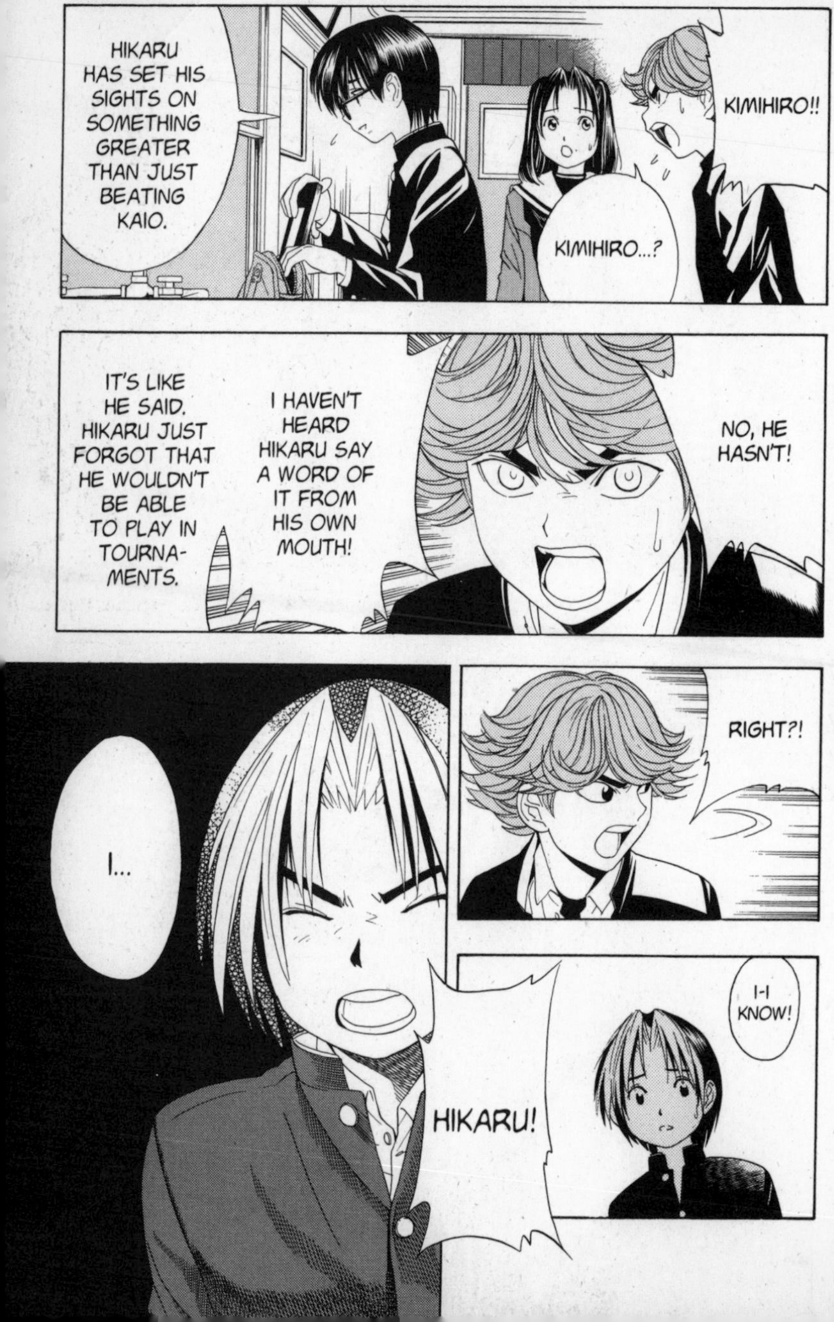
KIMIHIRO!!
KIMIHIRO...?
HIKARU HAS SET HIS SIGHTS ON SOMETHING GREATER THAN JUST BEATING KAIO.
NO, HE HASN'T!
I HAVEN'T HEARD HIKARU SAY A WORD OF IT FROM HIS OWN MOUTH!
IT'S LIKE HE SAID. HIKARU JUST FORGOT THAT HE WOULDN'T BE ABLE TO PLAY IN TOURNA-MENTS.
RIGHT?!
I-I KNOW!
HIKARU!
I...

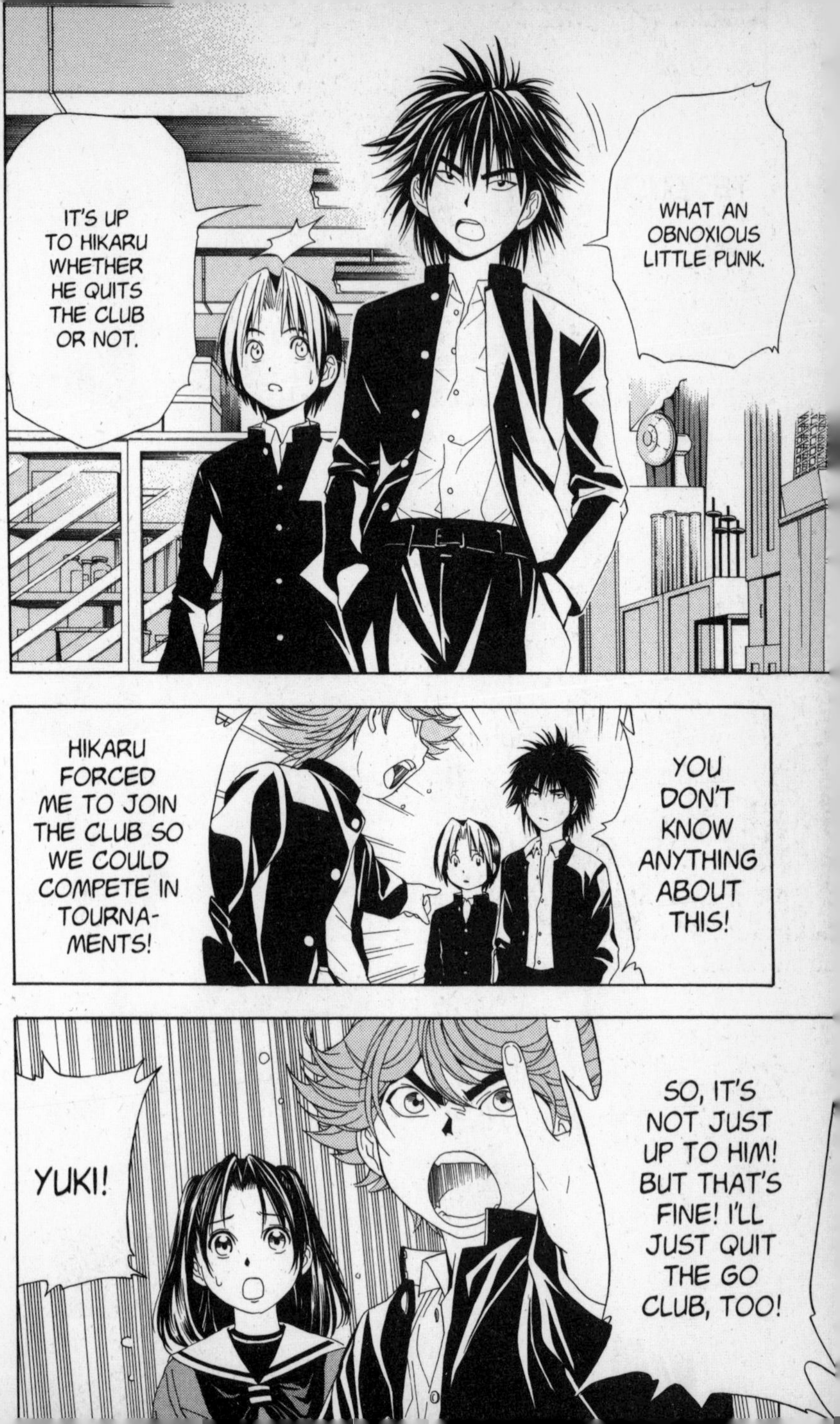
WHAT AN OBNOXIOUS LITTLE PUNK.
IT'S UP TO HIKARU WHETHER HE QUITS THE CLUB OR NOT.
YOU DON'T KNOW ANYTHING ABOUT THIS!
HIKARU FORCED ME TO JOIN THE CLUB SO WE COULD COMPETE IN TOURNA-MENTS!
SO, IT'S NOT JUST UP TO HIM! BUT THAT'S FINE! I'LL JUST QUIT THE GO CLUB, TOO!
YUKI!

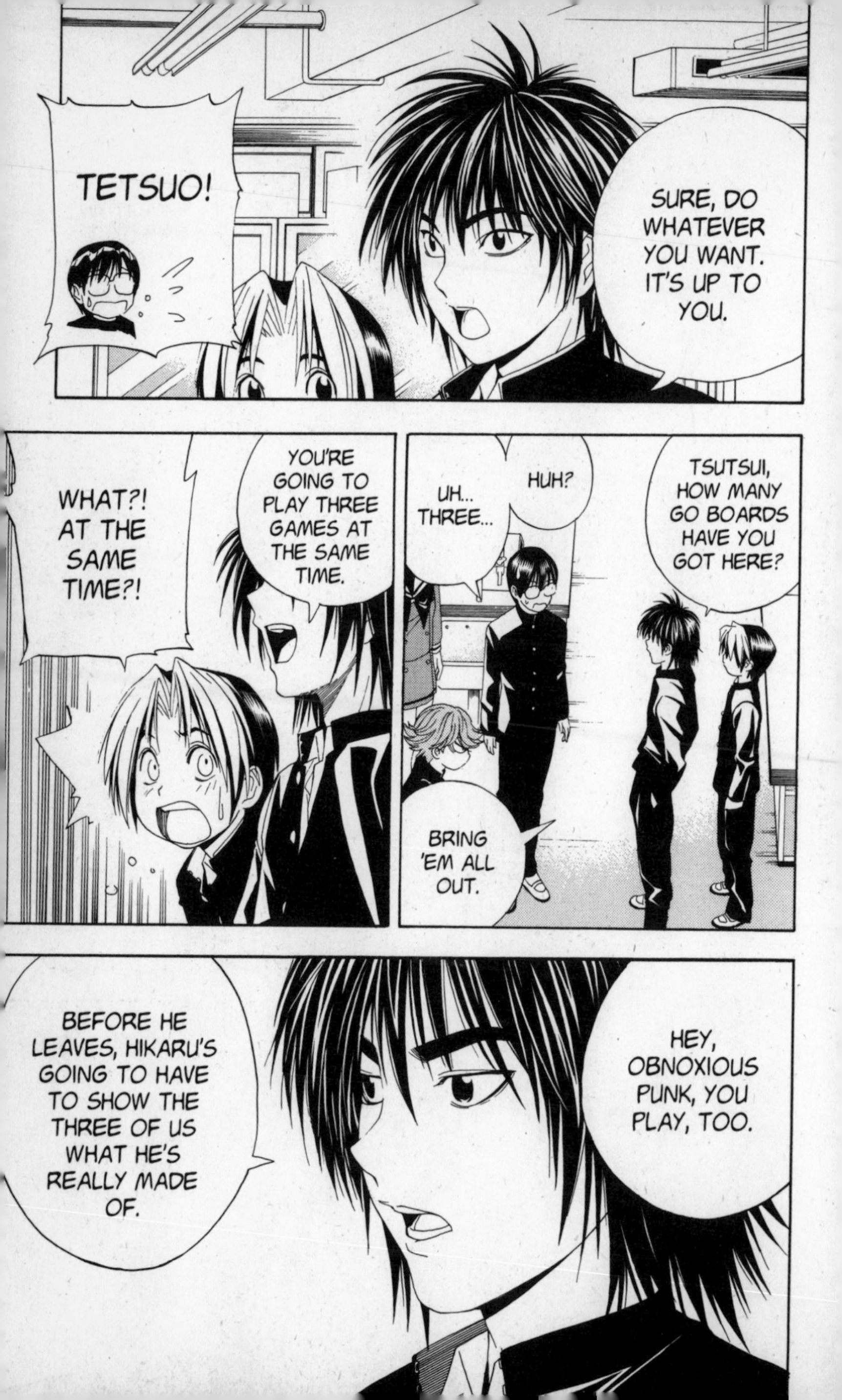
SURE, DO WHATEVER YOU WANT. IT'S UP TO YOU.
TETSUO!
TSUTSUI, HOW MANY GO BOARDS HAVE YOU GOT HERE?
HUH?
UH... THREE...
BRING 'EM ALL OUT.
YOU'RE GOING TO PLAY THREE GAMES AT THE SAME TIME.
WHAT?! AT THE SAME TIME?!
HEY, OBNOXIOUS PUNK, YOU PLAY, TOO.
BEFORE HE LEAVES, HIKARU'S GOING TO HAVE TO SHOW THE THREE OF US WHAT HE'S REALLY MADE OF.

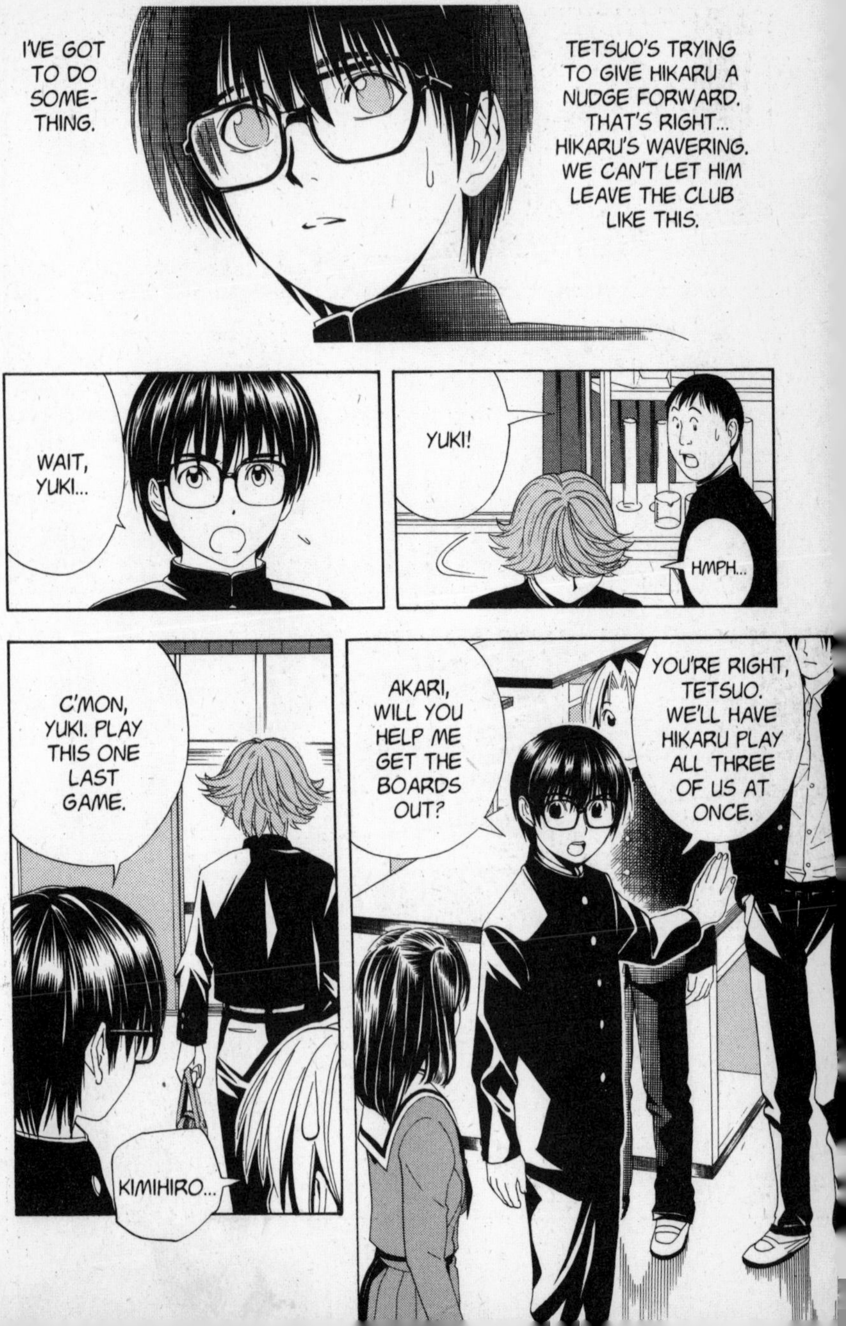
TETSUO'S TRYING TO GIVE HIKARU A NUDGE FORWARD. THAT'S RIGHT... HIKARU'S WAVERING. WE CAN'T LET HIM LEAVE THE CLUB LIKE THIS.
I'VE GOT TO DO SOME-THING.
YUKI!
HMPH...
WAIT, YUKI...
YOU'RE RIGHT, TETSUO. WE'LL HAVE HIKARU PLAY ALL THREE OF US AT ONCE.
AKARI, WILL YOU HELP ME GET THE BOARDS OUT?
C'MON, YUKI. PLAY THIS ONE LAST GAME.
KIMIHIRO...

HEH HEH... HAVEN'T PLAYED A GAME OF GO IN A WHILE!

FWAP

C'MON, YUKI. LET'S PLAY A GAME!

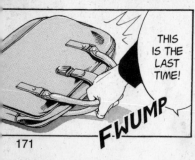

THIS IS THE LAST TIME!

FWUMP

171

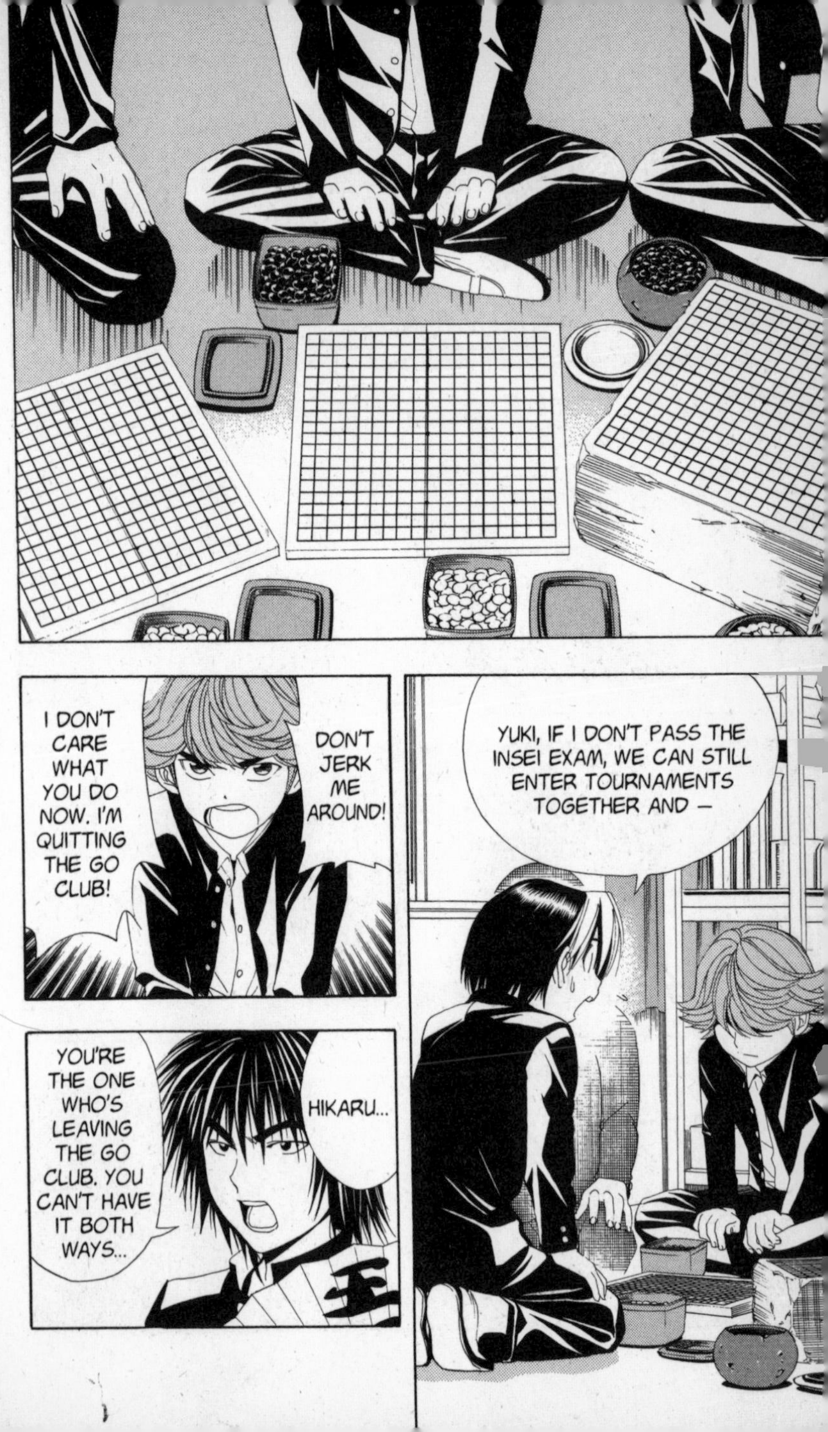
YUKI, IF I DON'T PASS THE INSEI EXAM, WE CAN STILL ENTER TOURNAMENTS TOGETHER AND –
DON'T JERK ME AROUND!
I DON'T CARE WHAT YOU DO NOW. I'M QUITTING THE GO CLUB!
HIKARU...
YOU'RE THE ONE WHO'S LEAVING THE GO CLUB. YOU CAN'T HAVE IT BOTH WAYS...

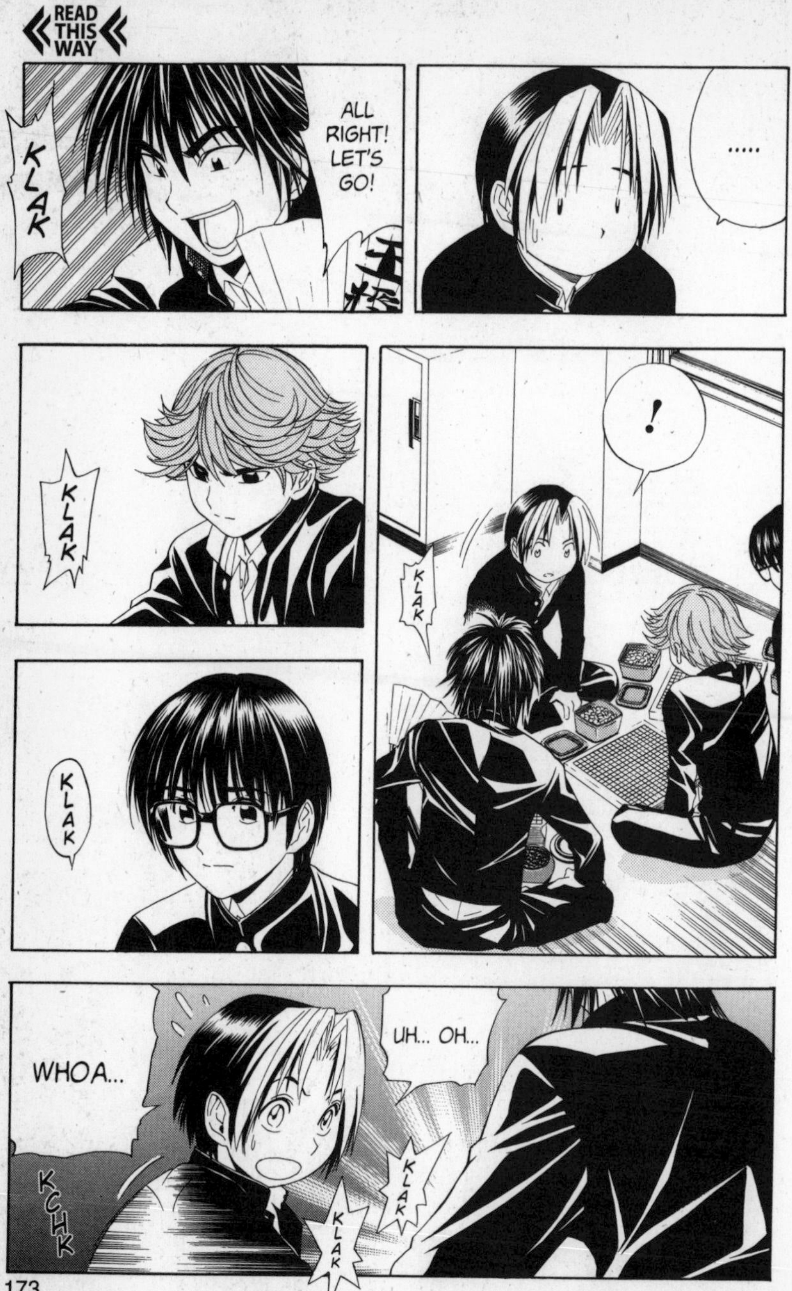
READ THIS WAY
.....
ALL RIGHT! LET'S GO!
KLAK
!
KLAK
KLAK
KLAK
UH... OH...
KLAK
KLAK
WHOA...
KCHK

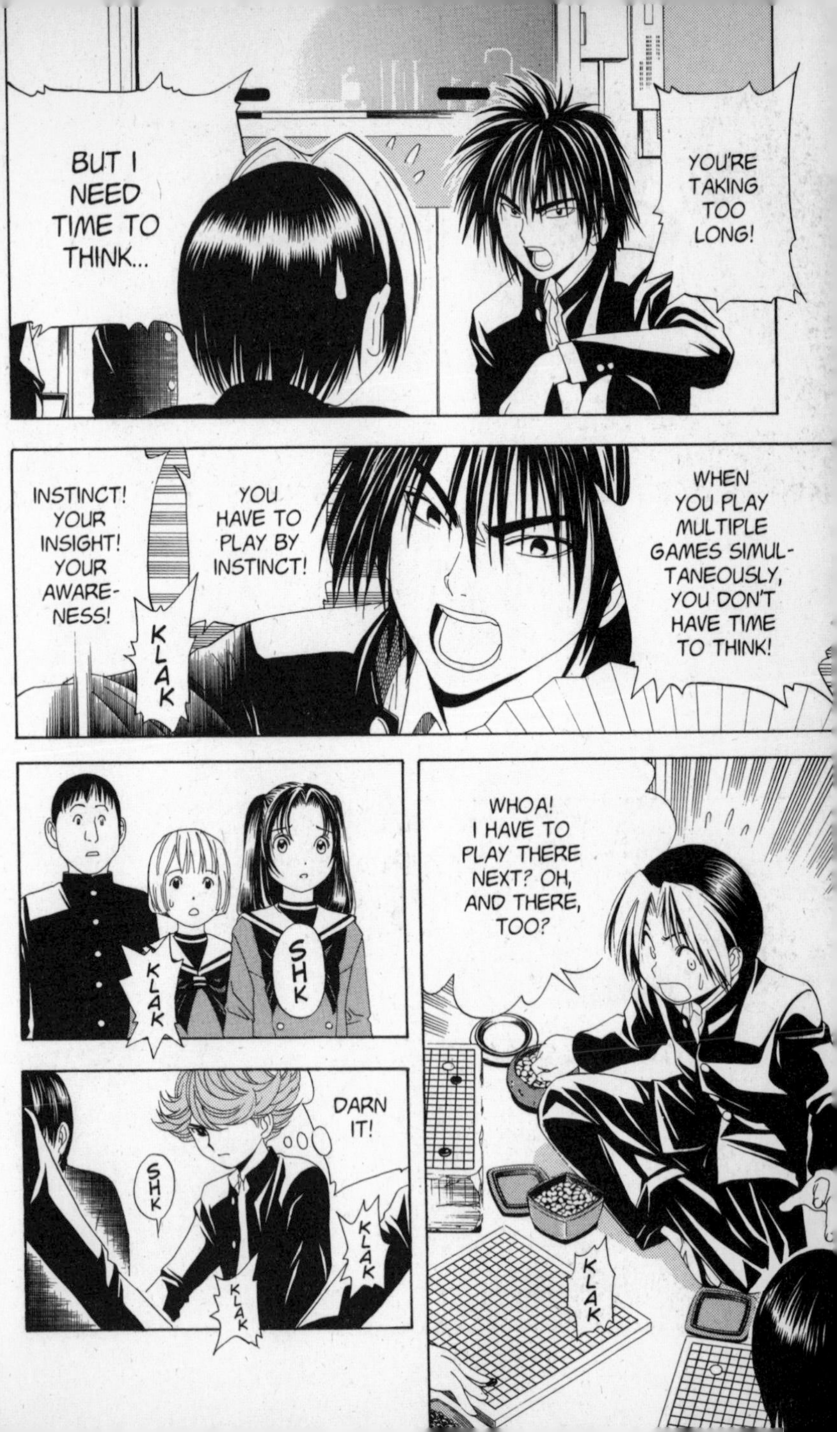
YOU'RE TAKING TOO LONG!
BUT I NEED TIME TO THINK...
WHEN YOU PLAY MULTIPLE GAMES SIMUL-TANEOUSLY, YOU DON'T HAVE TIME TO THINK!
YOU HAVE TO PLAY BY INSTINCT!
INSTINCT! YOUR INSIGHT! YOUR AWARE-NESS!
KLAK
WHOA! I HAVE TO PLAY THERE NEXT? OH, AND THERE, TOO?
KLAK
SHK
KLAK
DARN IT!
KLAK
SHK
KLAK

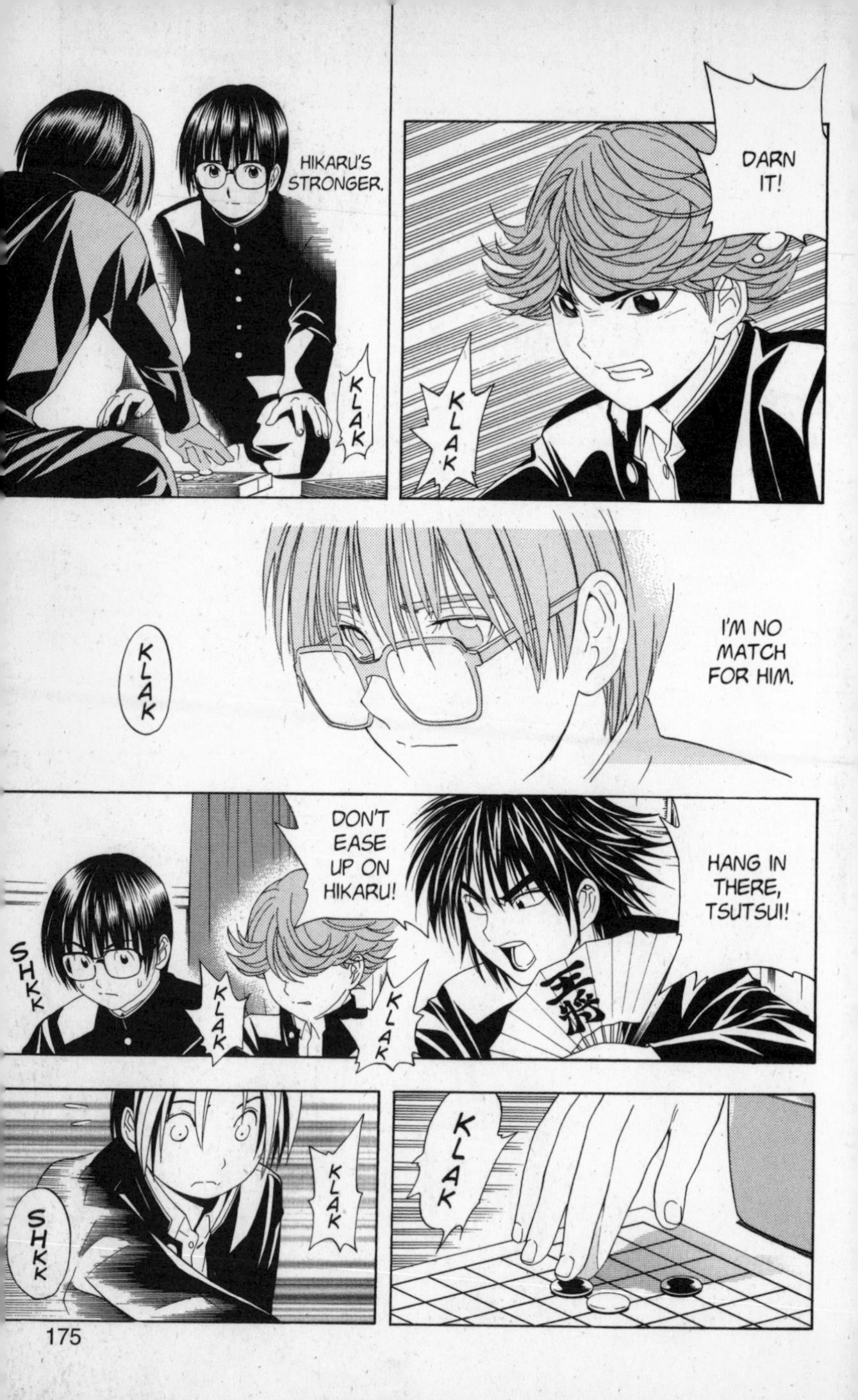
DARN IT!
KLAK
HIKARU'S STRONGER.
KLAK
I'M NO MATCH FOR HIM.
KLAK
HANG IN THERE, TSUTSUI!
DON'T EASE UP ON HIKARU!
KLAK
KLAK
SHKK
KLAK
KLAK
SHKK

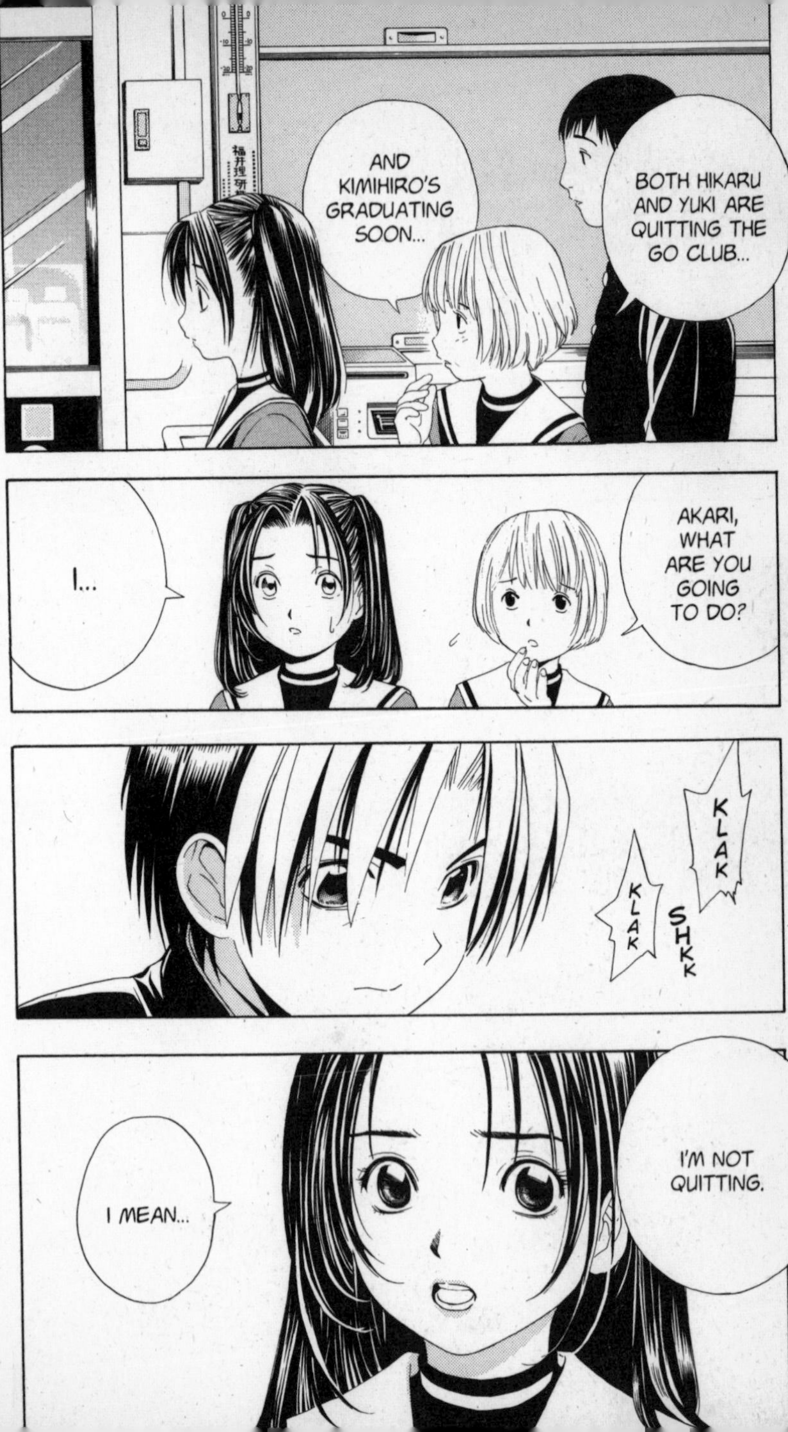
BOTH HIKARU AND YUKI ARE QUITTING THE GO CLUB...
AND KIMIHIRO'S GRADUATING SOON...
AKARI, WHAT ARE YOU GOING TO DO?
I...
KLAK
KLAK
SHKK
I'M NOT QUITTING.
I MEAN...

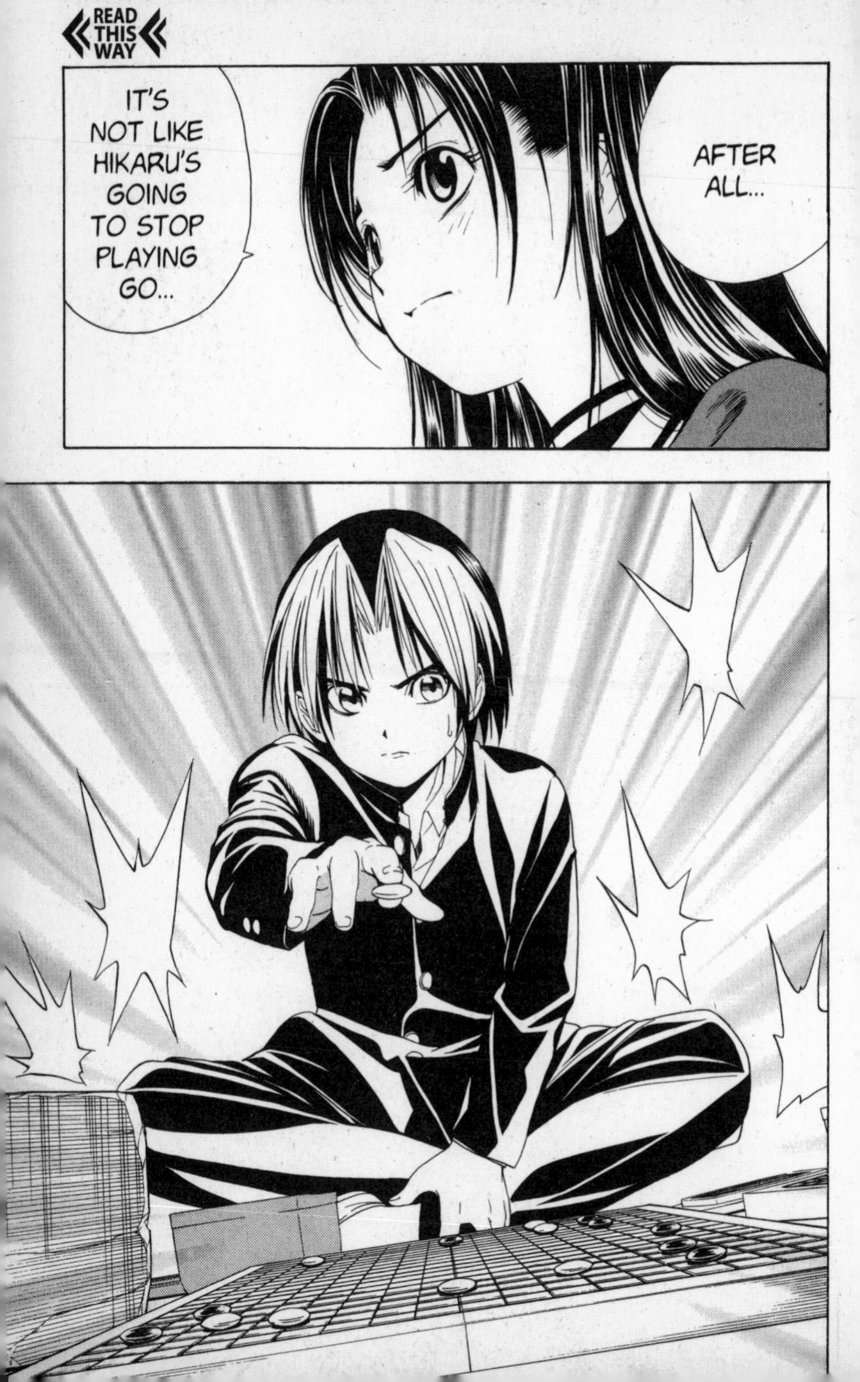
READ THIS WAY
AFTER ALL...
IT'S NOT LIKE HIKARU'S GOING TO STOP PLAYING GO...

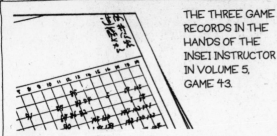

THE THREE GAME RECORDS IN THE HANDS OF THE INSEI INSTRUCTOR IN VOLUME 5, GAME 43.

HIKARU NO GO

STORYBOARDS ⑭

YUMI HOTTA

PART OF AN EDITOR'S JOB IS TO MAKE MINOR CORRECTIONS TO THE ILLUSTRATIONS.

Right here.

Their names should be written on this.

KIMIHIRO'S AND HIKARU'S NAMES ARE WRITTEN IN VERY SMALL WRITING ON THE TOP SHEET. MY EDITOR TAKAHASHI IS ACTUALLY THE ONE WHO WROTE THEM DOWN.

THAT'S EASY FOR HIM TO SAY...

Also, filling in black areas that have been missed and whiting out smudges, too.

And then I might try to draw over the white areas before they dried completely!

Then, I'd try to fix that and the white areas would go too far into the black.

After all, what if I went outside the lines as I filled in the black?

I'D BE TOO SCARED TO DO ANY OF THAT.

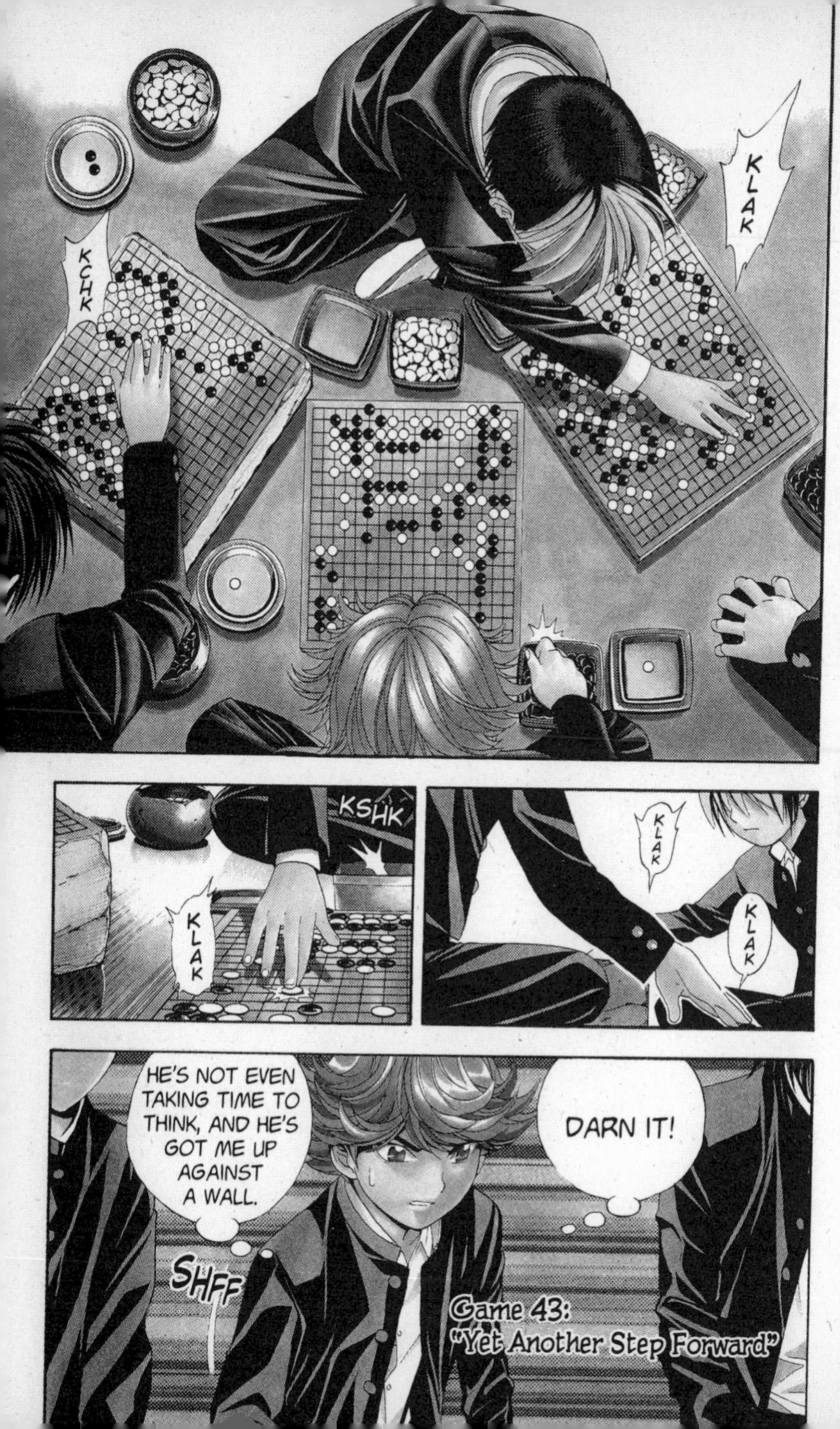
KLAK
KCHK
KLAK
KLAK
KSHK
KLAK
HE'S NOT EVEN TAKING TIME TO THINK, AND HE'S GOT ME UP AGAINST A WALL.
DARN IT!
SHFF
Game 43:
"Yet Another Step Forward"

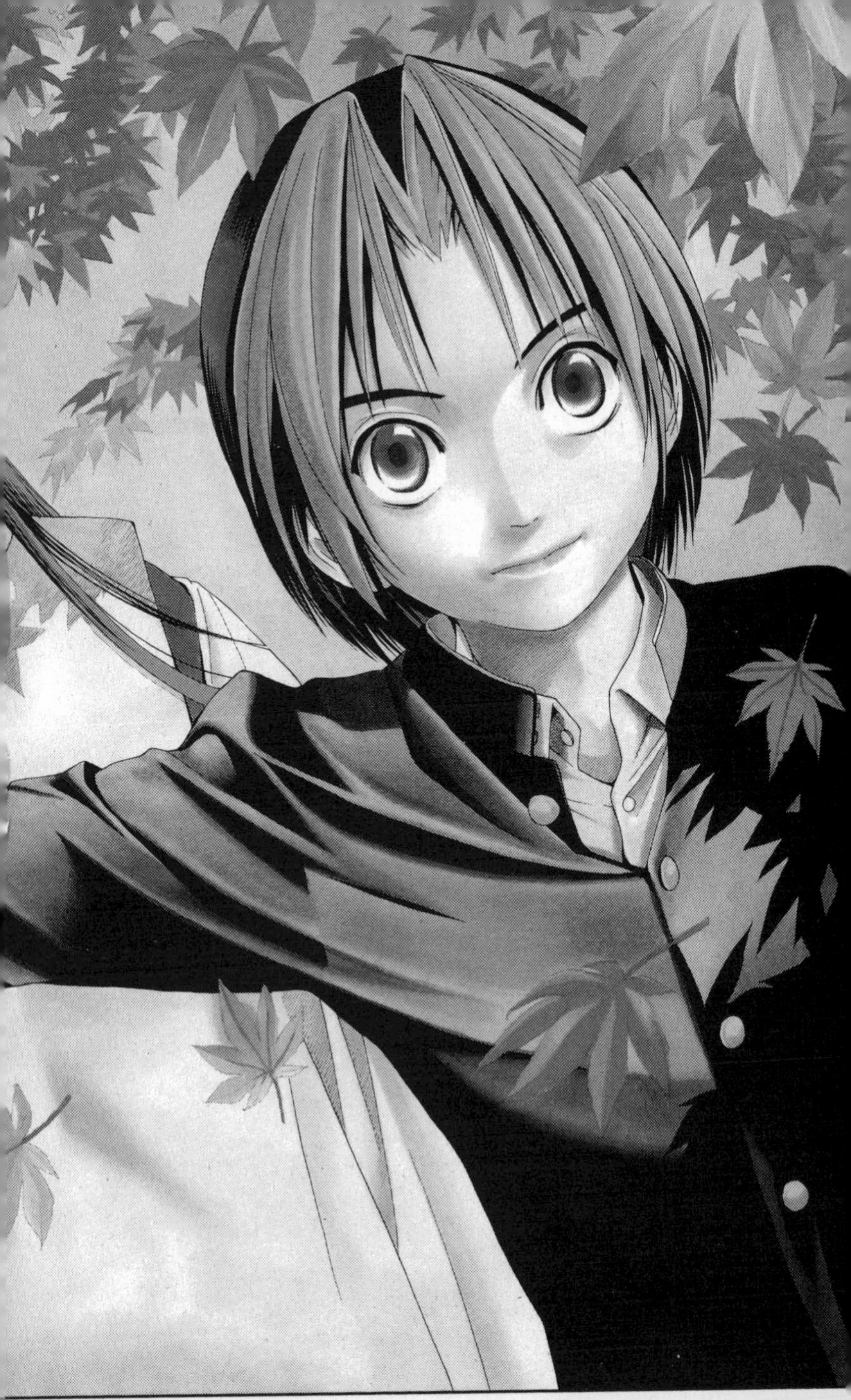

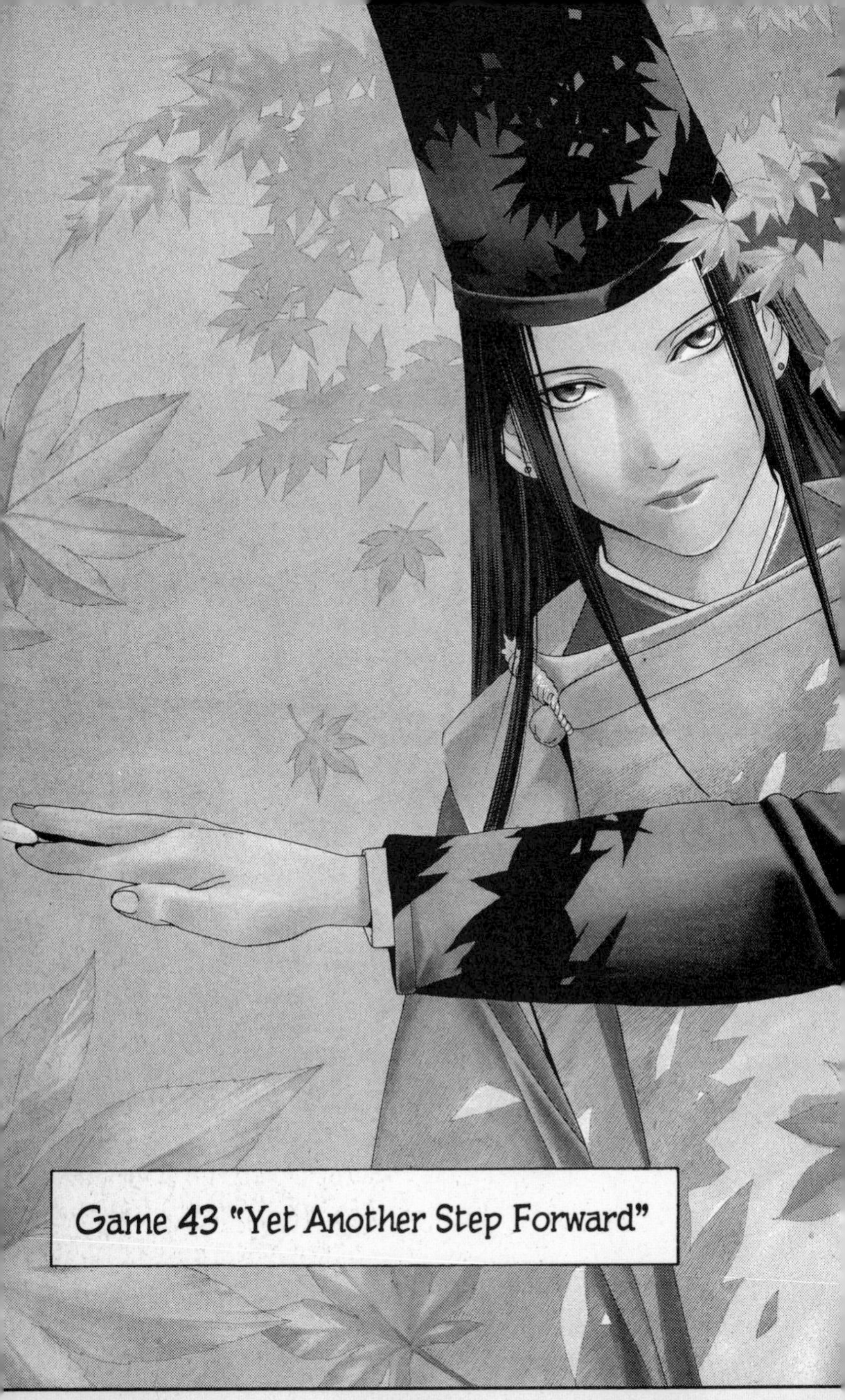
Game 43 "Yet Another Step Forward"

KLAK

KLAK

KLAK

THAT'S IT... I'LL HAVE TO RESIGN.

.....

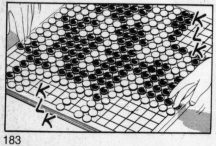

KLK

KLK

.....

HIKARU'S PRETTY AMAZING.

183

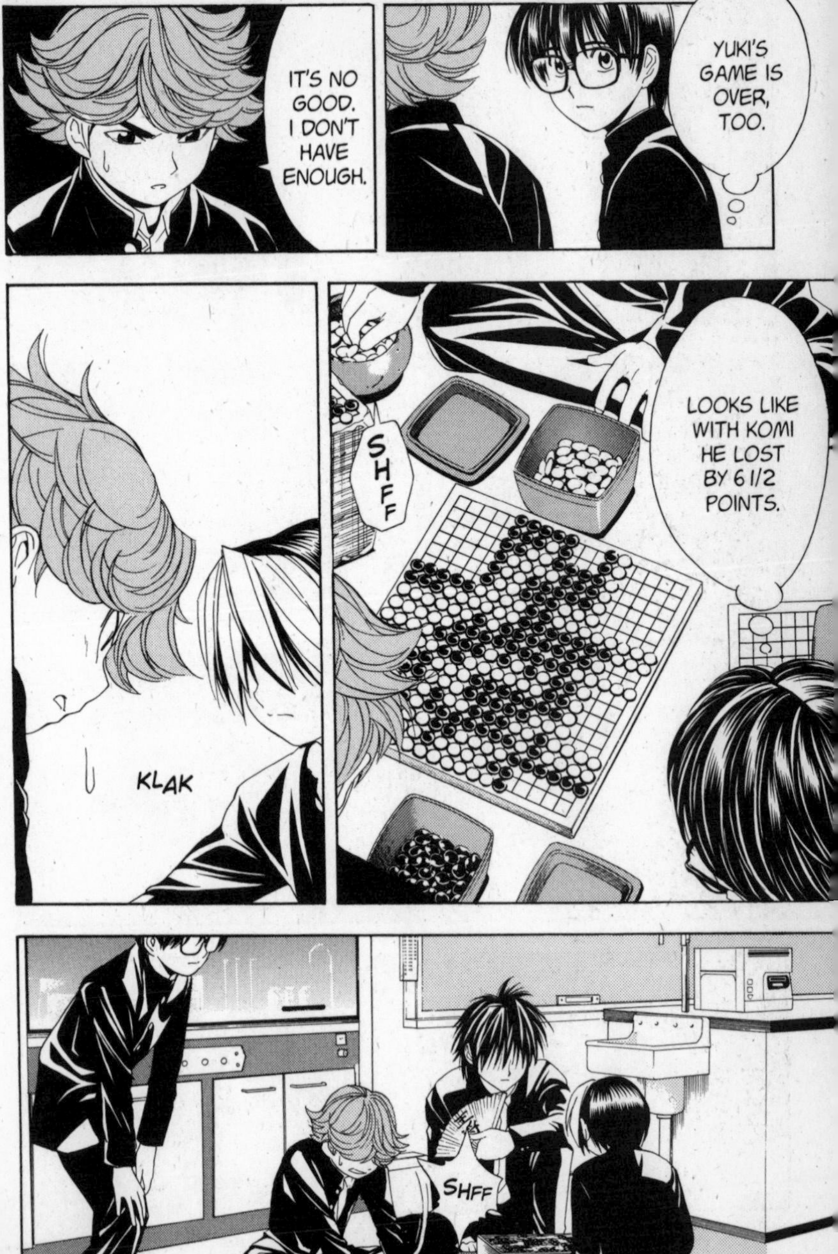
YUKI'S GAME IS OVER, TOO.
IT'S NO GOOD. I DON'T HAVE ENOUGH.
LOOKS LIKE WITH KOMI HE LOST BY 6 1/2 POINTS.
SHFF
KLAK
SHFF

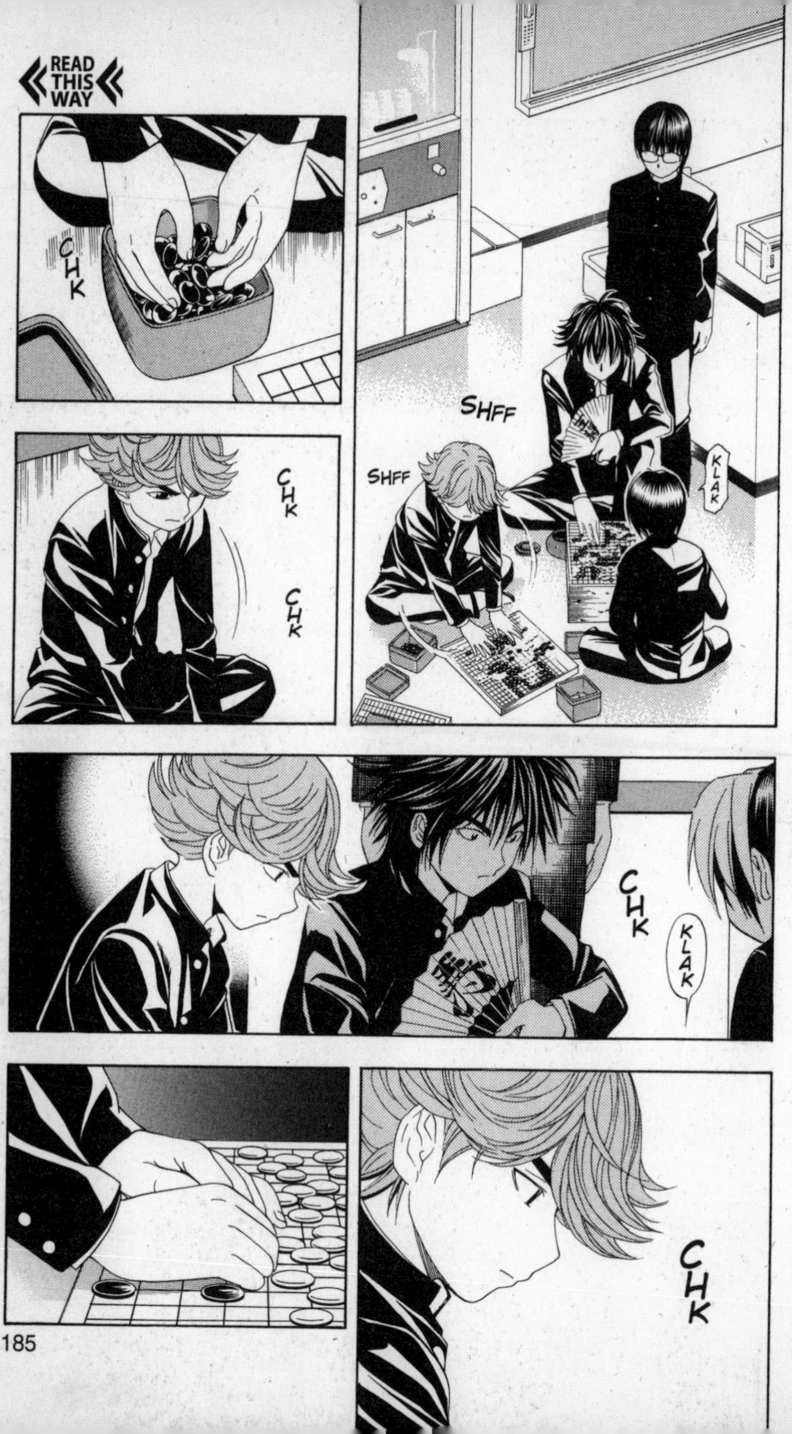
READ THIS WAY
SHFF
SHFF
KLAK
CHK
CHK
CHK
CHK
KLAK
CHK
CHK

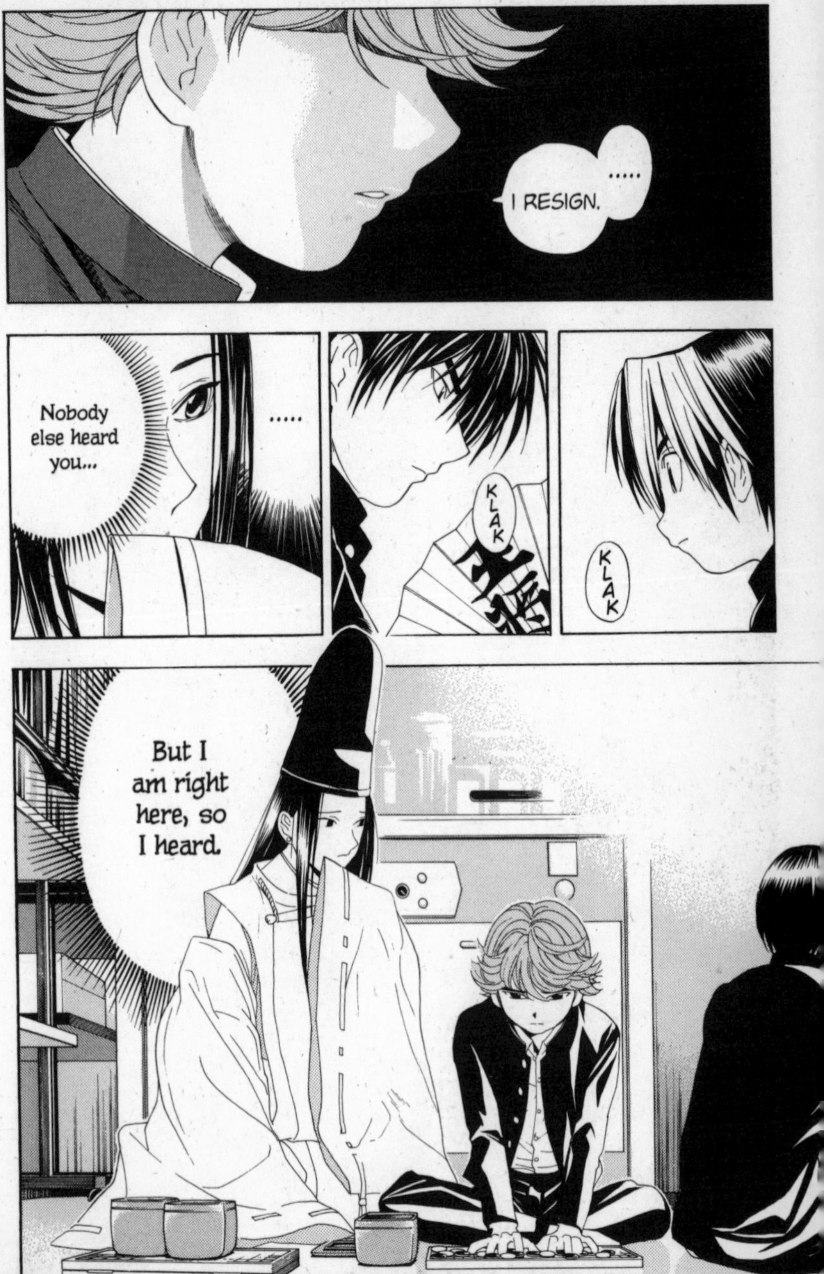
.....
I RESIGN.
KLAK
KLAK
.....
Nobody else heard you...
But I am right here, so I heard.

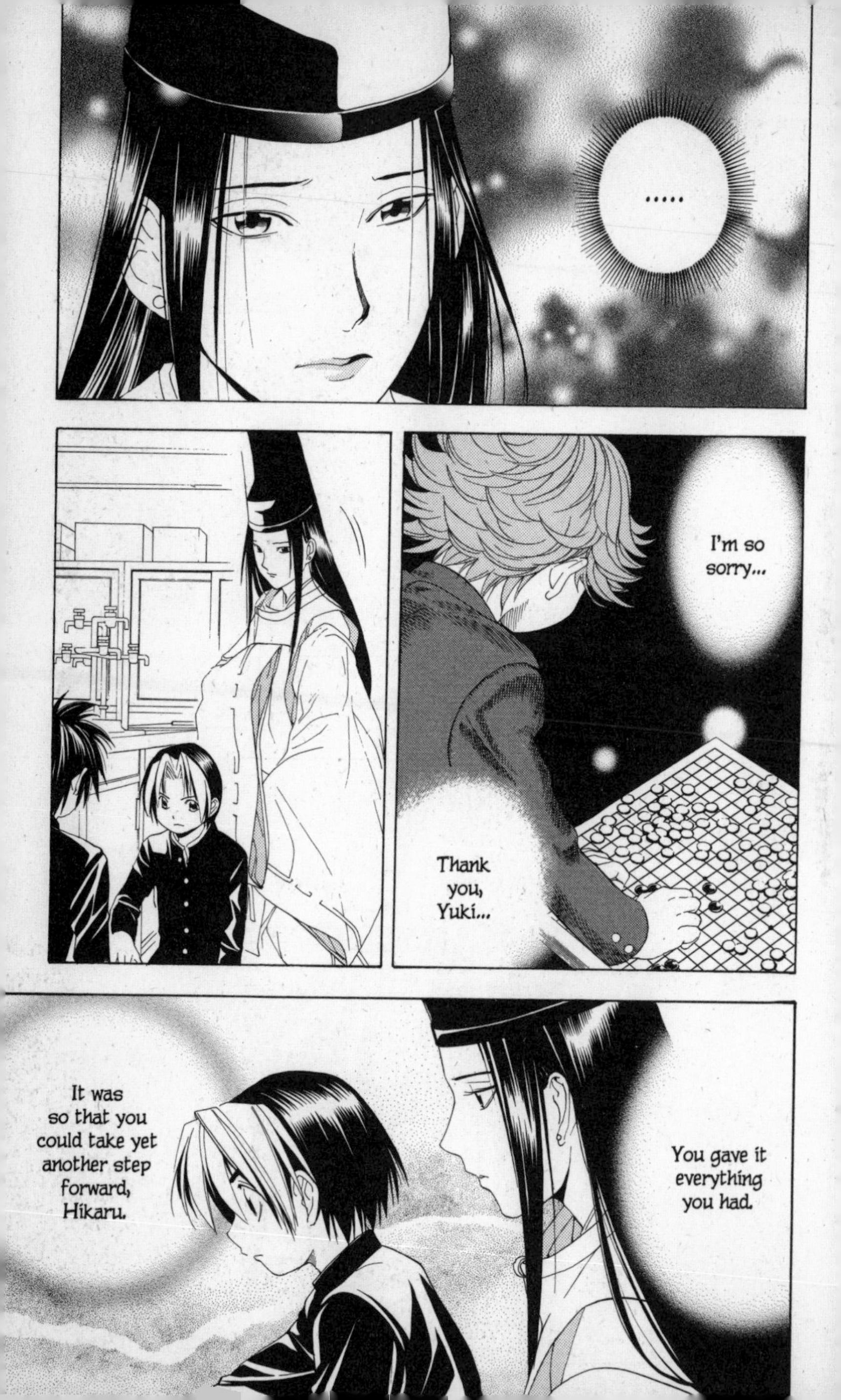
.....
I'm so sorry...
Thank you, Yuki...
You gave it everything you had.
It was so that you could take yet another step forward, Hikaru.

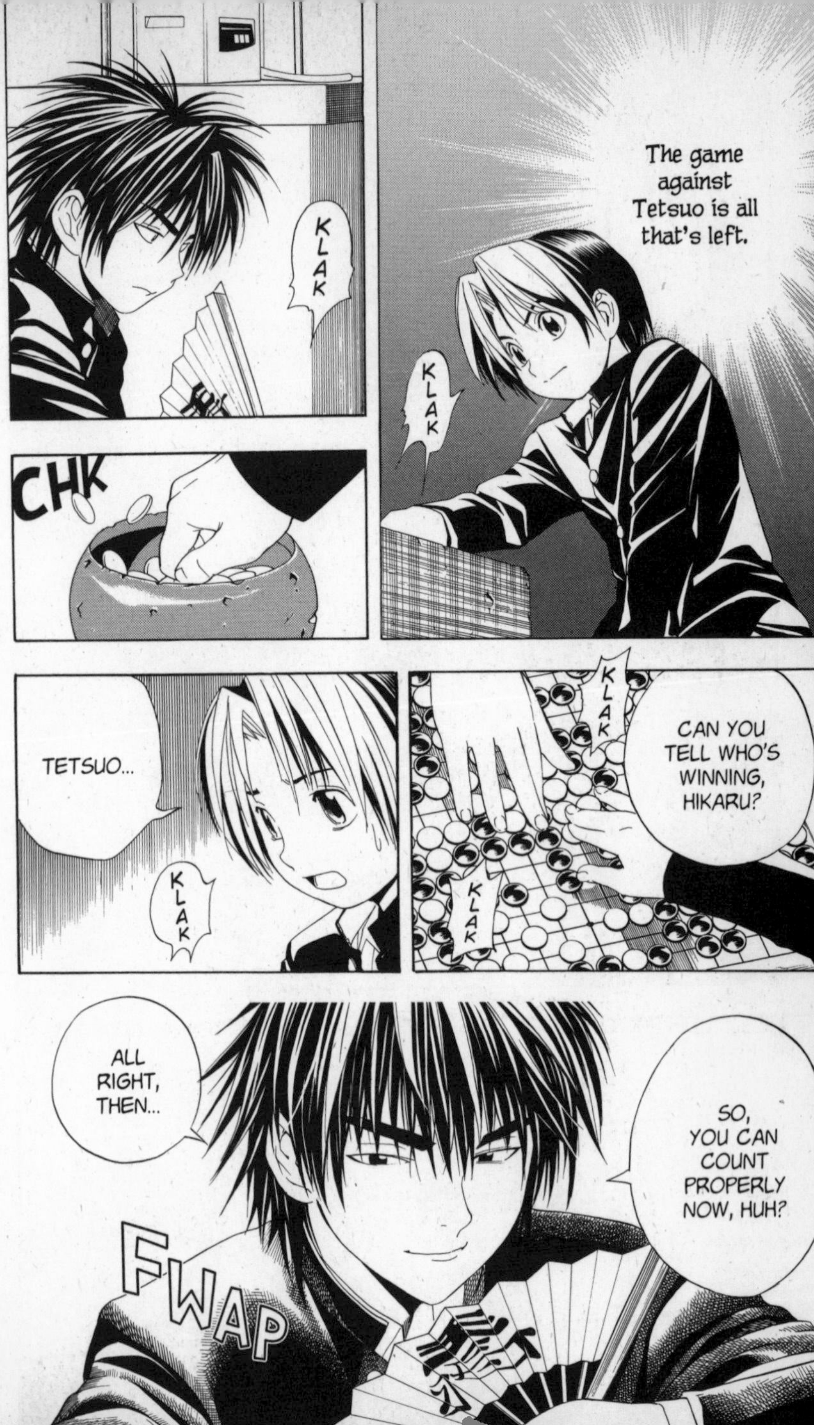
The game against Tetsuo is all that's left.
KLAK
KLAK
CHK
KLAK
CAN YOU TELL WHO'S WINNING, HIKARU?
KLAK
TETSUO...
KLAK
SO, YOU CAN COUNT PROPERLY NOW, HUH?
ALL RIGHT, THEN...
FWAP

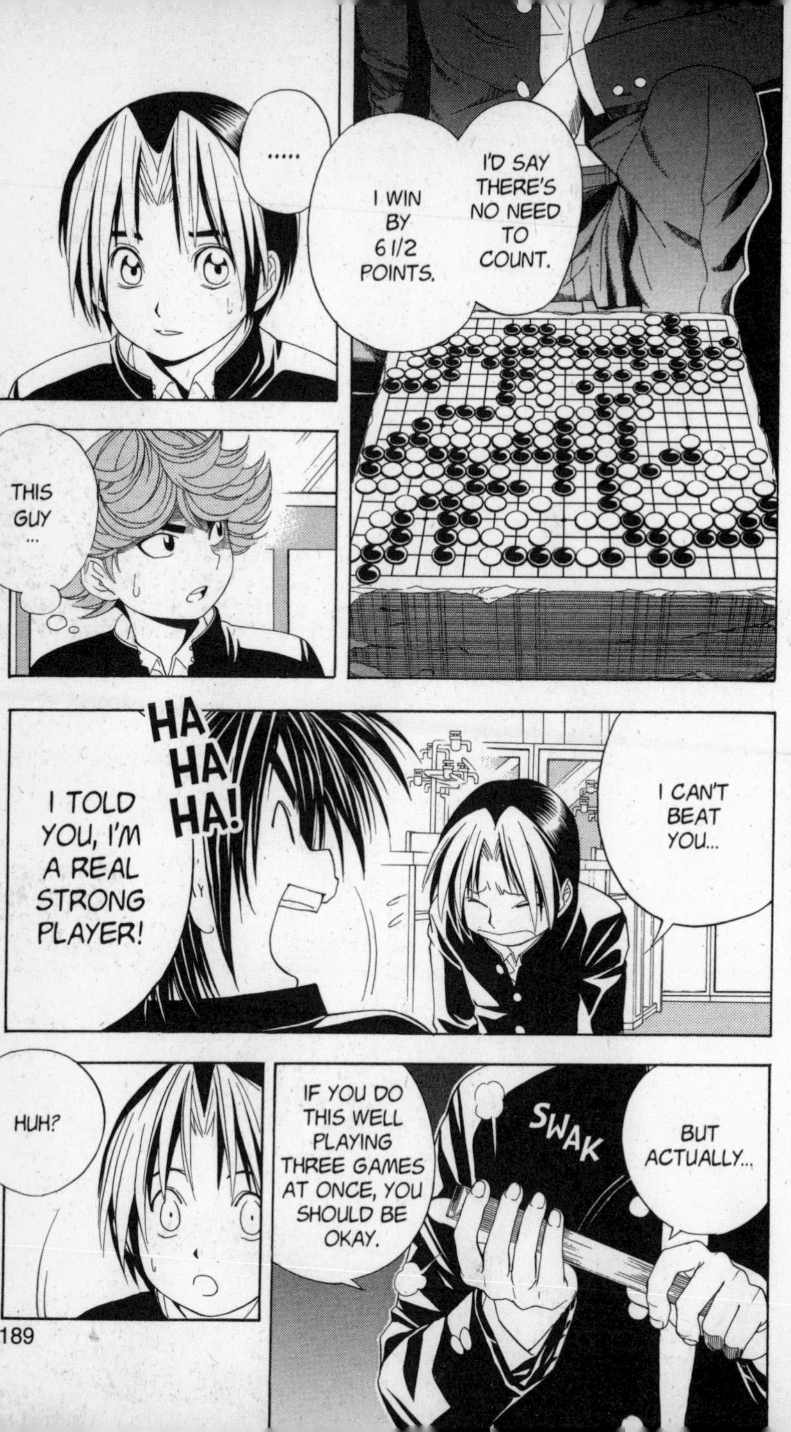

I'D SAY THERE'S NO NEED TO COUNT.
I WIN BY 6 1/2 POINTS.
......
THIS GUY ...
I CAN'T BEAT YOU...
HA HA HA!
I TOLD YOU, I'M A REAL STRONG PLAYER!
BUT ACTUALLY...
SWAK
IF YOU DO THIS WELL PLAYING THREE GAMES AT ONCE, YOU SHOULD BE OKAY.
HUH?

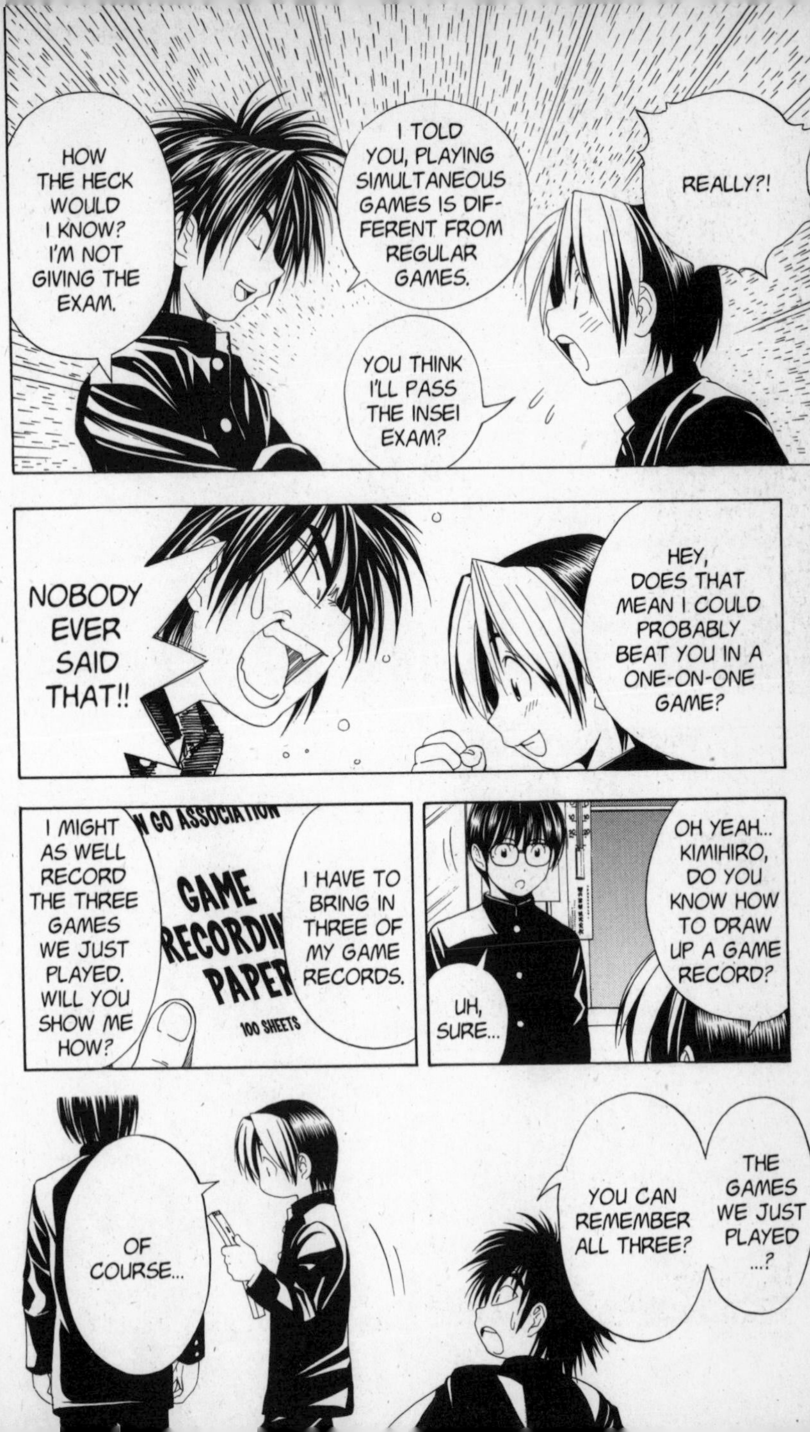
REALLY?!
I TOLD YOU, PLAYING SIMULTANEOUS GAMES IS DIFFERENT FROM REGULAR GAMES.
YOU THINK I'LL PASS THE INSEI EXAM?
HOW THE HECK WOULD I KNOW? I'M NOT GIVING THE EXAM.
HEY, DOES THAT MEAN I COULD PROBABLY BEAT YOU IN A ONE-ON-ONE GAME?
NOBODY EVER SAID THAT!!
OH YEAH... KIMIHIRO, DO YOU KNOW HOW TO DRAW UP A GAME RECORD?
UH, SURE...
I HAVE TO BRING IN THREE OF MY GAME RECORDS.
N GO ASSOCIATION
GAME RECORDIN
PAPER
100 SHEETS
I MIGHT AS WELL RECORD THE THREE GAMES WE JUST PLAYED. WILL YOU SHOW ME HOW?
THE GAMES WE JUST PLAYED ...?
YOU CAN REMEMBER ALL THREE?
OF COURSE...

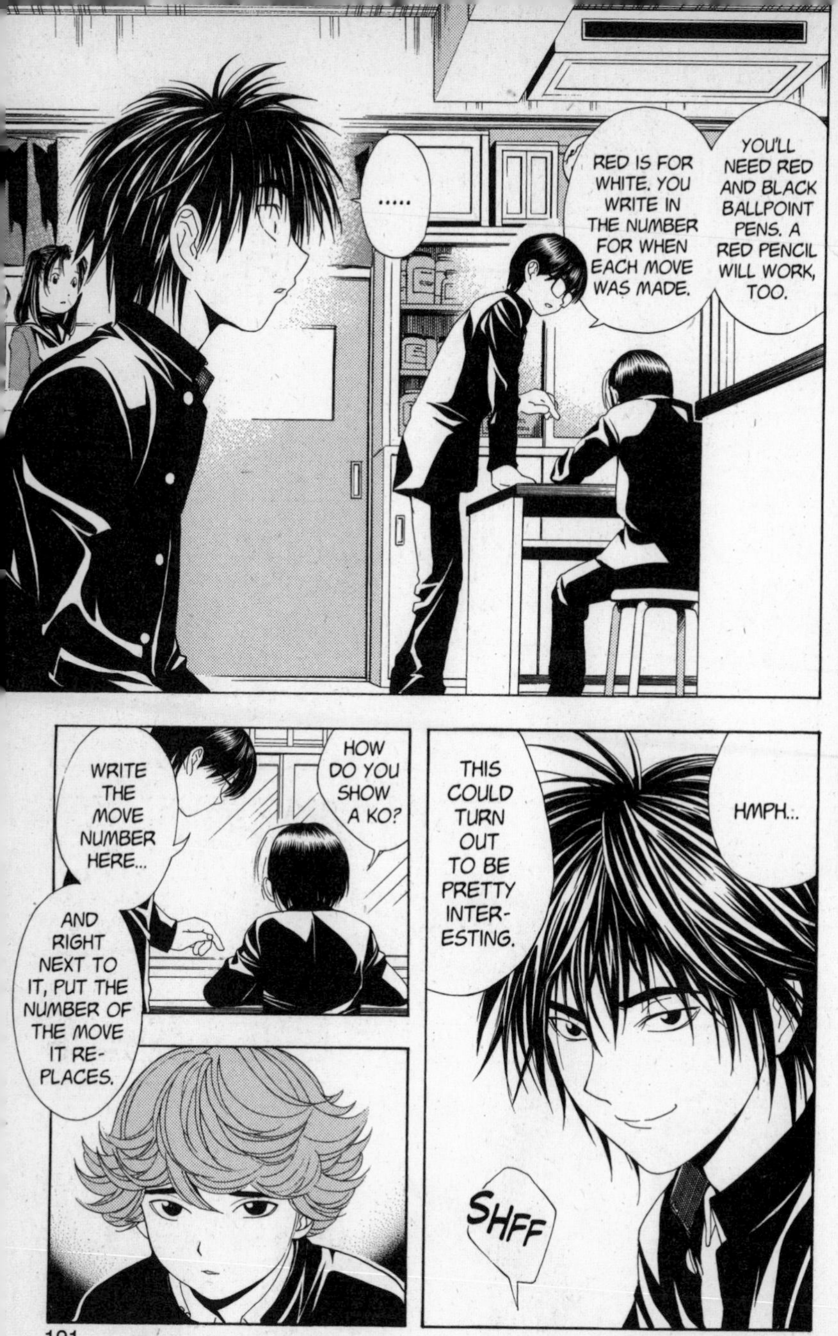

YOU'LL NEED RED AND BLACK BALLPOINT PENS. A RED PENCIL WILL WORK, TOO.
RED IS FOR WHITE. YOU WRITE IN THE NUMBER FOR WHEN EACH MOVE WAS MADE.
......
HMPH...
THIS COULD TURN OUT TO BE PRETTY INTER-ESTING.
SHFF
HOW DO YOU SHOW A KO?
WRITE THE MOVE NUMBER HERE...
AND RIGHT NEXT TO IT, PUT THE NUMBER OF THE MOVE IT RE-PLACES.

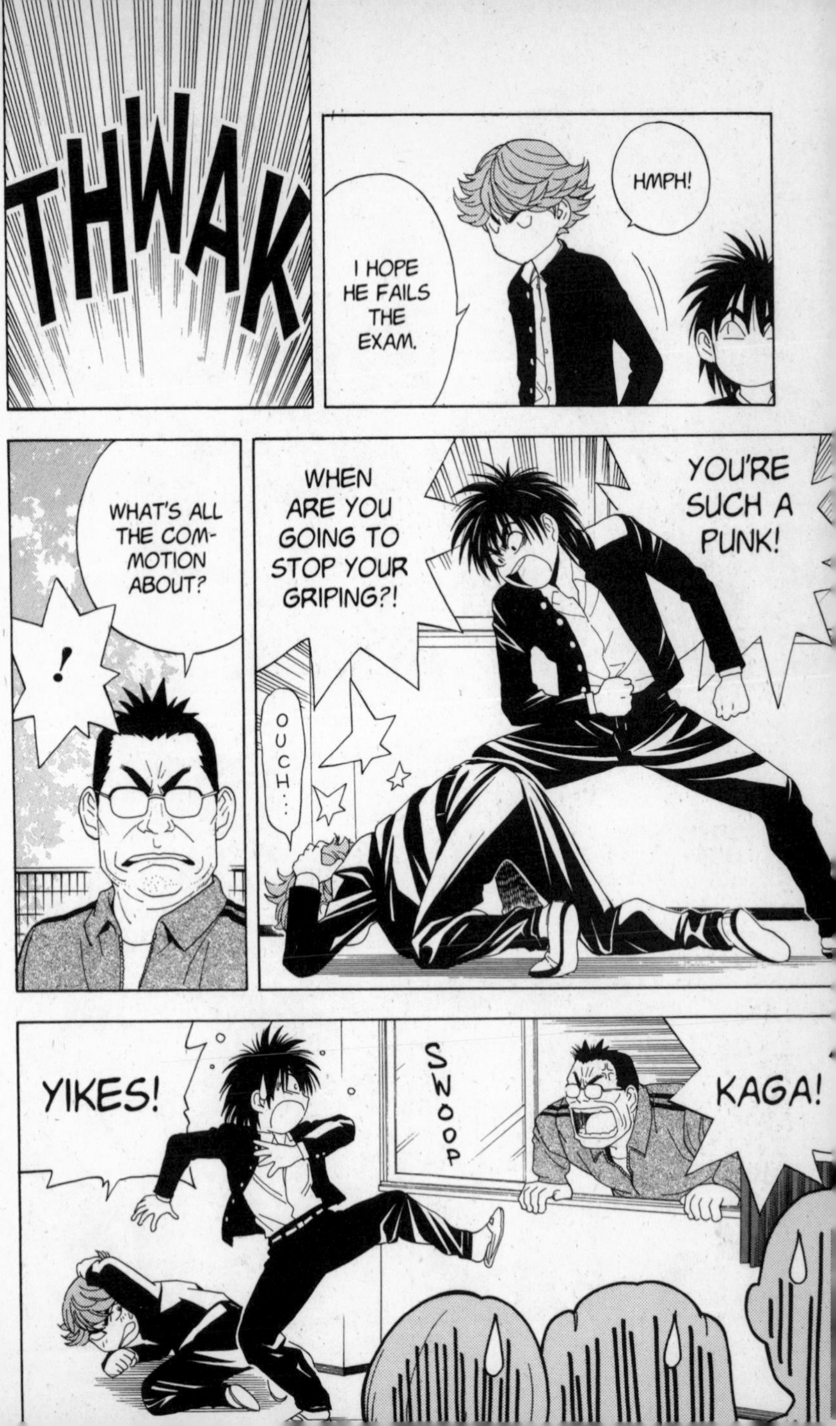
HMPH!
I HOPE HE FAILS THE EXAM.
THWAK
YOU'RE SUCH A PUNK!
WHEN ARE YOU GOING TO STOP YOUR GRIPING?!
OUCH...
WHAT'S ALL THE COM-MOTION ABOUT?
!
KAGA!
SWOOP
YIKES!

READ THIS WAY

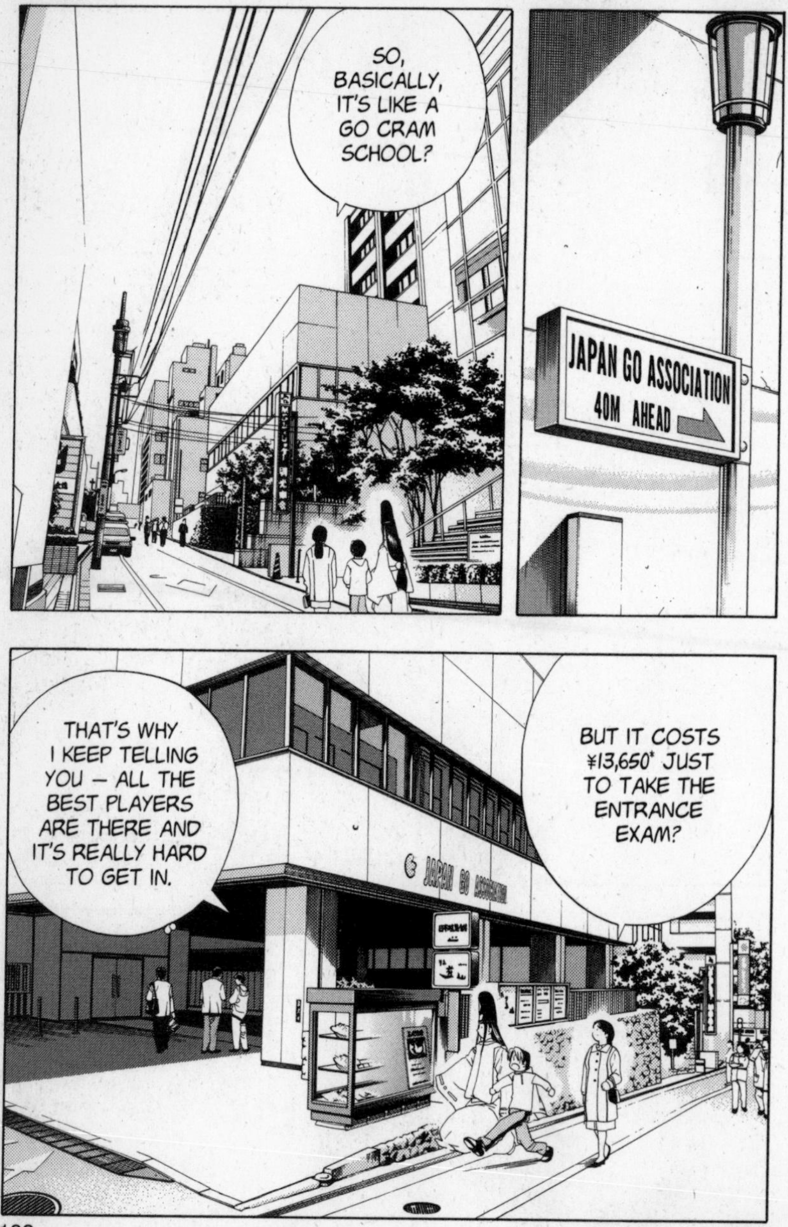
JAPAN GO ASSOCIATION
40M AHEAD
SO, BASICALLY, IT'S LIKE A GO CRAM SCHOOL?
JAPAN GO ASSOCIATION
BUT IT COSTS ¥13,650* JUST TO TAKE THE ENTRANCE EXAM?
THAT'S WHY I KEEP TELLING YOU — ALL THE BEST PLAYERS ARE THERE AND IT'S REALLY HARD TO GET IN.

*About US $136

ISN'T THAT GO CLASS YOU USED TO GO TO GOOD ENOUGH?
IT WAS SO CLOSE TO OUR HOUSE.
THAT CLASS IS FULL OF OLD LADIES WHO JUST WANNA HAVE FUN. THEY NEVER GET ANY BETTER.
WELL, YOU'VE NEVER SHOWN THIS MUCH INTEREST OR INITIATIVE IN ANY-THING BEFORE, SO I GUESS IT'S OKAY.
IF ONLY YOU WERE LIKE THIS ABOUT YOUR STUDIES.
......
hee hee
YOU'RE HIKARU SHINDO, RIGHT? LET ME SHOW YOU WHERE TO GO.
5 6 7
DING
VWSH
消火器
BA-BUMP BA-BUMP

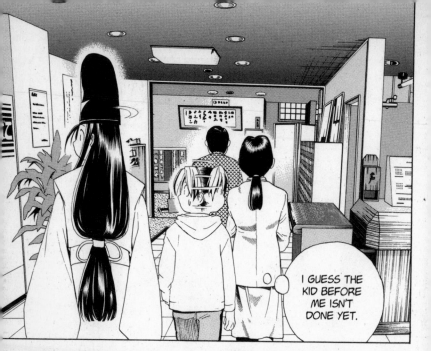

I GUESS THE KID BEFORE ME ISN'T DONE YET.

I'M GETTING REALLY NERVOUS.

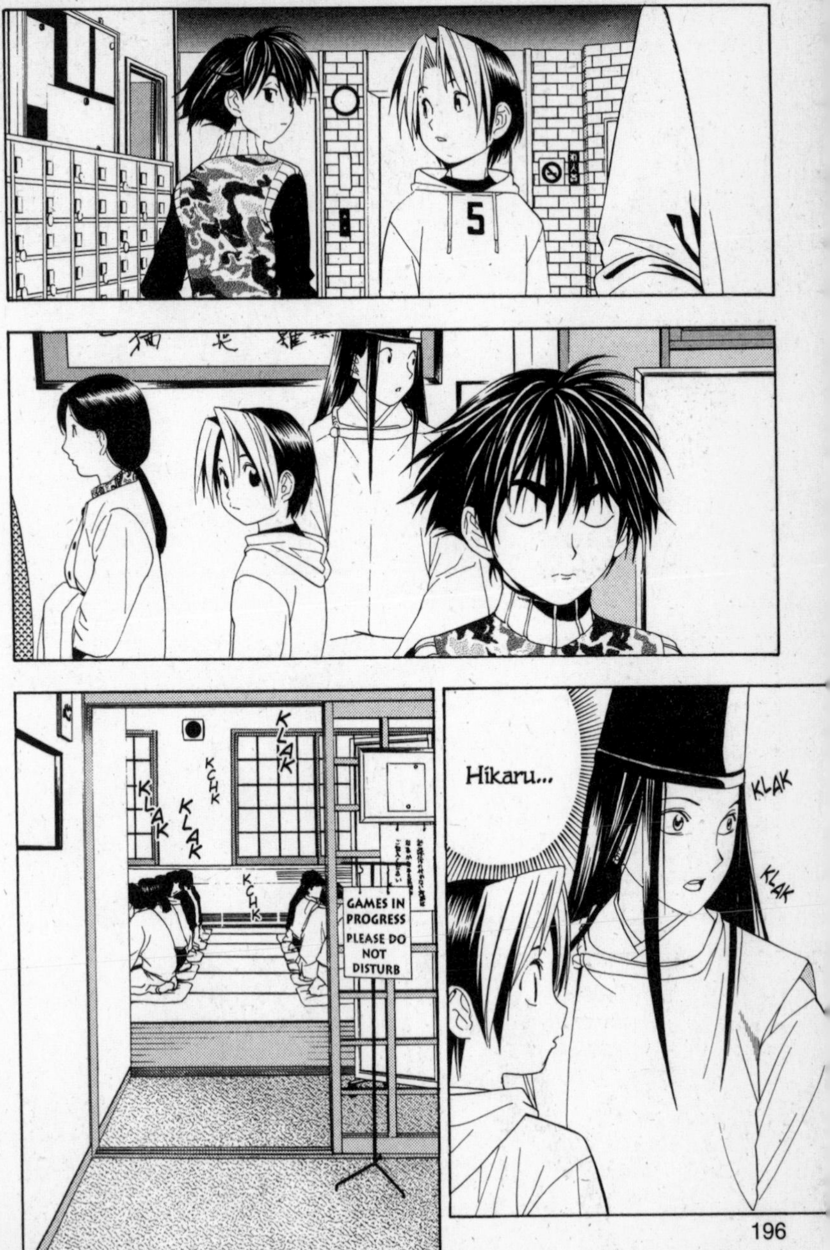

Hikaru...
KLAK
KLAK
KLAK
KCHK
KLAK
KLAK
KCHK
GAMES IN PROGRESS PLEASE DO NOT DISTURB

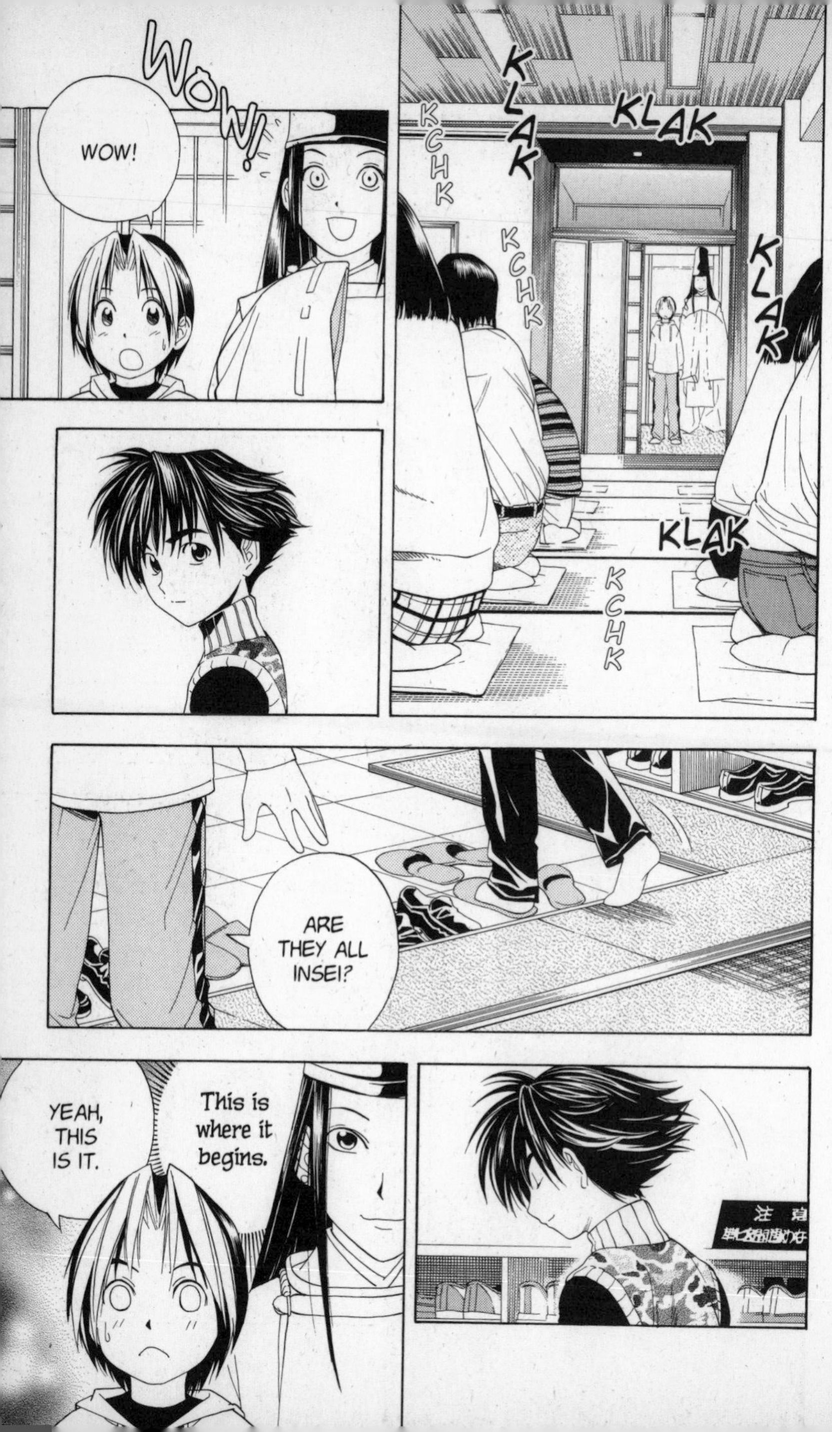
KLAK
KLAK
KCHK
KCHK
KLAK
KLAK
KCHK
WOW!
WOW!
ARE THEY ALL INSEI?
YEAH, THIS IS IT.
This is where it begins.

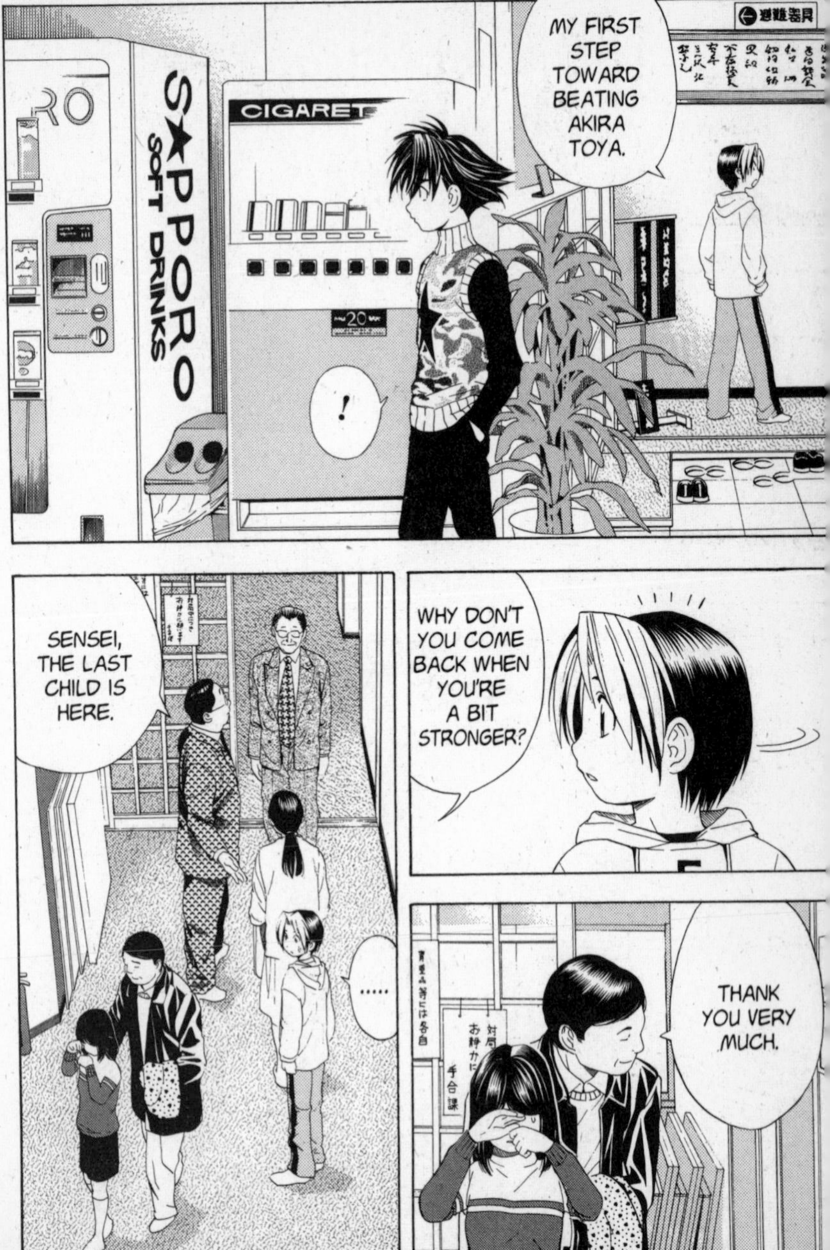

MY FIRST STEP TOWARD BEATING AKIRA TOYA.
CIGARET
S★PPORO SOFT DRINKS
RO
!
WHY DON'T YOU COME BACK WHEN YOU'RE A BIT STRONGER?
SENSEI, THE LAST CHILD IS HERE.
THANK YOU VERY MUCH.
......

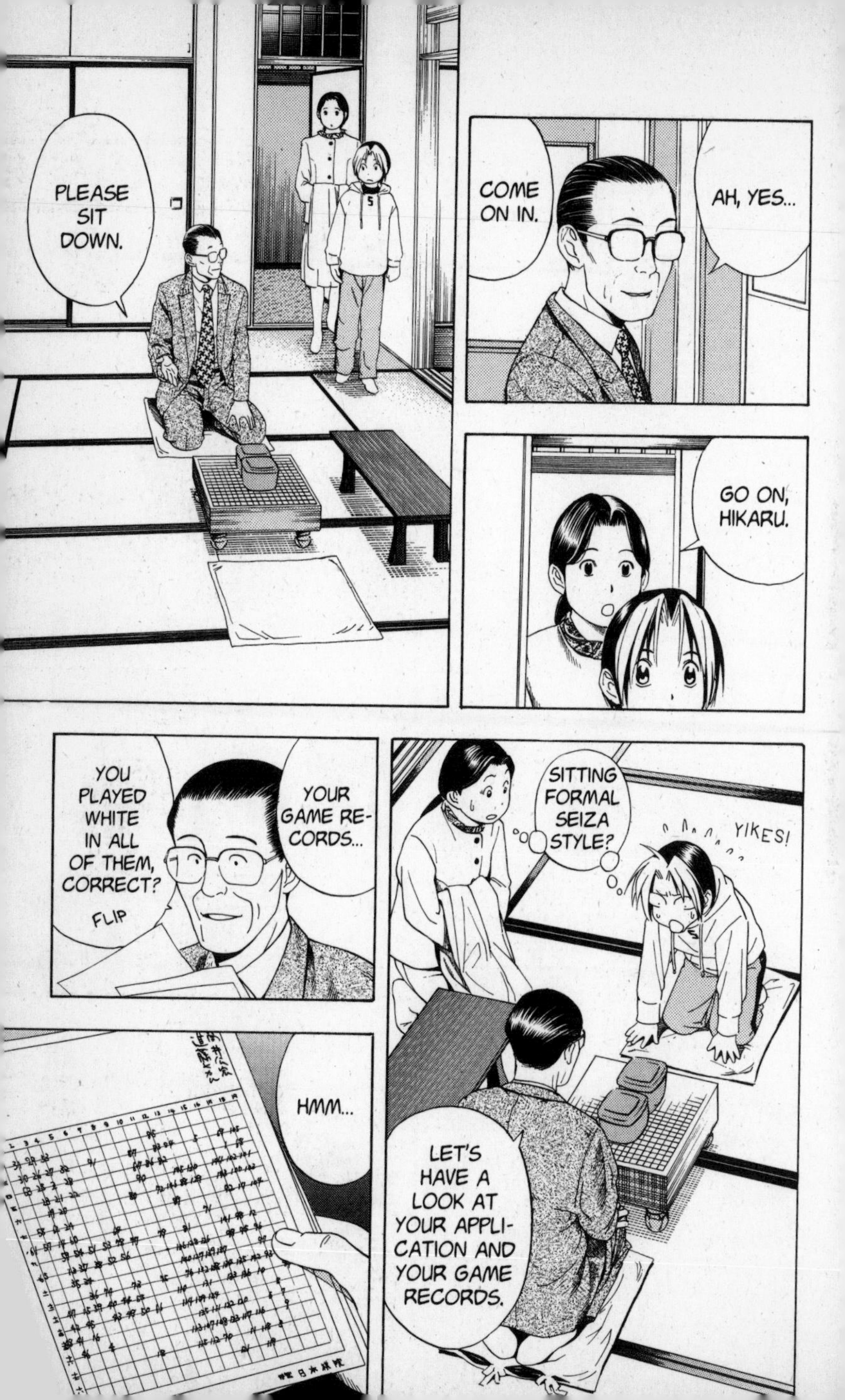
AH, YES...
COME ON IN.
GO ON, HIKARU.
PLEASE SIT DOWN.
SITTING FORMAL SEIZA STYLE?
YIKES!
LET'S HAVE A LOOK AT YOUR APPLICATION AND YOUR GAME RECORDS.
YOUR GAME RECORDS...
YOU PLAYED WHITE IN ALL OF THEM, CORRECT?
FLIP
HMM...

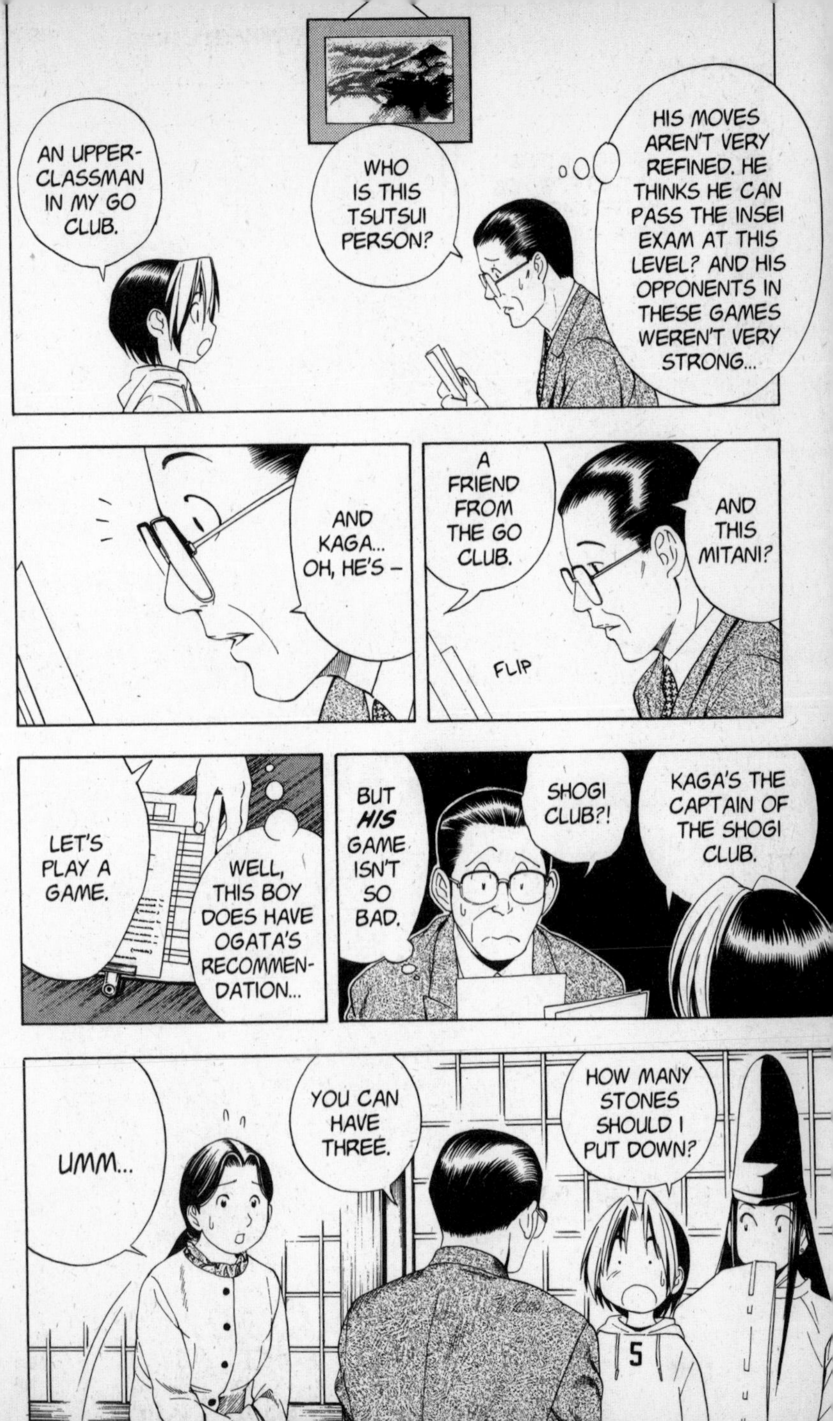
HIS MOVES AREN'T VERY REFINED. HE THINKS HE CAN PASS THE INSEI EXAM AT THIS LEVEL? AND HIS OPPONENTS IN THESE GAMES WEREN'T VERY STRONG...
WHO IS THIS TSUTSUI PERSON?
AN UPPER-CLASSMAN IN MY GO CLUB.
AND THIS MITANI?
FLIP
A FRIEND FROM THE GO CLUB.
AND KAGA... OH, HE'S –
KAGA'S THE CAPTAIN OF THE SHOGI CLUB.
SHOGI CLUB?!
BUT *HIS* GAME ISN'T SO BAD.
WELL, THIS BOY DOES HAVE OGATA'S RECOMMEN-DATION...
LET'S PLAY A GAME.
HOW MANY STONES SHOULD I PUT DOWN?
YOU CAN HAVE THREE.
UMM...

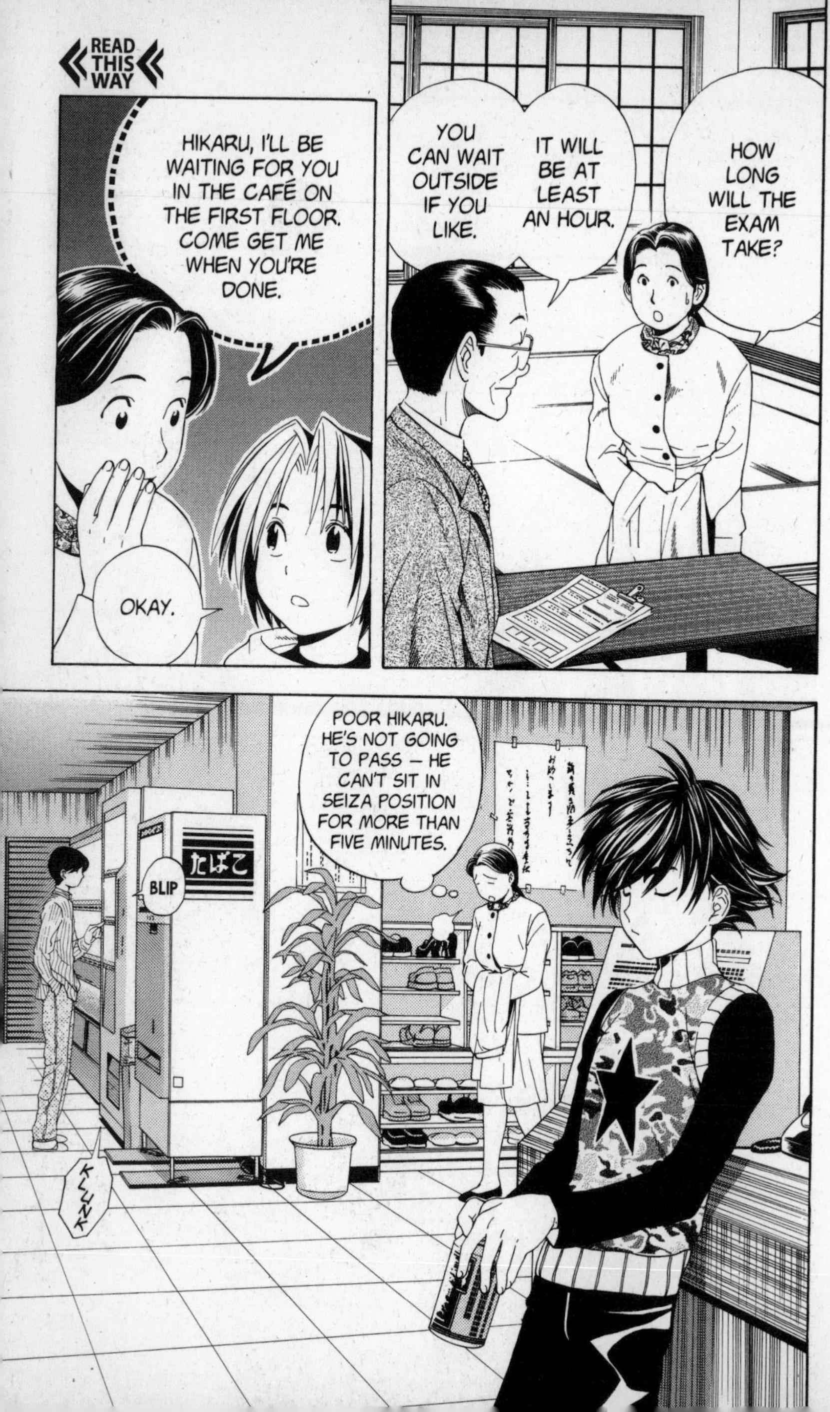
READ THIS WAY
HOW LONG WILL THE EXAM TAKE?
IT WILL BE AT LEAST AN HOUR.
YOU CAN WAIT OUTSIDE IF YOU LIKE.
HIKARU, I'LL BE WAITING FOR YOU IN THE CAFÉ ON THE FIRST FLOOR. COME GET ME WHEN YOU'RE DONE.
OKAY.
POOR HIKARU. HE'S NOT GOING TO PASS — HE CAN'T SIT IN SEIZA POSITION FOR MORE THAN FIVE MINUTES.
たばこ
BLIP
KLUNK

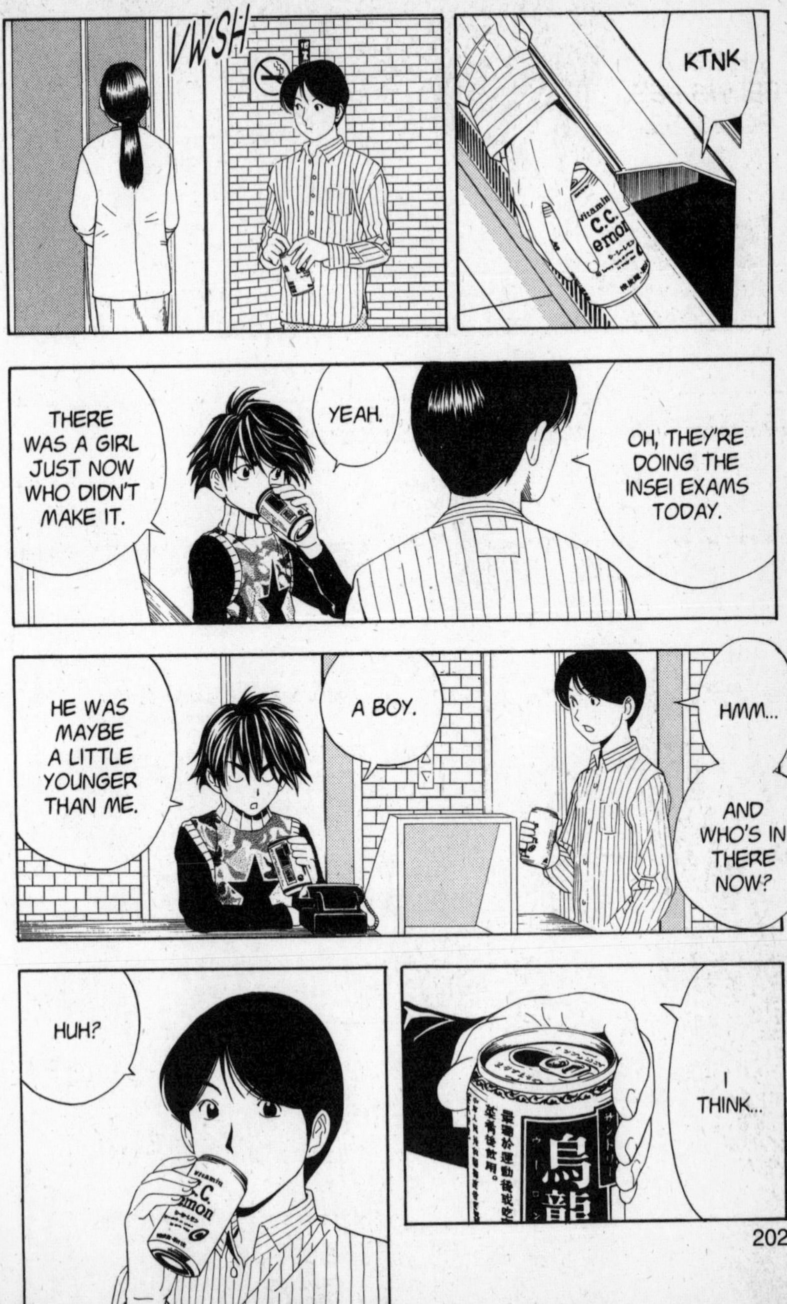
KTNK
VWSH
OH, THEY'RE DOING THE INSEI EXAMS TODAY.
YEAH.
THERE WAS A GIRL JUST NOW WHO DIDN'T MAKE IT.
HMM...
AND WHO'S IN THERE NOW?
A BOY.
HE WAS MAYBE A LITTLE YOUNGER THAN ME.
I THINK...
HUH?

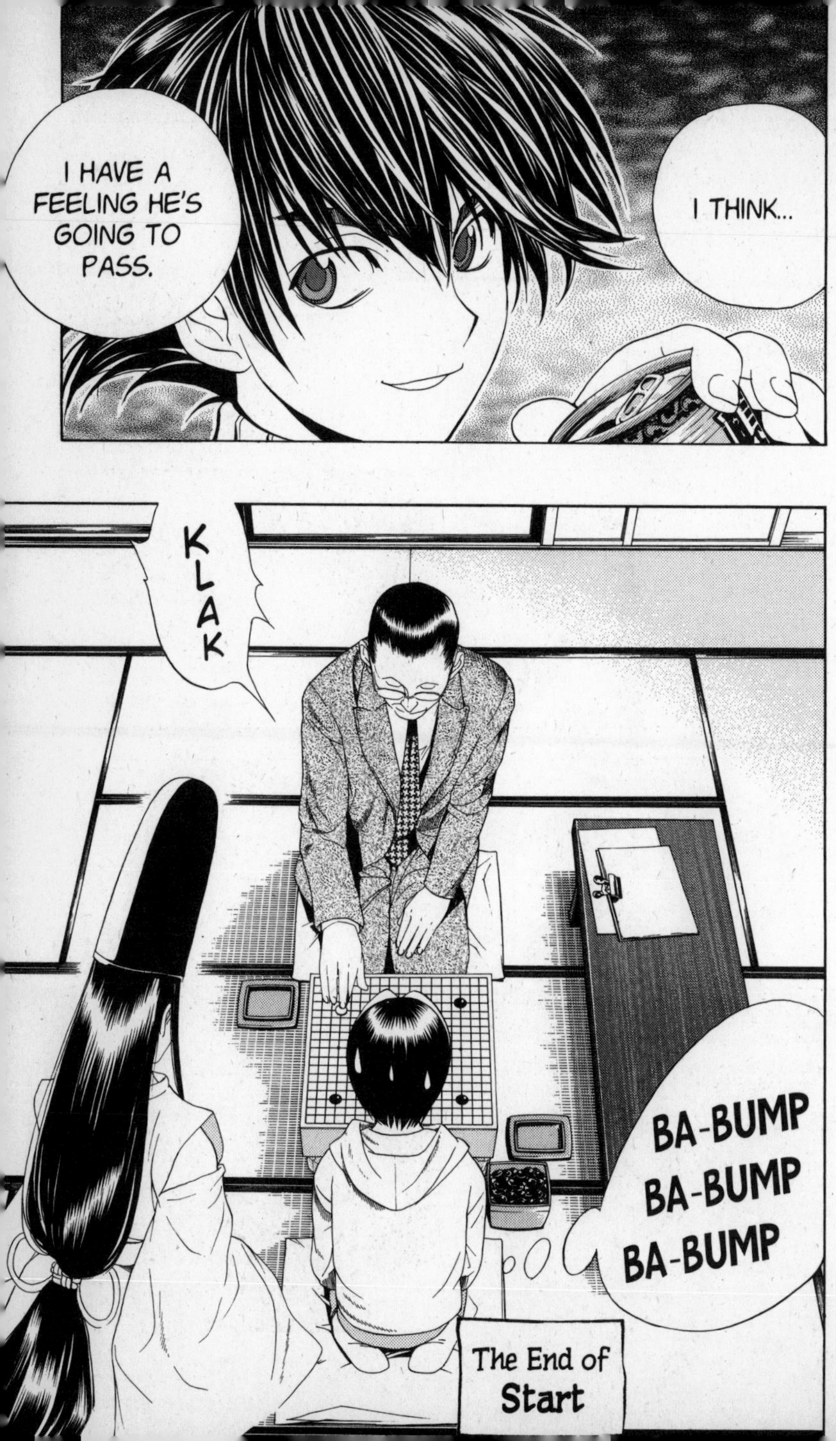
I THINK...
I HAVE A FEELING HE'S GOING TO PASS.
KLAK
BA-BUMP BA-BUMP BA-BUMP
The End of Start

Next Volume Preview

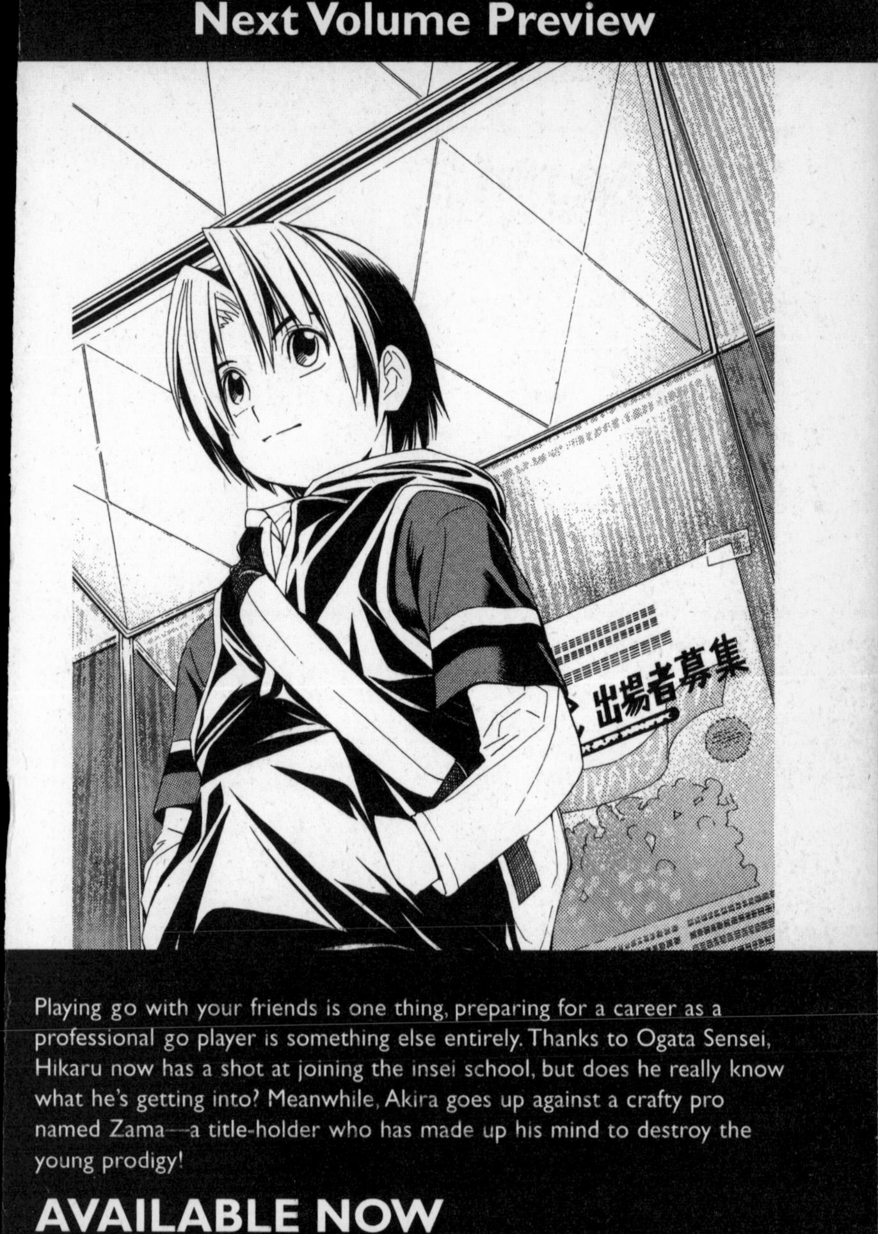
出場者募集

Playing go with your friends is one thing, preparing for a career as a professional go player is something else entirely. Thanks to Ogata Sensei, Hikaru now has a shot at joining the insei school, but does he really know what he's getting into? Meanwhile, Akira goes up against a crafty pro named Zama—a title-holder who has made up his mind to destroy the young prodigy!

AVAILABLE NOW

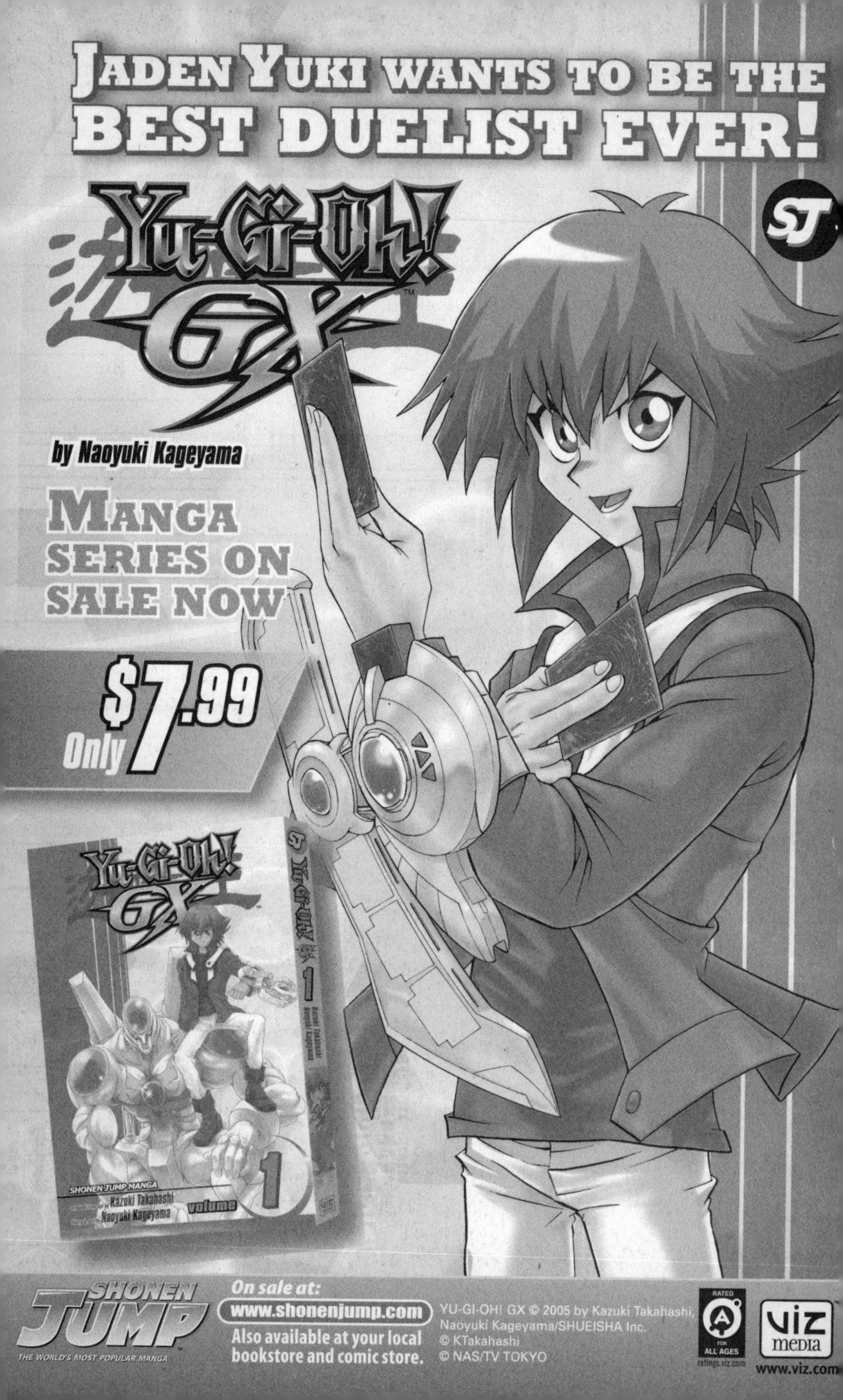

JADEN YUKI WANTS TO BE THE
BEST DUELIST EVER!
SJ
YU-GI-OH! GX™
by Naoyuki Kageyama
MANGA
SERIES ON
SALE NOW
Only $7.99
YU-GI-OH! GX
SHONEN JUMP MANGA
Kazuki Takahashi
Naoyuki Kageyama
volume 1
SHONEN JUMP
THE WORLD'S MOST POPULAR MANGA
On sale at:
www.shonenjump.com
Also available at your local
bookstore and comic store.
YU-GI-OH! GX © 2005 by Kazuki Takahashi,
Naoyuki Kageyama/SHUEISHA Inc.
© KTakahashi
© NAS/TV TOKYO
RATED
FOR
ALL AGES
ratings.viz.com
viz media
www.viz.com

SAVE 50% OFF
THE COVER PRICE!
IT'S LIKE GETTING 6 ISSUES
FREE!

OVER **350+** PAGES PER ISSUE

THE WORLD'S MOST POPULAR MANGA

This monthly magazine contains 7 of the coolest manga available in the U.S., PLUS anime news, and info about video & card games, toys AND more!

❏ **I want 12 HUGE issues of SHONEN JUMP for only $29.95*!**

NAME

ADDRESS

CITY/STATE/ZIP

EMAIL ADDRESS   DATE OF BIRTH

❏ YES, send me via email information, advertising, offers, and promotions related to VIZ Media, SHONEN JUMP, and/or their business partners.

❏ **CHECK ENCLOSED** (payable to SHONEN JUMP)   ❏ **BILL ME LATER**

CREDIT CARD: ❏ **Visa** ❏ **Mastercard**

ACCOUNT NUMBER   EXP. DATE

SIGNATURE

CLIP&MAIL TO:
SHONEN JUMP Subscriptions Service Dept.
P.O. Box 515
Mount Morris, IL 61054-0515

P9GNC1

* Canada price: $41.95 USD, including GST, HST, and QST, US/CAN orders only. Allow 6-8 weeks for delivery.
ONE PIECE © 1997 by Eiichiro Oda/SHUEISHA Inc. BLEACH © 2001 by Tite Kubo/SHUEISHA Inc.
NARUTO © 1999 by Masashi Kishimoto/SHUEISHA Inc.

www.viz.com